Morgan Sports Cars

Pit work before success for David Van Dal in the 1952 Northam Flying Fifty. (*Photograph D. Van Dal collection*)

David Van Dal in the 'Letterbox' Plus 4 at Northam, ahead of Maurice's Chrysler Special. They are taking the left-hand bend by the Railway Hotel. The year is probably 1953. (*Photograph D. Van Dal collection*)

Morgan Sports Cars

The Early Years

J.D. Alderson & Chris Chapman

Sheffield Academic Press

Published by Sheffield Academic Press Ltd
Mansion House
19 Kingfield Road
Sheffield S11 9AS
England

Printed on acid-free paper in Great Britain
by Bookcraft Ltd
Midsomer Norton, Bath

Typeset by Carnegie Publishing Ltd
Carnegie House, Chatsworth Road
Lancaster LA1 4SL

British Library Cataloguing-in-Publication Data
A catalogue record for this book is available from the British Library

ISBN 1-85075-680-5

Contents

Foreword

Some years ago one of the authors, together with another Morgan enthusiast, wrote a book covering the history of the Morgan Three-Wheeler Cyclecar with particular emphasis on the competition performance of the cars for the years they were in construction. The book *Morgan Sweeps the Board* was extremely well researched and is undoubtedly the foremost reference book for the three-wheeler cars.

Dr Jake Alderson, along with Chris Chapman, has repeated this historical record with this book which covers the history of the Morgan four-wheeler in similar great detail.

For my part it is of particular interest as either by 'design' of my father or events that occurred over the years the Morgan four-wheeler has neatly covered my whole motoring life, the only exception being one year driving an F2 Morgan three-wheeler on a motor cycle licence in 1936.

Before that I had learned to drive the prototype four-wheeler around the driveways of my father's home Cannon Hill, Maidenhead.

Having always enjoyed driving Morgans I am glad to report that at the age of 77 my everyday transport is a Plus 8, and I hope it may continue for a number of years.

Like myself I am sure all who read this book will find it both fascinating and of great interest.

Peter Morgan 1997

Introduction

HFS Morgan built his first three-wheeler runabout in 1909–10, a single-seater for his own use. Encouraged to go into production, he very soon realized that to sell any he had to demonstrate the soundness of his design in competition with other manufacturers.

Thus began a relationship with motor sport for the Morgan Motor Company Limited that continues today.

With falling three-wheeler sales in the 1930s it was apparent that a four-wheeler was required to save the Company. It was natural for such a Morgan to be a sports car, for the Company directors and their families were all keen motor sportsmen and it was therefore the market they knew best. With such enthusiasm for motor sport it was clear that much development work would be undertaken with factory cars in competition, and it therefore follows that to research Morgan history a competition bias is essential for the researcher.

The idea for this book was really that of Peter Morgan who approached one of us (J.A.) on several occasions following the successful publication of the three-wheeler history *Morgan Sweeps the Board.*

Having agreed with Peter that this story should be told, it was natural to recruit another keen researcher and an acknowledged expert (on Morgan Lawrencetune racing in the 1960s, [C.C.]) holding similar views that such a book needed writing. With two researchers the workload has been shared and has been most enjoyable.

All of this started some ten years ago, and this book has required an immense amount of research both in the UK and overseas to see it to fruition. We found that researching Morgan history from a competition viewpoint revealed much new information, and clarified several controversies.

Trying to trace Morgan racing activities around the world has been difficult in view of the many far away places in which Morgan sports cars provided enjoyable competitive drives for motor sportsmen. Tracing the owners themselves has been difficult and time consuming and sometimes not always possible, but we feel we have traced a sufficiently representative selection to tell our Morgan story. Similarly, finding photographs to illustrate the book has literally led us around the world.

We hope you will enjoy our story. It differs in many ways from previously written books on the marque, but we believe because of the way we have researched this book that our version is factual. Should anyone reading this book be able to add to our story we would be delighted to hear from them.

J. A. and C. C. 1997

CHAPTER ONE

The Birth of the 4/4

Henry Frederick Stanley Morgan was born, the son of a Herefordshire Clergyman, at Moreton Jeffries on 11 August 1881. Harry, or HFS as he later became known, was brought up with his three sisters at nearby Stoke Lacy rectory. A vocation in the Church, however, was not for him. During schooling he developed an interest in engineering and, after attending Crystal Palace Engineering College, was apprenticed to the Great Western Railway in Swindon. HFS worked there as a draughtsman until 1905, when he decided to go into partnership with his longtime friend, Leslie Bacon.

They set up business in a garage in Malvern Link on the Worcester road, adjacent to HFS's house, 'Chestnut Villa'. As well as being automobile engineers, the partnership developed a bus service. Useful as it was to the rural inhabitants of Malvern, it did not meet with universal acclaim. Motorists were still regarded by many as nuisances for driving such 'noisy, smelly things'!

Meanwhile, HFS's inventive brain was busy designing a simple and light three-wheeler, in collaboration with Mr Stephenson-Peach, the engineering master of Malvern College. When this single-seater machine appeared, registered CJ 743 on 9 June 1910, it attracted much favourable comment from enthusiasts. Weighing a claimed 2 cwt it incorporated several unique design features that were to form the basis of future Morgan models for over 50 years. For example, the sliding pillar independent suspension is still in use to this day and the central torque tube, linking the front-mounted engine to a remote bevel box (later a gearbox), persisted into the 1970s.

The prototype vehicle was powered by a vee

The experimental twin-cylinder four-wheeler, being driven by Geoffrey Day, outside Stoke Lacy rectory. To the right is Dorothy Morgan's own three-wheeler, CJ 1348. (*Photograph: Morgan Motor Co. collection*)

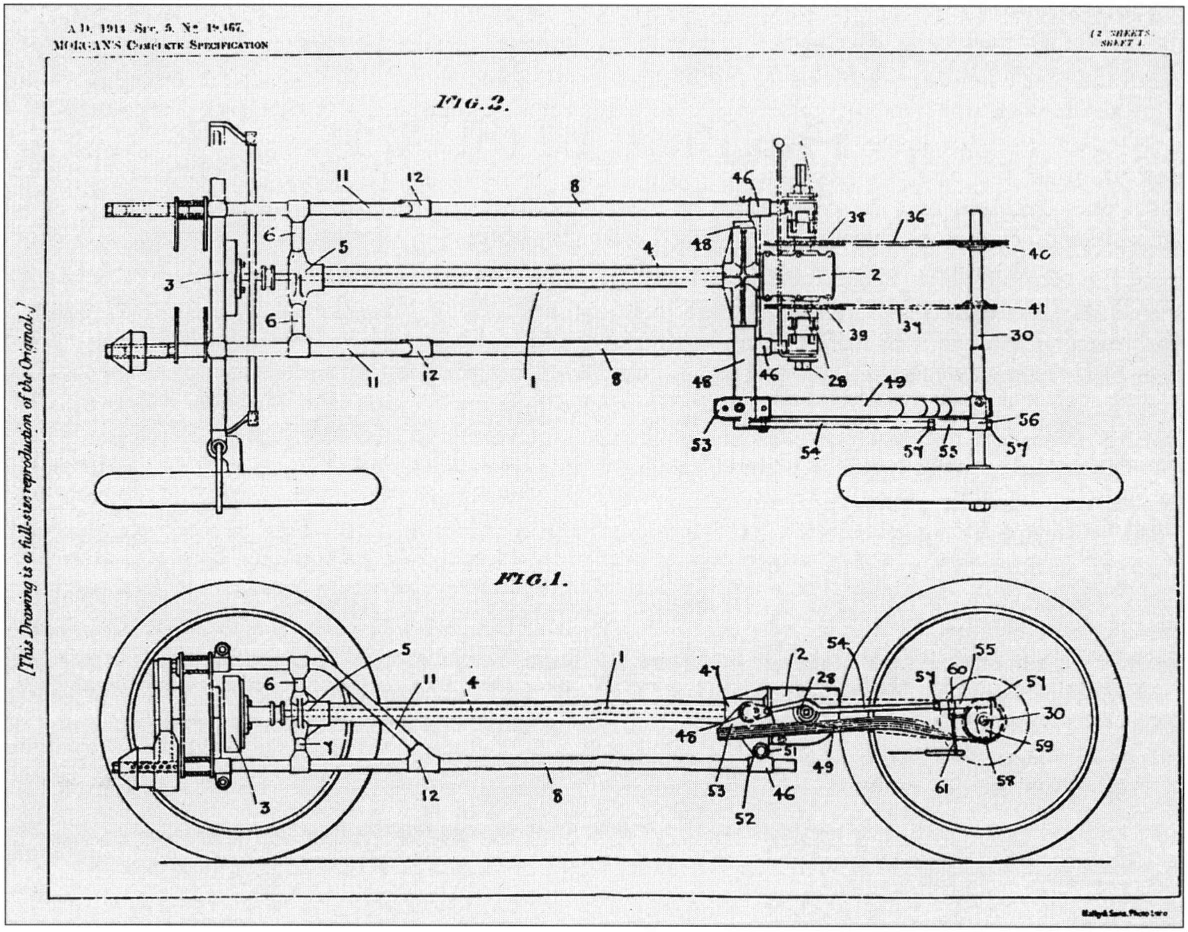

The patent drawing of the four-wheeler. (*British Patent Office*)

twin Peugeot motorcycle engine, attached via tubes to the front of the suspension. Drive to the single rear wheel was by bevel box, via two dog sprockets with chains, to sprockets fixed either side of the rear wheel. This gave a choice of two forward gears with no reverse.

Spurred on by the encouragement he received from many quarters, HFS built two further single-seaters, with JAP engines. He exhibited these at the Olympia motorcycle show in November 1910 but, surprisingly, few orders were forthcoming. HFS's partner decided that the whole venture was too risky and quitted.

To be commercially viable, HFS realized that a two-seater was required. An example was shown at Olympia in 1911 and it was a resounding success. HFS also knew that he would have to prove his 'Runabout' by competing against other vehicles in his class – the cycle cars. Thus began a commitment to motor sport that has continued throughout Morgan history.

Competition successes came quickly and, with the popularity of the two-seater, HFS found himself deluged with orders. Having only a small garage, he tried to get other manufacturers to take on the venture. This proved unsuccessful so he made arrangements with two local concerns. A nearby wheelwrights (Clares) made the wooden bodies, which were then taken for panelling to a sheet metal firm (Langleys) at the back of HFS's works. Clearly this system was not satisfactory, so in November 1913 HFS purchased two acres of land at the far end of Pickersleigh Road (the current factory location). The operation developed until, by 1934, the complete Morgan operation was located at the present site.

Although the light and sporting Morgan three-wheeler went from strength to strength, HFS decided in 1913 to investigate a four wheeled derivation of his design. Indeed, *The Cyclecar* magazine suggested that the vehicle would make its appearance at the Cycle Car Club's open hillclimb on 28 June. It failed to appear but a group photograph, taken at Stoke Lacy Rectory early in 1914, shows the four-wheeler in the hands of HFS's brother-in-law, Geoffrey Day.

The car has a modified 'De Luxe' three-wheeler body and it appears to be in primer. It has standard three-wheeler front wings extending into running boards and the rear wings are of similar shape to the front. The engine appears to be a vee twin and the front track is noticeably less than that of the sporting model three-wheeler in the same photograph (reg. CJ 1348). This belonged to HFS's sister, Dorothy.

In September 1914 HFS applied for a patent for the four-wheeled Morgan. This was granted on 13 May 1915 as patent 19,467.

HFS described the patent as referring to the rear of the vehicle 'there being little change in that part which is forward of the gearbox'. He commented that the car could be narrower in track with equal or greater stability than the three-wheeler.

Modification to the rear end consisted of a new bevel box casting, with extensions laterally to act as anchorage points for first, the quarter elliptic rear springs and second, the radius rods. The latter had screw threaded adjusters to alter their length and hence the tension of the two chains to the solid back axle.

Whatever the reason the project was not proceeded with – although a complete rear-end casting was saved from the Morgan scrap tip in the 1930s by a young employee and is still in existence.

Experiments continued in 1914 with an in-line four-cylinder Dorman engine of 1024 cc (64 × 88 mm). This engine, of type number KL30, serial number 1069, was delivered to Morgan on 26 May 1914. It is believed to have been fitted to another experimental four-wheeler.

Quite how this engine was fitted is lost with the passage of time but the extra length,

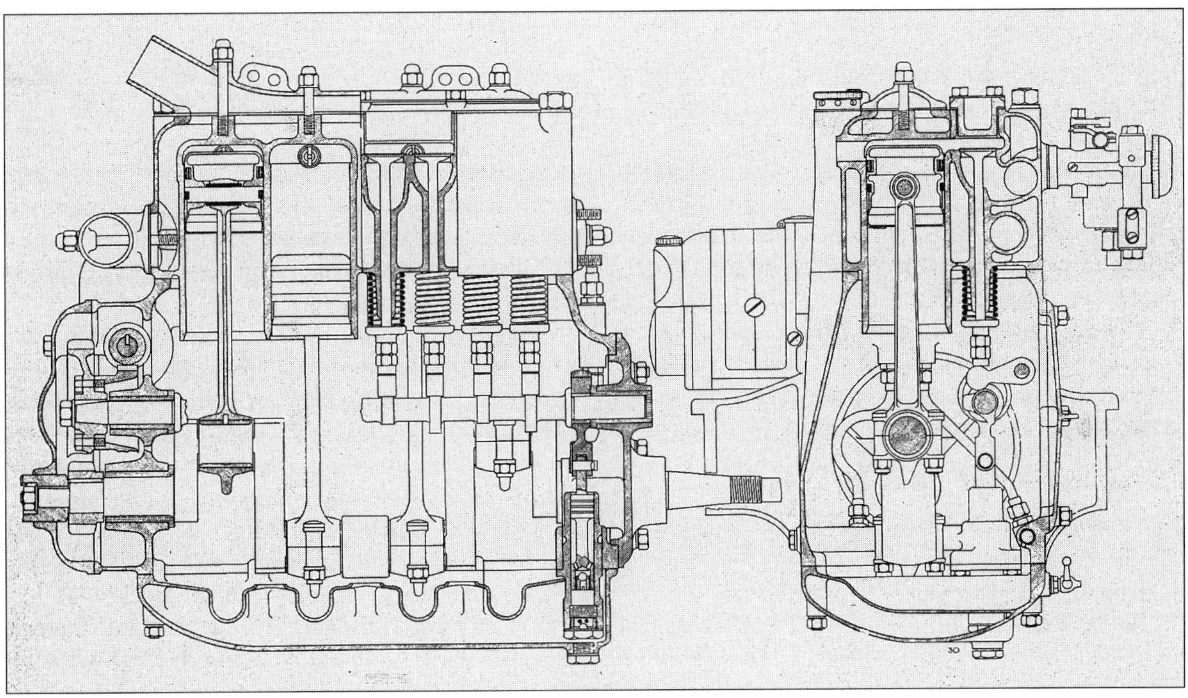

The Dorman Light Car engine, type KL 30. (*The Automobile Engineer*)

compared to the compact vee twin, would pose a problem. Dormans, however, supplied spares for this engine (new timing chain and timing sprockets) on 18 November 1919, so clearly several years of use was obtained from it.

The four-wheeler project was quietly shelved as sales of the vee twin three-wheeler proved very successful and lucrative at that time. By the late 1920s, however, sales were beginning to drop. The new cheap baby cars, such as the Austin 7 and Morris Minor, which had small, smooth-running, four-cylinder engines, were capturing the market. Experiments with fitting a four-cylinder, 750 cc, Coventry Climax engine into a two-speeder three-wheeler chassis were not successful. It became obvious that a different mounting system would be needed for the longer four-cylinder engine.

A new three-wheeler chassis was designed using Z section side longerons to replace the side tubing of the twin. The engine was now located behind the front suspension crosshead. The body frame was fastened directly to the top of the Z section flanges, with the floorboards being attached to the lower flanges. This new chassis also took advantage of the new rear-mounted three-speed and reverse gearbox, recently introduced on the twin cylinder machines. Production models of the new Morgan were known as F4s (Ford engine, four seats) and were fitted with the new Ford 8 side-valve, 933 cc engine, or Y type.

When this new chassis was introduced in 1933 it caused HFS to rethink the whole concept of the four-wheeler. Back in 1914 there had been two major problems. The first, which he had now overcome, was to fit a four-cylinder engine into a Morgan chassis. The second major problem had been the extreme rigidity of the twin-cylinder chassis, being constructed from linked tubes – an early space frame concept. While this was ideal for three-wheeler construction, it proved a problem in the four-wheeler version. The limited suspension travel could leave one wheel airborne on rough ground! It was possible that the model F chassis might be a suitable basis for conversion, so in 1934 an F4 was converted to a four-wheeler.

Before describing this vehicle it might be worth mentioning that, in late 1913, the Morgan factory received an unusual request from an Indian railway company. They wanted a four-wheeled track inspection vehicle to run on 5 ft gauge railway track. Clearly, suspension travel would not have been a problem on railway lines but whether or not the ex-GWR engineer took up the challenge we shall probably never know.

The new four-wheeler chassis that took to the road in 1934 contained a virtually standard F4 front end but with narrower track. It had a shortened central torque tube which mated with a Meadows gearbox, located amidships. From the gearbox, a short open propshaft took the drive to a Moss spiral bevel rear axle. This was located by quarter elliptic springs fastened to the outside of the chassis side longerons. A standard F4 bonnet scuttle and windscreen assembly was used; F type wheels were fitted all round but the rear ones were shod with trials tyres, to allow testing on rough ground. With rudimentary rear bodywork, the little 8 hp Ford-engined Morgan took to the roads and hills. While the basic design proved satisfactory, the location of the rear axle was inadequate, with just quarter elliptic springs.

The solution to the problem came from an unexpected quarter. Way back in 1912 HFS had married Ruth Day, the daughter of the vicar of Malvern. Their eldest daughter, Sylvia, was born in May 1913 and at the age of five she was privileged to unveil a foundation stone, situated in part of the Pickersleigh Road factory. In 1934 she was living with her parents at 'Fern Lodge' in Malvern and was driving a Hillman Aero Minx, a gift from her father. Peter Morgan remembers his father getting down onto his hands and knees at this time to study the Hillman's rear suspension for further inspiration.

This vehicle was fitted with an underslung chassis, the rear axle being located by semi-elliptic springs. Influenced by this, HFS redesigned the suspension of his four-wheeler. The design was to be incorporated into a further prototype that was now constructed.

The new chassis was designed with a Morgan sports car in mind. Based on the earlier Ford-engined car, it was wider and longer to allow a better seating position. The rear axle, a Moss, was now located by semi-elliptic rear springs positioned inboard of the chassis side longerons, the chassis being underslung. Rear location of the

The Coventry Climax-engined prototype nearing completion at the Morgan factory. Note the similarly shaped front and rear wings. (*Photograph: Morgan Motor Co. collection*)

The completed, original Ford 8hp-engined prototype WP7490 in the grounds of Fern Lodge. (*Photograph: Morgan Motor Co. collection*)

back springs was by trunnions in a chassis member that doubled as a support for twin spare wheels. This gave good weight distribution and the twin spares were so useful for the off-the-road trials that they were very popular with the sporting motorist at this time.

The gearbox was still amidships but the engine had been replaced by the tried and trusted Coventry Climax overhead inlet, side exhaust unit. Initial experiments were with an engine of around 1090 cc. Trials experience made the lowest part of the vehicle the floorboards, the exhaust being routed alongside the chassis longeron.

The bodywork was to take some time to satisfy Mr Morgan. He initially wanted to use the same wing pattern front and rear, in the interests of economy, but when the car began to take shape it lacked the flowing style of the earlier Morgan designs.

With the decision to proceed with the Climax car having been made, Peter Morgan suddenly found himself the proud new owner of the earlier Ford-engined car. His father brought it home to their new family house at Cannon Hill near Maidenhead and told the 15-year-old 'You can learn to drive that around the garden'! By now it was fully bodied, painted green and had a sloping tail panel on which was mounted the spare wheel. In keeping with three-wheeler custom the chassis number was inscribed on a St Christopher Badge fitted to the dash. It was given the 'identity' of D1281, a cancelled order from the Derby agent for the family vee twin three-wheeler. Its registration number WP 7490 was allocated on 1 December, 1934 but it was not kept for long. It was reassigned to the Climax prototype as soon as it was ready for the road.

By the summer of 1935 the Climax-engined new car had been taken by HFS and George Goodall to the trials hills of Somerset and Devon for testing. George was HFS's General Manager and had been with the company since 1927. Both were noted competition drivers and they believed explicitly that, as with the three-wheeler, the four-wheeler version would have to prove itself in competition.

In July the car was taken to Brooklands for

The Coventry Climax prototype at Drewsteignton in Devon while being tested on nearby trials hills (such as Fingle Bridge). (*Photograph: Morgan Motor Co. collection*)

HFS Morgan testing the new car on a trials hill. (*Photograph: Morgan Motor Co. collection*)

testing at the time of the Morgan factory three-wheeler team's entry in the Light Car Club Relay Race. It easily reached a good 70 mph.

Present on that occasion was Joe Huxham, the Bournemouth Morgan agent since 1932, who was

The Coventry Climax car at Brooklands. The engine was stated to be of 1090 cc in a caption written by Henry Laird. (*Photograph: Henry Laird collection*)

racing his three-wheeler. Joe, too, was an excellent competition driver but he also enjoyed the social side of Morgan competition. He was a close friend of George Goodall, whom he called 'Uncle George' and Harry Jones, the Service Manager, whom he called 'Cousin Harry'. Joe was later to show his talents in poetry. He composed his own version of the origin of the new four wheeled Morgan, which he titled 'The Birth of the 4/4'. For fear of reprisals, however, he dared not put it in print until 1973!

The Birth of the 4/4

Uncle George and Cousin Harry,
Sometimes at an Inn would tarry,
Each one having filled his belli,
Found he could not drive intelli-
gently; and through inability,
Had to have some more stability.

Being much averse to hiking,
They had always favoured triking;
But after both had overturned,

WP9590. (*Photograph: Morgan Motor Co. collection*)

Not only heads, but bottoms burned
So the need was made to feel
Of an extra driving wheel.

Out of Evil cometh good,
As does Courage from the Wood.
Thus the good old firm of Morgies
Benefited from their orgies.
For so that they could drink yet more
They built and drove the new 'Four-four'.

The success of the Climax-engined prototype prompted the construction of another works car which was later campaigned by Harry Jones. Registered as WP 9590, on 1 August 1935, this car too had the same wings, front and rear but with running boards between them. It did, however, have much neater tail end panels, which covered the fuel tank and spare wheels.

The major differences was in the engine bay. It had the 10 hp s.v. Ford 'C' engine of 1172 cc that was introduced late in 1934, for Ford's new range of light cars. Why this engine was fitted is not clear. Peter Morgan is sure that the decision was made very early on to use a Coventry Climax engine for production cars.

Another feature of this car was its Girling front brakes. The Climax car had been built with three-wheeler 8 in rear brake drums up front but with the chain drive sprockets turned off. This system, however, had not proved satisfactory. Both Morgans were fitted with the three-wheeler 2 to 1 steering reduction box, attached near the top of the steering column.

While WP 9590 was a better proposition than the Climax car, it still lacked the usual excellence of line of which HFS was rightly proud. As a result, the decision was made to abandon the policy of using the same patterns for front and rear wings. It was the Climax prototype, however, that went back into the factory for rebodying. It re-emerged with flowing front wings, incorporating running boards, and a tidier rear end in the manner of WP 9590.

The new body was much more satisfactory and it was clear to HFS that the new four-wheeled Morgan was at last ready to launch. Was it a coincidence then, that the Motor Cycling Club (MCC) announced that the 1935 Boxing Day London–Exeter Trial would contain a special class? This was for 'Veteran' members who had taken part in the very first Exeter Trial twenty five years earlier. As this had represented HFS's competition debut, with his three-wheeler in 1910, it was too good an opportunity to miss. Thus the motoring world saw a new type of Morgan make its successful debut. HFS, accompanied by his son Peter, became the only member of the Veteran Class to collect a Premier Award.

Morgans at this time were not into naming models in the manner they had before the 1930s. In keeping with this recent policy, George Goodall decided that the new car should be simply called the 4–4. This stood for four wheels and four cylinders, presumably to differentiate it from the three-wheeler vee twins. Following the car's successful introduction in competition, arrangements were made for production to commence in 1936, using the 1122 cc version of the 90 mm stroke range of Coventry Climax engines.

The first competitive event for the four-wheeler. HFS with his son Peter attacks Fingle Hill, in the MCC's Exeter Trial, on his way to a Premier award. (*Photograph: Quadrant Picture Library*)

CHAPTER TWO

1936

It was to be several months before production Morgan 4–4s began to leave the Morgan Factory. Meanwhile, the Coventry Climax-engined prototype, WP7490, had featured in several very favourable press reviews, and had now been fitted with the mechanically operated Girling brakes specified for production models.

The 63 mm bore version of the 90 mm stroke range of Coventry Climax engines (1122 cc) that Morgan had decided to use was manufactured to an overhead inlet valve side exhaust valve design. The cylinder head was manufactured to the patented design of W.A. Whatmough, a prominent consultant engineer. Each engine was to be bench tested to produce 34 bhp at 4500 rpm before delivery. Engines supplied to Morgans received an M prefix to the engine number.

As well as making sure an engine produced adequate performance for the chassis into which it was to be installed, there was another important factor to be taken into consideration by vehicle manufacturers. At this time all car owners in Britain had to pay an annual road tax for their cars, based on a scale of derived 'horsepower' by applying a formula originally introduced by the RAC in 1906. A very important factor in the formula was the size of the cylinder bore. The 1122 cc engine, having a bore of 63 mm, was rated at 9.8 hp, making the annual tax £7 10*s.* 0*d.* (£7.50) just under the 10 hp ceiling. The 10 hp to 11 hp scale would have been £8 5*s.* 0*d.* (£8.25), the rate being 15 shillings (75p) per 'horsepower'.

Production Morgans were to be fitted with the Moss BA8 rear axle, having a ratio of 5 to 1. With the four-speed Meadows gearbox this gave overall ratios of 17.5, 12, 7 and 5 to 1 with a reverse of 22.6 to 1. With a dry weight of only 11 cwt excellent performance for the day was obtained and the low slung chassis with independent front suspension gave excellent roadholding.

Car ownership was regarded by most as a luxury item, and the roads were comparatively traffic free. The roads were almost all of single carriageway construction. The universal 20 mph speed limit had been rescinded in 1930 for all except heavy commercial vehicles but in 1935 a 30 mph limit had been deemed necessary for built up areas. Traffic lights were rare, and had not begun to appear in the nation's capital until 1932. 'Cats eyes', to help locate the centre of the road at night, did not begin to be installed until 1936. There were also many horse-drawn vehicles to be encountered on British roads.

Competition motoring for the enthusiast was usually catered for by trials, rallies or racing. Trials had begun at the turn of the century initially as reliability events, timing motor cars against a schedule on long inter-city runs over the poor roads of the time. As motor cars became more reliable the organizers began to seek out unmade tracks up very steep gradients to test the drivers and cars still further. The MCC with its London–Exeter Trial held just after Christmas, the London–Lands End traditionally over Easter, and the London–Edinburgh traditionally at Whitsun, provided the most well-known events. Since its inception, the Morgan Motor Company has always had a strong interest in trials, particularly MCC events, and in fact still competes to this day.

Rallies had become popular on the continent of Europe, the famous Monte Carlo Rally commencing in 1911 with a winter time run from the snow-bound capitals to the Monte Carlo resort, to which much publicity was thus forthcoming. In Britain the RAC ran its first rally in 1932. Most British rallies had the usual format of long road sections involving navigation against strict time schedules, with driving tests interspersed along the way, and particularly at the finish, to decide the winners.

The racing motorist had been catered for at the banked track of Brooklands near Weybridge since 1907, and at the narrow and twisty former

Harry Jones in the Ford-engined car, on Station Hill, Lynton in the Lands End Trial. (*Photograph: W. J. Brunell*)

motor cycle road racing circuit at Donington in Derbyshire since 1933. There were also speed trials or sprints held at various locations in the county, such as the Shelsley Walsh hill climb in Worcestershire, and sand racing on the beach at Southport.

Racing on public roads had been prohibited by law since 1925, following an unfortunate accident to a spectator at the Essex MC's event at Kop.

When production Morgans began to leave the Morgan factory in March, one of the first changes in specification was the replacement of the three-wheeler-derived 2–1 steering reduction by a proprietary steering box manufactured by Burman-Douglas.

For the MCC Lands End Trial held on 10 and 11 April the two works Morgans, WP 7490 and WP 9590, were entered for HFS Morgan and Harry Jones respectively. HFS climbed all the observed sections of the hills and won a Premier Award, while Harry, with the Ford-engined car, failed on Barton Steep and Crackington to win but a Bronze.

By the time the Edinburgh Trial came around on 29 May, another works Morgan had been completed for George Goodall to use. With chassis number 032, engine number M54 and registered AUY 33 on 13 May, this blue Morgan had rear hinged doors, the front opening of the doors being a feature of a few early production 4–4s.

This time it was Harry Jones who won a Premier Award with WP 9590, while HFS and George Goodall, in WP 7490 and AUY 33 respectively, could only claim Silver Medals, each having failed the observed sections on Hard Knott pass.

Not long afterwards WP 9590 went back into the factory for a major refit, including a replacement experimental chassis from the rough stores (given chassis number 069). It was to be repainted black and at long last the old three-wheeler pattern Morgan badge on the radiator was to be replaced by the correct 4–4 type. It is our belief that WP 9590 had originally been given chassis number 1, fitted with engine number C07357, and had been coloured grey, while the Climax-engined prototype WP 7490 had been given chassis number 2.

At this time many foreign countries attempted to protect and encourage their own car industries by imposing stiff import duties on complete cars brought in for sale from abroad. One such country was Australia, and so the new Morgan agent Brylaws of Elizabeth Street, Melbourne made an arrangement with the Morgan factory to import just rolling chassis to get round the duty. They had the chassis bodied locally by the company of Cheetham and Borthwick. The first such chassis (079) was despatched in September.

Brylaw Motors, the Australian agency, at 330, Elizabeth Street, Melbourne. Morgans and BSA's abound. (*Photograph: T. Wright collection*)

Meanwhile Joe Huxham, the enthusiastic Bournemouth Morgan agent felt he should actively compete with the new 4–4 if he wanted to sell any, so his famous racing three-wheeler Morgan was sold off to a policeman, and he began competing with a standard 4–4, registration CEL 505.

Every autumn the MCC ran a day's speed event at Brooklands for their clubmen, which only allowed road equipped cars (lights, mudguards and silencers fitted) to take part. The main features of these events were the one-hour high-speed trials (known as hour blinds) in which

Joe Huxham at Brooklands, awaiting the start of a handicap event during the MCC's meeting. (*Photograph: Quadrant Picture Library*)

entrants were let loose on the banked outer circuit to see what distances they could cover in one hour. There were also handicap races. This year Joe Huxham was delighted to put 75.01 miles into his hour, an excellent performance for a new car of 1122 cc on bumpy Brooklands and useful publicity for the Malvern factory just before the Paris and Olympia Motor Shows.

Since the autumn all new Morgans had been leaving the factory with revised, and more attractive, front wings and also a revised version of the Coventry Climax engine. This had an improved dynamo drive, better cooling, modified valve rockers and larger inlet valves among other improvements. The engine now developed more power and the number was prefixed MA.

The first motor show to feature the 4–4 was the 30th International Automobile Exhibition, held for a week beginning 1 October at the Grand Palais des Champs-Elysees in Paris. Three 4–4s were exhibited, all right-hand-drive cars, and featuring spoke pattern steel wheels (Dunlop Easiclean?) One week later the British motor show was held at Olympia, possibly featuring the same 4–4s. This was the first time Morgans had exhibited at the Motor Show, as the three-wheelers had been shown at the motorcycle shows. The Morgan 4–4 attracted much favourable comment, and was competitively priced at £194 5*s*. 0*d*. well under the £222 of the newly introduced MGTA.

A Cornwall garage owner, J. Cameron Harris, took along his young 16-year-old son Raymond and remarked to him that the new Morgans resembled 'a young Bentley'. George Goodall was asked if they could have the Cornwall agency but he told them that there already was an agent in Cornwall. Not long after, the previous agent withdrew and so the Central Garage of Probus, near Truro, became the address of the new Cornwall Morgan agent.

CHAPTER THREE

1937

The MCC's Exeter Trial was held on 1 and 2 January. Two works cars were entered, this time both fitted with 1098 cc Coventry Climax engines (62.3 mm bore). These engines were specially tuned by Coventry Climax for racing in the 1100 cc category. Of the two works entries only Harry Jones started, driving WP 7490 (Goodall being the absentee). Joe Huxham's 1122 cc, CEL 505, kept Harry company, but neither was very successful, failing the observed sections on Fingle Bridge and Simms.

The RAC Rally this year was run from 9 March until 13 March, and finished with tests at Hastings. HFS Morgan had entered two works cars, to start from Leamington Spa. These were a new, very smart 1122 cc car, registered as BAB 765 on the start day of the rally, for HFS himself to drive, and George Goodall accompanied by his son Jim in the other works car, AUY 33, which we believe was running with a 1098 cc engine. Jim Goodall had joined the Morgan factory in 1936 after previous employment at the local electricity power station, and was achieving notable success in trials with the works Matchless MX2-engined trials three-wheeler, WP 6271. It was the intention for Jim to concentrate on driving the special tests.

Harry Jones on Fingle Bridge, during the MCC Exeter Trial. (*Photograph: W. J. Brunell*)

The third member of the Morgan team was E. D. Bowman, starting from Harrogate with a standard 4–4, AUY 229.

E. D. 'Jack' Bowman was the sales director of Bowman and Acock, the new Malvern Link Morgan distributors. His passenger was his partner W. H. 'Bill' Acock. They had purchased the original Morgan factory and adjacent Chestnut Villa (in which Peter Morgan had been born) in 1935, and were to remain enthusiastic Morgan agents for over forty years.

The weather proved atrocious, with snow, ice and fog all encountered during the one thousand miles but the Goodalls were victorious in the group for the open cars up to 10 hp, a superb achievement in this, their first RAC Rally. We

HFS Morgan beside his RAC entry, in the Morgan factory despatch bay. Also present are Sonny McCann and Jim Goodall. (*Photograph: Morgan Motor Co. collection*)

Jim Goodall during the RAC Rally driving tests at Hastings. (*Photograph: Quadrant Picture Library*)

Cornwall agent Cameron Harris at the bottom of Bluehills Mine during the Lands End Trial. (*Photograph: Morgan Motor Co. collection*)

suspect their fast times in the deciding tests were partly explained by the special 1098 cc engine.

For the Lands End Trial, held on the weekend of 26 and 27 March, Harry Jones was reunited with his refurbished Ford-engined 4–4, WP 9590. George Goodall and HFS Morgan were both entered with 1098 cc engined cars, these probably being AUY 33 and WP 7490 respectively. Joe Huxham was in CEL 505 and J. Cameron Harris had his demonstrator, DAF 400. Also entered was L. H. (Len) Coney (in his 4–4 with personalised number plate, CON 502), T. Wagner, J. A. Kyd and T. G. Meeten, all with 1122 cc 4–4s. T. G. Meeten was the Morgan agent in New Malden, Surrey. Cameron Harris was extremely annoyed to have the crown wheel and pinion of the back axle break on the slippery restart on Bluehills Mine – in front of the very enthusiasts he wanted to impress, being the Cornwall agent.

Harry Jones, HFS Morgan and T. Wagner all won Premier Awards, and George Goodall took a Silver, having failed the special test on Crackington Hill. Harry, HFS and George had also entered as the Morgan Motor Company's team in the team competition – which they won, beating the 1½ litre Singers into second place.

This was a major achievement for the Morgan Factory, beating the other works-sponsored teams including the powerful ones from MG.

The MCC was obviously impressed, for on Saturday 24 April the Morgan Motor Company was chosen to represent the MCC as their 'A' team, in the Sutton Coldfield and North Birmingham Automobile Club (SUNBAC) Interteam Trial, starting at Buxton. This was a formidable afternoon's event and most of the top trials teams were entered, including the two teams of works modified MGT As – the cream and brown 'Cream Crackers' and the red 'Three Musketeers', a team of 1½ litre Singers and a team of green supercharged Austin 7s, the Grasshoppers. Although all the Morgans were nominally entered as having 1122 cc engines, Harry Jones was in the Ford-engined car WP 9590 (1172 cc). HFS, accompanied by Peter Morgan, was in WP 7490 (1098 cc) and George Goodall we suspect was using AUY 33 (1098 cc). At the end of the day a mixed Lancashire team proved the victors, just ahead of the two MG teams. The Morgan team finished a creditable sixth, just beating the Singer team once more.

Harry Jones practises for the SUNBAC Inter Team Trial on 'Washgates', with Jim Goodall observing. *(Photograph: Harry Jones collection)*

The MCC Edinburgh Trial was held on 14 and 15 May. This time there were four works entries, all entered rather surprisingly as being of 1122 cc, these being the entries of George Goodall, Harry Jones and HFS Morgan. Also, in the first trial on his own, was the young 17-year-old, Peter Morgan. Peter was looking forward to the day when he could join his father working at

HFS Morgan on Summer Lodge in the Edinburgh Trial. *(Photograph: Quadrant Picture Library)*

the factory but was currently studying automobile engineering at the College of Automobile and Aeronautical Engineering in Chelsea. Passengered by his sister Bobby, Peter was given the prototype, WP 7490, for the event. Harry Jones was in his usual Ford-engined car, WP 9590, and HFS was using BNP 370, a new red works car, Chassis No. 259, registered on 28 April. We suspect George Goodall was in AUY 33. Harry, HFS and George made up the Morgan team entry once more. Also entered was J. Cameron Harris with DAF 400, R Thomas with his 4–4, FPA 500, J. A. Kyd with his 4–4 (he non-started) and Len Coney with CON 502. Premier Awards were obtained by Harry Jones, George Goodall, Cameron Harris and R. Thomas, in what was generally considered to be a very easy trial, owing to the dry weather. Peter Morgan failed Park Rash when he was deemed to have 'ceased forward motion' in attempting to snatch first gear from second, and HFS stopped astride the wrong line on the Tan Hill test. Coney failed on Humble.

The sixth Scottish Rally to be organized by the Royal Scottish Automobile Club was held from 17 to 21 May and based in Glasgow. George Goodall entered in the Open Car Class up to 1300 cc, a solitary Morgan up against twenty-six other entries, including a vast number of MGs. Jim Goodall confirmed his ability as a rally driver by driving his father's entry, AUY 33, to a fine fifth in class.

The regulations for a most interesting race to be held at Donington on 4 September were

Jim Goodall throws AUY 33 around a hairpin during the Scottish Rally. (*Photograph: National Motor Museum collection*)

announced in June by the RAC. This was the 1937 Tourist Trophy (TT), which was being held on the British mainland for the first time. For the previous nine years this famous race had been held on the Ards circuit of closed public roads in Northern Ireland, but in 1936 an out-of-control Riley had killed eight spectators in the town of Newtownards. Down County Council had immediately banned further racing through built-up areas.

The 1937 TT was to be held over one hundred laps of Donington (312 miles), and was restricted to modified sports cars. A handicap system was to be used for cars of different engine capacity. The Morgan Motor Company were definitely interested, and set about designing and building a suitable 4–4.

The previous organizer of the TT, the Ulster Automobile Club, was not to be defeated in its desire to continue to run an annual road race in Northern Ireland. The nearby Antrim Council gave permission for a new circuit of 4.14 miles to be used, near Ballyclare, and the event was to be called the Ulster Trophy. Held over thirty-six laps (149 miles), on 19 June, it too was a handicap event, and it was to provide Morgan with their first win in a major race.

Mrs R. E. Parish, the wife of Belfast Morgan Agent Jack Parish, entered a 4–4. The driver originally nominated was unable to produce his competition licence in time, so one of the mechanics, Robert Campbell, came in as a last-minute substitute. The 4–4 was one of the four limit cars on a handicap of eight credit laps, but the steady consistency of Robert's driving of the fully road equipped (lights and wings fitted) 1122 cc 4–4 earned much praise (his lap times never varied by more than nine seconds, with fastest lap at 54.8 mph). Into the race by three-quarters of an hour he was lying fourth in handicap but his trouble-free drive gradually gave him the advantage (only nine cars out of twenty-three starters completed the course). He finished first after 2 hr. 9 min. 30 sec., 2 minutes ahead of two supercharged MG K3s. This was a superb achievement for Morgans, as this race had many top quality racing cars among the field – including single-seater Alfa Romeos, and Maseratis – the Alfa P3s setting joint fastest laps at 72.73 mph. At last the

Morgan Motor Company had achieved a competition success for the 4–4 to rival those achieved earlier by their potent three-wheelers, and they lost no time in advertising this fact.

Also delighted by the success were Fred and Larry Gorman, who ran a garage in Dublin. The Republic of Ireland (then known as the Irish Free State) was another country that imposed heavy import duties on complete cars brought in from abroad, and the Gorman brothers had arranged to get round this by assembling Morgans in their own works from 'knock down kits'. These were purchased from Morgans in batches of three, the first batch, comprising chassis 329, 330 and 331, leaving the factory on 25 June. They had prevously imported a Chassis, No. 265, in April as an experiment. The cars were assembled by mechanic, Peter Pidgeon, and sales assistant, Simon Heritage. Virtually the only Irish components were glass, paint and batteries, but the original wooden frame for the bench seats was replaced with steel. An edging strip which they added to the front wings to reduce spray was later adopted by Morgan themselves. Tongue and groove floorboards were fitted and each car took nearly one month to assemble.

Similar arrangements had been made for the French agent, Stuart Sandford, who also imported bare chassis, these being bodied locally.

Back at the factory several interesting lines of development were taking place. HFS Morgan had always wanted his 4–4 chassis to be versatile and to be able to carry other types of bodywork, including a four-seater version – just as his three-wheeler chassis could take two- or four-seater bodies. Chassis 303 was taken off the production line early in 1937 to receive four-seater bodywork, although a production version was not introduced until the October Motor Show.

At a similar time, chassis number 238 was subjected to a most interesting experiment, when it was fitted with a 22 hp Ford V8 borrowed from Ford Industrial Units who supplied Ford engines to Morgan for the 'F' type three-wheeler. Ford were rightly proud of this engine, which was basically a small bore scaled down version of the 3.6 litre 30 hp V8 originally designed in Dearborn in the USA by Carl Shultz and Ray Laird. The advanced design had allowed Ford to pioneer the production of an inexpensive but robust V8 engine, by casting the cylinder banks, crankcase and exhaust passages in a single integral unit. The 22 hp version of 2,229 cc (2.6 in. × 3.2 in.) had been specifically designed for Europe, and was in production in Britain from 1936 onwards. The 90° V8 developed 60–65 bhp at 3,500 rpm, with maximum torque of 94 lb ft at 2,500 rpm, and was of side-valve configuration.

Also being constructed at the Morgan factory was a shortened wheelbase car designed as a 'one off' factory car for trials. Given chassis number 380, this car was to be fitted with a Ford 10

engine and finally registered for the road as BWP47 in October.

Finally, a standard 1122 cc Climax-engined car was fitted with a Centric supercharger by Carburettors Limited of Willesden Green in London. Peter Morgan, after preliminary testing of this car on short journeys around Malvern, was allowed by HFS to take it home to Cannon Hill, near Maidenhead. It appeared to go very well but on winding it up to 85–90 mph on the Oxford bypass a main bearing failed. Peter coaxed the car home, trying not to make the bearing rattle terminal. HFS commented that he was not surprised, as he did not think the bottom end was up to supercharging.

On 30 June the third annual Welsh Rally began, organized by the South Wales AC, using eight different starting venues, before converging on Llandrindod Wells. Only one Morgan was entered, DAL 360, belonging to O. M. Scott who started from Harrogate. He was to win the award for the best performance by a Harrogate starter.

The MCC ran its own rally on 16 and 17 July – the Torquay Rally. Despite entries from George Goodall (AUY 33), Cole (DOB 77), Cameron Harris (DAF 400), and Len Coney, only the latter obtained a Premier Award.

Over the sea in the Irish Free State, another handicap race on closed public roads took place on 17 July and again this Irish race was to provide Morgans with a major victory. The international Leinster Trophy competition had been initiated in 1934 at the Skerries circuit, but from 1935 onwards was held on a six-mile course at Tallaght in the foothills of the Dublin mountains. Three 1122 cc Morgan 4–4s were entered for the 154-mile race in 1937, receiving five credit laps from the Leinster Motor Club. One of these was to be driven by Robert Campbell, being the Ulster Trophy winning Morgan, entered by Mrs R. Parrish of Bangor. A second Northern Ireland entry was by Mr Duignan of Belfast for Freddy Smyth to drive (registered EZ 7368). The third, however, was the first Irish assembled Morgan, carrying registration ZC 1176, entered by Fred Gorman himself but to be driven by a Dublin law student, Desmond McCracken. Desmond had previously shown his ability in Irish road racing by winning the 1935 'Round the Houses' Bray race in his Frazer Nash.

Many top drivers were present, including Tony Rolt with one credit lap in the ex-Monte Carlo Rally, supercharged Triumph Dolomite. Practice on a wet evening on 14 July showed Desmond McCracken to be the fastest of the Morgans, lapping at over 60 mph.

Thirty drivers started on a fine day, in five groups according to handicap. Robert Campbell found himself balked at the start and oiled a plug, putting himself behind his team mates, McCracken and Smyth. After ten laps local driver Willie O'Riordan's Riley Brooklands overtook McCracken to take the lead and began to pull away. However, with only seven laps to go he

O. M. Scott tackles the first test on the road to the golf course at Llandrindod Wells, during the Welsh Rally. (*Photograph: National Motor Museum*)

Len Coney on his way to a Premier Award in the MCC Torquay Rally. (*Photograph: National Motor Museum*)

tangled with Charlie Manders' Adler and both went out, leaving the three Morgans in first, second and third positions. Sadly, however, Campbell was forced to slow over the last two laps with 'oiling problems', and eventually dropped to fifth, while Freddy Smyth, attempting a fast final lap, completely misjudged Templeogue Bridge and was forced to retire. McCracken made no mistakes, and after a trouble-free drive won at 61.95 mph, over three minutes ahead of the second-placed MG of Dublin engineer, Cox.

This was truly excellent publicity for the Morgan Motor Company and even more so for the Gorman Brothers' business.

Fred Gorman and Desmond McCracken, with supporter John Laird standing in the front of the successful Morgan racer. (*Photograph: Gorman collection*)

Back in England a virtually complete green 4–4, missing just its engine, and with a special 4½ to 1 back axle ratio, left the factory on 28 July bound for Yorkshire. This car, chassis number 148, was on its way to the famous Scott Motor Cycle Co. at Shipley, where it was to become the mobile test bed for a new car engine that the company hoped other manufacturers (including Morgan) might be interested in.

Scott were famous for their two-stroke twin-cylinder motorcycles, but in 1935 had put into limited production a 980 cc (73 × 78 mm) three-cylinder two-stroke motorcycle. The designer, William Cull, thought that with little adaptation a suitable 1100 cc engine for a car could be devised and thus the 3SM Scott light car engine came into being. Of cylinder dimensions 78 mm × 78 mm (1108 cc), this two-stroke three-cylinder produced over 40 bhp at 4,000 rpm. More on this car later.

Preparation for the TT race continued at the factory with the construction of the Morgan entry. The factory nominated two drivers for their entry – Henry Laird with RMV Sutton as reserve. Henry Laird was a well-known driver of Morgan three-wheelers and had been a member of the factory team for the Relay Races at Brooklands.

It was at Donington where he had particularly made his mark, however, making him an obvious choice for Morgan. He had several times broken the lap record with his Morgan in the three-wheeler classes and had also raced four-wheeled vehicles around the Leicestershire circuit, including the McEvoy Special and an Aston Martin.

The Morgan was entered in Class 6, for cars exceeding 1100 cc up to 1500 cc, but received a special handicap credit of five laps and five seconds for being under 1200 cc, the others in the class of above 1200 cc receiving just two credit laps and 52 seconds start. It is likely the 1122 cc engine had been specially prepared for the event, possibly by Coventry Climax themselves. A Solex carburettor and KLG sparking plugs were used. The engine was fitted into a modified two-seater 4–4, with tuned exhaust system. The standard heavy front wings were replaced by well-made cycle wings, there was a mandatory bonnet strap, and twin aero screens were fitted for practice, although only the driver's side was used for the race. The rear portion of the panel work consisted of a flat sloping panel, on to which a single spare wheel was fitted. Dunlop 'Easiclean' spoked pattern wheels were fitted – such wheels had been in use on works cars for some time – and were probably used to improve air flow to cool the brakes on such a demanding circuit.

Practice began on 31 August. In attendance was Charlie Curtis, the enthusiastic Morgan factory mechanic whose expert knowledge was always much in demand whenever Morgan entered a factory racer, either in earlier three-wheeler, or now four-wheeler form. Charlie Curtis was affectionately known as 'Fatty Curtis' by Henry Laird. He had joined the Morgan Motor Company in 1917, working in the repair shop at Worcester

Charlie Curtis, wearing his famous cap, takes charge of work on the TT entry. (*Photograph: Henry Laird collection*)

The Morgan on the grid. Working on the engine is Charlie Curtis. Jim Goodall stands by the passenger door. Jack Woodhouse wears a beret and stands behind the front wheel, and Henry Laird is by the driver's door. (*Photograph: Henry Laird collection*)

Road until the late 1920s before moving to the new factory in Pickersleigh Road.

There was considerable foreign interest in the TT. Entries had been received from the French manufacturers Delahaye and Darracq, from the Franco-Italian combine of Simca-FIAT, and of particular interest was the team of immaculate white German BMWs, entered by the importer as Frazer Nash BMWs. In practice the Delahaye and BMWs were impressive, and looked likely to win.

The 4th of September turned out to be a fine hot day for the race. Charlie Curtis, Jim Goodall, George Goodall, HFS Morgan, Jack Woodhouse and Barbara Laird (Henry's wife) were all present in the Morgan pits, with Barbara keeping the lap charts. Jack Woodhouse was the esteemed secretary of SUNBAC, of which Henry Laird was a member, and he was also famous for his organizational skills, being an ACU approved timekeeper.

The racer was immaculately prepared for the starting grid and from the start immediately impressed the spectators with its exceptional cornering, as indeed did the BMWs. Henry was lapping consistently at 56–59 mph. He made two pit stops, the first of $59\frac{3}{5}$ seconds to take on five gallons of Cleveland Discol fuel, top up the radiator and check the oil. The second stop, for 1 min. 52 sec., was to take on more water and adjust the brakes. On the eighty-fourth lap, however, the Morgan's race came to an end when a stub axle broke, as Henry accelerated at 80 mph down the straight from Red Gate Corner towards Holly Wood. Henry managed to bring the three-wheeler to a stop in the adjoining field before retrieving the errant wheel.

The TT itself was won by Gianfranco Comotti's 4-litre Darracq, ahead of another Darracq, a BMW and then the first British car – Donald Barnes' Singer. The Morgan was not the only car to lose a wheel as Charles Martin's Lagonda had a similar incident at Melbourne corner.

Naturally the stub axle failure caused some concern at the Morgan factory and was put down to insufficient radius at the change of section of the stub axle at the sites of the bearings. Slightly

Henry Laird inspects the retrieved wheel. (*Photograph: Quadrant Picture Library*)

tapered stub axles were to be introduced on all 4–4s after chassis number 493, which left the factory in January 1938. Later the 1¼in. width brake shoes were increased to 1½in. with chassis number 545 (despatched in March 1938), and finally fully tapered stub axles were introduced with chassis number 578 (despatched in May 1938).

The famous Phoenix Park circuit in Dublin was the venue for the annual races organized by the Irish Motor Racing Club (IMRC) on 11 September. This circuit of four and a quarter miles featured a long straight of almost two miles, and had been used for motor races since 1929. For the September meeting two separate one hundred mile races were planned, one a scratch race and the other a handicap. Desmond McCracken entered ZC 1176 for the latter. He enlivened practice on a wet 9 September when he encountered a flock of peacocks wandering on to the track from the park zoo. He cleared the track in a flurry of feathers!

The handicap event was run off first on 11 September and included in the field such famous drivers as Raymond Mays with a supercharged 1½-litre ERA, and 'B. Bira' with a supercharged 3-litre Maserati, both on scratch. McCracken had the misfortune of losing a minute by having to secure a loose carburettor float but came through to finish fifth at a speed of 70.07 mph after a handicap credit of seven laps. The race was won by David Yule's supercharged CMY (Cox Morris Yule Special) but Bira very nearly caught him, averaging 105.01 mph on the very fast circuit.

Brooklands on 25 September saw the MCC running its annual High Speed Trials, bad weather reducing the expected speeds. Joe Huxham still managed to put 74.72 miles into his hour, driving CEL 505, but R. Thomas could only cover a disappointing 67.61 miles.

The following weekend Desmond McCracken was back in action, this time in the Leinster Motor Club's October Trial, a reliability event with a driving test at the finish. He showed the versatility of his Morgan by winning a First Class Award and coming second overall. He had also managed tenth place in the Irish Rally held the previous month, confirming the competitiveness of ZC1176.

This year the Motor Show had been transferred to the newly completed Exhibition Centre at Earls Court, and was held from 14 to 23 October. The Morgan Motor Company featured the four-seater for the first time showing a Nile Blue car. The Carnation Red prototype had already been reviewed by some motoring magazines in August. The new four-seater was advertised at £225, the two-seater costing £210.

On 23 October the MCC ran its Sporting Trial in the Buxton district of Derbyshire. Sporting trials used much reduced road distances compared with classic trials but included stiffer gradients on the observed hills, often with appalling surfaces. Jim Goodall entered in the brand new short chassis works trials car, which was registered BWP 47 only four days before the event. It was fitted with an 1172 cc Ford 'C' side-valve engine, and Jim was to make this car a very successful trials car, using it extensively. He was accompanied by E. F. Tomkinson's standard 4–4, BAB 11. Torrential downpours made the event particularly unpleasant for the crews and Bamford Clough was especially demanding.

Jim was 'clean', however, and went on to win a Premier Award. To aid traction Jim would position an old two gallon petrol can, filled with lead, behind the seats to add weight over the rear wheels. Tomkinson had a disastrous day, failing every hill.

The North West London MC's Gloucester Trial held on 4 December was now more of a sporting trial than its original classic predecessor, with *The Autocar* calling it 'Tough, mighty tough'. Even hills used previously only for the British Experts Trial for motorcycles, were included, such as the appropriately named Breakheart. Jim Goodall was one of only thirteen who managed to clear this hill, but he did not finish in the awards.

Overseas

Australia

While Australia did have some circuit racing, the dare-devil racers who broke records travelling from one city to another had attracted more public attention. The Phillip Island circuit, situated offshore, nor far from Melbourne, Victoria, had

The two Morgans of Jim Boughton (31) and Gus Collins (32) at Phillip Island. (*Photograph: Terry Wright collection*)

been given a gravel covered six and a half mile rectangular circuit for the 1928 Australian Grand Prix. It had staged all the annual Australian Grand Prix up to and including 1935. Maintenance of the circuit deteriorated, however, and combined with complaints from local residents, led to the circuit being downgraded into a three and a quarter mile triangle. It never hosted the Grand Prix again. All was not bad news for circuit racing, as £25,000 was being spent on a new circuit at Bathurst, New South Wales, around the slopes of Mount Panorama. It was hoped the racing would encourage tourism to the area.

There were also dust speedway circuits available in the major cities of Sydney (Maroubra) and Melbourne (Aspendale). The Victorian Light Car Club had constructed a loose gravel surfaced half-mile hillclimb on private property at Rob Roy in the Christmas Hills, approximately twenty miles east of Melbourne.

Home-constructed specials were a particular feature of Australian events, partly because of the difficulty in getting up-to-date equipment from the distant automobile factories of Europe and the USA.

In November 1937 the Victorian Sporting Car Club held its Cup Day races on the shortened Phillip Island circuit.

Two Morgans took part, both stripped 4–4s, driven by James Boughton and A. Collins. All the races were handicap events, James Boughton managing fourth place in the third race over five laps, and sixth in the 15 lap (50 miles) final race, at a speed of 58 mph, despite breaking a cam follower.

Twenty-seven-year-old Jim Boughton had acquired his Morgan from the Melbourne agents 'Brylaws' in which his mother had invested some money. Jim was to work for Brylaws on the management side in 1938 and 1939. On his racing exploits he was often accompanied by Brylaw mechanics and his younger brother, Russell.

'Gus' Collins was also employed by Brylaws, the Morgan agents set up by Jack Bryson and Wally Lawson, but he was their main salesman.

CHAPTER FOUR

1938

The year 1938 began with the MCC's Exeter Trial, held on Friday and Saturday, 7 and 8 January. The Morgan factory was represented by the Ford-engined cars of Jim Goodall and Harry Jones (BWP 47 and WP 9590 respectively) along with the Climax car of George Goodall, now claimed as 1122 cc (probably AUY 33). These three also made up the Morgan team. Among the private entries were L. Coney, G. Lilley, E. F. Tomkinson, Joe Huxham, D. H. George, R. Thomas and E. G. Boutle. From Dublin came Desmond McCracken with his famous 4–4. Of these, Harry Jones, having won Premier Awards in the previous two MCC Trials (Edinburgh and Lands End), was one of thirteen entries eligible for a triple award – a highly coveted award among trials drivers for winning Premier Awards in all three classic MCC Trials held in one year.

Sadly, Harry picked the worst possible starting place – Stratford on Avon. Beset with severe ice just two miles from the start there was considerable damage to many entries in the treacherous conditions. The entire MG Three Musketeers' Team went off in wild skids, one rolling and another embracing a telegraph pole. Sadly, Harry Jones had to retire along with another Stratford starter, Desmond McCracken, with unreported maladies.

E. F. Tomkinson on Knowle Lane in the MCC's Exeter Trial. (*Photograph: Quadrant Picture Library*)

Premier Awards were claimed by Joe Huxham with CEL 505, Len Coney with CON 502, Jim and George Goodall with their works entries; Lilley won a Silver and Tomkinson, Thomas and Boutle won Bronzes, the second part of the Fingle Bridge being particularly difficult in what was generally thought to be an easy trial.

George Goodall was found to be quite a difficult man to deal with by many Morgan agents. Several believed he had 'favourite agencies' for whom all was roses, whereas the others were to be given inferior treatment. Certainly he could be difficult. Joe Huxham, who got on comparatively well with him, recalled writing to him about a problem with a JAP engine, experienced by one of his customers in a three-wheeler. In his reply George blamed the customer, assuring him that only Joe's customers experienced this problem. He added that while he himself drove fast, he always drove intelligently. Joe always remembered this and when, on a subsequent visit to the factory, he noticed Goodall's three-wheeler with a front wheel, wing and front tubes bent back into the body, he inquired of the cause, to be told that George had hit his front gate post! Joe subsequently incorporated the remark about intelligent driving into his poem on the birth of the 4–4 (see chapter 1).

HFS Morgan also had reason to be angry with George Goodall's driving abilities when, in the winter of 1937–38, George had an almighty crash with WP 7490 in the Worcester Road in Malvern, destroying the car and being lucky not to be injured. The car was returned to the works, and HFS insisted this unique prototype was rebuilt. It was finally sold on the 6 March 1938, carrying the unusual chassis number FW 123.

Meanwhile, George Goodall himself was having his own car AUY 33 modified with cycle-type front wings and outside exhaust system, as used on the TT car. In this form it was to become a very potent competition car. At some time it also acquired a 1232 cc Coventry Climax engine as fitted to the Triumph Gloria (66 mm × 90 mm with 46 bhp) and having different tappet adjustment to the smaller Morgan engine. Goodall, however, rather naughtily would always enter the car as being a standard capacity 1122 cc. Quite when this engine was fitted is not known.

HFS Morgan was now considering another body version for his chassis. He was impressed with the coupe bodies produced by the Warwick firm of Avon Bodies on various manufacturers' chassis, in particular those of the Standard Motor Company. Accordingly, he commissioned the firm to build a coupe body on chassis number 500 during the winter of 1937. The Avon coupe bodies had been originally designed by either Alan Jensen, one of the Jensen brothers later to found their own motor company, or A.H. Meredith, who became a post-war director of Avons. When this car returned to the factory early in 1938 it attracted much favourable comment. Henry Laird called it 'Uncle George's Winter Carriage'.

Back on the Irish trials hills, Desmond McCracken was on his home territory for the

'Where's George?' was the caption given to this photo by Harry Jones. (*Photograph: Harry Jones collection*)

Uncle George's Winter Carriage. (*Photograph: Henry Laird collection*)

Dublin University MC and LCC Grafton Cup Trial on the 5 March, over a fifty-three mile course. He set fastest time in two of the special tests, becoming a worthy winner of the Grafton Cup, excellent compensation for his Exeter retirement.

At Brooklands on 26 March the Junior Car Club (JCC) ran its rally, consisting of seven different driving tests. Three Morgans were entered, those of J. A. Andrews, Miss Dorothy Bean and M. A. C. Simmonds. The two men won Second Class Awards.

On 8 April Joe Huxham acquired a new Morgan for competition use. With chassis number 575, fitted with a 1098cc engine, spoked disc wheels with competition tyres and a Burgess silencer, this black two-seater was registered EEL 200. The engine (MA 591) was one of a batch of twenty-two (MA 576–597) 1100cc engines (62.3mm bore) ordered by the factory.

While Joe did not enter for the MCC Lands End Trial held on 15 and 16 April, he did follow the trial to take part in the post-event drinking at the St Ives hotel. Two Morgan teams were entered. In one team were the two Ford-engined cars of Harry Jones (WP 9590) and Jim Goodall (BWP 47), along with George Goodall and his modified 4–4 AUY 33, entered as 1122cc.

In the other team were Len Coney with CON 502, HFS and Peter Morgan. HFS Morgan was driving CAB 652, a new red works two-seater

George Goodall in AUY 33, has a break with Harry Jones and Sonny McCann, while queuing for an observed section in the Lands End Trial. (*Photograph: Sonny McCann collection*)

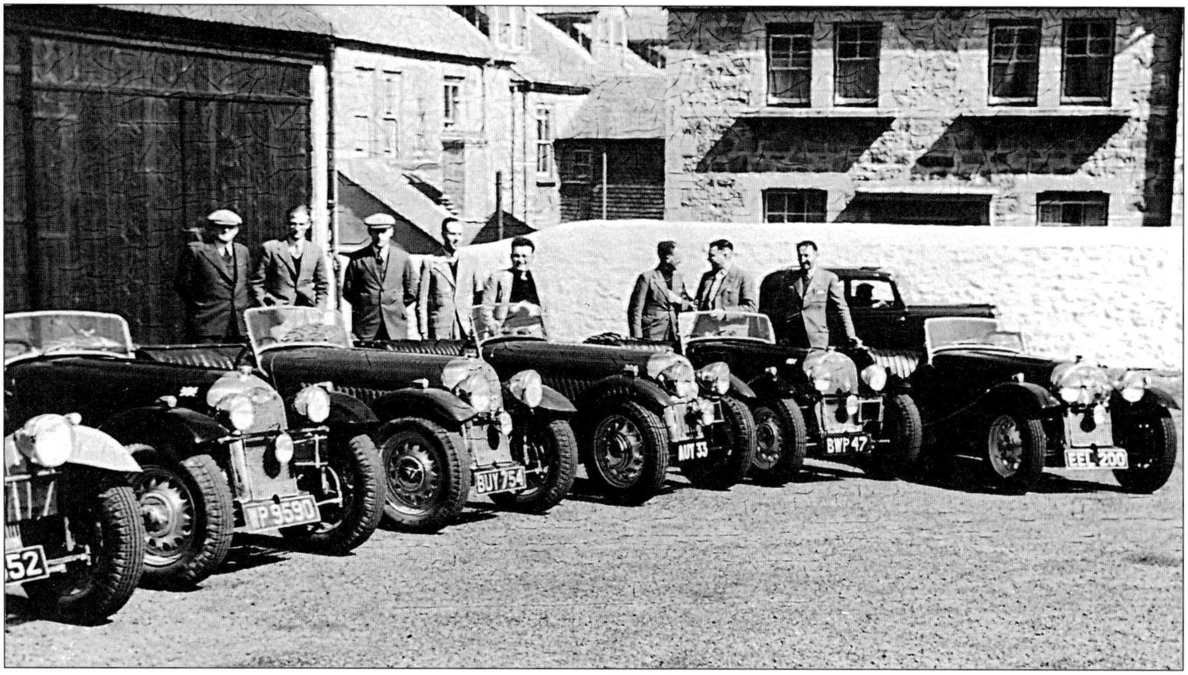

Morgan entries at St Ives, after the finish of the Lands End Trial. Behind the cars can be identified HFS and Peter Morgan (left), Jim Goodall (behind AUY 33), Harry Jones (behind BWP 47) and Joe Huxham (far right). (*Photograph: Morgan Motor Co. collection*)

registered on 7 April, fitted with a 5½ to 1 back axle to make it more suitable for climbing trials hills. Peter Morgan was driving BUY 754, a blue works two-seater, chassis number 373 first registered on 16 September 1937, which had now been allocated to him for trials work.

Also entered were R. Thomas, R. S. Mantle, F. E. Whipp and Cameron Harris in their 4/4s. The latter was driving a new 4–4, reg. EAF 735. This he had collected from the factory the day before the trial. Chassis number 587, the black two-seater was another of those fitted with an 1100 cc engine (MA 581), and it had 5.50in. × 16in. tyres and a 5½ to 1 back axle ratio.

There were mixed fortunes for the competitors. While the Morgans, both father and son, Jim Goodall and Mantle were all clean and received Premier Awards, Harry Jones failed Bluehills Mine for a Silver, and the others, except poor Thomas, all received Bronze Awards.

Towards the end of 1937 a new Morgan agency received its first car from the factory. This was the Winter Garden Garages in Holborn, London. It was owned by Lancelot and Charlotte Prideaux-Brune who were keen supporters of British sports cars, and already agents for Aston Martins. Indeed, in 1932 they had briefly owned the company!

Their workshop was managed by a meticulous self-taught mechanic by the name of C. M. 'Dick' Anthony, whom Lance had persuaded to leave his own Mews garage and join his business in 1932, along with his assistant Joe Penny.

Dick Anthony was a regular competitor in racing events and trials with a 2-litre experimentally engined MkII Aston Martin BGF 557, which he prepared himself. The Prideaux-Brunes had previously accompanied the Aston Martin company to Le Mans for the 1933 24-hour race, working alongside Aston Martin team manager 'Sammy' Davis in the pits. Dick Anthony had also been to Le Mans, manning the pits for the private Aston Martin entries of Reggie Tongue and John Noel in 1934.

With such racing experience available it was not surprising that an enthusiastic, young London-based daughter of a Sheffield solicitor should approach Winter Garden Garages regarding the organization of a drive in the 1938 Le Mans 24-hour race in June. Prudence Fawcett, although now living in London, had previously been living near Genoa in Italy. Some years earlier she had raced an Alfa Romeo 1750 in a minor event there, finishing second. She had also been importing Alfa Romeos into England and these had been sold in London on her behalf by Winter Garden Garages. A trip to the 1937 Le Mans 24 hour race in the Duke of Kent's aircraft had convinced her that she herself must have a go, having watched Miss Dorothy Stanley-Turner and Miss Enid Riddell finish sixteenth with their little MG.

Prudence Fawcett had been fascinated by sports cars all her life, and had been encouraged by her Bugatti owning Uncle Percy, of nearby Hope in Derbyshire. She had learned to drive at the age of seventeen, and her first sports car was a Wolseley Hornet. Not only did she maintain her own cars, but took such pride in them that she would always leather them off following a wet journey, even after returning from a party at 3 a.m.!

A Morgan seemed the ideal small sports car for Prudence to enter, and so discussions were entered into with HFS Morgan about the possibility of a Morgan for Le Mans. Meanwhile Prudence put in her application.

HFS agreed to supply a Morgan, based on the 1937 TT car, but wanted the Prideaux-Brunes to run the whole operation, aiming for a finish with a good average speed and hence to qualify for the final of the biennial cup sponsored by Rudge-Whitworth (a handicap competition held over two successive years). By April, Prudence was able to confirm to the Automobile Club de l'Oest, the organizer, that she would be driving a Morgan, and construction was put in hand at the Morgan factory. She had managed to obtain some sponsorship from Lord Wakefield of Castrol oils.

Another vehicle being completed at the factory, but of very different type, was an experimental coupe. This was the Morgan factory's version of the Avon Bodies design, and was fitted to chassis 600, which had a 1100 cc Climax engine. This proved satisfactory and production was to begin in the summer.

This year's five-day RAC Rally began on Tuesday 26 April, with starts in London, Torquay,

Harrogate and Leamington. As usual HFS Morgan wanted to impress the press and spectators and had the factory team comprising CAB 652, for himself, George Goodall with AUY 33 and Jack Bowman with BWP44, turned out in the patriotic colours, red, blue and white respectively, attracting much attention.

Also starting from Leamington was Miss Dorothy Bean in EJJ 63, and completing the Morgan entries was J.F. Heaton from Harrogate.

Dorothy Bean was another enthusiastic amateur lady driver, and a close friend of the Prideaux-Brunes. Consequently she was a favoured customer of Winter Garden Garages. She had competed previously in Aston Martins in the early 1930s, and formed part of the Aston Martin pit crew at Le Mans in 1933.

The one thousand mile road sections of the RAC rally were relatively mild this year and most cars reached Blackpool. It was either in this rally, or the previous year, that Jack Bowman experienced an elusive misfire that resisted all efforts to cure it. His passenger, Ken Acock, finally resorted to the unusual measure of lying on the front wing with the bonnet up while Jack drove along. Finally he spotted the trouble – the distributor was lifting on its pedestal and soon the misfire was no more.

Come the special test and George Goodall, AUY 33 (probably with Jim Goodall driving), did exceptionally well, winning the class for up to 10hp open cars, while HFS finished fourth, and Heaton seventh. Dick Anthony, incidently, won the class for open cars from 10 to 15hp with his Aston Martin, and Prideaux Brune also competed with an Aston.

For the MCC Edinburgh Trial on 3 and 6 June two factory teams were entered once again.

Dorothy Bean raises dust in the RAC Rally. (*Photograph: National Motor Museum*)

George Goodall with AUY 33, Harry Jones with WP 9590 and Jim Goodall with BWP 47 made up one team. HFS Morgan with CAB 652, his son Peter with BUY 754 and Len Coney with CON 502 made up the other. Cameron Harris, passengered by his wife, was in EAF 735. His son Raymond was in DRL 339. R. Thomas was in FPA 500, and also competing were R. Mantel, W. Webb and H. Reuben. Three days of rain made the Scottish hills particularly treacherous, so no doubt HFS and Peter were delighted each to claim First Class Awards, with their team finishing second in the team competition to the works-prepared big-engined MGTA 'Cream Crackers'. Silvers were won by the two Goodalls, Mantel and Cameron Harris. Unlucky Harry Jones retired, in his last trial with the Ford-engined prototype, WP 9590.

The following week J. F. Heaton took part in the Scottish Rally and after five days of rallying managed to finish sixth behind five MGs in the class for open cars up to 1300 cc.

Early in June the Le Mans car was delivered to Winter Garden Garages ready for the Le Mans 24-hour race to be held on 18 and 19 June. It closely resembled the TT car, having a flat sloping tail on which was fastened the spare wheel, but differed from the TT car in having slightly different cycle-type front wings, and two bonnet straps. It had been given the registration number BNP 370 from the 1937 works 4–4, to enable it to be driven on the French roads down to the circuit.

The engine was a specially built and balanced Coventry Climax unit of 1098 cc, fitted with a down draught carburettor, and magneto ignition for better sparks at high revs. The compression ratio was 8 to 1, giving well over 50 bhp (the standard 1098 cc competition engine had a compression ratio of 6.5 to 1 and produced 48 bhp). An extra large fuel tank of approximately twenty-four gallons was fitted behind the seats, with twin fuel fillers protruding through the tonneau cover. A wire gauze stone screen was fitted for the driver in addition to an aero screen, but was not needed.

Prudence and Dick Anthony gave the car a thorough check in the Winter Garden workshops, before setting off for Le Mans on Saturday, 11 June. The car was shipped across the Channel and then driven onwards to Le Mans by Prudence, accompanied by a female companion, arriving at the Hostellerie des Ifs at Le Mans on the 12th.

This hotel had several stables, and they had arranged to rent one of these for 5 francs a day as a garage for testing and preparation.

Preparation of the Morgan by Dick Anthony continued here, and Prudence was able to put in three days' practice between the regulation hours of 1 a.m. to 6 a.m., sticking to a rigid schedule of lap times and resisting the temptation to 'have a go' at the faster cars. The Morgan's top speed was quoted at just under 100 mph by the British newspapers, suggesting a non-standard back axle ratio.

Cameron Harris needs some help on Adderstonshiels in the MCC Edinburgh Trial. (*Photograph: National Motor Museum*)

J. F. Heaton in the Scottish Rally. (*Photograph: National Motor Museum*)

Prudence Fawcett, Geoff White and Dick Anthony preparing the Morgan at the Hostellerie des Ifs. (*Photograph: Prudence Fawcett collection*)

The Morgan is positioned for the Le Mans start. (*Photograph: Prudence Fawcett collection*)

A pit stop for Prudence. Note her special seat cushion behind her back to bring her further forward than the normal seat back allowed. (*Photograph: Prudence Fawcett collection*)

Prudence's co-driver was to be Geoff White, the Sales Manager of Winter Garden Garages. The arrangement was for each driver to undertake four-hour shifts, with Geoff doing the start.

Of the forty-two starters, no fewer than twenty-seven failed to finish. The race was won by the 3½ litre Delahaye of Chaboud and Tremoulet at an average of 82.36 mph, but for most of the race the remarkable pace set by Sommer and Biondetti in their 2.9 litre Alfa Romeo 862900B Berlinetta Special Coupe looked uncatchable and caused havoc among those who tried to keep up. It led for twenty-one hours at an average of 94 mph and was reaching over 150 mph on the Mulsanne Straight before a burst tyre led to mechanical failure and retirement.

The little Morgan, meanwhile, had been circulating happily to schedule, the driver changing every twenty-five laps. Lap speeds varied between 57 and 65 mph and the only notable happening was at half distance during the night, when the Morgan pit manager fell into the adjacent MG pit, complete with a door, felling six bewildered people in the process!

Prudence was thoroughly enjoying herself, and the initial nerves soon settled. By noon on the Sunday there was jubilation in the Morgan camp when they realized they had a four-lap lead over their nearest rival. Unfortunately a misfire, caused by valve trouble, then intervened and lap times had to be reduced to ensure a finish, losing their position. Eventually the Morgan finished thirteenth overall, having covered 1,373 miles at an average of 57.20 mph.

Only two British cars crewed by British drivers finished, the other being the 1½ litre HRG of Peter Clark and Marcus Chambers, which finished tenth. When the band struck up the British National Anthem in honour of these achievements, Prudence received a bouquet and was warmly applauded.

The Morgan had done all that was expected. It qualified for the Biennial Cup covering the required distance in just twenty-two hours, and HFS immediately began advertising the superb achievement.

After the celebrations were over the engine was stripped and new valves fitted before Prudence once more took the wheel. This time she was

Prudence Fawcett visits her parents at Sheffield. (*Photograph: Prudence Fawcett collection*)

J. A. Andrews at speed on Brooklands during the JCC meeting. (*Photograph: The Light Car*)

Joe Huxham at Brooklands during the three-hour race, the club house in the background. (*Photograph: Quadrant Picture Library*)

racing across France to Calais at over 60 mph average on her way home to visit her family in Sheffield! With her was a set of broken goggles – hit by flying tyre tread from the stricken Sommer Alfa Romeo. These are still in the family's possession.

The 1100 cc class had been won by Jacques and Pierre Savoye with a Singer, covering 1,467 miles. The Savoyes were later to become the post-war Paris Morgan agents, and were able to use their Le Mans experience to assist the factory with their entry in 1962, of which more much later.

The Le Mans Morgan was soon to return to the factory for preparation for the Tourist Trophy race to be held at Donington on 3 September. This year the rules had been changed to allow freer engine preparation, and also enough fuel had to be carried for the full 312 miles, as refuelling was not allowed. This made the Le Mans car most suitable for the event, and Henry Laird was again to be nominated as driver, with Joe Huxham as reserve.

Summer brought the usual number of race meetings in Britain and Ireland. At the JCC's members' day at Brooklands on 2 July J. A. Andrews finished third in a one-lap handicap. He then went on to win a two-lap handicap convincingly from the limit position at 71.56 mph, beating an AC and a Terraplane.

The weekend of 16 and 17 July saw three important events taking place, two race meetings and a rally.

At Brooklands on 16 July the Light Car Club organized a three-hour race for sports cars, over the Campbell road circuit. Joe Huxham and his business partner Tom Bryant, who also prepared the car, entered in EEL 200, their 1098 cc 4–4. They had an absolutely trouble-free run, with two stops for change of driver, and finished a creditable eighth at 52.73 mph. They were also class winners for up to 1100 cc, in fact the only entrants in the class!

The MCC Torquay Rally had four Morgan entries for the Friday, 15 July start. W. F. Webb and Raymond Harris started from Exeter. Len Coney and Jim Goodall started from Stratford upon Avon. This mixed trial and rally finished in Torquay, with Jim Goodall, in BWP 47, winning the class for open cars up to £7 10*s.* 0*d.* car tax, and the others all taking Premier Awards.

Over in Ireland the Leinster Motor Club's Leinster Trophy race meeting was held once more

Jim Goodall with Sonny McCann gets away from the stop and restart test at Babbacombe, on his way to a class win in the Torquay Rally. (*Photograph: National Motor Museum*)

over the Tallaght circuit on 16 July over twenty-six laps (154 miles). Two Morgans were entered, Bobby Campbell from Belfast and Desmond McCracken from Dublin with ZC 1176. The slower Morgan of Campbell was given five laps and one minute start, compared with four laps and two minutes for Desmond McCracken.

Sadly, McCracken ran a newly fitted big end bearing after just three laps and retired, after lapping at 66.77 mph. At the sixteen-lap stage Campbell was lying fourth, but by then the scratch men were coming through the field, and at the flag he finished eleventh at 62.47 mph.

The following week saw the Fourth Welsh Rally start on Wednesday 20 July. Just two Morgans took part, Miss Dorothy Bean starting from London, and R. Richards from Leamington. Richards did very well, finishing second in the open cars up to 10 bhp class while Dorothy suffered from oil on the brakes, hitting some of the final driving test barriers.

Over in Ireland the Irish Motor Racing Club had reintroduced the 'round the houses' Limerick Grand Prix on 1 August after a one-year absence. The twisting street circuit of 2.76 miles included the main thoroughfare, O'Connell Street, and was to be of fifty-five laps (151 miles). Sadly only eighteen entries were attracted to this handicap event, but one of them was Belfast's Bobby Campbell with his ex-Ulster Trophy winning 4–4 who received fifteen credit laps over scratch man Tony Rolt with an ERA. Also on fifteen credit laps was another Belfast driver, J. D. McClure with an MGTA, and for the first twenty minutes of the race McClure and Campbell held uncontested first and second positions, the former lapping consistently 4–6 seconds faster than Campbell.

No one could touch McClure, who finished first after 2 hr. 9 min. and 50 sec. Campbell finished second, 5½ minutes behind at 51.96 mph, after Aubrey Thompson's much modified Ford 8 Special retired with engine trouble just a mile from a certain second place finish having previously passed Campbell. Of the meagre grid of seventeen eventual starters, only a handful finished and this was to be the last of the Limerick 'Round the Houses' races. The ERA unfortunately retired with transmission failure.

Desmond McCracken smiles for the camera before the start of the Leinster Trophy race. (*Photograph: Brendan Lynch collection*)

Dorothy Bean knocks off the barriers during the final driving tests of the Welsh Rally, held near the City Hall in Cardiff. (*Photograph: Morgan Motor Co. collection*)

During the summer months Peter Morgan was having much fun using the 22 hp V8-engined experimental Morgan. The engine gave remarkable performance to a ceiling of 90–92 mph, when it was as if a 'governor' was applied to the engine. This made it a very safe car to drive – except for the brakes. The car suffered badly from brake fade, a subject little known about at this time. Peter was keen to have a Morgan entry for races himself, but his father first wanted him to have more experience on the road and in trials, so he contented himself with spectating at the various events of the day, the V8 Morgan being excellent for post event 'dices'.

Back at the Morgan factory Harry Jones took delivery of his new works Morgan on 18 July.

Joe Huxham's Morgan at the Donington pits. (*Photograph: Sonny McCann collection*)

Henry Laird sits in the TT car, whilst Charlie Curtis and Jim Goodall attend to the car. Over the pit counter can be seen HFS Morgan (partly hidden by wooden support), Barbara Laird, with cigarette, and George Goodall, holding his chin. (*Photograph: Morgan Motor Co. collection*)

Registered CNP 507, it was a black four-seater, chassis number 666. It was to become the works road test four-seater that was borrowed by the motoring press for evaluation tests. We wonder if they were aware of the special Climax engine of 1098 cc that powered this innocent looking car – no less than one of the special 8–1 compression racing versions! Harry decided to 'run-in' the new car on a trip to the French Alps with his wife Lola and her sister Dagmar Cotton, spending much time with the Paris Morgan agent Stuart Sandford and his wife. Harry's old car, WP 9590, a significant prototype, was finally sold second-hand from the factory on 17 August.

Following successes in the Poole Speed Trials in Poole Park on 16 August, where he finished third in the sports cars and racing car classes of up to 1100 cc, Joe Huxham now prepared for the RAC Tourist Trophy Meeting at Donington for which he was reserve driver to Henry Laird. He took EEL 200 up to the Derbyshire circuit for some practice and met up with the Morgan factory's entry – the ex-Le Mans car, still carrying registration BNP 370. Only two British cars had been entered by manufacturers – the Morgan and an Aston Martin being among the thirty-one entries, but several other British cars were private entries.

Again the French Darracq team was present, and this year no fewer than six of the BMW sports cars were entered as Frazer Nash-BMWs. The Morgan being of 1098 cc this year, was one of eleven in class 5, 500 cc–1100 cc, there also being two Franco Italian Simca FIATS, one FIAT, two Rileys, two MGs and two Singers in this class.

Supporting the Morgan entry was Charlie Curtis as mechanic, George and Jim Goodall, HFS Morgan, Barbara Laird with Henry's dog Lou, Jack Woodhouse, and the Lairds friend 'Zug' Sugden, a three-wheeler enthusiast.

The start this year was a mass start. When Ebblewhite dropped the Union flag at midday the drivers had to start their engines and were then on their way. Initially the course was dry

The TT car, with Barbara Laird sat inside, at Melbourne following the race. 'Zug' Sugden has his hand in the air behind his own three wheeler; next to him is Henry Laird, then Charlie Curtis and finally George Goodall behind his own car. Note the BMW transporter on the right. (*Photograph: Henry Laird collection*)

Desmond McCracken calls at the shops on his way to Phoenix Park! (*Photograph: Gorman collection*)

but by half distance heavy rain had begun, making the course treacherous and, indeed, it flooded in parts. Sadly the Morgan began to lose water from radiator pipes, and required frequent stops for attention – recurrence of a problem that had occurred to a lesser degree towards the end of the Le Mans race.

The French 3-litre Delage of Louis Giron won the event at 67.61 mph. Henry Laird was flagged off in twenty-fourth place, having completed ninety-three laps.

In Ireland the IMRC's Phoenix Park Grand Prix Meeting took place on Saturday 10 September. Again, as in the previous year, there were two races, the scratch race being preceded by a handicap race. Desmond McCracken duly entered ZC 1176 for the handicap event, which was over eighteen laps (76¾ miles) of this fast circuit. He received four credit laps and two minutes start over the scratch 2-litre Bugatti of Charles Brackenbury, in a field of thirty-two.

The handicapping proved excellent and exciting racing was enjoyed, particularly by a group

Just before the start of the first High Speed Trial, with Dick Anthony and Geoff Hunt in the Morgan (10), alongside two MG TAs (8 & 9). (*Photograph: Quadrant Picture Library*)

of six Dublin drivers off the same handicap. For lap after lap Willie O'Riodan's Riley, Charlie Mander's Adler and McCracken's Morgan travelled tail to bonnet until sadly McCracken had to retire.

Back in England Peter Morgan was delighted when his father offered him a drive in CNP 507, Harry Jones' four-seater, for the MCC high-speed trial meeting at Brooklands on 10 September. Also representing the factory was Jim Goodall, but he was driving the ex-Le Mans, ex-TT racer, BNP 370, which had to be fitted with lights (in three-wheeler fashion) to allow it to comply with the 'touring' specification required by the MCC. There were two one-hour high speed trials. Only one Morgan competed in the first event – Dick Anthony with a 4–4 in the rather unusual engine size of 1087 cc.

Accompanied by Geoff Hunt, a Winter Garden Garages junior salesman, Dick successfully obtained a Premier Award, putting seventy-four miles into his hour.

The second hour high speed trial had three Morgans entered. Peter Morgan, driving bareheaded, was accompanied by his sister Bobby, Jim Goodall was passengered by Cecil 'Sonny' McCann, who worked in the machine shop, and also entered was Joe Huxham in EEL 200, probably accompanied by his partner Tom Bryant. These three also made up the Morgan team entry, and it is interesting that this team of Morgans all had 1098 cc engines rather than the production 1122 cc versions.

As expected, Jim Goodall shot away in the Le Mans car, but was delayed by some mechanical problems, eventually putting 79.43 miles into his hour. Joe Huxham managed 67.76 miles, and Peter Morgan out-distanced them all in his first speed event by managing 80.72 miles. All received Premier Awards.

The start of the second High Speed Trial, with Peter Morgan in CNP 507 (27), Jim Goodall in the TT car (28) and Joe Huxham in EEL 200 (25). (*Photograph: Quadrant Picture Library*)

Peter was naturally very pleased with his performance, although he had found the drive around Brooklands very bumpy. HFS Morgan was also absolutely delighted, as 81 miles in the hour was a masterful achievement for a four-seater. Then Charlie Curtis sought out Peter and told him that he could not start the car, as all the piston rings were broken. Peter was horrified; he envisaged the end of his racing career on his first event, having wrecked the engine. He went, rather crestfallen, to tell his father. 'Oh don't worry,' he replied, 'you did a fine speed. In fact, you probably did better because you had no piston rings. When racing three-wheelers we often removed piston rings to reduce high speed friction!'

Peter was thankful that his father could behave in such a down-to-earth way. Quite what Harry Jones thought of the whole affair is not recorded!

During 1938 the Bugatti Owners Club had constructed a hill climb using 880 yards of the private drive to Prescott House, situated near Gotherington in Gloucestershire. They ran their first event on 10 April, but the first event to include a Morgan was held on 25 September when J. A. Andrews finished sixth in the class for unsupercharged sports cars up to 1500 cc, with a time of 63.65 seconds.

Back at the factory Morgans were announcing their models for the coming year. Joining the two- and four-seater was the new Coupe model. HFS had been concerned about the noise levels inside

George Goodall, Sonny McCann and Charlie Curtis behind the ex-Le Mans and TT car, parked on the Brooklands Finishing Straight. (*Photograph: Sonny McCann collection*)

this almost closed body, and, therefore, the engine and gearbox were supported by four Silentbloc rubber bushes. The Meadows gearbox was also rather noisy, and so HFS arranged for Moss gears to supply their version, which had quieter double helical gear profiles. The gear ratios differed little from the Meadows, and with the 5 to 1 back axle ratio gave overall ratios of 19.3, 11.95, 6.7 and 5 to 1, with a 22.35 reverse. The first gearbox was fitted to the first production Coupe, chassis number 648, which took some time to leave the factory, eventually departing in November. Meadows gearboxes continued to be available alongside the new Moss for other models, and were still being fitted into the late 1940s.

The new Coupe was retailed at £225. It also had 16 in. wheels taking 5.50 section tyres, and a new slotted radiator grille. It was a true flagship to the Morgan range.

Over in Ireland Desmond McCracken was now having better luck. In the IMRC Ballinascomey Hill Climb he won the handicap section of the over 1100 cc class, and came tenth in the unlimited capacity handicap class. Desmond now decided to have another go at a MCC event in England, and duly entered the Sporting Trial, held in Derbyshire on 22 October. He formed part of the Morgan team, accompanying Peter Morgan with BUY 754 and Jim Goodall with BWP 47. In what was generally reckoned to be an easy trial he unfortunately experienced overheating with ZC 1176 and had to retire. Only Jim gained a First Class Award. Peter would have gained a First as well. He was 'clean' on all the hills, enjoying himself singing to his sister Bobbie and speeding on his way to the finish when, to his horror, he discovered a control around a blind bend. He was unable to stop in time and therefore disqualified for overrunning the line!

McCracken returned to Ireland, and the following weekend he made up for his disappointment by soundly winning the IMRC Autumn Trial, gaining twice as many bonus marks as any other starter in the forty-six miles event. In this event the Irish Morgan team, consisting of McCracken, Sydney Booth and Fred Gorman, won the team prize, with the latter two drivers also winning First Class Awards, and Sydney being second overall.

McCracken continued his winning ways with the Leinster Night Trial on 5 November, but by only a half second time mark from Miss Pringle in a Wolseley. Sydney Booth was third and won a First Class Award.

Sydney Booth was a regular member of the Irish Morgan Trials team that was entered by Gormans. His sister, who was also his passenger, worked as the book keeper in the Gorman Brothers business, and Sydney had purchased his Morgan two-seater second-hand from that company in March. It was registered ZC 2138, and was unmodified.

Captain John Black was one of the top men in the British motor industry. He had moved to the ailing Standard Motor Company in 1929 from Hillman and within a year was Managing Director. He completely revitalized the company, rearranging working practices, and had an eye for markets which he could exploit. In 1932 he had formed an agreement with William Lyons to manufacture engines for the SS/Jaguar concern.

Before joining the motor industry John had been articled to a solicitor in the patent field. As such he had been involved with the drawings submitted with HFS Morgan's patent for the first three-wheeler in 1910–11.

John now asked for a meeting with HFS. He wanted to manufacture an engine especially for the Morgan sports car. While Standard used sidevalve engines, the ones supplied to Lyons were o.h.v. Morgan wanted o.h.v. engines, so it was agreed that the Standard designer, Ted Grinham, would convert the Standard Flying 10 s.v. engine to o.h.v. operation. The first engine was delivered in late 1938 and HFS decided it would be best tested in a Coupe that was being built for him. No engine number was evident, so for registration purposes the new engine was given the number of the chassis into which it was fitted (712), being registered as engine S712. The completed Coupe was registered as CUY 831 on 2 January 1939.

Sadly, McCracken's racing career with ZC 1176 was coming to an end. Although he had put in an optimistic entry for the 1939 Exeter Trial, he was fighting a losing battle against tuberculosis and reluctantly decided the Morgan had to go. On impulse, it was purchased by the famous Irish motorcycle racer Stanley Woods, who was looking for a suitable car for the 1939 RAC Tourist Trophy at Donington. He was to set in hand various modifications to improve its competitiveness. This sale did not mark the end of McCracken's involvement with the Morgan, for he was to driver it in one or two events on invitation from Stanley in 1939.

Peter Morgan finished 1938 with an entry in the Gloucester Trial. For 1939 the RAC Motor Sport Standing Joint Sub-Committee had decided that competition tyres would no longer be permitted in trials; an attempt to make trials hills competitive without becoming too extreme. The North West London MC decided to run to these new rules for the Gloucester on 3 December, and only two 'cleans' resulted, for Guy Warburton and Martin Soames, both with Allard Specials. Sidney Allard's concept of a large 30 hp V8 engine set well back in a strong light chassis was proving to be the way to go to win trials.

Overseas

Australia

With the Christmas and New Year holidays being in the midst of summer in Australia, this was a popular time for sport, including motor racing. At the end of 1937 Jim Boughton set off with a couple of Brylaws mechanics on the long circa five hundred mile journey to Lobethal, a town of mainly German settlers nestling in the Adelaide hills. The event that had attracted Jim was the second South Australian Grand Prix, to be held

Jim Boughton's Morgan arrives at Lobethal! (*Photograph: Mrs. Boughton collection*)

on 3 January 1938. The Morgan was transported on the back of a Morris Commercial truck, and the journey took nearly two days, including around a hundred miles of desert dirt roads. Russell Boughton travelled separately, in his Morris 8 (known as the Morris 8/40 in Australia).

The circuit was roughly triangular, of 8.75 miles over two approach roads to Lobethal, joined by the main road through the village of Charleston. Two events were held, both handicaps. The first was the South Australian Grand Prix, over one hundred miles. Jim drove a consistent race to finish fifth, the winner being Noel Campbell's little Singer Bantam. The second event was a fifty-mile handicap, and the excellent handicapping saw Jim in the lead with two laps to go. However, Colin Dunne's very rapid supercharged MG K3 overtook Jim's Morgan on the approach to the dangerous Mill Corner, to demote Jim to a fine second at the finish after an exciting race. No doubt much beer was consumed by Jim's happy party, which included Emrhys Jones as main Brylaws mechanic. Also entered for the racing had been another Morgan. It was entered by Eric Morgan as a 'Morgan Special supercharged', but non started. Perhaps it was not a product from Malvern Link but just a special of his own construction.

On 19 March the town of Albury on the Victoria–New South Wales border ran its Interstate Grand Prix as a finale to the local 140th anniversary celebrations. Over 9,000 people lined the virtually rectangular 4.25-mile Wirlinga circuit of

The Lobethal pits, with Jim's Morgan (27) to the centre. Nearest the camera are an MG (21) and a Riley (22). (*Photograph: Mrs Boughton collection*)

Jim Boughton at Quarry Bend at Bathurst during the Grand Prix. (*Photograph: Terry Wright collection*)

closed public roads, and they frequently surged on to the course itself, luckily without injury. Jack Phillips from Wangaratta won the 148½ mile race in his Ford V8 special. Jim Boughton failed to finish in the awards with his 4–4.

Easter Monday, 18 April, was the date of the Australian Grand Prix to be held on the new Bathurst circuit in New South Wales. Jim Boughton duly entered, and this time his mother also came, riding with Russell in the Morris 8 and accompanying the Morris truck. They went cross country, giving a rather rugged drive, especially for the truck occupants.

The new circuit, with its graded gravel surface was of 3.84 miles, and Jim was given twenty-four minutes start over Englishman Peter Whitehead's ERA on scratch. The passenger compartment of the Morgan was now faired over with a metal tonneau, and the legend MORGAN painted on the bonnet. The 150-mile race was easily won by Peter Whitehead while the circuit cut up badly and many cars retired. Jim is not listed in the results.

Several hundred miles away in Albany on the south coast of Western Australia, Easter Monday, was also the date of the third annual 'round the houses' fifty-mile Albany Grand Prix. Based on the concept of the famous Monte Carlo circuit, the two-mile street circuit had seven acute bends, including a hairpin, and three flat bends, and twisted and dipped along the sides of the town's two mountains, Mts Clarence and Melville. Local

Jack McIntosh, young son of Australian aviation pioneer Lt. J. C. McIntosh, entered his 4/4, with the Climax engine fed by a single SU carburettor, and sparked by a Scintilla magneto. He had considered running supercharged, but in fact ran unblown. Giving 4 min. 40 sec. handicap credit, Jack drove very smoothly to finish seventh, but he later reported that his brakes partially failed on the seventh lap, necessitating caution on the many corners. A crowd of over 10,000 people had watched the race on the beautiful autumn day.

Just a few miles north east of Goomalling is the agricultural town of Dowerin, and the Western Australia Sporting Car Club arranged to hold some races in conjunction with the Dowerin Car Club on Monday, 6 June. The venue was the Dowerin Showgrounds 'D' Shaped, 1 mile, 220 yards, speedway type course, with dust surface allowing broadside cornering. The event attracted many of the Perth enthusiasts to make the one hundred mile journey, of which the last thirty-five miles to the venue were over gravel-surfaced roads.

The day before the event was devoted to practice and several aeroplanes also made an appearance, landing inside the track.

The first race on the Monday was a match race between Jack McIntosh and his Morgan, and Norm Kestel, with an MG, the Morgan leading all the way to win a close and exciting race, by a wheel.

The racing continued with the heats of the three-lap handicaps, and the first was easily won by Jack Nelson in his Ford V-8-engined Ballot, with McIntosh battling with Kestel for second, until the latter spun through 360 degrees. Although Jack McIntosh also contested the final of this event, Neil Baird won in his Vauxhall 10.

Jack McIntosh now took part in another match race – this time against Cliff Nicholas's De Havilland Moth aeroplane! Despite lapping in 1 min. 11.2 sec., Jack had to accept defeat.

The main race of the day was the twenty-lap (23-mile) Dowerin Cup handicap. The sun had now dried out the course, making dust a real hazard for the back markers, and some eighteen cars crowded on to the little track.

The race was won by Harris's Terraplane, and poor McIntosh lost a wheel while lying sixth on the last lap, spinning to a stop in a cloud of dust.

In the state of Victoria, Les Murphy was a well known competitor with his P Type MG – he had won the 1935 and 1936 Australian Grand Prix with this car. Brylaw Motors obviously were keen to see him driving a Morgan, and he was loaned the demonstrator for the Speed Trials at Cowes on 28 June, recording 22.0 sec. for the S/S ¼ mile, and 12.0 sec. for the flying ¼ mile (75 mph).

For the Experts Trial held on 13 July, Les was again given the demonstrator. He was passengered by Jim Gullan, an enthusiast on both two and four wheels who had also raced in the 1936 Australian Grand Prix using his Wolseley Hornet. The event led from Melbourne to Warragul, over the mountains to Mt Donna Buang, to Healsville and to the finish at Queenstown, a journey of over two hundred miles including many forestry tracks which were deeply rutted and inches deep in mud. The attrition rate was high, fewer than half finishing, and the Morgan did not go unscathed: it lost the rear of the bodywork on the ruts, the windscreen cracked and fell out, and the lampbrackets collapsed, leaving the headlamps pointing at the number plate. Despite all this, they finished, and the mud-caked wreck was proudly displayed in Brylaws showroom as a sign of Morgan durability!

The 1938 Australian Grand Prix had marked the end of a long and illustrious racing career for 'Barney' Dentry with his Rileys. Jim Boughton, however, wanted to go yet faster with his Morgan, and had decided he needed to convert it to a single-seater. It was no longer his everyday car (he now had another Morgan for work), and so he approached Barney, who had a workshop at St Kilda, about building an ultra lightweight body for his Morgan Special. Making a 4/4 into a single-seater was not easy. The steering column, in being moved to a central position, put the steering wheel at an angle to the dashboard. The seating position was, of necessity, high, having to sit over the propshaft, with the gearbox between the legs. A long streamlined tail was fitted containing the fuel tank. In front of the driver was the speedometer, to the left a rev-counter, and to the right a single auxiliary gauge.

We believe that the Morgan single-seater was

completed just in time for the 1 November Rob Roy hillclimb. A Morgan had been entered by Jim's brother Russell for this event, but Russell recently told us that his own car would only have been entered because there was some doubt whether Jim's own car would be completed in time. Jim was always the intended driver.

Rob Roy had received a sealed bitumen surface earlier in the year, and Jim achieved times of 46.30 and 45.30 sec. Les Murphy had also entered this event in a Morgan (perhaps he was sharing Jim's new racer), and he recorded times of 46.19 and 44.89 sec.

The success of the Albany race had prompted the Western Australian agricultural and holiday town of Bunbury, famous for its surfing beaches, to run the Bunbury 'Flying Fifty' on 14 November as part of the King's birthday celebrations. Two Morgans entered for this round the houses race, Jack McIntosh from Albany, and Tony Forrest. On the way to Bunbury Jack hit a culvert, badly damaging the back axle and wheels. A total strip-down at Bunbury was required and using non original wheels, Jack finally made the start after burning much midnight oil putting the car right. The two Morgans started together, with a handicap of 4 min. 30 sec. credit, and McIntosh took the lead from his colleague, but then skidded out of the race on one of the first corners, a sad end to his endeavours.

Forrest ran in second place to Lee's Riley 9 for eight laps, and then passed him to take the lead, only to crash immediately onto the sandbags at Jane's corner, to overturn and retire. The race was won, as had been the Albany Grand Prix, by Allan Tomlinson's supercharged MG TA, watched by nearly 15,000 spectators.

Ceylon (now Sri Lanka)

Englishman Lawson Annesley took part in the Ceylon Motor Sports Club's hill climb held over six furlongs (¾ mile) of the Bogala mines private road in the Ruanwella District of Ceylon on 16 October. This was the Ceylon MSC's first hill climb in the low-country, and started with a one in seven gradient leading to a right-angled bend, a straight, another right-angled bend and a further straight. Then followed five hairpin bends leading to a loop and the final straight. Lawson was using his Ceylon registered four-seater 4/4, reg. Z–6377 and took the class for sports cars between 1000 and 1500 cc.

CHAPTER FIVE

1939

The 1939 competition year began with the MCC Exeter Trial on 6 and 7 January, the first MCC event under the 'standard tyre' RAC decree. As a result the organizers eased the route, and in fact it proved too easy, with Premier Awards being collected by 103 out of the 130 car starters.

Of the eight Morgan starters, only Harry Jones went home without a Premier Award. Indeed, he went home with a very bent CNP 507, as a result of sliding into a six-wheel lorry on ice just a mile or so from his starting point of Stratford on Avon. George Goodall was in AUY 33, Jim Goodall in the Ford-engined BWP47, Len Coney in his usual CON 502 and HFS and Peter Morgan were probably in their trials cars, CAB 652 and BUY 754. Tomkinson was in BAB 11 but Joe Huxham was in his new car, a Coupe, reg. ELJ 860.

When the new Coupe had appeared at the 1938 Motor Show, Joe decided that he ought to campaign one of these to publicise the new model, so his tuned Climax car, EEL 200, was replaced on 18 November 1938 by a blue Coupe with black wings (chassis number 697). The engine was a Coventry Climax (MA 787), mated to a new Moss gearbox, although *The Motor* reporter of the Exeter Trial had heard about the new Standard engine being tested in a Coupe and intimated one was in Huxham's car.

Following the Exeter Trial the MCC was able to award its coveted Triple Awards for obtaining

E. F. Tomkinson attempts Simms during the Exeter Trial. (*Photograph:* The Motor)

Joe Huxham gets away well from the start on Woodhaynes during the Exeter Trial in his new Coupe. (*Photograph:* The Motor)

Peter Morgan in Jim Goodall's usual car, the short chassis 4/4, tackling the JCC driving tests at Brooklands. (*Photograph: National Motor Museum*)

premier awards in the previous year's Land's End, Edinburgh and Exeter Trials. Of the sixteen awarded there were two for Morgan drivers, these being for HFS and Peter Morgan. Peter Morgan was extremely proud to have won such a prestigious award so early in his trials career.

Over in Ireland snow and ice curtailed the route of the Dublin University night trial held on 21 January, but Sydney Booth successfully won a First Class Award with his black two-seater ZC 2138.

At the end of February, a new Morgan model was announced in the motoring press. This was the Morgan Le Mans Replica, selling for £250, and based on the 1938 Le Mans entry. This two-seater was advertised as having a tuned 1098 cc Coventry Climax engine, outside exhaust and cycle front wings. It is interesting that 80 mph was guaranteed to be exceeded 'in full trim', as the photograph accompanying the announcement was of BNP 370, the actual Le Mans car, shown in the 'touring trim' in which Jim Goodall had driven it in the September 1938 MCC high-speed trial – when it completed just under eighty miles in the hour.

In Ireland Sydney Booth continued his winning ways by taking home another First Class Award on 4 March in the Leinster Motor Cycle Night Trial.

On 25 March action returned to Brooklands, this time for the annual JCC Rally. As usual, J. A. Andrews was there with his Morgan, and gained a First Class Award for completing the seven varied driving tests without penalty. Peter Morgan was also present, driving BWP 47, but made one mistake and had to settle for a Second Class Award.

Once again the MCC was to take its brave competitors on the long journey to Lands End over the night of Good Friday, 7 April, and the following Saturday. Eleven Morgans were entered. Len Coney was in CON 502 as usual. Harry Jones was in the rebuilt CNP 507, still with 1098 cc Climax engine, and Peter Morgan was in BUY 754. HFS Morgan was in the o.h.v. Standard-engined Coupe, CUY 831, looking as though it was in unpainted primer. Jim Goodall was in BWP 47, but it too had a new engine. The new relationship with the Standard Motor Company had made available to Morgan their range of engines, and Jim's car was now fitted with a side-valve 1267 cc engine, as used in the Standard Flying 10. This engine was capable of 36 bhp at 4,000 rpm, and had 6.5 to 1 compression ratio, compared with the 38.8 bhp at 4,500 and 6.8 to 1 of the o.h.v. version being used by HFS.

Joe Huxham was in his Climax-engined Coupe, ELJ 860, L. Hyland in his 4/4, GPA 307, and W. Sandiford was in CCV 464. Morgans were also entered by H. L. Dunne, L. F. Phillipson and F. E. Whipp.

George Goodall was entered in AUY 33 but on the morning before the trial he felt unwell, so Jim Goodall was despatched to visit Cecil (Sonny) McCann and offer him the drive. George Goodall was keen for the Morgan team of Harry Jones, Jim and himself to be seen to be competing, as this was good for publicity and sales, even though Sonny would inevitably be disqualified from receiving an award. Sonny had joined Morgan in 1936 in the machine shop, and it was not long before his previous trials exploits with motorcycles, as a member of the Sutton Coldfield Motor Cycle Club, had come to the attention of George. As a result Sonny had passengered for the works since 1937, but this was his first offer of a drive. His passenger, Smith, was a friend of Jim's from his power station days.

Premier Awards were collected by the two Coupes of HFS and Joe Huxham, and Len Coney's two-seater, while Silvers were obtained by Harry Jones, L. Hyland and Jim Goodall, the latter's Standard side-valve-engined car attracted comment for its 'most unfamiliar exhaust note'.

On 25 April the Chancellor of the Exchequer, Sir John Simon, devastated the British Motor industry by announcing a rise in the horse power based road tax on private cars of 66% to commence on 1 January 1940. From that date the tax was to rise from 15*s.* (75p) per hp to £1 5*s.* 0*d.* (£1.25) raising the tax on the 10 hp Morgan from £7 10*s.* 0*d.* to £12 10*s.* 0*d.* (£12.50). As a result of this decision, HFS Morgan decided there was no point in continuing with the development of the 22 hp Ford V8-engined car. In later months the engine was to be removed from the chassis and returned to Fords, but this car had made a lasting impression on Peter Morgan, who never forgot its impressive performance.

This year the RAC Rally was to finish at Brighton, on Friday 28 April, with starting points at either London, Torquay, Blackpool or Stratford on Avon on the previous Tuesday. As usual HFS Morgan had the factory Morgan entries specially prepared at the factory, to give the best possible impression. He and his son, Peter, were to compete in CUY 831, the Standard-engined Coupe, now painted and running in the up to 10 hp closed car class, by virtue of running with the hood up.

George and Jim Goodall were in faithful AUY 33, running in the up to 10 hp open class. The idea was for Peter and Jim to do the driving tests, the rest of the driving being shared. All went well with HFS and Peter, until, approaching Brighton for the final tests, with Peter driving, the Meadows gearbox stuck in top gear. HFS told Peter to get out. He grabbed the lever and managed to force it free with much brute force. Luckily the problem did not recur and, come the awards, not only had HFS and Peter won the 10 hp closed car class, but George and Jim had also won the 10 hp open class: two Morgans entered and two class wins, the best possible result, with considerable beneficial publicity.

From this time on HFS insisted that the Moss gearbox should replace the Meadows in the 'up market' Coupe specification. Not all had been well with early Moss gearboxes, however, as several were replaced in the first few months, including that in Huxham's Coupe.

By now entries were in for the 1939 Le Mans 24 hour race, to be held in June. The Winter Garden Garage's Morgan of Prudence Fawcett and Geoff White was eligible for the Biennial Cup but this year Prudence was unable to drive the car – she had become engaged and as part of this engagement she had agreed to give up motor racing if her fiancé gave up flying. As a result it was decided that Dick Anthony would take her place as a driver, with Morgans offering the services of Charlie Curtis to help run the pits. Meanwhile the car was being prepared at the Morgan factory. Its first test was in the hands of Dick Anthony at the North West London Motor Club's Lawrence Cup Trial. This was held on non-damaging loose sand, on War Department land on Bagshot Heath and Pirbright Common on 20 May. Acting as 'shake down' tests for the Le Mans car, Dick Anthony won the Almond Cup for a class win.

The MCC Edinburgh Trial was held on 26 and 27 May. The factory entries consisted of HFS and Peter Morgan, Harry Jones and Jim Goodall. They were accompanied by R. Thomas, Len Coney, L. Hyland and L. F. Phillipson. Jim Goodall, accompanied by Sonny McCann, was using his father's car, AUY 33, and then staying on in Edinburgh for the start of the Scottish Rally. R. Thomas was using a Le Mans Replica, HFS was in his Coupe, CUY 831, Peter in his usual BUY 754 and Harry Jones in CNP 507. Coney was in CON 502. Brilliant weather made the

HFS in his Standard-engined Coupe approaches Hustyn Hill behind Alderton's MG in the Lands End Trial. (*Photograph: Morgan Motor Co. collection*)

event easy, with Gold for Coney, Thomas, HFS, Peter and Jim. Harry took home a Silver for failing Addestonshiels, while Hyland failed Park Rash.

The Scottish Rally, organized by the Royal Scottish Automobile Club, began in Glasgow on 29 May and finished in the same city with a coachwork competition on 2 June.

Jim Goodall, with Sonny McCann, was in AUY 33, the only Morgan entered in the class for open cars of up to 1300 cc. They trounced the opposition, and secured the highest total in marks of all entries to win the class, and some very nice rosebowls to go back to Malvern as a result.

Meanwhile the motoring press was at last able to confirm the availability of the new o.h.v. Standard engine for Morgans, these being mainly destined for the Coupe, which was unchanged in price at £225. The same engine was also available for the 2- and 4-seaters, at an additional charge of £5.

The 1939 Le Mans race was to take place on 17 June. Although the Morgan had been entered by Prudence Fawcett, it was confirmed that Dick Anthony and Geoff White would drive. It looked considerably different in appearance to that used in 1938, although the information we have available from those who were there at the time suggests it was, in fact, the same car. The body was completely rebuilt. There were no doors, and the spare wheel was now recessed into the sloping rear panel. The twin fillers of the twenty-six gallon fuel tank protruded through the sloping tail panel, rather than, as in 1938, through the rear tonneau cover, which was now replaced by a metal one. Under the bonnet the 1098 cc engine had been bored out to 0.070in. oversize, taking the bore to 62.48 mm and the capacity to 1104 cc. This took the Morgan into the next class for 1100 to 1500 cc, a class which Dick Anthony had thought

HFS and Peter Morgan during the RAC Rally. (*Photograph: Morgan Motor Co. collection*)

Jim Goodall and Sonny McCann making light work of the tricky test at Moulin, near Pitlochry, on their way to the best scores of the Scottish Rally. (*Photograph: Morgan Motor Co. collection*)

The Le Mans Morgan is lifted off the Channel ferry. (*Photograph: Lancelot Prideaux-Brune collection*)

Harry Jones on Summer Lodge in the four-seater during the Edinburgh Trial. (*Photograph:* The Motor)

to be less competitive than the under 1100cc class they had entered in 1938. The carburation had been changed with the addition of two down-draught SU units, one at each end of the cylinder head. The dynamo was moved to a special cradle, and away from the top water manifold, in view of the difficulties with the cooling system in the 1938 TT.

The radiator now sported the early type wire mesh stone guard, but sported a Morgan three-wheeler type badge! It was registered FXD 280.

As in the previous year, the team lodged at the Hostellerie des Ifs, Charlie Curtis travelling down with Dick Anthony. Also in attendance were Lance and Charlotte Prideaux-Brune, the owners of Winter Garden Garages. Only one racer was taken, although the garage-owned, ordinary two-seater 4–4 also accompanied the team.

Dick Anthony (driving) and Geoff White leave the pits during practice, letting a Delahaye (12) go by. (*Photograph: Lancelot Prideaux-Brune collection*)

Ready for the Le Mans start, with the Morgan parked outside the pits. Charlie Curtis is by the pit wall, and Dick Anthony is visible third from the right behind the pit wall. (*Photograph: Lancelot Prideaux-Brune collection*)

The regulations insisted on a minimum distance of twenty-four laps between refuelling, so a race plan was formulated for Dick and Geoff to each drive 28-lap stints before stops for refuelling and changing drivers. Dick was to drive the first stint.

Practice was comparatively uneventful, apart from Charlie Curtis having to change a head gasket.

The start was also uneventful and, quickly, Dick Anthony settled into lap times of around 7 min. 20 sec. to 7 min. 30 sec., well over 40 seconds faster per lap than in 1938. After twenty-eight laps Dick came into the pits, the car was refuelled and after a stop of 1 min. 22 sec. Geoff White joined the race at 7.31 p.m. He continued the good work, coming in on his fifteenth lap to have the headlight covers removed, ready for the night session, and handed over to Dick once more after a 1 min. 52 sec. refuel stop at 11.03 p.m. Again consistent lap times were the order of the day and the only excitement at the Morgan pits was when the Mazaud-Mongin Delahaye caught fire approaching the pits area, being finally abandoned right in front of the Morgan pit where it was eventually extinguished, but too damaged to continue. And so it went on, with another 1 min. 39 sec. pit stop just before 2.32 a.m. to refuel and for Geoff to take over once more, and a stop of 1 min. 38 sec. just before 6 a.m. for Dick to take over. All was well until on his 26th lap when Dick came into the pits for nearly a 19-minute stop, before restarting. It is likely the stop was related to petrol feed, and the Morgan was not alone in having problems – one of the Singers was withdrawn because of 'muck' in the pit fuel tanks getting into the fuel lines, and the subsequent flushing through causing it to run out of fuel.

Geoff took over again at 9.53 a.m. after a 13 sec. stop to change drivers, but the lap times were now lengthening, probably due to the fuel feed problems. At the end of his allotted twenty-eight laps he came in for refuelling, and a long delay of 12 min. 24 sec., ensued before Dick Anthony took over for the final laps of the race at

13.41 p.m. He only managed four laps before a stop of 6 min. 8 sec., but the car then continued on its way to the finish at 4 p.m., covering 1,548.8 miles at an average of 64.4 mph. They finished fifteenth overall, but the idea of Dick Anthony to rebore into the higher capacity class proved worthwhile as they were second in this class. The Rudge Whitworth Biennial Cup was won by the Simca-FIAT of Gordini and Scaron, but the Morgan was the highest placed British entry.

No doubt there were celebrations that day for the Morgan drivers, and the pit crew, at the Hostellerie des Ifs.

Outside the Hostellerie des Ifs for the celebrations. (*Photograph: Lancelot Prideaux-Brune collection*)

Back in England, Peter Morgan had persuaded his father to let him enter a works car in the MCC's Donington race meeting on 1 July. Registered as CAB 652, this racer had rear end bodywork as used on the 1937 and 1938 TT cars. Whether it was one of these, or HFS's trial's car of the same registration rebodied to TT specification, we have been unable to verify. Dick Anthony has stated that the 1939 Le Mans car was the previous year's car rebodied, so it seems unlikely it was that car (the 1938 Le Mans car also took part in the 1938 TT). Possibly it was the 1937 TT car updated, if it still existed, or perhaps the old body removed from the 1938 Le Mans/TT car was fitted to HFS's car. As yet we do not know the answer.

Peter Morgan in his first race at Donington. (*Photograph: Louis Klemantaski*)

In event three, a five-lap handicap, Peter demonstrated his driving ability by finishing second to runaway victor, C.E. Truett's SS. The last event of the day was a twenty-lap handicap race, and Peter Morgan was showing well among the light cars until a valve rocker broke and ended his fun. Peter was now looking forward to racing on the Brooklands Campbell circuit in the autumn.

The racing scene now turned to Ireland for the Leinster Motor Club's Leinster Trophy race meeting, which was held once more as a handicap event over 153 miles of the Tallaght circuit on 8 July. Two Morgans were entered, Stanley Woods with the ex-McCracken car, and Ken Besson with his own car. Stanley Woods had been busy racing motorcycles, but had found time to fit separate exhaust pipes to each cylinder, these passing down the near side of the car, like organ pipes, terminating before the left rear wheel. A single downdraught SU carburettor was fitted. In practice Stanley ran a big end which was changed with the help of his mechanic Tom Leonard, who had also helped McCracken when he raced the car.

Ken Besson's car was also fitted with a tuned engine, of 1122 cc. Ken's racing activities were frowned upon by his father, who ran the Hibernian Hotel, so he had entered under the name 'R. Hare'.

The race started in the rain, on treacherously slippery roads. Stanley Woods first attracted attention by lapping closest to his handicap speed, but sadly did not last long as the same big end gave out on lap nine, sidelining him. The same fate had befallen Desmond McCracken the previous year.

Tom Leonard (left) and Stanley Woods prepare the latter's Morgan for the Leinster Trophy race. Note the organ pipe exhausts. (*Photograph:* Evening Mail)

Meanwhile the slippery road had caused Donald Maclure's SS100 to somersault near Old Bawn, and D. O'Kane to slide into Templeogue Bridge with his MG, as did Dudley Colley with his Frazer Nash. The race was won by Belfast driver, Ernie Robbs, in his Alvis Special, at 64.10 mph. 'R Hare' finished eighth at 58.34 mph, with a fastest lap of 67.19 mph.

Stanley Woods was now preparing for the RAC TT, to be held at Donington on 2 September. He was unhappy with the wide ratios of the Meadows gearbox, which he thought quite unsuitable for racing, having far too low first and second gears. Stanley's motorcycle racing experience had made him value close ratio gears, so he had a set of pinions made to reduce the reduction on first gear from 3.5 to approximately 1.8, on second from 2.4 to 1.33 and on third from 1.4 to 1.1. He was to send the car over to Morgans for the gears to be fitted, and also for Dunlop to fit a set of special race tyres. Stanley reasoned that if the car performed well in the TT then over the forthcoming winter he would fit an improved camshaft, and also a separate carburettor to each cylinder, ready for racing in 1940.

Back at the Morgan factory, the news of the severe car road tax for 1940 had led to the experimental V8 Ford engine being replaced with a side-valve Standard unit of 1021 cc (57 × 100 mm) which was tax rated at only 8 hp. Taken from the Standard Flying 8 model, this engine only produced a maximum of 31 bhp at 4,000 rpm, obviously not much use for a sports car, but the Willesden Green firm, Carburettors Limited,

Ken Besson looks proud to have won the Frank O'Reilly Trophy for his performance in the Leinster Trophy Race. This impressive cup was awarded to the first Leinster MC member to finish. (*Photograph: Gorman collection*)

The supercharged Standard 8 s.v. engine in the Morgan. (*Photograph: Quadrant Picture Library*)

had fitted an Arnott supercharger, blowing at 3–4 lbs/sq inch to give it some 'pep', and it proved capable of around 80 mph, suggesting that it might make a nice economy sports car.

The fifth Welsh Rally of the South Wales AC began on Wednesday 16 July from various points all over the country, finishing on Friday the 21th, at Cardiff, and followed by a coachwork competition on Saturday 22 July. There were three Morgan entries in class one, open cars upto 10 hp. Jim Goodall, after winning his class in the RAC and Scottish Rally had high hopes with AUY 33. Dick Anthony was surprisingly driving Jim's trials car, BWP 47, and F.E. Whipp was presumably in his own 4–4. Also entered was R. K. Russell but he was rather oddly in class three, open cars 10–15 hp. It was run in monsoon conditions, and it was a FIAT Balilla that took the class win, with 404.2 marks against second-placed Dick Anthony with 403 marks. Jim Goodall was only just behind with 402.8 marks, to be third in class but he did take away the Leamington Spa starters' award and the Yearling Prize. *The Light Car*, in its report of the event, described both Jim and Dick's Morgan as 'TT Replicas', this being a common term for two-seaters with cycle type front mudguards

The Class One entries marshalled outside Cardiff Civic Centre, with BWP 47 nearest the camera. (*Photograph: Quadrant Picture Library*)

and outside exhaust. These items were available as 'extras' from the Morgan factory on new models.

For some months war with Germany had been looking more and more certain, even to the most optimistic of the British population, despite the efforts of the Government to seek peace. The various motor clubs continued to apply for permits to run events, however, hoping to continue racing until the last possible moment. One week before the date of the RAC TT at Donington, Stanley Woods went to collect his Morgan from the factory and took it to the circuit for practice. This year his was one of three Morgans entered, the other two being works entries, one of which was for the experienced Singer racer, Donald Barnes. We suspect the other was for Henry Laird once more, and that the two cars were the Le Mans car and CAB 652. Sadly, the RAC decided it was inappropriate to continue with the race in the political circumstances and reluctantly cancelled it. The day after the race was to have been run, the news everyone was dreading, but expecting, was given to the nation by the Prime Minister, Neville Chamberlain – Britain was now at war with Germany. Obviously all motor sport was now at an end for the foreseeable future in Britain. Stanley Woods was Irish, however, so he made a dash for Liverpool and the ferry home to Dublin. Within a week of war being declared he had joined the Irish Army Supply and Transport Corps, as officer in charge of base workshops and training. The Irish government was to declare Ireland a neutral country, and motor racing was to continue there for some time ahead, to the envy of the British.

Despite the onset of war, the Irish Motor Racing Cub went ahead with the organization of its Phoenix Park races in Dublin on 9 September. It was originally planned that there would be a 1500 cc scratch race, but as the nine English entrants could not get to Ireland, the race was replaced by a motorcycle race. The club was able to go ahead with the one hundred mile handicap race, and of the twenty entrants fifteen finally faced the starter. There were two Morgan entries, Stanley Woods with his racer, having an engine capacity of 1087 cc, and Ken Besson in his racer. Both received three credit laps and thirty seconds start but Ken Besson hardly finished his warming-up lap before a big end went, although he had lapped at 74.8 mph on the fast circuit.

After about forty minutes racing Stanley Woods lay third, behind Thompson's 1100 cc TRS in second place, with Cahill's MG leading. The latter later developed clutch-slip, allowing Thompson into the lead to win. Stanley Woods had been pleased with his drive in the Morgan, until the gear lever broke off leaving just a short stump. His left hand had been badly damaged in a crash on his Velocette motorcycle in the 1938 Belgian Grand Prix, and gear changing became very painful. Nevertheless Stanley struggled on finally to finish fifth at an average speed of 76.32 mph.

The IMRC followed the Phoenix Park race with its hill climb at Ballinascorney, on 23 September. Desmond McCracken was feeling sufficiently fit to return to racing, and he shared his old Morgan with its new owner Stanley Woods, winning the class for up to 1100 cc and beating Stanley by over one and a half seconds, with a time of 58.26 sec. The Morgan was running with its low-compression cylinder head fitted.

McCracken borrowed his old car again on 30 September for the Leinster Motor Club's Lincolan Cup Trial. He proved untouchable and walked off with the Lincolan Cup. A First Class Award was also collected by Sydney Booth, and to complete the success, McCracken, Booth and J. Stokes, who won a Second Class Award, also took the team prize as the Morgan team. This event was held on the last day before petrol rationing was introduced by the Irish government.

The IMRC ran its Autumn Cup Trial on 28 October but, because of petrol rationing, the distance was restricted to twenty-five miles, with six driving tests. George Mangan's Austin 14 took the Premier Award but Desmond McCracken was best open car, and Sydney Booth was right behind with a First Class Award.

On 17 November the Leinster GVB Cup Trial was held over a thirty-mile course. Charlie Manders' Chevrolet took the GVB Cup, but Sydney Booth won a First Class Award.

McCracken was out in his old Morgan on Boxing Day in the IMRC Trial, and once again was unstoppable, and came away with the Premier Award. Sydney Booth finished ten points behind with a Second Class Award.

The sole Sandford-Morgan. (*Photograph: Didier Coste*)

While sport continued in a somewhat restricted form in Ireland, things were different in England, with motor sport having stopped completely. Petrol rationing had been introduced within three weeks of the outbreak of war, based on the horse power of the vehicle. Branded fuel had been replaced with decidedly inferior 'Pool' petrol. Road signposts were removed in anticipation of a German invasion, and headlamps had to be specially masked to restrict light being shone on the road. Bumpers, or the edges of the wings, had to be painted white to enable vehicles to be seen in poor light.

In France, during 1939, Stuart Sandford had built a Sandford-Morgan. This was simply a Morgan 4–4 into which Stuart had installed a French 6 CV Ruby engine, and to which he had fitted a distinctive Sandford radiator grille.

Stuart only got as far as making the one prototype, which sadly was later to be requisitioned by the German Occupation authorities, together with all the drawings and even the accounts of his little Paris company. Sandford, being British, was imprisoned at Saint-Dennis with other Allied nationals.

Overseas

Australia

This year the New Year Lobethal meeting was upgraded to be the Australian Grand Prix for 1939 and was held on 2 January. Once again Jim Boughton was entered, this time in his new single-seater. His brother Russell also undertook the long journey, taking their mother in his own road-going Morgan. There were three full days of practice before the three races on 2 January. The first was the South Australian Junior Grand Prix, a handicap event held over nine laps (75 miles) of the circuit. Jim started with a gaggle of MGs with eleven minutes credit over scratch man Jack Saywell's Alfa Romeo P3, but failed to feature in the results. Following the next race, the Australian Stock Car Road Championship, came the Australian Grand Prix, held over seventeen laps (150 miles). Jim was now on twenty-one minutes credit over scratch man Saywell's Alfa Romeo.

All went well for Jim in the early stages, lapping steadily between 7 min. 30 sec. and 7 min. 40 sec., but he had a long stop on his seventh lap, and finally retired on his tenth, after two hours' racing. He had been running as high as fifth place on the fifth lap before the engine trouble intervened.

Boughton's Special receives attention. Note the cockpit layout, and the unusual body construction. (*Photograph: Norman Howard*)

Jim Boughton goes speedway racing at Aspendale, a one-mile slightly banked oval dirt track. (*Photograph: Terry Wright collection*)

Back in Melbourne Jim had more luck on the Aspendale speedway on 21 January, collecting four third places in three five-lap handicaps, and in the sporting cars scratch race. Also at this meeting was held a novel Relay Race, involving teams of three cars, with each completing two laps before handing a baton over on the start line to the next member. Jim competed in the 'A' team of Oliver's Lagonda, Jim's Morgan and Ralph's Morgan, and they won. 'Teddy' Ralph was a Brylaws mechanic, so Brylaws could feel well proud with their day's entries.

On 10 April Jim returned to Bathurst for the 150-mile road race over the Mount Panorama circuit, now with a bitumen surface. With a handicap of thirty minutes credit over scratch man Jack Saywell's Alfa Romeo P3, Jim hoped for good things but it was not to be as he only completed five laps before retiring with engine trouble in the Morgan Special, now painted white.

On 12 June, the King's birthday, action moved to Albury for the Albury and Interstate Gold Cup Motor Race Meeting over the Wirlinga circuit. Apart from Jim Boughton's Morgan Special there were two other 4–4s, entered by Teddy Ralph and Ted Gray respectively. Just the latter two entered the restricted handicap of six laps (25½ miles) both having 3½ minutes credit over scratch. Gray led for most of the race, but was overhauled by Worth's Hudson Six, and Crouch's Alfa Romeo.

The next race was over eighteen laps (76½ miles) for the Albury and Interstate Gold Cup. Only fourteen of the twenty-nine entered eventually started, Jim Boughton having nine minutes credit, and Ralph and Gray 10½ minutes. Gray took an early lead, completing two laps before the scratch man had set off, and was followed closely by Ralph, but then retired on lap nine. Boughton and Ralph were closely matched with lap speeds, but Ralph was forced to stop on lap ten, letting Boughton through. They finished

Jim Boughton (25) and John Pike's Singer Le Mans (26) waiting to start at Bathurst in the 150-mile race. (*Photograph: Terry McGrath collection*)

sixth and seventh, the winner being Wangaratta driver Jack Phillips with his Ford V8.

The final race for six laps was the Open handicap. Boughton had three minutes credit, and Gray and Ralph 3 min. 30 sec. over scratch. Jim did not survive long, retiring after two laps, but Ralph drove consistently to finish eighth, the winner being Les Burrow with his Hudson.

The outbreak of the Second World War in September resulted in Australia, like other countries of the British Empire, eventually becoming caught up in the conflict. Motor sport was able to continue for some time, however, and on 28 October Jim Boughton was in action at Rob Roy hillclimb. He recorded 44.79 seconds to clinch second in class behind T Skeene's MG TA.

CHAPTER SIX

1940– 45

1940 began as 1939 ended, with no let-up from the restrictions of war on motor competition in Europe. Despite severe petrol rationing, it was only in the neutral country of Ireland that some form of motor sport could continue, at least in minor events.

On 18 March the Irish Motor Racing Club ran its spring trial over a forty-four mile course in the Dublin mountains, with seven driving tests included to determine the results. Ken Besson surprised the opposition by failing to lose a single mark, obviously winning the event, while Fred Gorman, whose garage built the Irish Morgans, finished second to win a First Class Award, probably driving his 1938 Coupe (Chassis No. 721). Stokes was the other Morgan entrant, but he failed to be successful.

One month later the Dublin University Club's Grafton Cup Trial was held over a figure-of-8 course. This time Ken Besson, after a great struggle with D. Gill's MG, eventually had to concede, finishing second but taking home a First Class Award. Stokes did better this time with a Second Class Award to collect.

Back at Malvern car production had ceased at the Morgan factory on the outbreak of war in 1939, apart from the despatch of a handful of three- and four-wheelers that had been nearing completion. The skills of the workforce were much in demand, and those not serving in the armed forces were busy supporting the war effort at home.

Most of the sheet metal workers had been sent to work on aeroplane production, and the machine shop was busy with munitions, also becoming involved on such contract work for the manufacture of components for aircraft undercarriages produced by Dowty of Gloucester.

Meanwhile, Sir Alan Cobham, who had been researching in-flight refuelling, had been advised that his current base at Ford airfield in Sussex

Fred Gorman attacks a trials hill with his Coupe. (*Photograph: Gorman collection*)

A stack of Morgan-manufactured munitions. (*Photograph: Jim Goodall collection*)

was vulnerable to enemy action. In May 1940 he visited his cousin in West Malvern during the course of a search for new premises, and was advised to call in at the nearby, mainly deserted, Morgan factory. It seemed ideal, so he requisitioned the body shop for the work of his company, Flight Refuelling Limited. Captain John Black, the Managing Director of the Standard Motor Company, also made an arrangement with George Goodall to requisition the sheet metal shop and finishing shops to form part of his aircraft production factories, the Morgan shops being involved with carburettor manufacture.

HFS Morgan was very pleased that George Goodall was able to secure all the contracts to keep the factory busy. HFS himself tended to be something of a pacifist, and found the reallocation of his factory to help the war effort difficult for him to become involved with. His son, Peter, had enlisted in the Royal Army Service Corps and was to spend a considerable part of the war in Africa, often with many men working under his authority – something he found very valuable for his future days at the Morgan factory.

The Government-enforced masking of car headlights at night led to a considerable increase in pedestrian fatalities, and so in 1940 the 20 mph speed limit was reinstated in Britain. In October 1940 the government also introduced purchase tax on the ex-works wholesale price of new cars at 33⅓%, although very few cars were available to purchase at this time.

By June 1942 there was a further tightening of the motoring belt for British motorists, when the petrol rationing was further restricted to ban any motoring for pleasure, with the removal of the basic ration for private motorists.

Meanwhile, at the Morgan factory an interesting vehicle was being assembled on a 4–4 chassis. This was to be a pick-up for the factory! As the sheet metal workers were working elsewhere in aeroplane production, the body was made mainly of wood, and it was constructed by Arthur Frith, who was the pattern maker for Morgan Motors and worked in the woodshop, along with Arthur Cridland, the foreman of the woodshop. Coloured grey, it was registered EAB 460 on 8 January 1943 as a Morgan Truck weighing 15 cwt, 2 qr. 1 lbs.

The Morgan factory truck, photographed in the 1950s. *(Photograph: Chas. Smith collection)*

By the end of 1944 it was clear that the Allies were winning the war. As a result the Chancellor of the Exchequer, Sir John Anderson, announced the Government's post-war policy on car tax – it was to be levied at the rate of £1 per 100 cc of engine capacity, with the unpopular RAC-devised horsepower tax, which favoured long stroke engines, being scrapped. This was to be good news for the British motor industry, allowing the development of higher-revving, squarer bore and stroke, engines which were more desirable for future export markets.

At the Morgan factory HFS Morgan had begun to experiment with a new chassis. One of the problems with the 4–4 chassis was the poor turning circle, which was restricted by the front tyres rubbing on the tapering front end of the outer chassis rails. Indeed for trials use the upper flange was often cut away to increase the steering lock. HFS Morgan had therefore devised an experimental chassis with the normally tapered outer rails bent inwards, in front of the pedal board chassis member. These were bent, to join on to two parallel channel members which passed alongside the engine and joined the conventional rear of the chassis at the pedal board cross member. These two new channel members also continued forwards to a fabricated cross head, and through this to act as radiator mountings.

When the chassis was built up HFS used an experimental o.h.v. Standard engine of 106 mm stroke giving 53 bhp at 5,000 rpm, directly attached to a four-speed gearbox with remote gear

HFS Morgan testing the experimental chassis, fitted with the experimental Standard engine and gearbox. Behind is Harry Jones. (*Photograph: Morgan Motor Co. collection*)

change, the latter being as manufactured by the Standard Motor Company solely for SS Jaguar. The Standard Motor Company had been making special o.h.v. conversions of the 1776 cc Standard s.v. 14 hp engine especially for SS Jaguar since 1937. These engines, of 73 mm bore, produced 63 bhp at 5,000 rpm. We suspect that the special engine sent to Morgans was a smaller bore version of this engine that Sir John Black (knighted in 1943 for his services to the war effort) had been keen for Morgan to consider using.

This Morgan chassis did not prove successful. Eventually the chassis was dismantled and discarded to the side of the factory, where it lay in the weeds until a tidy-up in 1989.

When HFS Morgan contemplated a new design his methods of communicating this to his workforce tended to be rather unusual. He often performed measurements with his pocket handkerchief, which he held taut, or even a piece of string, and body designs were often sketched onto a dark wall in chalk for the hapless Mr Frith to interpret to his employer's satisfaction. HFS Morgan's greatest design attribute was an ability to think simply with designs that were light, functional, easy to manufacture and repair, yet exceedingly versatile. In his office he would often hold up photographs of Morgan chassis to the light and draw, on the reverse, new body shapes to enclose them – usually for his own amusement rather than serious production.

In the spring of 1945 the war in Europe was all but won, victory finally coming on 8 May. The Far East involvement with Japan took a further few months before the Allies brought the war to a close by atomic means, Japanese surrender taking place on 15 August.

In March 1945 HFS and Ruth Morgan gave a party at the Winter Gardens in Malvern for three hundred employees and friends as a 'thank you' and to remind them that Morgans were soon to be back in production. Sadly, many pre-war faces were missing and among the competition drivers this included Henry Laird who had been killed in a despatch riding accident. Of the British racing circuits, Brooklands had been sacrificed in the cause of aeroplane production at the adjacent Vickers factory, and Donington Park was to remain a large military vehicle base for many years to come.

Although the war was won the British economy was in a very sorry state. Food rationing was to remain in operation for many years, as was petrol rationing, although the basic ration for private use was reintroduced in June allowing approximately 150 miles of personal driving per month.

Factories were very slow to get back to civilian activity. Raw materials were in short supply and the workforces were often still to be stationed around the world on peace-keeping duties for some time to come. The Morgan factory, of course, had bays sublet to others, and it was to be another year before the occupants left and production could begin. Meanwhile the machine shop remained in demand for general engineering.

Enthusiasm for motor sport had remained high throughout the war time restrictions, and enthusiasts were now keen to return to their sport. The MCC organized an informal rally at Wrotham Park on 3 July, which over one hundred cars attended. Also in July, A. F. Rivers-Fletcher, an enthusiastic supporter of top flight British motor racing, organized a meeting at Cockfosters in North London, to which Bill Boddy, the editor of *Motor Sport*, then stationed in Harrogate on Ministry of Aircraft Production duty, decided to go. Not wishing to use his Austin 7 on such a long journey, he borrowed the Scott-engined 4/4 from the helpful Scott Chief Engineer, William Cull.

Despite having been used as a works 'hack' throughout the war the Morgan proved trouble free, apart from some plug oiling in London traffic, averaging 23 mpg for the five hundred miles, and doing an impromptu acceleration test of 0–50 mph in 17 sec.

The first event to be held under the RAC permit for nearly six long years was a hill climb, organized by the Bristol MC and LCC on 18 August on the grassy road on Joe Fry's estate in Naish, near Portishead. Local enthusiast, Ken Burgess, secured two first places, in the classes for war time 'hacks' up to 1100 cc, and sports cars up to 1100 cc with his 1122 cc Climax-engined 4–4. Presumably the extra 22 cc was not thought to be worth reclassification into a higher class.

On 1 September the SUNBAC ran an abbreviated trial over a fifteen-mile course near Halesowen, in which that great trials enthusiast C. A. N. May competed, having just managed to complete the clutch replacement on his 4–4 before the 6 p.m. start.

The MCC was keen to restart its long distance classic trials in 1946 but by late 1945 the unavoidable continuation of the severe petrol rationing led to these being abandoned for the foreseeable future. This led to the cancellation of the Exeter Trial due to be held in the New Year of 1946, for which a route had been planned.

Overseas

Australia

Despite the World War involving the countries of the British Empire, the annual New Year South Australia races at Lobethal went ahead as usual on New Year's Day 1940. Once again Jim Boughton entered the two races on the programme, the South Australian Hundred and the Lobethal Fifty. This time the car was shipped over by coastal freighter. Russell drove over with a friend in his own Morgan, and Mrs Boughton, their mother, accompanied them with a girl friend of Jim's, in her own BSA Coupe. Jim took his own road-going 4/4.

Practice was enlivened by blowing the racer's engine, so Jim and a mechanic took the engine out of Jim's ordinary 4/4 and installed it in the racer. It seemed a bit 'tight' so Russell was told to drive it around the course to 'put some miles on it'. Meanwhile the same mechanic borrowed Russell's Morgan to drive to Adelaide, and promptly went off the road in the mountains on the way back, damaging the left front sliding axle! In the South Australian 100 itself Jim had further engine trouble. With little more than two laps to go, Jim's limping Morgan was hit from behind by the flying, supercharged MGTA Special of Allan Tomlinson which was cresting the blind rise near Kayannie Corner. The MG eventually ended up embedded in a gum tree after several frightening somersaults, injuring its driver quite seriously. Jim retired, and does not appear to have started in the Lobethal Fifty.

Once the racing was over a stub axle was

Jim Boughton's Morgan at Lobethal. (*Photograph: Terry McGrath collection*)

removed from the racer to get Russell's Morgan mobile once more. On the return journey to Melbourne, the troubles continued when Russell's Morgan lost its nearside front wheel about twenty miles from Murray Bridge, the wheel nuts having worked loose. With the help of another motorist, the front of the car was lifted up and the spare wheel fitted before continuing to Murray Bridge to have the front cross head straightened!

Apart from keeping the lap charts, Russell's main function was 'general support and help with the drinking', so he got a bit more than he had anticipated on this particular adventure.

CHAPTER SEVEN

1946

The continuing imposition of severe petrol rationing meant that it was only local club events with limited mileage that the frustrated sportsmen could enter, and most of these were trials. The Bristol MC and LCC went ahead with two trials during the winter months. The first, held on 5 January was the 'Full Moon Cup Trial', held over thawing hills which proved real stoppers. Birmingham trials enthusiast, C. A. N. May, found his Climax-engined 4–4 unable to get into motion at all on Burledge.

On 23 February the Bristol Club ran its Roy Fedden Trophy Trial. Austen May was given the privilege of being the first car, but succeeded in climbing just a single hill! Certainly the Morgan was not Austen's most successful trials car. Also entered were D. C. D. Campbell with a pre-war two-seater and Ken Burgess, the latter carrying an enormous compressed air cylinder in his 4–4 as combined ballast and tyre reinflator after the observed sections. Neither featured among the awards.

The first major trial after the war was to be SUNBAC's Colmore Trophy Trial held on 9 March in the Cotswolds. Clerk of the Course was none other than Austen May again, who used his Morgan to test out the route. Three Morgans took part. Jim Goodall was driving a gleaming blue Morgan, thought by *The Motor* reporter to be a new post-war model. We suspect, however, that it was none other than the trials 4/4, BWP 47, which had been refurbished and repainted at the works. We know that around war-time, the Standard side-valve engine was replaced by a tuned version of the o.h.v. Standard engine used for production Morgans, but quite when this was fitted we are unable to be certain. Jim himself had been kept busy during the war years running the expanded and hard-worked Morgan factory machine shop.

D. C. D. Campbell needs assistance on Nailsworth Ladder during the Roy Fedden Trial. (*Photograph: Morgan Motor Co. collection*)

The second Morgan entry was that of Horace Roberts, who helped run the family garage business in the village of Ombersley in Worcestershire. Horace's introduction to Morgans had been through his father's Aero, but just before the war he acquired a 1938 Climax-engined two-seater, reg EKF 495. During the war his future wife, Hilda, had used the Morgan to tow a trailer of Fordson tractor engines on a regular run to Hereford, for reconditioning. By the end of the war the Morgan was worn out, and Horace set about reconditioning it for trials use. He enlisted Jim Roberts, the Morgan factory repair shop foreman, to help on Saturdays, and together they rebuilt the Morgan from the chassis up into what was then described as TT replica style (outside exhaust and cycle wings). The engine was found to have no piston rings left; so it was replaced by another 1122 cc Climax. Horace was no newcomer to trials, having previously competed on motorcyles. The third entry was that of Ken Burgess of Portishead, Bristol, with his pre-war 4/4. The event was held on a sunny, frosty day, and Jim Goodall only missed a Second Class Award because of failing the stop and restart test on Laverton, losing a total of eighteen marks. Horace Roberts had trouble with the bonnet, eventually securing it with Hilda's scarf and missed out on an award, with thirty-four penalties. Ken Burgess sadly arrived too late at the finish.

Horace and Hilda Roberts on Laverton in the Colmore. (*Photograph: Horace Roberts collection*)

Ken Burgess had better luck on 25 March, gaining a Second Class Award in the West of England Club's Annual Spring Trial, which started from Tiverton. On 7 April Austen May (with his Morgan carrying ballast), had an enjoyable day at the Berkhamsted MC and CC's first post-war Winwood Cup Trial. In the 'Jeans' Gold Cup Trial, organized on 26 May by the Liverpool MC, Ken Burgess went a stage further by carrying a complete welding kit of oxygen and acetylene bottles etc. in the rear of his Morgan, but the weight failed to put him into the awards.

Back at the Morgan factory, hesitant production of new cars had begun, with the first deliveries in March. With the many suppliers struggling to get back into production themselves, it was initially a question of raiding the stores to see what could be built up.

There were a few Matchless o.h.v. vee twins at the factory, and these were built up into the last of the Morgan vee-twin three-wheelers that had made the Company's reputation, nine of these twelve Super Sports being exported to Brylaws in Australia. This left just the 'F' type Ford-engined three-wheeler to continue to represent the three-wheeler series.

With the 4/4s, production continued with the 1267 cc Standard engines (engine number prefixed Q, and suffixed E for engine). Sir John Black had confirmed the future availability of these engines, but only for a limited period as a new model policy was to be introduced by the Standard Motor Company, of which more later. There were also a few 1100 cc Climax engines in the stores, available for building into 4/4s. Post-war chassis numbers began at 1000 (F type, 600).

While engines were available for limited production, other items were not. Front shock absorbers could not readily be located, so George Goodall announced to the press that 'adjustment of the spring characteristics had made front shock absorbers unnecessary'. Gearboxes were thought to be a problem, and the Morgan factory actively considered manufacturing them at the factory with bought-in gears (as they did for three-wheelers). In the event this proved unnecessary. Moss and a few remaining Meadows gearboxes were able to be fitted. The biggest problem of all, however, was in obtaining steel. The Government was to tie supply to exports.

New to Morgan was an improved steering damper of saw leaf steel to the front sliding axle. It was suggested the back axle ratio would be raised to 4.5 to 1, but in fact 4.72 to 1 was to be adopted.

As well as changes to the new Morgan, there were also many changes to the agents. Gone was the famous Winter Garden Garages – sold by Lance Prideaux-Brune during the war. Dick Anthony had joined the company of John Mowlem Ltd, servicing mechanical plant at airports, but wanted to continue in motor sport, so he obtained a rather worn 1938 Coupe, chassis 718. This he took to the Morgan factory to be rebuilt as a blue two-seater, which he collected on 25 August.

New post-war Morgan agents were Central Garages of Barnstaple. When director Reg Hellier visited the Morgan factory in the spring of 1946 to see George Goodall, he noticed two Le Mans Replicas under dust sheets. Upon return to North Devon he mentioned this to his friends Murray Symons, his brother Vyvyan Symons and Bob Harris. As a result, Reg purchased the two Le Mans Replicas, the first a red one, chassis number 1097, being delivered to accountant Murray Symons on 1 June, registered JTT 703. Bob Harris, the head of a large building company, was to take its sister, a white Morgan with red upholstery, chassis number 1098, reg. JUO 177, in March 1947. Both cars were sold, like most post-war Le Mans Replicas, as if they had actually been prepared for the 1939 race, or had been reserves! Reg Hellier himself ordered a Standard-engined

A Standard-engined chassis in the factory yard. Note the steering dampers, but absence of front shock-absorbers. Behind can be seen the entrance to a war-time air raid shelter. (*Photograph: Quadrant Picture Library*)

two-seater, and after some persuasion, managed to get 'F' type three-wheeler front wings fitted as he preferred cycle type wings. This red Morgan, chassis 1024, was registered FUO 919 and delivered on 3 October. Vyvyan Symons ordered a Coupe, probably 1023, which was collected, the earliest of the four, on 17 April, registered JTT 96.

Reg Hellier and his customers could be well pleased with their purchases, for theirs were the exceptions. While many orders were received, often not bothering to specify colour, and taking the first available, most were to be disappointed as steel was only available for exports. As chassis numbers were allocated to orders, this led to huge gaps in the chassis numbers of cars actually built, as these orders were never completed.

Another of those lucky enough to acquire a new Morgan was the local Malvern doctor Dr Gavin Scott, who managed to get his directly from HFS Morgan. This blue Standard-engined two-seater, chassis number 1483, was collected on 26 July.

Those fortunate enough to obtain new cars could clearly make a fat profit by immediately re-selling at an exorbitant price. To counteract this the British Motor Trade Association was to require, from July, all new car purchasers to execute a deed of covenant to retain their cars for their own use for a period of six months.

It was the ambitious Ulster Automobile Club that was to stage the first race meeting in the British Isles, with Brooklands and Donington out of action, the former forever and the latter until the 1970s. The circuit to be used on 10 August was once again the closed public roads constituting the Ballyclare circuit of 4.14 miles as used previously. After the scratch Ulster International Trophy of 1½ litre racing cars, won by 'B Bira's ERA came the two heats of the twenty-five mile Ulster Trophy Handicap. On limit in the first heat of twelve was Frank Bigger from Castleknock in Dublin with his 1122cc Climax-engined 4–4 and he drove steadily to finish last of the six qualifiers from the heat for the final. In the final, over six laps, the one lap plus three minutes credit of Frank Bigger did not prove sufficient to get into the places. He finished eighth at 53.4mph, the winner being Noel Hillis with his 2276cc Talbot 90 special, with crowds estimated at 40,000 lining the course.

While circuit racing was not yet possible in England, sprinting was possible. On 7 September the Brighton and Hove MC ran their Brighton Speed Trials over a kilometre stretch of the Madeira Drive. Two Morgans were entered in Class 5, for unsupercharged standard sports cars up to 1500cc. Garage owner, Geoffrey Render, recently demobilized from the forces, was driving his brother's pre-war green 1100cc Climax-engined 4/4, reg. HPH 750. David Render had purchased the car in 1942 before joining the army in the November of that year, but was currently still away in an armoured regiment in the North African desert. The other entry was the 4/4 of P. J. Burke. Neither finished among the awards.

Just four days later Jim Goodall, probably in BWP47, beat an Allard, an HRG and a Riley by a single mark to win the open class of the SUNBAC Evening Trial, an excellent performance.

The uncertainty about engine supply earlier in the year had led HFS Morgan to commission Harry Hatch to design an engine especially for the firm. HFS had been very impressed with the KM Series of 1100cc Blackburne vee-twins that he fitted to Morgan three-wheelers in the 1920s. In particular he had been impressed with the racing KMB version which proved so successful, particularly for record breaking in the hands of Harold Beart. The designer of these engines was Harry Hatch, with whom HFS had become quite friendly. During the war Harry Hatch had been working for the Air Ministry, on the development of air-cooled engines. In 1948 he was to join the motorcycle firm AMC Limited as research and development engineer.

In October 1946 the drawings of the proposed Hatch Morgan engine arrived at the factory, and many still exist to this day allowing much of the proposed engine to be recorded, although it was never built.

It was a conventional four-cylinder o.h.v. engine, of 67mm bore by 77.5 stroke, with a capacity of 1093cc. The cylinder block and separate head were to be of cast iron, with a pressed steel sump measuring 17³⁄₁₆in. × 10in. The rocker cover was of aluminium. A three-bearing crankshaft was

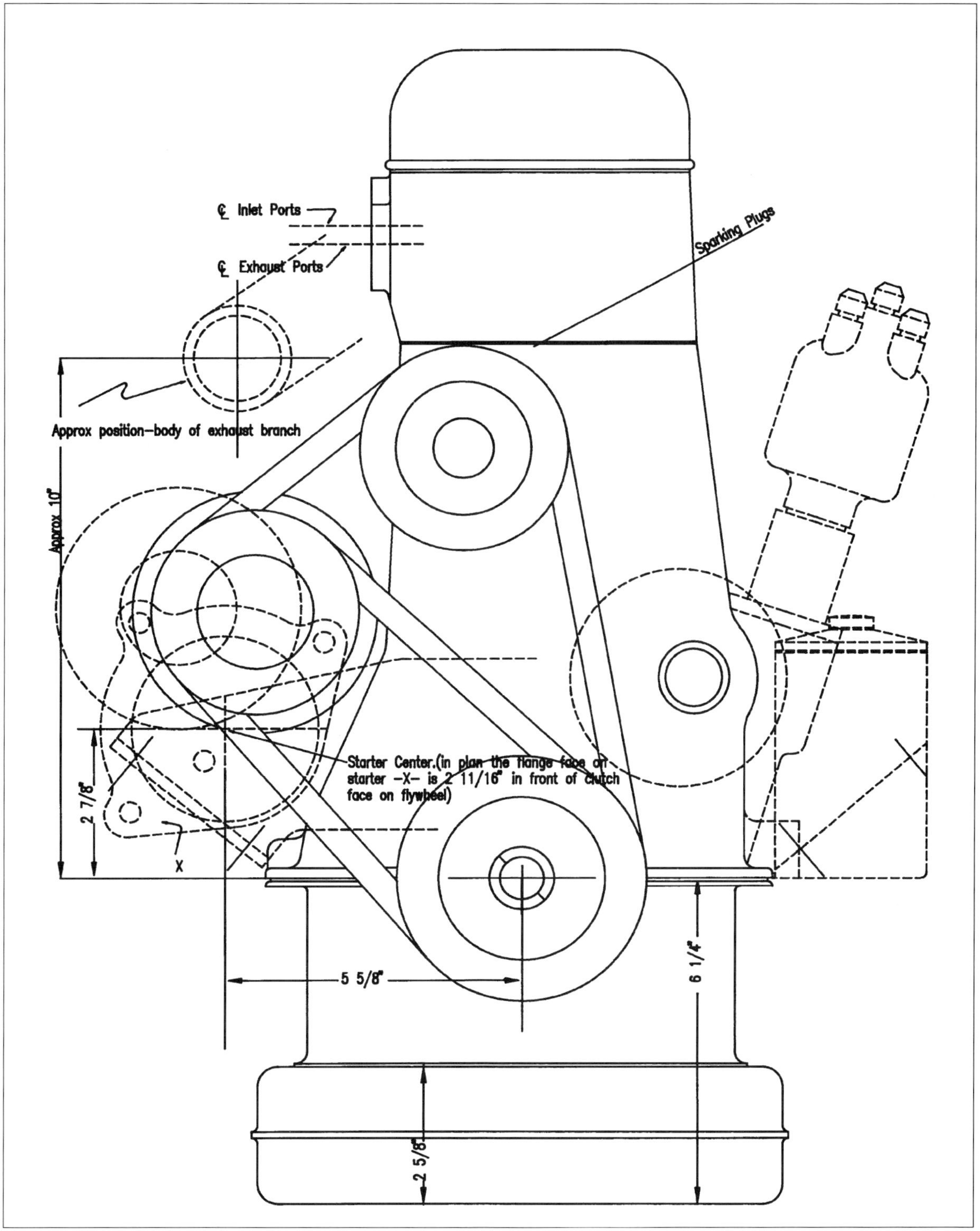

The front plan of the Harry Hatch designed Morgan engine, redrawn from the original by Dennis Rushton. Note that two fan belt schemes were submitted, depending on whether a water pump was to be specified.

fitted. The main bearings were 2 1/8in. diameter, and the big ends 2in. diameter, all plain bearings.

Aluminium con-rods of 6 9/16 in. length were to be used with 11/16in. little ends. A single vertical 1 1/2in. inlet valve and a single vertical 1 1/4in. exhaust valve were fitted to each cylinder, the latter valve being recessed within the combustion chamber. The ports were to the offside of the engine with the inlet ports slightly higher than the exhaust. Sadly the camshaft drawings appear to be missing, but the distributor drive is shown to be between cylinders two and three to the nearside of the engine.

The production and development of a new engine for a small manufacturer of inexpensive sports cars was clearly an uneconomic proposition. Whether HFS Morgan believed other small motor companies might be interested in his engine, and share the costs, is not known, but it was never to be built.

On 2 November the MCC ran again its famous Sporting Trial over the old 1938 route based on the Buxton area of Derbyshire. One Morgan was entered, an 1122cc Climax 4/4, driven by J. A. Thomson of South Croydon.

This was a very odd Morgan, as the original suspension had been heavily modified, the front now being independent to the Leslie Ballamy pattern, with transverse leaf springs, as used in Allards. The Morgan was also supercharged, but retired on route.

CHAPTER EIGHT

1947

Although the petrol rationing had been gradually eased during 1946 (allowing the average family car up to 180 miles per month from March and then 260 miles from August), the MCC reluctantly decided it still could not run the traditional long-distance Exeter Trial in January. It resolved, however, come hell or high water that the Lands End would run at Easter.

In February 1947 Peter Morgan was finally able to start work at the Morgan factory, having been demobilized from the Army. Initially he was to work in the various shops that would allow non-union labour, gaining experience in the way the Morgan was built.

The winter of 1947 was unusually severe, with much of the North of England and the Midlands blanketed by deep snow, accompanied by sub-zero temperatures, from February until close to Easter. As a result many trials had to be cancelled or postponed, giving a lean time for the motoring sportsman. One event that managed to beat the weather by moving its location from Tiverton to the Newton Abbot area was the West of England Spring Trial, held on 2 March. Campbell managed a First Class Award, while Ken Burgess, now transferred to an Allard, took home the Unlimited Cup.

The difficulty of purchasing new cars continued, and delivery from factories was still far from normal. As a result the BMTA covenant restricting the resale of new cars for six months from purchase was extended to twelve months as from 15 March to stop speculators. The Government was requiring 60% of new cars to be exported, and later in the summer was to increase this to 75%.

Because of the petrol rationing, Jackie Masters, the MCC Club Secretary, had of necessity decided to abandon the long overnight run for the forthcoming first post war Lands End Trial, to be held on 6 April. Back at the Morgan factory the previous trials stalwarts HFS Morgan, George Goodall and Harry Jones had all decided that advancing age necessitated retirement from active motor sport. Peter Morgan and Jim Goodall, however were keen for competition and duly entered. Peter, we believe, was driving his pre-war 4/4 BUY 754 which had been refurbished and was running with an o.h.v. 1267 cc Standard engine, as was Jim Goodall's usual Morgan, BWP 47. Completing the Morgan factory team was Joe Huxham from Bournemouth, entered with a 1098 cc Climax-engined Morgan, prepared as usual by his partner Tom Bryant. We believe this to be ELJ 837 (registered on 13 January 1941), as used by Joe throughout 1947. This standard-looking 4/4 with 1098 cc engine was chassis number 803, and was collected from the factory in March 1939. Perhaps it had been in stock for some time before registration.

A second team of Morgans comprised the West Country enthusiasts, Murray Symons and Bob Harris with the two Le Mans Replicas, JTT 703 and JUO 177 respectively, and Barnstaple agent Reg Hellier with the 'F' type front winged FUO 919. All looked very smart wearing white helmets. Murray Symons' brother Vyvyan was following the team with his Standard-engined Coupe JTT 96.

Also competing were J. A. Thomson with his unusual Climax 4/4 DEL 125, DCD Campbell with a smart red Standard-engined 4/4 Coupe, and D. J. Holliday with a Climax 4/4.

The appalling weather played havoc with the depth of the water splash at Crackington and caused the retirement of Vyvyan Symons' Coupe, due to a drowned engine. When the rather wet Vyvyan and his passenger opened their doors simultaneously, to escape from the rapidly rising water inside the car, they watched the 'float on air' cushions float away on water down stream!

Thomson and Huxham also retired, but Peter Morgan, Jim Goodall, D. Campbell, Reg Hellier and Murray Symons all took First Class Awards,

Bob Harris carefully wades his way through the swollen Crackington ford in JUO 177. (*Photograph: Reg Hellier collection*)

J. A. Thomson in his heavily modified Morgan blasts up Lynton Hill during the Lands End Trial. His passenger appears somewhat apprehensive. (*Photograph:* The Motor)

Bob Harris failing Darracott for a Second, and Holliday claiming a Third.

On the return journey to Malvern Link, Peter Morgan was stopped for speeding in Launceston, and subsequently summoned and fined. With commendable honesty he informed the MCC Stewards, who regretted they had no option but to withdraw his Premier Award.

The eventual contest of the Colmore Trophy Trial took place on 26 April (having been postponed because of the snowy weather), and this time glorious spring sunshine greeted the event. Jim Goodall came away with a Second Class Award with BWP 47, no mean achievement bearing in mind the proliferation of specials being built for trialing.

Horace Roberts went up to North Wales for another previously postponed event, the Liverpool MC 'Jeans' Trial, held eventually on 18 May. He too did well to collect a Third Class Award against so many specials, especially as the ceaseless rain made the course into a mudbath. Jim Goodall had success in another of the popular SUNBAC Evening Trials, held on 26 May in the Hagley area, and collected a First Class Award with BWP 47.

Following the success of the MCC's Lands End Trial at Easter, the club decided to run its oldest trial, the Edinburgh, at Whitsun, on 14 May, but running an abbreviated course based in Harrogate and using the Yorkshire Dales rather than going from London to Edinburgh. Five Morgans took part. The factory was represented by Peter Morgan with BUY 754, and Jim Goodall with BWP 47, the Morgan team being completed by Murray Symons with his Le Mans Replica JTT 703. Campbell was in his Coupe, and Thomson in his modified 4/4, DEL 125. The trial proved reasonably easy, with Firsts for Peter, Jim and DCD Campbell, a Second for Murray Symons for failing Park Rash and a Third for Thomson, who failed Summer Lodge also. The Morgan team also took the 'one make' team award.

Britain's first post-war rally was held at Blackpool on 6 and 7 June, organized by the Lancashire AC along the same lines as the popular pre-war Blackpool rallies. With 260 miles of road and then the traditional driving and manoeuvrability tests at the finish, the event was remarkable for the victory of Ken Wharton in his home made Wharton Special (Austin Seven chassis, Ford 10 engine). This event also saw Dick Anthony back among the awards with his rebuilt pre-war 4/4, HPC 13, taking the JCC club's prize.

The first post-war car racing in Ireland took place over a triangular course at the famous Curragh, the vast plain of grass and gorse east of Kildare on which stands the Irish military camp and the horse racing headquarters. Military personnel provided the majority of the marshalls and proved most efficient. Entered for this event was a blue Climax-engined 4/4, driven by Belfast motorcycle racer and automobile engineer Terry Hill.

In May 1946, Dublin garage owner, Fred Armstrong, father of another motor cycle racer, Reg Armstrong, had purchased second-hand one of the 1937 Gorman-assembled 4/4s, chassis 330, engine MA 343. He wanted the Morgan to be used for racing, and had approached Terry Hill to prepare the car for this purpose. Terry stripped the Morgan to the bare minimum, and worked on the engine, fitting larger valves, and opening out the ports. The compression was raised, and the carburation altered. It is possible a close ratio gearbox was also fitted, to bring the gearing up to motorcycle racing ratios.

The handicap events were run as two ten-lap heats (16.7 miles) followed by a fifteen-lap (25 mile) final. In the first heat Terry Hill made good use of his handicap award to win at 52.39 mph. In the final it was anticipated Terry Hill would be difficult to beat, but engine trouble intervened after a third of the distance forcing retirement.

The Ulster AC's second Ulster Trophy races were held on 9 August. Once again Frank Bigger from Dublin entered his 1122 cc 4/4 in the handicap event hoping for better things than in 1946 and this year he was joined by Terry Hill with the Armstrong Morgan, with reserve driver Desmond McCracken nominated for the Armstrong car.

The Ulster races were the only form of circuit racing possible in the United Kingdom, so they attracted all the keen racers from the mainland. In the scratch race which was to follow the handicap event there were no fewer than eight ERAs entered by owners, all desperate for the return of road racing. One of these drivers was the Siamese prince, 'B. Bira', with his ERA 'Hanuman'. On the Friday practice he ran a big end, and enlisted the help of Terry Hill and his mechanics to work all night fitting new bearings enabling him to run-in the bearings on the Saturday morning at a nearby airfield.

There were so many entries for the handicap that two fifty-mile heats were held, with the fastest eight in each heat going through to the fifty-mile final. Sadly Frank Bigger non-started, but the now rather weary Terry Hill managed to finish seventh for a place in the final, despite some clutch slip being evident.

In the final Terry Hill took the lead on the fifth lap, with some very fast driving but sadly the clutch slip began to return on the seventh lap. Thereafter it was a case of surviving to the finish but not before Donald Pitt's MGPB and two other drivers had passed him during the last couple of laps. Still, in the circumstances, fourth place at 56.17 mph was an excellent result for the Armstrong Morgan.

With the absence of circuit racing in the British mainland, most British racers had turned to hillclimbs for competition. As a result, the RAC officially recognised speed hillclimbing with a National Championship for 1947. Included as one of the rounds was the famous Craigantlet course in Ulster, of 1,883 yards length, average 1 in 16 gradient, and in use since 1925.

The 1947 event was held on 30 August, and the intense heat of the sun caused some melting

Terry Hill at Craigantlet with the tuned Reg Armstrong Morgan. (*Photograph: Terry Hill collection*)

of the tar surface, making life difficult for the powerful ERAs and Allards. Terry Hill took the Armstrong Morgan, but failed to feature among the awards despite a neat climb.

During August the British Government announced that the economic situation necessitated the imposition of even tougher petrol rationing as from October, with a reduction in the basic ration used for pleasure motoring, as opposed to essential travel. As a result many clubs brought forward their events to try and beat the deadline.

There was a record entry of 227 cars for the 1947 Brighton Speed Trials, held on 1 September in good weather. One of these was David Render, having a go in his first competitive event. Now demobilized from Army service in North Africa, he had reclaimed his pre-war 1100 cc Climax-engined 4/4, HPH 750, from his brother who had driven it the previous year. In the class for standard sports cars up to 1300 cc, he finished twelfth at 47.67 mph for the standing start kilometre.

In the class for standard supercharged sports cars up to 1300 cc was the non-standard, much modified Climax-engined 4/4 of J. A. Thomson, but he had problems and finished sixth at 46.60 mph.

On 6 September the West Hants and Dorset Car Club held their Poole Speed Trials in the grounds of the school of South Lychett Manor. Two 4/4s took part, the 1100 cc cars of local agent Joe Huxham and also that of David Render. Joe's Morgan appeared off-colour. Despite using an immense number of revs as he changed down for

A front wheel is lifted by David Render at Poole. (*Photograph: Guy Griffiths*)

Joe Huxham at Poole. (*Photograph: Guy Griffiths*)

the 'S', David Render did not appear in the awards either.

David Render's Morgan was recently described by him as a Le Mans Replica, but the photos clearly show the standard twin spare wheels rear bodywork of the normal 4/4. It had the optional cycle wings and outside exhaust available as extras for the pre-war 4/4 at £15, if ordered from the factory from new. The special 1100 cc Climax engines had been fitted to many pre-war 4/4s.

At the Morgan factory HFS Morgan was still concerned to locate a suitable engine to power the Morgan when the 1267 cc Standard engine was discontinued. One of the first jobs given to Peter Morgan by his father was to try and locate a suitable unit, which HFS wanted to be of o.h.v. type and less then 1500 cc, to keep the Morgan sports car in the inexpensive sports car market that he knew best.

The reason for the discontinuation of the Standard Special engine was the new one-model policy to be introduced by Sir John Black, which merits explanation. With the war coming to an end by 1944 and the proposed changes in post-war road fund taxation, Sir John had decided that the only way forward for the post war future was to concentrate on one model, which he would produce in large numbers, minimizing costs and thus enabling the Standard Motor Company to target export markets aggressively. He had been impressed by the Plymouth staff cars used by visiting United States Army officers. In 1945 his styling designer Walter Belgrove found himself sitting outside the US Embassy in London making sketches of the cars!

Having decided on the styling, Sir John had drawn up the specification that he required to be achieved by Ted Grinham, who had recently (October 1945) returned from war service with the De Havilland Aircraft Company. It must seat six in comfort, be capable of cruising at 60 mph, be economical and low in price. The new car was code named 20S.

In August 1945 Sir John Black had also made an agreement with Harry Ferguson to manufacture the Ferguson tractor – provided he could eventually use a Standard engine. Tractor production meanwhile began in July 1946, using an American Continental engine of 1966 cc.

Ted Grinham was now asked to alter the design of the proposed four-cylinder engine for the 20S to make its basic components adaptable for use in the Ferguson Tractor which necessitated the use of a simple, rugged and versatile design. Ted had been impressed by the wet liner engine used in the the Citroën Traction Avant which appeared in the 1930s (designed by Maurice Sainturat) and realized this system would suit the purpose admirably.

An engine of 1850 cc was envisaged for the 20S car and the TE20 tractor, and a prototype car with such an engine (80 × 92 mm) was built by mid-1946. The new car was now named the Vanguard after the British battleship, and announced to the motoring world in July 1947 with this engine, but it was to be well into 1948 before production could begin. Power of 65 bhp at 4,500 rpm was claimed.

Early contact with Sir John Black revealed that he would be prepared to let Morgan use his engine, but HFS was not keen, believing the engine to be too large. He asked Peter to pursue alternatives. There was little point in contacting Morris Motors as they supplied engines to Morgan's competitor, MG. Similarly, Singer engines were ruled out. Peter contacted the Managing Director of Coventry Climax, Leonard Lee, only to find they were still busy on wartime fire pump contracts, and work on fork lift trucks, and had no new engines to offer.

The Ford Motor Company was still supplying Morgan with the side-valve Anglia and Prefect engines of 1172 cc for the 'F' type three-wheeler, but Morgan did not want to use the same engine in the 4/4, and anyway wanted an o.h.v. engine. George Goodall, however, seemed quite keen to use this engine, which of course had been successfully used in factory 4/4s pre-war for trials use.

Then, in October 1947, the Austin Motor Company announced the new A40 Devon and Dorset range, powered by their first o.h.v. small engine of 1200 cc. This engine, which had been designed by Eric Bareham and colleagues at 'the Austin', with input from Harry Weslake on head design, was bang up to date and produced 40 bhp at 4,300 rpm. The capacity of 1199 cc (65.48 × 89 mm) was ideally suited for the 4/4, and so Peter Morgan made an appointment to see the Chairman and Managing Director of Austin, Leonard Lord at Longbridge, Birmingham to enquire about the possibility of Morgan using this engine. Peter remembers being received most courteously, but Leonard Lord expected the demand for the new A40 to be such that there would be no spare engines available for sale.

An approach was also made to the Vauxhall Motor Company at Luton. Powering the current Vauxhall 12, and later the soon to be announced Vauxhall Wyvern, was a four-cylinder o.h.v. engine of 1442 cc (69.5 × 95 mm) producing a modest 35 bhp at 3,600 rpm. Vauxhall replied that it was not General Motors' policy to supply engines to outside manufacturers.

Peter Morgan discussed his so far unsuccessful search for a future Morgan engine with his father. Peter had been impressed with the specification of the 1850 cc Vanguard engine, and managed to persuade his father to let him experiment with one of these prototype engines in a 4/4 chassis to see how it would work, despite the large capacity.

HFS Morgan, while always the first to instigate change in the three-wheelers, was happy to leave others to develop the four-wheeler. Peter therefore ordered a Vanguard engine of 1850 cc and enrolled the help of Jim Roberts, the repair shop foreman, to develop the new Morgan.

An announcement by the British Government to discontinue the basic petrol allowance completely late in the year shook the motoring sportsmen. As a result many trials were brought forward

Peter Morgan going well in the Sporting Trial. (*Photograph: H. R. Clayton*)

to avoid the ban. The MCC brought forward their One Day Sporting Trial to Saturday 25 October, and the Sheffield and Hallamshire Motor Club then advanced their High Peak Trial to the following day, allowing a weekend of trials activity in the Buxton area of Derbyshire.

Dry hills made the Sporting Trial less demanding than many, and Jim Goodall with BWP 47, and Peter Morgan both won First Class Awards. Peter Morgan had now taken over the use of George Goodall's Triumph-Climax-engined 4/4 AUY 33, although the 1232 cc engine had probably been replaced by an 1100 cc Climax. Also entered, and winning a Second Class Award, was Basil de Mattos, who worked for Laystall Engineering. His Climax-engined two-seater failed Jenkins Chapel and Litton Slack. J. A. Thomson was also entered, his engine capacity being given as 1089 cc, but he non-started.

Following the customary evening party at the Palace Hotel in Buxton, most of the drivers made their way to Sheffield for the High Peak Trial on the following day. Again dry weather gave competition an easy day, but Peter Morgan was truly outstanding, finishing in fifth place, and winning the award for the best performance by an MCC member. Jim Goodall lost marks on the rocky slabs of Dowlow, and finished forty-fifth.

Apart from minor local events, the last major trials event before the loss of the basic petrol ration was the Cheltenham Motor Club's Closed Invitation Trial in the Cotswolds on 22 November. The event was won by Ken Burgess with his Allard, but Jim Goodall's trials special, BWP 47, gave him a First Class Award.

Peter Morgan was also entered, and although he did not feature in the awards, he caused note by succeeding in climbing the difficult grass loop in Syde. C. A. N. May in his book *More Wheelspin* states that Peter was using a locked differential, but Peter has no recollection of this, and thinks it more likely he used very thick back axle oil.

And so the year ended with a return to a ban on private motoring through petrol rationing. It was to be several months before the Government eased the restrictions sufficiently to allow a restart of motor sport.

Overseas

Australia

Jim Boughton did not return to motor sport after the war. He had spent the war years as a pilot seconded to the RAF in England and India, and returned to Brylaw Motors when hostilities were over. Later, in the 1950s, he was to open his own service stations and specialize in Citroën cars.

Over in Western Australia the Western Australian Sporting Car Club was able to gain access to the World War 2 airstrip of the Royal Australian Air Force at Caversham, some fifteen miles north-east of Perth. On 27 January the Western Australian speed championships were held there in aid of the Air Force Memorial House Appeal, and drew a crowd estimated at over 7,000, giving problems with spectators encroaching on the track during races. Entered was the red Climax-engined Morgan of John Emery, instructor in Motor mechanics at the local technical college, but he failed to feature in the results. Also competing, and more successfully, was truck operator Barry Ranford with his Chrysler-engined special. He was later to drive a Morgan.

CHAPTER NINE

1948

With petrol only available for commerce, it was a rather austere start to the motoring year. A new system of road tax was introduced as from 1 January, whereby all new cars would be subject to a £10 flat rate. Obviously this removed another restriction against the development of larger capacity engines in Britain, thereby allowing British motor exports to compete favourably in markets where engine size was not restricted.

Meanwhile, back at the Morgan factory, Jim Roberts and Peter Morgan were working at fitting the loaned 1850 cc Vanguard engine into a 4/4 chassis. It turned out not to be too difficult a job, although the extra length of the engine necessitated an increase in the size of the chassis around the engine compartment. HFS Morgan did not show much interest in this construction, until the prototype was completed. He then took the car to the steep Croft Bank in West Malvern where it performed most satisfactorily. HFS was now pleased to agree with Peter that they should base their future sports car on this engine.

Standard-Triumph themselves had not yet begun production of the Vanguard, and Sir John Black promised to continue supplies of the Standard Special 1267 cc engine until the new engine was available. Jim Roberts and Peter Morgan were now to continue to develop the new Vanguard-engined Morgan, with Peter doing the drawings.

The Ferguson Tractor TE20 had now begun to be fitted with the 1850 cc tractor version of the common components engine. As the tractor chassis used the American Unified National Thread system for fastenings, the new engine followed suit. In later years this was to mislead enthusiasts into believing the new engine was derived from its predecessor, the Continental, which also happened to use that system.

During 1948, George Goodall, who was responsible for sales, targeted many overseas markets to boost exports. In Australia, Champion Motors in Adelaide joined Brylaws in Melbourne as agents. Cars were also shipped to Uruguay, South Africa, Denmark, India, Sweden and Malaya often using the buying and confirming agents, Tozer, Kemsley and Millbourne. Perhaps the most significant of all the exports, however, was the sale of a few cars (beginning in May) to the USA.

The stationing of United States forces on British soil both during the war and afterwards, exposed them to a new motoring expeience – the British sports car. Many of them fell in love with this sporting type of open motor car, so much so that they wanted them 'back home'. The invasion of the USA by British sports cars was to have profound future effects on the development and survival of many British car makers, including Morgan, of which more later. Exports were led by the MG company, which actually targeted the US Forces with its marketing. The Morgan sports cars were initially imported into the USA by Whitehall Distributors.

The summer of 1948 saw the first Vanguard leave the Standard-Triumph production line. The new road tax system had meant that there would be no tax penalty for British motorists if the engine was enlarged, and the trials with the 1850 cc engine had shown it was a little underpowered for the performance Sir John Black had specified. As a result Standard-Triumph made the late decision, just before production commenced, to increase the bore to 85 mm, giving a capacity of 2088 cc.

Peter Morgan was horrified, as the engine was now much bigger than originally intended, and, more importantly, missed the important cut off of 2 litres for motor racing classes. However, the development of the new car was proceeding well, and it was really too late to look again for a new engine. The 85 mm bore engine produced 68 bhp at 4,200 rpm.

From 1 June the British Government announced the reintroduction of a petrol ration for pleasure motoring, equivalent to 90 miles per month, only the name had now changed from 'basic' to 'standard' petrol ration. Still a pretty austere state of affairs, but some motor sport was able to restart. To try and stop the fraudulent use of commercial petrol for pleasure, the Government had introduced separate pumps at petrol stations for commercial petrol as from 18 May with this petrol having a red dye added. It was 'woe betide' anyone caught using 'red petrol' for pleasure, but we know of one Morgan fitted with a disguised extra fuel tank within the under bonnet tool box for such a purpose, with a secret tap beneath the dashboard to enable the driver to switch back to 'yellow' pleasure petrol if the police took an interest!

As a further boost to the motoring sportsman the RAC announced that they had taken a lease on a decommissioned wartime RAF airfield in Northamptonshire – Silverstone, with a view to establishing circuit racing once more. The RAC also was impressed with the redundant Westhampnett airfield in Sussex which the Junior Car Club, later to become the British Automobile Racing Club, sought permission to use for racing. This was to become Goodwood, with the perimeter road being considered suitable for racing.

Road racing in Ireland continued on 10 July with the resurrection of the international Leinster Trophy handicap race held on the Tallaght circuit in County Dublin over twenty laps of the six-mile circuit. Three Morgans were entered, all 1122 cc Climax-engined, but we believe only two started. All were driven by Dublin drivers, one by Frank Bigger, one by Fred Armstrong (the car recently prepared by Terry Hill), and one by Kenneth McLean. Interestingly all were given different handicaps, the car of Frank Bigger having five credit laps, the car of Fred Armstrong four laps plus four minutes credit and the non-starting car of Kenneth McLean four laps and 1½ minutes.

Tar melted by the blazing sun made the course difficult in places. It was the long markers who dominated the race, with Frank Bigger taking the lead on the ninth lap. Sadly he did not keep it for long as he had to pit to attend to the battery.

The race turned out to be a 'MG benefit', as they took six of the first seven places. The winner, though, was Leeper's Le Mans Singer. Fred Armstrong finished eleventh and Frank Bigger thirteenth.

Having been unable to run the 1948 Exeter, Lands End and Edinburgh Trials because of the petrol rationing, the ever resourceful MCC Secretary Jackie Masters organized a thirty-seven mile trial in Exmoor on 31 July now that rationing allowed. This Devon Trial attracted sixty-seven car entries, of which seven were Morgans. From the factory there was Jim Goodall with BWP 47, and Peter Morgan also with a Standard Special-engined car (possibly BUY 754). From Devon there was Reg Hellier with FUO 919 and Vyvyan Symons with JTT 96. Joe Huxham was with a 1100 cc car (possibly FLJ 837) and Basil de Mattos was in his 4/4, with its capacity given as 1140 cc. The other driver, Holliday, non-started.

Rain the night before the event made some of the hills tricky, but Reg Hellier and Jim Goodall were 'clean' to take Premier Awards. Peter Morgan failed Yeascombe to claim a Second,

Reg Hellier's 4/4 during the Devon Trial. The three-wheeler 'F' type front wings make the car unique. (*Photograph: Reg Hellier collection*)

Tom Bryant in Joe Huxham's Morgan on the wooded Boscombe hill climb course. (*Photograph: Guy Griffiths*)

while de Mattos, Symons and Huxham took Thirds.

It was Joe Huxham's business partner Tom Bryant's turn to drive Joe's 1100 cc Morgan on 7 August at the Boscombe hill climb, of just 708 yards, but he was lacking in success. Also entered, and of interest, was another Bournemouth motor trader by the name of Jeff Sparrowe, who was competing with an 1100 cc Crossley. We shall read more of him in the future.

Over in Ireland the Limerick Light Car and Motor Cycle Club held a sand race meeting on 8 August at the popular County Clare seaside resort of Lahinch. There were two fifteen-lap heats and a twenty-lap final run on handicap, each lap being just one mile long, but a delay in starting meant that the tide was on its way in for the final, giving the event a nautical flavour. The second heat saw Limerick quantity surveyor, Derry O'Brien, finish second with his 1087 cc Morgan (presumably a Climax-engined car), qualifying for the waterlogged final. Despite being hit from behind by Dr Gaskin's Ford Midget, Derry was able to finish a commendable third at 43.72 mph behind Le Fanu's winning LERA and Colley's Frazer Nash.

It was to be the Goodwood circuit that was to be the first of the two new airfield circuits to stage a motor race, and when the regulations were announced for the September meeting the three-lap scratch races included one for 1100 cc sports cars. This attracted the interest of several Morgan drivers, including Peter Morgan. Under dust covers at the factory were two pre-war racers – CAB 652 as used by Peter Morgan at Donington in 1939, and the 1939 Le Mans car. The latter, Peter found difficult to tune, the multi-carburettor system fitted by Dick Anthony at Winter Garden Garages not being easy to set up, so Peter concentrated on getting CAB 652 ready. As the event was for sports cars, CAB 652 was prepared in road trim, complete with lights and front cycle

Thomson sets off at Brighton in his extremely unusual Morgan. (*Photograph: Guy Griffiths*)

wings, although the windscreen was replaced by an aero screen. A racing mirror was fitted alongside it.

Meanwhile the speed trials continued. At Brighton on 4 September there was just one Morgan entered, the heavily modified supercharged 1089 cc Climax-engined 4/4 of J. A. Thomson, running in the class for supercharged standard sports cars of up to 1200 cc. Fitted with the unusual LMB front suspension, altered rear suspension and bodywork, and a hand clutch, Thomson's Morgan started well, but was caught by Baines' MG. He finished out of the awards at 46.8 mph.

When Thomson advertized this Morgan for sale in the 1951 motoring magazines, the 1937 Morgan was fitted with a Marshall supercharger, a special additional gearbox giving 1.33 overdrive and a BTH vertical magneto. We suspect all or most of these items were in place at Brighton.

At long last 18 September, the eagerly awaited day of the very first Goodwood race meeting, arrived. Entered were no fewer than three Morgans, all with 1100 cc engines. Peter Morgan was in CAB 652, as previously described. David Render was in HPH 750, and Dick Anthony in his 4/4, HPC 13.

The course was opened by the Duke and Duchess of Richmond and Gordon driving around the 2.4-mile lap in a new Bristol, watched by a large crowd despite the petrol rationing.

Event two was the three-lap scratch race for non-supercharged open sports cars of up to 1100 cc, and saw the three Morgans on the grid. Peter Morgan took an immediate lead, but had been passed by Harry Lester's much modified MG after the first lap, and Lester duly won with Peter Morgan an excellent second. The other two Morgans were not placed.

The Cheltenham Motor Club ran its trial in pouring rain on 16 October. Peter Morgan, with AUY 33, and Jim Goodall, with BWP 47, both

The start of the 1100cc race at Goodwood, with Peter Morgan leading the field. (*Photograph:* Daily Graphic)

Peter Morgan at speed at Goodwood. (*Photograph: Louis Klemantaski*)

excelled with First Class Awards, and, with Ken Delingpole's HRG, made up the winning team entry. Kenneth Delingpole and Ronald Low had begun manufacture of their own trials car, powered by 1172 cc Ford SV engine – the Dellow.

On 23 October the MCC once again ran its Sporting One Day Trial in Derbyshire. Peter Morgan, with a 1122 cc Climax-engined car (probably AUY 33) and Jim Goodall with a 1267 cc Standard-engined BWP 47 were both entered. Jim Goodall was passengered by Bromsgrove chemist Terry Hill. Terry was well known at the Morgan factory, having run a three-wheeler Super Sports for some time, and Jim had asked him to passenger for him when they had met while both marshalling a club event. The partnership was to last for many fruitful years.

Jim and Peter both won Second Class Awards, Jim failing Litton Slack, and Peter the second part of Jenkins Chapel.

Following the usual celebrations overnight in Buxton, the Sheffield and Hallamshire Motor Club ran its High Peak Trial on the following day (Sunday). Neither Peter nor Jim featured in the awards.

The first day of the first post-war British motor show opened at Earls Court on 27 October. The Morgan Motor Company took full advantage of this opportunity, exhibiting all three types of

Peter Morgan climbing Litton Slack in the Sporting Trial. (*Photograph:* The Motor)

bodywork and a bare chassis. Sensation of the show was undoubtedly the stunningly beautiful 3½ litre 2 o.h.c. Jaguar XK120, priced, with purchase tax added, at £1,263.

It is interesting to compare the prices (rounded to the nearest pound) of some British sports cars for 1949 as given by *The Motor*. Morgan priced their two-seater at £435, which with purchase tax sold at £557. The four-seater cost £576, and the Coupe £633. The MG TC was priced at £528 and the Singer 9 Roadster at £576. The 1100 cc HRG cost £1,004 and the 1500 cc version £1,087. The Allards cost from £1,238, the Frazer Nash £3,074 and the Aston Martin Spa replica £3,109.

While the Morgan Motor Company's advertiser was still faithful to the original hyphenated 4–4 model description in its advertisements, the factory itself in internal memoranda, and also the motoring press, had preferred the title 4/4 with an oblique since early in the model's pre-war history. We have previously used both descriptions, but will now standardize on the more generally used 4/4.

Dick Anthony during a driving test in the Chiltern Trial. (*Photograph: Guy Griffiths*)

Over seventy competitors started in the Chiltern Car Club's Tourist Trial on 12 December, starting at Chorley Wood Common and finishing at Wendover after an eighteen-mile course with two observed sections and five driving tests. Two Morgans were entered, both 1100 cc Climax-engined. One was David Render's and the other that of Dick Anthony. David won a First Class Award in HPH 750, and together with his brother's MG and Jim Mayers' MG also won the team award. Dick Anthony, with HPC 13, won a Second Class Award.

Overseas

Australia

For 1948 the honour of hosting the Australian Grand Prix fell to the state of Victoria. Not having a suitable purpose-built circuit available, the race meeting on Australia Day, 26 January, was held over the concrete runways and dispersal roads of the RAAF aerodrome at Point Cook, some fifteen miles from Melbourne. The circuit was of 2.4 miles, including a ¾ mile runway, with 90° bends at each end.

Two other races were scheduled for the day, a ten-lap scratch race for cars of under 1500 cc, which was to precede the Grand Prix, and an open handicap which was to follow it.

Entered for the scratch race were two Morgans, the 1946 Super Sport three-wheeler of Cec

John Emery taking part in the Narrogin parade. *(Photograph: Terry McGrath collection)*

Warren, and the 4/4 of R King. Both lined up for the start at 11 a.m. in blistering heat (98° in the shade), with fine ash blowing about from a recent shrubbery burn-off. Their main opposition came from some very fast MGs. After just one lap poor King was at the tail of the field, but Cec Warren was going well in sixth place. The heat took a dreadful toll, however, with overheating and fuel vaporization causing many retirements, and at the flag the winner was Alf Najar in his single-seater MG TB special with a time of 27 min. 22 sec. Finishing sixth behind more MGs and a Riley was Cec Warren in his MX4-engined three-wheeler in 23 min. 47 sec., with R. King seventh, some 53 seconds behind.

Of the two Morgans only Cec Warren started in the Grand Prix, but did not feature in the results.

In Western Australia John Emery continued his motor racing with his red 4/4. On 13 March he was at Caversham once more for the Speed Carnival, and by dint of good handicapping proved the victor in the six-lap handicap for racing cars, beating Arthur Collett's well-prepared MGTC and Jack Nelson's Ford 10 special. A partially obscured tree stump at the edge of the track caught out a motor cycle and a Bugatti in two other events, luckily without injury.

John was back at Caversham for the quarter mile records day on 22 May, but without success.

On Monday, 8 November the agricultural town of Narrogin situated approximately one hundred and twenty miles south of Perth held its 'round the houses' races. It formed part of a whole weekend of motoring carnival, including a car and motorcycle Gymkhana, an exhibition of the can-can!, and a presentation ball after the racing. Preceding the afternoon's races was a parade of the cars and drivers, which included John Emery once more with his red Climax-engined Morgan. He had recently been elected to the committee of the WA Sporting Car Club.

Sadly, John did not feature in the results for the Great Southern Fifty (twenty-one laps of the 2.2-mile street circuit), or the six-lap open handicap.

John Emery racing through Narrogin. *(Photograph: Terry McGrath collection)*

CHAPTER TEN

1949

Despite the continuation of petrol rationing, the MCC managed to run its first Exeter Trial for ten years on 1 January, but it was, of necessity, based around Exeter itself, with a meagre road mileage of under sixty miles. The small field of competitors included three Morgans, all from the factory. Peter Morgan was driving the ex-George Goodall Climax-engined car, AUY 33, Jim Goodall was in his usual short chassis trials car BWP 47, and the team was completed by machine shop employee Sonny McCann driving Peter Morgan's pre-war trials car BUY 754, fitted with the Standard Special engine. Torrential rain failed to prevent Jim claiming a First Class Award, but Peter and Sonny both needed assistance on Simms, claiming Seconds with the team finishing second overall in the team contest, but best one-make team.

Previous rain made the course of the Maidstone and Mid Kent MC's Tyrwhitt-Drake Cup Trial rather tricky on 16 January, but David Render, with HPH 750, helped his brother and Mayers, both with MGs, to take the team award.

The search for redundant airfields to use for racing had led the Bristol MC and LCC to investigate Lulsgate Bottom, and the club ran its first event there on 16 April, Easter Saturday. Although the public were not admitted, the event was well organized over a two-mile circuit, and even had a public address system and a beer tent. Entered in the first five-lap race for sports cars up to 1100 cc and super sports cars up to 850 cc was the Le Mans Replica JUO 177, but it now had a new owner – Ilfracombe enthusiast A. B. Napper.

A wet Peter Morgan grinds to a halt on Simms. (*Photograph: Quadrant Picture Library*)

There was no doubt that the original owner Bob Harris, had complied with the still in force BMTA covenant restricting sale of new cars for one year. Napper led from the flag, but the Morgan started to sound distinctly sick on the final laps, and he only just managed to hold off Barnes blown MG to finish first.

The same day saw the sister Le Mans Replica JTT 703 also in competition, this time still in the hands of the original owner Okehampton accountant Murray Symons. The event was the MCC Lands End Trial, which again was restricted by the petrol rationing to a short fifty-two-mile route based at Lynton. Murray had now had JTT supercharged with a low-pressure Arnott supercharger in a search for more power, the conversion being undertaken by the supercharger manufacturers, Carburettors Limited of North London. Also entered was the factory team of Peter Morgan with the 1122 cc Climax car AUY 33, Jim Goodall with BWP 47 and Sonny McCann with BUY 754, the latter two of course being Standard Special powered. Also entered was Barnstaple agent Reg Hellier with FUO 919, Bournemouth agent Joe Huxham, presumably with FLJ 837 and there were two non-starters – Thomson with his Morgan Special (still supercharged) of 1089 cc and Napper with JUO 177 – but obviously he could not be in two places at once! A fairly dry event gave Premier Awards to the factory team and Reg Hellier, while Murray Symons and Joe Huxham collected Third Class Awards. The best one-make team award went once again to Morgan.

Peter Morgan on Lyn Hill in the Lands End Trial. (*Photograph: Morgan Motor Co. collection*)

The lightweight 4/4 of Dr Gavin Scott at Prescott. (*Photograph: Bill Parkes collection*)

Jim Goodall fails to interest many cows as he climbs Park Rash in the Edinburgh. (*Photograph: Morgan Motor Co. collection*)

Back at the factory the 4/4 received larger 9in. rear brake drums for improved retardation (as from April) giving 9in. drums all round (original 4–4s had 8in.) Also, Standard Triumph had delivered a 2088 cc production Standard Vanguard engine, engine number V 14277E, for fitting to the pre-production Vanguard-engined sports car now nearing completion in the repair shop under the supervision of Peter Morgan and Jim Roberts.

It was a pleasant dry day for the Bugatti Owners Club (BOC) Prescott hill climb on 22 May. While Ken Delingpole's HRG easily won the class for sports cars up to 1500 cc unsupercharged, there had been a Malvern GP among its opposition. Dr Gavin Scott had lightened and tuned his Standard Special-engined 4/4, FNP 684, and climbed in 60.61 seconds finishing sixth.

Conditions improved for motor sport during the summer months of June, July and August when the British Government announced a relaxation in petrol rationing for this period as a concession to the holidaying public. The standard petrol ration was doubled for these three months only.

Despite relaxed petrol rationing the MCC decided to run their traditional Whitsun trial, the Edinburgh, over a shortened one-hundred mile course based at Harrogate. There were four Morgans entered for this event on 9 June. Peter Morgan was in AUY 33, Jim Goodall in BWP 47 and Sonny McCann in BUY 754. Murray Symons was in his blown Le Mans Replica, JTT 703. Of the thirty-nine cars that started, twenty-three gained First Class Awards, including all the Morgans. Once again the one-make team award went to the Morgan factory.

Over a glorious sunny weekend of 2 and 3 July the British Automobile Racing Club (renamed from the Junior Car Club) ran its annual Eastbourne Rally, with a record entry of 167. The local corporation closed several roads to allow the various hill climbs and driving tests which constituted the rally, to take place on the Saturday. Most impressive was Peter Morgan with AUY 33, such that he won a First Class Award, as also did Jim Goodall with BWP 47. Dick Anthony won a Standard Award with his 4/4.

On the Sunday was held the concourse d'elegance and J. Wimborne entered a Morgan two-seater (chassis number 1753) that had been most attractively bodied by Leacroft Limited, of Egham in Surrey.

On Saturday 13 August the BARC ran a 'members only' meeting at Goodwood on a glorious summer day. The two 'Devon' Le Mans Replicas of Murray Symons and A. B. Napper were both competing, Murray's blown Morgan JTT 703 being notable for carrying its race number on a large vertical disc on the tail, reminiscent of the JCC 200-mile Brooklands races of the 1920s. The events were all handicaps over three or five laps, but neither JTT 703 or JUO 177 featured in the first three.

Thanks to financial sponsorship from the national newspaper *The Daily Express* the BRDC was able to organize a major race meeting at Silverstone on 20 August, namely the Daily Express International Trophy Meeting. While the main attraction was obviously the International Trophy race itself for Grand Prix cars the BRDC also attracted entries from major British motor manufacturers for the one-hour race for production sports cars, and within this race was a class for up to 1½ litres. The Morgan factory managed to gain an entry in this oversubscribed race for Peter Morgan, and he drove CAB 652 with a 1098 cc Climax engine. This year a new perimeter road circuit had been developed of 2.97 miles around the old aerodrome, the same circuit in basic concept that is in use today, except the pits were then just after Abbey curve.

Within the 1500 cc class were also three works-supported 1500 cc Singer-engined HRGs, two works-entered Jowett Javelins, two works MGTCs and a sole 1100 cc HRG.

The start was Le Mans style, by sprinting across the track to the parked cars, and twenty-nine cars set off on the hour race. Peter Morgan's main opposition proved to be the three 1500 cc HRGs, and he finished an excellent fourteenth overall, and third in class behind the two HRGs of Eric Thompson and Peter Clark, but ahead of the third HRG of John Buncombe, and ahead of the MGs and Jowetts. His performance was all the more remarkable in view of the 400 cc that he was giving away to the HRG team, and that the regulations for the event stipulated that only tyres, ignition and carburettor settings were allowed to

The very modern looking Leacroft Morgan at Eastbourne. (*Photograph: Quadrant Picture Library*)

Peter Morgan corners ahead of a $4\frac{1}{2}$ litre Lagonda at Silverstone. (*Photograph: Guy Griffiths*)

be modified from standard. There was a huge crowd of over 100,000, so this was excellent publicity for the Malvern factory.

Motor racing events were now being held virtually every weekend through the summer as car clubs took advantage of the extra freedom allowed by the more liberal petrol rationing, and also continued to look for new venues for racing, particularly ex-military and ex-RAF facilities.

One such, venue found by West Hants and Dorset CC, was the army camp at Blandford and they arranged a race meeting there over a $3\frac{1}{8}$ mile circuit of camp roads for 27 August. The roads were very narrow, but had gradients, unlike the artificial ex-aerodrome circuits usually used. Sadly, there were several accidents, including one fatal, but the event was interesting and attracted four local Morgans, all entered in the race for sports cars up to 1100 cc. A. B. Napper was present with his Le Mans Replica JUO 177 with 1098 cc Climax engine.

Joe Huxham had a second-hand 1086 cc Climax-engined Morgan, registered FOH 812. This Morgan had been supplied new in 1939 to

Napper's Morgan ahead of Cluff-Miller's Riley at Blandford. (*Photograph: Guy Griffiths*)

a very lucky young lady as a 21st birthday present. Chassis number 879, this black Morgan had cycle wings, outside exhaust and 1100 cc engine from new. In his autobiography *Lucky Joe*, Joe Huxham describes all his 1100 cc post-war 4/4s as Le Mans Replicas, a common term at the time for the 1100 cc cycle wing cars, as we have shown, but these cars were not true Le Mans Replicas in the sense that JUO 177 was.

John Macklin, a Dorset enthusiast, who was present with his own Morgan, remembers Joe Huxham telling him that Joe's car was a 'TT car'. It clearly had not been in the TT so perhaps Joe was on this occasion using the term 'TT' to refer to the 1100 cc outside exhaust cars. It is a pity the Morgan factory did not give these 4/4 models with the optional 1100 cc engine, cycle wings and outside exhaust a name as the confusion caused by agents and enthusiasts calling them either TT Replicas or Le Mans Replicas is considerable!

John Macklin, a young twenty-one year old embarking on his first race, had a 1939, 1122 cc two-seater, registered HG 6876. To make it suitable for racing he fitted cycle wings to the front wheels and then took the car to Joe Huxham's garage at Parkstone where Tom Bryant sleeved the engine down to take a spare set of Joe's 1098 cc pistons.

Being impressed with the two-tone paintwork of the type 55 Bugatti, John resprayed the Morgan blue and cream in similar style, and very attractive it looked too.

The fourth Morgan entered was JTT 703 with Murray Symons, but just as a reserve.

Grid positions were allocated by drawing numbers from a hat, and John Macklin found himself one of the two on the front row for his first ever event. When he saw the starter approach he immediately selected first gear, held the clutch out and screamed the engine. Eventually the starter raised and lowered the flag whereupon John promptly let the clutch in, only to stand still!

The clutch was hot and bothered and had had enough, and as he crept off the line Joe Huxham, who was immediately behind had to take major avoiding action and take to the grass to miss him.

Only one Morgan finished, and not in the awards. John completed but a few slow laps before the clutch gave out completely. In the paddock afterwards Joe Huxham gave poor John considerable verbal abuse on his starting technique in his own inimitable manner.

This Blandford meeting had another interesting car entered in the Blandford Trophy Race, this being a Monoposto 'Formula 2' HRG driven by Peter Clark, and fitted with a Vanguard engine linered down to 83 mm and therefore 1991 cc, a pointer to the future. Special Martlet pistons giving 8 to 1 compression were also fitted as well as twin Solex carburettors. Unfortunately overheating put paid to its chances.

The famous trials club SUNBAC branched out with a club race meeting at Silverstone on 3 September, and attracted Jim Goodall from the factory for the first event over four laps for sports

John Macklin's pretty Morgan on the front row of the Blandford grid, alongside Harewood's MG. (*Photograph: John Macklin collection*)

cars under 1000 cc supercharged or 1300 cc unsupercharged. After a closely fought race Jim had to settle for second behind Gibbs Riley but beating Derek Buckler's 'Buckler' (a Ford special) into third place. Jim was driving a Climax car, which, sadly, we have been unable to identify.

The capacity was given as 1122 cc, suggesting AUY 33, but we wonder whether it was really CAB 652, the 1098 cc engined ex-TT car that he used.

The following week, on 11 September, there was action on Prescott Hill for the International Speed Hill-Climb, where Sydney Allard in his Allard clinched the championship. Dr Gavin Scott was present with his Standard-engined 4/4, FNP 684, climbing in a creditable 57.50 seconds, over three seconds faster than his climb in May.

Gavin's car was much lightened and modified. As he lived in the house next door to the one that HFS Morgan had owned in Worcester Road, Malvern (adjacent to the original Morgan factory, which was now the Morgan agency of Bowman and Acock), it was hardly surprising that it was to this company that he entrusted the preparation of the car. A special manifold system had been fabricated, to allow twin SU carburettors to be used, and the exhaust manifold had short stub exhaust pipes leading to an expansion chamber alongside the engine, from which the exhaust pipe descended vertically to follow the normal route.

On 16 September the new Standard Vanguard-engined sports car was registered for the road as HUY 982. This blue two-seater was a virtually all-new design from the Morgan factory although very much based on the current 4/4. The most important features of the specification were as follows:

The Rubery Owen manufactured chassis followed 4/4 practice, but a 4in. longer wheelbase of 8ft. was used. Similarly the track was increased by 2in. to 3ft. 11in. Improved space for the driver's feet was achieved by curving the chassis rails at the front, rather than using angles as on the 4/4.

The front suspension contained two new features. The first was the use of new Peter Morgan designed upper crosshead lugs – the 'swan neck' lugs, which increased suspension travel by 3in. (A smaller version was soon to be fitted to F-type three-wheelers.)

The second was the tapping of the engine lubrication system to allow supply of oil to the centre pins, and thence via holes to the sliding pillars and their bushes. This 'one shot' lubrication system was to save much greasy maintenance and was thought up and designed by HFS Morgan.

The engine, V14277E, was connected to a mid-mounted Moss gearbox (as produced for Jaguar), by an Elektron clutch shaft housing, machined from a solid casting for the first time, whereas previous models had always been fabricated.

Behind the gearbox a Hardy Spicer propeller shaft took the drive to the rear axle. This was produced by the Birmingham company, Salisbury Transmission Limited and based on the USA designs of the Dana Corporation. The Salisbury axle was of type 3HA (hypoid axle), and based on the Dana type 23 axle as used in the USA by Studebaker. The 37-tooth crown wheel and 9-tooth bevel pinion gave an axle ratio of 4.11 to 1, and this, in conjunction with the Moss gearbox gave overall ratios of 13.87, 8.15, 5.62 and 4.11 to 1 for the four gears.

Hydraulic 9in. Girling brakes were fitted for the first time, the front being twin leading shoe.

Steering was by the usual Burman worm and nut box, but Peter Morgan had been unhappy with the amount of play in post-war Burman boxes and had really wanted a change. His father, however, remained loyal to his long-time supplier (they had also supplied gears for the three-wheeler), and reasoned that they would soon make them to pre-war standards once again solving the problem.

The radiator was reduced in height, giving a purposeful look to the car, and trials continued with Dunlop disc wheels. (HFS disliked wire wheels, which were so difficult to keep clean.)

In view of the increased performance of the new car, and its change of class for competition purposes, the directors wished to use a new model name to indicate these changes. As usual it was George Goodall who came up with the suggestion of the Plus 4 (for four-cylinders).

The modest compression ratio of the Vanguard engine (6.7 to 1) may seem low by modern standards, but it must be remembered that only Pool petrol was available and this did not look likely to change for some time. It is estimated that using the research method of octane rating, this petrol could only achieve 72 (pre-war 80, wartime 60).

Preparations were now in full swing for the Motor Show in October, but it was too soon to debut the new model. Only one prototype was available, and anyway sufficient Standard Special engines were available for the 4/4 to continue, so just the latter model was shown. The event was noteworthy for the appearance of Henry Ford II, who spent much time on the Morgan stand examining the front suspension. In common with other major manufacturers Ford wished to use independent front suspension on future models, and indeed the future Consul/Zephyr range was in the final months of development at Dearborn in the USA – using the MacPherson Strut patented a year of so earlier by Earle S. MacPherson.

Back at the factory the new prototype was being put through its paces. HFS Morgan borrowed the car to take to his home in Cannon Hill, Maidenhead – all the way in top gear! This was a not unusual way of assessing the torque of an engine at this time and he had performed a similar feat with an 'F' type three-wheeler many years earlier.

Despite the return of petrol rationing the MCC was able to run its Sporting Trial based at Buxton on 22 October.

Four Morgans entered – the factory team of Peter Morgan in AUY 33, Jim Goodall in BWP 47, and Sonny McCann in BUY 754. Non-starting was J. A. Thomson in his supercharged Morgan special. Much rain had fallen in the week before the event and continued to fall on the day, making the hills very difficult for standard sports cars, and the awards went to the many home-made short wheelbase trials specials now being specially constructed by trials enthusiasts from old pre-war cars (mainly Austin 7s and Ford 10s). None of the Morgans took an award, and the lack of suitability of this one-day MCC event for standard sports cars meant that it was to be several years before Morgans tackled this trial again.

The new Plus 4, HUY 982, was run in, and

Jim Goodall prepares for the start of the MCC's Exeter Trial in BWP 47. Note the three-wheeler type front wings. Sonny McCann in BUY 754 is just visible alongside. (*Photograph: LAT Photographic*)

then satisfactorily put through its paces on journeys around the Malvern area. With the pre-war motor industry test track of Brooklands being no longer available in the post-war period, the British motor industry had jointly funded with the British Government the development and running of a testing complex close to the A5 near Nuneaton. Known as 'MIRA', from the initials of the Motor Industry Research Association, it was now possible for the motor manufacturers to put new cars through their paces in relative secrecy over a variety of conditions and surfaces. HUY 982 was taken to MIRA by Peter Morgan. Performance testing demonstrated brisk acceleration for the time from the Vanguard engine, but once 85 mph had been reached the engine behaved as if a governor was fitted and no more was available. Of course it had been designed for powering a family saloon, so top end performance was not a priority for the Standard Motor Company.

Peter Morgan also took HUY 982 on to the MIRA Pavee surfaced area; 'a bit uncomfortable, but nothing fell off,' he told us recently.

Minor changes to the front suspension and steering geometry had been found necessary for the new model. The king pin inclination was reduced from the three degrees of the 4/4 to two degrees, with the camber angle following suit, while the caster angle was increased one degree to four degrees. The turning circle was one foot better for the Plus 4, at 32 ft.

This winter the MCC's Exeter Trial did not, as usual, mark the beginning of the new year. Instead, it was held on the last day of 1949. Once again petrol rationing curtailed this long-distance event to just eight observed trials sections on a sixty-mile route on and around Dartmoor. Five Morgans were entered. The Morgan factory had the usual team of Peter Morgan with AUY33, Sonny McCann with BUY 754, and Jim Goodall with BWP47, the latter now fitted with three-wheeler twin front wings. Supporting them were Murray Symons with his supercharged Le Mans Replica, JTT 703, and West Country enthusiast Ted Dennis with his purchase from Barnstaple agent Reg Hellier of FUO 919. None of the Morgans was able to climb Simms and Peter and Jim took Second Class Awards. The other three took home Third Class Awards.

Murray Symons in JTT 703, carrying two spare wheels, in the Exeter. *(Photograph: LAT Photographic)*

Overseas

Australia

Undoubtedly a most significant event for the Australian Morgan enthusiast was the setting up of a new Morgan agency early in 1949 in Perth, Western Australia. Bill Richards Motors was run by Bill Richards, who following his demobilization from war service in the Middle East returned to Australia and decided to sell used cars, working with Merv McAlinden as a car salesman. Bill was then to meet an agent from the English buying and confirming house, Tozer, Kemsley and Millbourne who worked out a deal to supply Bill with some Morgans. Having sold a few he was to become a Morgan agent in his own right, trading from a weatherboard shed some 50 ft. by 30 ft. in Fitzgerald Street, North Perth. Immediately opposite was the Rosemount Hotel, which become known as his branch office.

Joining Bill as a mechanic was Colin Uphill, a keen motor sport enthusiast. Colin purchased a Standard Special-engined, green 4/4, and, with help from Bill, began to prepare it for racing. As he wanted to continue to use the Morgan on the road, the engine etc. was always left standard, except for fitting twin Solex carburettors and an extractor type exhaust manifold. Various steel panels, such as doors and bonnet were eventually to be replaced with aluminium versions and the car was to be lightened as much as possible.

On 25 September Colin took his then still

Colin Uphill at Narrogin (*Photograph: Colin Uphill collection*)

Ted Reid at Mount Cargill (*Photograph: Ted Reid collection*)

virtually standard Morgan to the airstrip at Mooliabeenie some fifty miles north of Perth.

This airstrip had been a reserve fighter base for Kittyhawks and Spitfires during the Second World War, and now the WA Sporting Car Club were to use a circuit based on the ¾ mile North/South runway with the dispersal 'D' forming the back of the circuit. In the five-lap up to 1500 cc scratch races Colin finished second to Arthur Collett's MGTC.

The town of Narrogin was once more thronged with thousands of spectators for the annual 'round the houses' Motor Racing Carnival on 7 November. A number of small races were held before the main event, the 'Great Southern Fifty', and Colin Uphill did well in these, finishing third in the three-lap scratch race for up to 1500 cc behind Jack Nelson's Ford Special and Claude La Motte's Fidget Special, and then winning the six-lap Norman Hall Handicap from Glendenning's Mercury Special.

The main event saw gruelling and exciting racing with several cars sidelined with mechanical problems. Also Sid Barker's Ford V-8 Ballot shed a wheel which injured two children. At the finish it was Collett's MGTC which took the honours, with Nelson's Ford 10 Special second ahead of Colin Uphill's reliable Morgan in an excellent third place.

New Zealand

The New Zealand hill climb championship for 1949 held its first event at Paekakariki on 12 February on a 2-mile course. The 1500 cc class was contested by four MGs, an Alvis and the Standard Special Morgan Coupe driven by Gordon Vogtherr. Vogtherr was off the pace with the fully road equipped car, but won first place in the handicap event. The Morgan actually belonged to Gordon's father Ernie, a keen motor enthusiast from Hastings. He sometimes hill climbed this car himself.

Winning the 1949 South Island hill climb championship in a 1939 Ford V8 was a radio dealer from Dunedin, Ted Reid. Also in 1949 he purchased a 1936 Coventry Climax-engined Morgan 4/4 which had been brought out to New Zealand by an English airman in the war years. Ted's first event with the Morgan was the Mount Cargill hill climb on 15 October, when he finished equal third in the 1100 cc and over scratch event, and first in the all comers handicap, after stripping the car of all surplus weight.

By the time the Otago Sports Car Club Inc. ran its Otago Provincial quarter-mile sprint on 19 November Ted had lightened the flywheel, pocketed the valves and fitted on aluminium bonnet. He finished third, in 21.23 sec., in the open class and also third in the 1101 cc to 1500 cc class.

Singapore

On 5 June the Singapore MC ran its Seremban Speed Trial over a half mile course. Morgans did very well, Loke Yaik Heng's three-wheeler winning the class for touring cars up to 1000 cc, J. L. Seaton's 4/4 the similar class up to 1195 cc, and a further 4/4 of Lee Soon Lee came second in the class up to 1595 cc, their times being 39.4 sec., 37.7 sec. and 38.4 sec. respectively.

United States of America

We mentioned during the 1948 chapter that

Ted Reid at the Dunedin Sprint. (*Photograph: Ted Reid collection*)

several 4/4s had been exported to the USA in that year, beginning the marque's inroads into this important export market.

This was not the first attempt by Morgans to enter the USA market, for in the 20 January 1947 edition of the American magazine *Automotive News* a quarter page advert was carried inviting enquiries for the 4/4 to be made to 'The Reciprocal Trade Corp' of New York.

The first race in the USA that we have been able to locate that featured a Morgan was the rather grandly titled 'Florida Grand Prix', held on 27 February 1949 at Fort Lauderdale. The National Association for Stock Car Auto Racing (NASCAR) had arranged a circuit on the ex- wartime naval airfield, then called the Broward Speedway. As part of their programme they invited the local branch of the Sports Car Club of America to run a twenty-five lap race for sports cars. Such hospitality from the professional NASCAR to the amateur racers of the SCCA was extremely unusual, and did not last through future years.

When founded in the Boston, New England area in early 1944 the SCCA had been a club for owners of vintage sporting vehicles, but within a few years it was to take on the role of the club for modern sports cars, with regional centres throughout the USA to encourage local enthusiasts. Its famous emblem was a Rudge-Whitworth wire wheel, with black tyre and red brake drum.

Just seven cars lined up for the race, split into two groups. The first group of two unblown MGs and the Morgan of Tom Comisky had 40 sec. start over three blown MGs and a rare Cisitalia. From the start the Morgan settled down into third place behind the two MGs, the straw baled 'L' and 'S' shaped bends causing some interesting lines.

A pit stop was required to take on five gallons of fuel, but by the twentieth lap Tom Comisky was running in fifth position behind three MGs and the Cisitalia. To everyone's surprise the chequered flag was waved at this point, making this the final order. Apparently an approaching cloudburst, which soon hit the circuit was responsible for the race being stopped early.

Many wealthy sports car owners from the North East would spend the cold winter months in Florida, and no doubt the entries had mainly come from this source.

CHAPTER ELEVEN

1950

With the design of HUY 982 proving successful the body shop was now asked to develop the bodywork for the Coupe and four-seater versions, the former first. HUY 982 itself was sent to Standard Triumph in order that the engine modifications required by the Morgan factory for its version of the Vanguard engine could be determined and productionized (mainly water pump and manifold differences).

Sir John Black was impressed by the simple yet functional construction of the Plus 4 – in return he was to lend HFS Morgan one of the newly introduced Triumph Mayflower saloons – which HFS quite liked. Standard Triumph themselves (Standard had bought the Triumph marque in 1945), were developing a successor to the Triumph Roadster – the Triumph TRX, using a twin SU carburettor version of the Standard Vanguard engine giving 71 bhp, but this was a complex car. We suspect Sir John was having second thoughts.

Having been approved by the RAC in February a new motor racing track had become available, initially just for Formula 3 – 500 cc cars – Brands Hatch in Kent. Developed from the pre-war motorcycle grass track this 1-mile track was roughly oblong in shape, but with a 'bulge' at one end.

Brian Lister in his stripped Morgan at Bedwell Hey. (*Photograph: Guy Griffiths*)

On Sunday 12 March the Cambridge University Automobile Club held speed trials and driving tests on some of the roads of the decommissioned war-time bomber aerodrome of Witchford near Ely. These roads were now within the farm of Bedwell Hey.

Among the nearly thirty club members enjoying their day of competition were three Morgan drivers in 4/4s. A. H. Gray was driving a two-tone Climax-engined Coupe, FLN 382; W. Wallace was using a two-seater Standard-engined roadster, HF 5687, and B. Lister was in a Climax-engined two-seater, FHU 351.

Fastest of the three was Brian Lister in his much lightened car. He was beginning an involvement with sports cars that would eventually lead to the manufacture of cars of his own, notably the famous Lister-Jaguars.

Once again petrol rationing reduced the mileage of the MCC's Lands End Trial on Easter Saturday, 8 April, to a paultry fifty-three, but sixty-two cars set off from the start at Lynton for the Exmoor sections. Five Morgans were entered, the usual factory team of Peter Morgan, Jim Goodall and Sonny McCann with AUY 33, BWP 47 and BUY 754 respectively, Joe Huxham with FOH 812, and Ted Dennis with FUO 919. BUY 754 now had three-wheeler type front wings fitted, similar to those on BWP 47. Despite the dry weather of the days before the event suggesting the climbs would be easy, last-minute driving rain changed the conditions somewhat, and only Jim Goodall received a First Class Award, Peter and Joe claiming Second and Ted Dennis Third.

On 15 April the Bristol MC and LCC ran another of its race meetings at Lulsgate Aerodrome. Jeff Sparrowe, the proprietor of Sparrowe's Motor Services in Northbourne, Bournemouth, had recently been a keen competitor in the new Formula 3 (500 cc) racing with his Sparrowe Marwyn Special but he decided to go to this meeting to spectate. He chose to travel in the Morgan that he had bought the previous day for £450, as a part of his business. This was the ex-Napper Le Mans Replica, JUO 177. When he arrived Jeff met several of his 500 cc racing friends, who suggested he should enter the Morgan. This he did, and he duly won the first race for sports cars up to 1100 cc having led all the way! Racing was relatively carefree, and crash helmets were not mandatory.

Later, in the handicap challenge race, Jeff again proved that he could really make the Morgan go by finishing second to Lyons' Connaught, of 1767 cc. From the beginning Jeff always felt at one with the Morgan, which he found so predictable and easy to drive.

One of the great annual long-distance European rallies of the post-war period was the Dutch 'de Tulpen Rallye'. Those English drivers lucky enough to be able to get adequate petrol joined their Continental competitors for the start of the rally on the 16 April, there being ten starting points, spread as far afield as Rome and Glasgow. Some two thousand miles of high-speed motoring was to ensue over the next four days, while the weather dished up snow, hail and rain at different times. Of the 278 starters only sixty-three had clean sheets on arrival at the Noordwijk control. After a welcome overnight hotel stop came the eliminating test to determine the winners at Zandvoort. In Class 2 was the Dutch Morgan, reg. H 83163, of Leiden driver W. F. Verhey van Wijk, navigated by his wife. They failed by just 24 thousands of a second to beat the export specification Ford Anglia (with 1172 cc Prefect engine) of the Reece cousins, taking second place in this class for cars of 1100–1500 cc, and finishing eighteenth overall.

We shall come across the Reece cousins Jack and Peter later on in the Morgan story. Both were directors of the Liverpool Ford agency, J. Blake and Co., and Peter in particular was a keen racer.

The Tulip Rally, as it was known in England, helped publicize the Dutch bulb growing industry, and the procession of flowers at Noordwijk was a grand finale to the week, preceding the evening's prizegiving and dance.

While rally navigation techniques were at an early evolutionary stage at this time, the Tulip Rally was to achieve fame for developing a type of route card for the navigators where the route was indicated by a line drawing, junctions being shown as meeting lines, with arrows to indicate the direction to take.

A notable absentee from the list of entrants for the last MCC Lands End Trial had been Murray

Symons and his supercharged Le Mans Replica, JTT 703. Murray had decided to sell the Morgan (he had two other cars) and advertized it locally, where it was spotted by an enthusiastic Dawlish garage owner John Cowperthwaite. John thought he could sell the car to the granddaughter of some local customers of his and so he contacted Aileen Jervis, a Warwick hospital secretary, at her home in Gloucester to see if she was interested. She asked John to vet the car for her, and he bought it on her behalf for £520 at the end of April. Aileen found it to be a superb little car, but she disliked the Arnott supercharger, which used a lot of oil.

In April the British Government announced that the doubling of the petrol ration for the three summer months, as in 1949, would again occur in 1950, but this time it was intended for the double ration to continue for a full twelve months as the British economy improved. There was a downside, however, in that petrol tax was to increase by a hefty 9*d.* (3½p) a gallon. At least the motoring clubs could now contemplate a full programme of events for the future year.

On Saturday, 6 May the BARC held a 'members only' meeting at Goodwood, which attracted one hundred and twenty entries. Jeff Sparrowe was one of these with his Morgan, JUO 177, which he was now preparing seriously for club racing. Jeff, through his many years of racing, had come to believe strongly that the easiest way to make a car go faster was to remove surplus weight, and he began an aggressive preparation of JUO. The normal steel louvred bonnet had now been replaced by an alloy version, with the louvred sides replaced by a wire mesh grill to allow surplus heat to escape. *The Autocar* was impressed by the 'surprising turn of speed' of Sparrowe's Morgan when it was just beaten for third place in the final handicap by the MGTC-engined Cooper of Eric Brandon. Second had been David Render – but now in an Allard.

In mid-May the MCC announced that the Edinburgh Trial due to be held at Whitsun had had to be cancelled through lack of entries. Many of the pre-war hills were no longer difficult and the shortened course (around Harrogate) was not particularly challenging to the trials enthusiast.

Jeff Sparrowe fills up with derationed petrol at Blandford. (*Photograph: J. Sparrowe collection*)

The unusual rear end treatment for JNP 239. (*Photograph: Quadrant Picture Library*)

The MCC was to rethink this event for future years.

On Friday, 26 May the government announced the immediate end of petrol rationing, following agreements with Standard Oil of New Jersey USA and the California-Texas Oil Company, to supply extra petrol as part of an interim arrangement until the new Fawley oil refinery was completed at the end of 1951. Pool petrol was still all that was to be available for several years hence however. This was obviously the news the motoring enthusiasts had dreamed of, and motoring clubs were now at last really free to plan their competitive events.

The new availability of petrol encouraged a crowd of around 15,000 to visit Blandford on Whit Monday, 29 May to support the West Hants and Dorset CC races. Once again Jeff Sparrowe was present with JUO 177, this time running with conventional bonnet, in the production car class for under 1500 cc. He was out of luck, the race going to Dick Jacobs semi-works MGTD, followed by two 1500 cc HRGs, although Jacobs' MG was later disqualified for having non-standard shock absorbers.

Back at the Morgan factory the prototype Plus 4 Coupe was tested by works tester Charlie Curtis during the week ending 19 June, and was registered JNP 239 the following day. Fitting the Coupe body on to the Plus 4 chassis had been a fairly simple exercise for the bodyshop involving scaling up the 4/4 version to fit the larger chassis, but as JNP 239 was to be a works car HFS Morgan gave instructions for a modification to the tail of the car to suit his own requirements. HFS's wife Ruth kept chickens and HFS was required to pick up a crate of between eight and ten pullets every so often from Malvern to take back to Ruth in Maidenhead. Having just one spare wheel instead of the usual two meant a small luggage tray could be fitted, which could be extended to carry the crate of pullets!

While HFS preferred plain disc wheels for the Coupe, Peter Morgan liked the drilled version fitted to HUY 982 and destined for the roadster models, these being more attractive in his eye, and also lighter than the disc version. The fifteen holes were drilled in the 4J × 16in. Dunlop type LP 643 wheels at the Morgan factory.

The Morgan specification Vanguard engines were now being supplied to the factory, and the very first was fitted to this Coupe, engine number V1ME, the prefix indicating Vanguard, and the suffix Morgan Engine. These engines were much heavier than the Standard Special engine, weighing 3 cwts 3 qtrs 24 lbs (444 lbs or 202 kgs) as supplied, compared with 2 cwts 3 qtrs 1 lb (309 lbs or 140 kgs) for the latter, although the latter weight is without the starter.

As yet the series of chassis numbers for the new Plus 4 model had not been determined, so a 4/4 number, consistent with the time of build, was allocated (2038) for this blue Coupe.

Over in Northern Ireland the long-running Knock Motor Cycle Club's all-night trial for cars and motorcycles started on 23 June from the Logan Embankment. We suspect this is the occasion when the ex-Reg Armstrong racer, ZC 3038 (now in the hands of Belfast motoring enthusiast and garage owner Marshall Watson) took part. It was now painted cream, and the event proved to be so tough that Marshall and his navigator Terry Hill almost wrecked the car, but they had had the pleasure of overtaking R. Dorndorf's BMW.

On 8 July the Leinster Motor Club ran the

V1ME fits neatly in the Coupe. (*Photograph: Quadrant Picture Library*)

Leinster Trophy race over twelve laps of the new eight and a half mile circuit on the outskirts of Wicklow. Frank Bigger was entered with his Climax-engined 4/4, but we have been unable to discover whether he actually started.

The same day saw the Bristol MC and LCC trying out a new airfield circuit to replace the no longer available Lulsgate Bottom, which was now destined to become the future Bristol civil airport. This was at Castle Combe, a few miles north west of Chippenham. All the races were held over five laps of the 1.84 mile circuit of the perimeter road. The race for cars up to 850 cc supercharged or 1100 cc unsupercharged saw Jeff Sparrowe score an easy victory with his rapid Morgan, and he completed an excellent day by finishing second to Gerry Ruddock's 1500 cc HRG in the race for supercharged cars up to 1100 cc or 1500 cc unsupercharged.

One of the most interesting sprint courses of the 1950s was Great Auclum at Burghfield Common, near Reading. This was a quarter-mile event held on the drive leading to the house of a wealthy motor enthusiast Neil Gardiner, who so enjoyed motoring that he had even banked one of the corners on his drive, Brooklands fashion. After a downhill start, the banked right-hand first corner then led via several lesser bends to the finish near the house.

Holland Birkett managed to get Neil to lend the course to the Hants and Berks Motor Club on 23 July, and three Morgans entered the event.

Jeff Sparrowe, who recently described the event as 'quite fun', had now undertaken an extensive lightening process on JUO 177. Where regulations allowed, as in this event, the original Morgan steel mudguards were replaced by smaller and lighter motorcycle aluminium items. Likewise the headlamps were replaced with smaller ones and of course the alternative recently made aluminium bonnet was used. The two six-volt batteries were discarded and a small 12-volt battery from a Fiat 500 substituted. The wooden seat backrest received liberal hole drilling and all unnecessary upholstery was removed. The cast radiator mountings were replaced with two pieces of 1in. angle Dural, and a similar fate befell the front number plate brackets which were replaced

Jeff Sparrowe drives a lightened JUO 177 around the banked corner at Great Auclum. (*Photograph: Guy Griffiths*)

The start of the 1100cc race at Goodwood. Jeff Sparrowe (8) shares the front row with Hall's MG (9), Gibbs' Riley (10) and Metcalfe's Fiat (5). (*Photograph: Jeff Sparrowe collection*)

by two pieces of 16g aluminium 1in. × 6in., bent to fix the number plate horizontal, allowing cool air to get at the engine sump as well as reducing wind resistance.

Twin SU electric fuel pumps were used and the Scintilla magneto gave sparks to KLG FE80 spark plugs. The Coventry Climax engine Jeff carefully polished and assembled with the inlet valves having just 1/16in. contact. Little was done with the brakes – Jeff said he did not use them much!

Jeff's efforts proved worthwhile for he gained an excellent second place in the class for sports cars up to 1100 cc, with a time of 26.85 seconds, and he was only beaten by the potent Austin/Ford special of Arthur Mallock. He in turn beat such well developed machinery as Harry Lester's Lester-MG and a Treen Riley.

In the class up to 1500 cc were the two 1122 cc Climax-engined Morgans of R. J. Ellis and A. Hess, but their times were some three seconds slower than Jeff had managed. One other racer managed to go over the top of the banking!

On 12 August the BARC held another members' meeting at Goodwood. Jeff Sparrowe contested the five-lap scratch race for sports cars up to 1100 cc, his Morgan using the lightweight alloy bonnet allowed by the rules. He was unable to hold the works MG of Dick Jacobs, the very special Lester-MG of Harry Lester, or Len Gibbs Riley, finishing in fourth place.

Probably the biggest British motor racing event of the year was the Daily Express International Trophy meeting, held at Silverstone on 26 August. The one-hour production-car race for up to 2 litres contained a class for up to 1100 cc, which Jeff Sparrowe entered, his only opposition being David Price's 1100 cc HRG. The start was Le Mans style, with a sprint across the track to the waiting cars, and off for one hour's racing. Jeff quickly disposed of Price, and then set about the 1500 cc class cars, going around the corners as if on rails and lapping Price in the process, finally finishing at 68.28 mph average. He clearly won his class, but also finished twenty-fifth overall, just behind Peter Clark's 1500 cc HRG. Being a production car race, Jeff refitted the production Morgan bonnet, wings and full lights for this event.

Jeff Sparrowe at speed during the Daily Express Silverstone meeting. (*Photograph: Guy Griffiths*)

The revised exhaust manifold system on Gavin Scott's Standard-engined 4/4. (*Photograph: Bill Parkes collection*)

On 9 September it was the MCC's turn to use Silverstone for its annual race meeting. Joe Huxham took part in a one-hour high-speed trial, presumably in FOH 812, but had the disadvantage of losing his offside front wheel before the finish.

The new availability of petrol had put greater pressure on the new and used car market to satisfy the demand for cars. In 1950 there were just over 2,300,000 cars registered for the road. Steel quotas were being tied by the British Government to exports, and even then a shortage of steel imports from abroad had led to several motor manufacturers having to reduce production, Ford among others working a four-day week during the coming winter months. With such a shortage of cars for the home market it was not surprising that in September the BMTA covenant restricting the sale of a new car by its owner for one year should be increased to two years.

On Sunday 10 September Gavin Scott took FNP684 onto Prescott Hill, but recorded 57.67 seconds, just slower than his climb in 1949. We believe that it was following this that Dr Gavin Scott used the new opportunity afforded by availability of petrol to tour Scotland, with his wife, in his Morgan FNP 684, taking in a hill climb at Bo'ness, probably that held on 30 September. A Mk II manifold system had now been devised in conjunction with Morgan agents Bowman and Acock, which featured a different exhaust system, the individual short exhaust stubs feeding into a large exhaust pipe leading out through a slot in the bonnet to a silencer under the door.

One of the most memorable Morgan races for Jeff Sparrowe took place at Castle Combe on 7 October at the national meeting held by the Bristol MC and LCC. The Bristol Club had managed to attract many top flight drivers for a series of ten-lap scratch races, including such notables as Stirling Moss, Peter Collins and Bob Gerard, with cars as diverse as 500s, ERAs and Connaughts. Jeff had entered the race for sports cars up to 2000 cc by virtue of supercharging his Morgan, JUO 177, with an Arnott blower obtained from the Aston Martin DB2 driver, Patsy Burke, whose father owned a garage near London. Driven off the front of the crankshaft by a belt, the supercharger delivered approximately 3½ lbs/square inch boost, and the alloy bonnet received a scoop to allow air to the high mounted carburettor, which sat on top of the supercharger.

Opposition for Jeff in the ten-lap race was formidable, there being several Frazer Nash Le Mans Replica models entered, and driven by such notable drivers as Stirling Moss, Tony Crook and Mrs Joan Gerard. John Cooper was driving a Cooper MG, Gerry Ruddock a 1500 cc HRG, R. F. Peacock had his BMW 328, and Ernest Stapleton a 2-litre Aston Martin.

From the start Tony Crook took the lead, followed by Peacock and Sparrowe, but then Stirling Moss came through the field to dispute the lead with Tony Crook, taking it on lap two.

Jeff puts up another amazing performance, at Castle Combe. (*Photograph: Guy Griffiths*)

Soon the two Frazer Nashes were on their own in the lead followed by Peacock's BMW. Also way ahead of the field by a large margin in fourth place was the amazing Jeff Sparrowe, despite the presence of such high-powered opposition as the other BMW-engined cars and the Cooper.

So it remained until the final lap, when sadly Jeff's crankshaft pulley broke and a piece became mixed up with the timing chain giving engine failure. It had been an amazing performance however, and Jeff had put many very expensive sports cars to shame.

While Jeff was enjoying himself at Castle Combe the BARC was running a rally on the Yorkshire coast at Scarborough, this containing a series of driving tests for open or closed, long or short wheelbase cars. Two Morgans featured among the awards, one being A. C. 'Bert' Westwood's 4/4 which finished second in the class for 'short wheelbase open cars'! The other was the 4/4 of Derek Howard, who finished an excellent second overall in the event behind J. M. Richmond's HRG. Derek, a Bridlington dentist, had recently finished his service in the RAF, and caused comment for having a radio aerial on his Morgan, car radios being very rare in these pre-transistor days.

The Motor Show this year was held from 18 to 28 October and saw the debut of the new Morgan Plus 4. At the factory a batch of Plus 4s had been finished before the 4/4 model finally ceased production, with the Motor Show in mind. These four cars, given chassis numbers P2101 to 4 were tested by Charlie Curtis during the week prior to the show. There were two Coupes, one two-seater roadster and a l.h.d. export specification two-seater. No four-seater Plus 4s had been completed so, to indicate the complete future model range, a four-seater 4/4 was also prepared for the Motor Show (chassis number 2069). A specially prepared Plus 4 chassis was also shown, with many features chrome-plated.

The new Plus 4 attracted much favourable comment, with the range competitively priced at £510 basic price for the two-seater, £525 for the four-seater and £565 for the Coupe. *The Motor* magazine was moved to comment that 'the position of the old established Morgan Motor Company as maker of the fastest car at the price should be secure'.

Among those impressed was Sir John Black of the Standard Motor Company. Standard Triumph themselves were showing the twin carburettor Vanguard-engined Triumph TRX, but at £975 basic price it was very expensive and more a roadster than a sports car. Sir John had an 'eye' for markets and believed the Vanguard-engined sports car had a promising future, especially in the USA. He, therefore, invited HFS and Peter Morgan to his office on the Standard Triumph stand and made an offer for Standard Triumph to take over the Morgan Motor Company in order to produce the new Plus 4 in greater numbers than Morgan could manage at Malvern. He promised that whatever the Morgan family's decision the supply of Vanguard engines would not be compromised, and guaranteed Peter a job at Standard Triumph.

HFS was flattered that Sir John should rate the new car so highly and wish to take over the factory, but he wanted to discuss the offer further before making his decision. Several weeks later Morgan's company secretary, Major Kendall, wrote to Sir John informing him that the Morgan family wished to keep their company in their ownership, and therefore rejecting his offer. HFS Morgan did not think that Standard Triumph would pursue the development of a sports car any further. Peter, however, believed that Standard Triumph would do just that and Peter was to be proved to be right.

Sir John Black was used to getting his own way, and was doubtless angry that his plans had been thwarted. His development team, headed by Ted Grinham, were busy, however, with a new Standard small car, so there was little he could do for the next year.

The removal of petrol rationing in the summer had allowed the MCC to develop an idea of a one-thousand mile rally to fruition, and, with sponsorship from the *Daily Express* newspaper, this new event started on Wednesday, 8 November, with starting points at Plymouth, Norwich, Leamington Spa, London, Manchester, Harrogate and Glasgow. After separate seven-hundred mile runs the routes converged at Chester for a 423-mile common route through Wales into the West Country, finishing in Torquay on 10 November, where the final driving tests were held to decide the winners. Over eight hundred entries were received, demonstrating the increasing popularity of rallies with the motoring sportsman, but the RAC restricted starters to 470.

Several Morgans were entered, but none by the factory, which was saving the debut of the Plus 4 for the end of the year MCC Exeter Trial. Some 337 cars checked in at the finish at Torquay, two thirds of them without losing marks, for the final deciding driving test. None of the Morgans won an award, but Newquay driver Peter Musitano in his blue Standard-engined 4/4, MCV 227, had a win in the concours held the next day, in the class for open cars built since 1 January 1947 and costing lest than £450.

Peter Musitano's Morgan had been purchased from the Devon agent. A friend of Mr Goodall had tipped off Peter that a car was due to be delivered to this agent, so he went along, prepared to pay a bit extra to acquire the 4/4. The agent gave him a stiff lecture about the honesty of his company, and its waiting list of customers. So Peter left with his tail between his legs, expecting to hear no more. Two weeks later the agent rang up and mentioned that a Morgan was being sent to Newquay if he was still interested. The deal was completed.

The last few months of 1950 saw two interesting cars change hands. Jeff Sparrowe's success with JUO 177 had not gone unnoticed at the Morgan factory, and while visiting the factory on business Jeff was taken by Peter Morgan to see the 1939 Le Mans car which was still stored under dust sheets. This Morgan had had little post-war use following Peter Morgan's decision to concentrate his post-war racing on CAB 652. The Le Mans car still had the multi-carburettor set-up devised by Dick Anthony, with two supplementary carburettors in addition to the usual single SU, the extra carburettors having been fitted at each end of the cylinder head where the blanking plates had been removed to expose the inlet tracks. A series of complicated rods and levers connected the three carburettors together.

Peter Musitano's 4/4 beats the MGs to win the Daily Express Rally concours. Peter and brother Bill stand alongside. (*Photograph: Autosport*)

The Le Mans car had had doors fitted at some stage since the 1939 race, but still retained the three-wheeler pattern Morgan badge on the radiator, helping to differentiate this Morgan from others. Jeff decided to purchase the car, although it was designed specifically for Le Mans and therefore more solidly built but heavier than JUO 177.

The other Morgan to change hands was Dr Gavin Scott's much modified Standard-engined Morgan, now red, which was sold by Bowman and Acock's garage to T. A. Parkes on 14 November for approximately £550 together with several spares, including the special manifolds. 'Bill' Parkes, who worked in his family's market garden business in Pershore, Worcestershire had previously been driving a 1933 MG J2, but wanted a more up-to-date, competitive car for racing. He sold his MG to another future Morgan driver – Ray Meredith.

Peter Morgan on Meerhay Hill with the Coupe in the Exeter Trial. (*Photograph: The Motor*)

The Morgan Motor Company had developed the tradition of introducing its new models to the competition world with entries in the MCC's Exeter Trials. The Morgan three-wheeler had made its competition debut in the hands of HFS Morgan in the very first Exeter Trial way back in 1910; the first 4/4 made its debut in the 1935 event. The year 1950 was to mark the entrance of the new Plus 4, with Jim Goodall using the two-seater prototype, HUY 982, and Peter Morgan the Coupe JNP 239. The works team was completed by Sonny McCann who could now inherit Jim Goodall's old trials 4/4, BWP 47.

Other Morgans entered for the trial on 29 December were the Standard-engined 4/4, MCV 227 of Peter Musitano, Joe Huxham's usual 1086 cc Climax-engined 4/4, FOH 812, and T. H. Wood's early 1122 cc Climax-engined 4/4, ETV 996.

The trial itself was, at last, back to its full length now that petrol rationing had disappeared, and it attracted 256 entries, 169 being cars. Frost, snow, sleet then rain were the order of the day, but both of the new Plus 4s attracted favourable comment for their speed and handling qualities.

Peter Morgan proved unstoppable, claiming a Premier Award along with Sonny McCann. Jim ground to a halt with wheelspin on Simms, taking home a Second Class Award, as did Joe Huxham and Peter Musitano, but all in all it had been a fine debut for the new model.

Back at the factory the last Standard-engined 4/4, chassis number 2081, had been tested by Charlie Curtis in the week ending 13 November, and production had now changed over completely to the new Plus 4. The prototype, HUY 982, had been allocated the chassis number P 2100 retrospectively, the P prefix indicating Plus 4, and the engine was changed to a Morgan specification Vanguard, number V24ME, perhaps before the Exeter Trial.

Of the Show cars the red two-seater, P 2103, had been acquired by the Belfast agent Victor Limited on behalf of motor sport enthusiast Stanley Porter, who ran a newspaper distribution business and had been competing successfully with

Jim Goodall grinds to a halt on Simms. (*Photograph: Morgan Motor Co. collection*)

Mundaring Weir, with Bill Richards setting off up the hill. (*Photograph: Terry McGrath collection*)

an 1100 cc MG. It was to be registered OZ2343 on 21 February 1951.

One of the show Coupes, P2102, was to go to Holden and Hunt Limited, the suppliers to Morgan of front stub axle forgings.

Overseas

Australia

Colin Uphill, a mechanic working for Perth Morgan agent, Bill Richards, continued his success with his lightened green 4/4 at the WA Sporting Car Club Inc.'s hill climb on 25 February. Only one driver managed to beat him – Syd Negus with his Plymouth Special who became WA Hill Climb champion for 1950, but Colin took the class for racing cars 1101–1500 cc beating several MGs. The course, on the road from Kalamunda at Mundaring Weir, obviously suited the Morgans, for John Emery's 4/4 also took the class for sports cars 750–1101 cc. In the handicap competition Colin took another victory with Jack Nelson's Ford 10 Special in second place, then John Emery in third.

Mooliabeenie airstrip was once again used for races by the same club on 23 April. Practice was enlivened by Claude La Motte, who caught his trousers around the open propshaft of his 'Fidget', losing them completely. He had to sit naked and ashamed in the car until a 'good Samaritan' rescued him with a spare pair. Two Morgan 4/4s took part, the demonstration model of Bill Richards and the lightened 4/4 of Colin Uphill. Much useful publicity for Bill Richards Motors was to come from this meeting, starting with the five-lap handicap in which Bill himself came second to Claude La Motte's Fidget (A Fiat/Ford 10 single-seater). In the three-lap scratch race it was Colin's turn, with a win in the 1500 cc class and also fastest lap, beating Noel Aldous's MGTC. In the fourth car event, the ten-lap handicap, both did well, Colin wining the event from Syd Negus's fast Plymouth Special with Bill an excellent third.

On 5 June the WA Sporting Car Club ran its round the houses events at Goomalling, attracting crowds of around 3,000 to watch the racing. Three Morgans were entered, the 4/4s of Bill Richards and Colin Uphill as before, and the 4/4 of A.K. 'Digger' Wright, a soldier who had bought a new Morgan from Bill Richards. Colin Uphill was the only one to taste success, however, finishing third behind Jack Nelson's Ford 10

Colin Uphill guides his lightened 4/4 through the streets of Goomalling (*Photograph: Colin Uphill collection*)

Special and Claude La Motte's 'Fidget' in the three-lap scratch race up to 1500 cc.

Jack Nelson completed his excellent day by winning the fifty-mile Goomalling Flying Fifty, with the Morgans unplaced.

Back at Mooliabeenie on 23 October were 'Digger' Wright and Colin Uphill, but this time without success.

In the State of New South Wales Brian and Betty Sheaffe had been regular entrants of the events of the Vintage Sports Car Club of Australia with their new 4/4. In the Club's Annual 1½ day Trial, held on 20 and 21 May, they took turns to drive, and collected a Second Class Award.

Brian then finished sixth in the same Club's 100 mile Lapstone Trial, held on 24 September, and, on 29 October took part in the class for modern cars under 1500 cc at Foley's Hill Climb, where he recorded 30.50 seconds.

New Zealand

Dunedin driver Ted Reid's successes with his pre-war 4/4 continued during 1950. Much lightened and with engine of 1125 cc, the Morgan finished second in the championship hill climb stock sections organized by the South Canterbury Car Club on 25 March.

A further second place was obtained on 20 May at the Otago Sports Car Club's hill climb, held on Norwood Street in Dunedin on 20 May, this being in the up to 1500 cc scratch class. Dunedin was the major city in the New Zealand province of Otago.

Ted was very impressed with the handling of the elderly Morgan, especially on loose surfaces. He continued to race other vehicles, however, including modified speedway midgets, in a variety of events, including beach races.

United States of America

The introduction of the new Plus 4 at the Motor Show in England in October did not go unnoticed in the USA and led to the setting up of two distributorships, one for the West and one for the East. This system of distributorships was to be retained throughout the 1950s and 1960s period of exports of Morgans to the USA.

The initial West Coast distributor was to be Angell Motors of Pasadena in California, and they took the very first left-hand-drive car, chassis P2104, one of the first batch of four built in 1950, a green two-seater. Angell Motors were also Jowett distributors, and enthusiastically advertized the Jupiter sportscar. Surprisingly, the company did not give the new Morgan the same support.

CHAPTER TWELVE

1951

Despite the new Plus 4 being now in production, it was to be some time before the British enthusiasts would get hold of any, as most cars were to be exported, the early ones going to Australia, Belgium, New York, Sweden and Uruguay.

With the increasing interest in rallies among motor sportsmen, the Morgan Motor Company was keen to set up a team for the forthcoming RAC rally, which was to be reintroduced in 1951 for the first time since the war, as part of the Festival of Britain celebrations. With Peter Morgan having the Coupe, and Jim Goodall the two-seater the team would be completed by a four-seater. The question was who was to drive it? They needed someone with RAC rally experience.

George Goodall was an enthusiastic member of the Worcestershire Motor Club, the club that had run the famous Madresfield Speed Trials in the 1920s and '30s which did so much to publicize the speed of the Morgan three-wheelers. George was to become the club's chairman and, later, President. Also a keen member was Dr William Steel, a family doctor and hospital anaesthetist from Worcester. Doc Steel had taken part in the 1937 RAC Rally as a crew member in a Rover 14. In 1939 he completed that year's rally in his own car, a Lancia Aprilia. Clearly he had the experience, so George asked him if he would like to become the third team member with the four-seater, which was nearing completion at the factory. At the time Doc Steel was running an ex-police Morris 8 tourer that he had had converted to four speeds, but the offer of a new sports car at a time when any new vehicle was very difficult to acquire was a great privilege and too great an opportunity to miss. The black prototype four-seater, chassis number P2121 was fitted, rather surprisingly, with Vanguard engine number V45039E rather than one numbered as a Morgan engine, and was tested by Charlie Curtis during the week ending 1 March and finally registered for the road, as JWP 537, on 21 March.

The Worcestershire Motor Club's own auto-tests quite probably witnessed the testing during the previous year of the prototype Plus 4. Club members had thought it odd that no-one was allowed to see under the competing Morgan's bonnet, especially as the driving test times had been exceptional, but the mysterious vehicle disappeared before the end of the day's competition with them none the wiser.

The MCC's Lands End Trial was back to full length this year starting on Good Friday, 23 March and finishing the following day. Among the 182 cars entered were six Morgans, including the factory team which was as in the preceding Exeter Trial. Also entered was Joe Huxham with FOH 812, and two pre-war Climax-engined cars for E.C. Cameron and L. V. Cruttenden. The weather was kind this year, and thirty-seven cars claimed First Class Awards, including the Morgan factory team. Joe Huxham claimed a Third.

The marvellous Morgan team performance meant that they beat three Dellows to the one-make team award, the two Plus 4s impressing generally with their 'immense power'.

In Ireland the Easter weekend marked the start of the Ulster Automobile Club's Circuit of Ireland one-thousand mile rally which finished in Belfast on the Tuesday after four days' driving. Stanley Porter with OZ 2343, Ulster's only Plus 4, took part and achieved third best performance to two Allards in the timed climb of the famous Tim Healy Pass, but overall failed to feature in the results.

On 31 March the Castle Combe circuit was host to the Bristol MC & LCC race meeting, which took place in very damp conditions. The opening race, a ten-lap scratch race for sports cars up to 1100 cc featured Jeff Sparrowe, in JUO 177, running in lightweight form, but the Morgan was no match for the amazing Riley of Leslie Hawthorn, the proprietor of the Tourist Trophy Garage in Farnham, Surrey, who finished over a

Jeff Sparrowe trying to stay ahead of Len Gibbs' Riley on a wet Castle Combe track. (*Photograph: Jeff Sparrowe collection*)

minute ahead of the second-placed Riley of Len Gibbs, with Jeff just a few seconds further behind.

On 4 April Doc Steel collected his four-seater Plus 4 from the Morgan factory, and began a period of careful running-in and preparation for the forthcoming RAC Rally in June.

The Government's Chancellor, the Rt Hon. Hugh Gaitskell MP, put further restrictions into place for those struggling to purchase new cars when, in his 1951 budget, he doubled the purchase tax on new cars from 33⅓% to 66⅔% as from April, while leaving that on goods vehicles at 33⅓%. Petrol tax was also increased by 4½*d.* (2p) per gallon.

Once again the *Daily Express* newspaper was to sponsor the BRDC's prestigious International Trophy Race at Silverstone on 5 May. Besides the Formula 1 International Trophy Race the programme included the usual one-hour production car races, and this year three Morgans were entered. In the first race, containing the classes for production cars up to 2 litres, was Jeff Sparrowe with JUO 177, running in 'production car' trim, with the normal Morgan bonnet, wings and lights of the Le Mans replica. This year there was little opposition in the 1100 cc class, just several Morris Minors. Jeff had a successful day, winning the class and also finishing eighteenth overall in the general classification – just behind Frank Bigger who was in an MG.

In the class for cars over 2 litres, two Morgans, both Plus 4s, were lined up for the Le Mans type start. Their drivers were Peter Morgan, with the works Coupe JNP 239, and David Price with a roadster, WHX 280. David Price, who ran a windscreen glazing company in North West London, had managed to acquire one of the few Plus 4s to reach the home market, chassis number P2127, colour red, which was despatched on 4 April 1951.

This race naturally went to the big-engined Jaguars, with Stirling Moss victorious in an

Jeff Sparrowe is followed by a Jowett Jupiter and an MG TD during the *Daily Express* up to 2 litre race. (*Photograph: Guy Griffiths*)

David Price at the *Daily Express* meeting. (*Photograph: LAT Photographic*)

Peter Morgan follows an Allard, during a very impressive drive at Silverstone. (*Photograph: Guy Griffiths*)

XK120. Peter Morgan impressed all with his 'remarkable speed', throwing the Coupe through the corners, hanging on to Spiller's Healey for several laps and finally finishing in twentieth place, just ahead of it.

David Price was three laps down – possibly his engine was not fully run-in. He finished just behind the rather slow Ferrari 'Inter' of another future Morgan driver, Roy Clarkson.

The average speeds of Jeff, Peter and David's Morgans in this meeting worked out at 64, 74 and 66 mph respectively.

Just prior to this event Peter Morgan had had the hood of his Coupe modified. He had been concerned that he would become too hot during one hour of summer racing with the normal Coupe hood in place, so he arranged for Bert Gulliver in the trim shop at the factory to modify it by fitting a flap around the rear window which could be let down. The top fixing was by press studs, and the sides by zip fastenings. As a bonus, visibility to the rear was found to be much improved with the flap lowered, such that it became very useful for driving tests in future rallies.

Peter Morgan stands behind his Coupe at Silverstone, prior to the Le Mans start. The modified rear window is clearly visible. (*Photograph: Morgan Motor Co. Collection*)

The 500 Motor Racing Club of Ireland had excellent weather for its first hill climb of the year, at Cairncastle on 5 May. Stanley Porter entered the scratch class for open cars, other than racing cars, over 1500 cc. He must have been pleased with a win in his Plus 4, OZ 2343, some two seconds faster than two Jaguars, demonstrating well the handling qualities of the new Morgan.

Sonny McCann tackles the 'regularity' test at Oughtershaw during the Edinburgh Rally. (*Photograph: Morgan Motor Co. collection*)

Paul Hughes lines up alongside Bill Parkes and a Jowett Javelin for the VSCC handicap race. (*Photograph: Bill Parkes collection*)

We mentioned the cancellation of the MCC's Edinburgh Trial in 1950 through lack of entries. This Whit Friday, 11 May, saw the start of the MCC's replacement, the first Edinburgh Rally. There was the usual MCC overnight run from three different starts, via Warwick to Harrogate for breakfast, then on via North Yorkshire and Lakeland to Edinburgh, with various special tests en route. The Morgan team comprised the Plus 4s of Peter, JNP 239 and Jim, HUY 982, along with the 4/4, BWP 47, of Sonny McCann. They found this new event somewhat tricky, but Sonny won a Second Class Award in Class III, and Jim and Peter a Second and Third respectively in Class IV.

That same weekend saw Jeff Sparrowe at Castle Combe on Whit Saturday. The first race, a ten-lap event for sports cars up to 1100 cc saw the Leslie Hawthorn prepared 1100 cc Riley take an easy win – but this time driven by his son Mike – a future world champion. Second was Jeff Sparrowe, with JUO 177.

In the third race, a ten-lap event for sports cars up to 1500 cc, it was again Mike Hawthorn victorious, but this time driving his father's ex-works 1936 Riley TT Sprite of 1496 cc. Once again, Jeff had to accept second place with JUO 177.

The following weekend the Vintage Sports Car Club ran a race meeting at Silverstone, and included some events for other cars. The four-lap handicap race for non vintage cars attracted a field of twenty-one, of which two were Morgans. One was the ex-Gavin Scott Standard-engined 4/4 appearing in the hands of its new owner 'Bill' Parkes. The second was the Morgan factory's car, CAB 652. This car had been recently rebuilt with a Standard Special engine number Q2ES, replacing the 1100 cc Climax which Jim Goodall has been accused of blowing up. Probably at the same time, the special fuel tank had been replaced by one with a conventional fuel filler fitted through the rear panel, to the left of the spare wheel. It had been painted ivory.

The driver was a Morgan factory employee, Paul Hughes, from Worcester, who had initially worked in the chassis erection shop just after the war, but was now in the offices.

It was Bradford's MGTC that took an early lead which it held until the last one hundred yards, when Margulies's Talbot went through to win with Bill Parkes finishing third.

After an officials' conference, the runners for the first heat of the *Motor Sport* Silverstone Handicap Challenge Trophy were announced for the next race, over four laps. Chapman's 4½ litre Bentley came through from the 52 second mark to win with Bill Parkes, off 1 min. 35 sec., coming second.

Bill Parkes was back at Silverstone the following weekend for the Maidstone and Mid-Kent MC meeting. In the third event, a five-lap scratch race for up to 1500 cc unsupercharged or 1300 cc supercharged sports cars he finished fifth, and in the second heat of the *Motor Sport* Trophy handicap he finished ninth. 'Bill' was finding the Morgan very competitive, the tuned engine (lightened flywheel, balanced crank, uprated valve springs, raised compression, polished ports etc.) making it difficult to beat. The 'pool' petrol of the time was not ideal for speed events, so, on advice from the petrol company 'National Benzole', he added some benzole. FNP 684 had a close ratio gearbox, and also the radiator fan was removed – there was never a problem with overheating, even in traffic. Only one headlight was used, this being road legal at this time and saving weight. For racing the spare wheels were removed and a plywood cover was fitted over the gap. The improved valve springs acted as a 'governor' for engine revs, producing valve bounce above 6,000 rpm, but the spring makers advised Bill not to go for even stronger springs, or the engine would blow.

The same day, 26 May, saw a large crowd at Boreham, near Chelmsford, for the West Essex-CC's opening circuit race meeting. 'Bert' Westwood, perhaps better known for his exploits with his pre-war Fiat Balilla 'Black Diamond', was entered in his Morgan 4/4 for the five-lap race for sports cars up to 1500 cc, but he failed to feature in the awards.

The *News of the World* newspaper's sponsored Ulster Trophy Races in Northern Ireland was held on 2 June on the 7 mile 732 yards Dundrod circuit, which had been constructed in 1949. The Ulster Automobile Club had managed to attract an excellent field of Formula 1 cars for the Ulster Trophy Race itself, but among the supporting programme was a ten-lap handicap race, and Stanley Porter entered his Plus 4, OZ 2343, for this event.

Excellent weather was the order of the day, and the carnival atmosphere was to be enlivened by a visit from Her Majesty the Queen, who, with her daughter Princess Margaret, toured the circuit to the cheers of the crowd. First, though, were the preliminary races, the first of which was a five-lap scratch race for cars up to 1300 cc running on 80 octane fuel. Entered for this was J. Maitland of Armagh, with his 1125 cc 4/4, but we have no record of his performance, the race being won by Ron Flockhart's J. P. Vincent.

After a 500 cc race came the handicap race, featuring Stanley Porter and his red Plus 4. Tuning for the event just consisted of replacing the windscreen with an aero screen, removing the spare wheels and substituting a 140 main jet for the standard 135 in the Solex 32BI carburettor, as recommended by the makers. Some fifty cars had entered, ranging from a 750 cc MG to Sydney Allard's 5.4 litre Cadillac-engined Allard. One of the features of the course was a timed kilometre on the straight, and the winner, Mike Hawthorn's TT Riley, went through at 111.9 mph. Stanley Porter, although not in the awards, acquitted himself well. He was timed at an amazing 96 mph through the kilometre, and finished the seventy-four mile event at an average of close to 68 mph.

Stanley Porter is passed by Ron Flockhart's single-seater J. P. Vincent at Quarry during the handicap race at Dundrod. (*Photograph: Quadrant Picture Library*)

The RAC International Rally commenced on 4 June with starting places in Brighton, Cheltenham, Harrogate and Skegness. Some 265 cars were entered, of which four were Morgans. The Morgan factory team consisted of the three 'prototype' Plus 4s. Jim Goodall was in the blue two-seater, HUY 982, navigated by Bromsgrove Chemist Terry Hall. Peter Morgan was in the blue Coupe JNP 239 navigated by his brother in law Dr Michael Scott. Doc Steel was in his black four-seater, JWP 537, navigated by Sonny McCann. Also competing was Dave Price, with his daughter Pamela as navigator in his red two-seater Plus 4, WHX 280. All chose to start from Cheltenham; they were competing in the class for open cars of over 1500 cc, which also contained the formidable XK120 Jaguars.

From Cheltenham the route lay via Bredon to Silverstone where a predetermined number of laps (thirteen for the open Plus 4s) had to be completed in thirty minutes. Too many laps as well as too few were penalized and the navigator was not allowed on the circuit. From Silverstone the next time check was Scarborough, and thence on to Jedburgh, Edinburgh, Stirling and Amulree control. Leaving Crieff the bumpy 'road' to Kenmore was tackled, then the Braemar road via Devils Elbow to Grantoun-on-Spey. Reaching Fort William the route took the Glencoe road to the timed hill climb at Rest-and-Be-Thankful. First and second in the sub-class for over 1500 cc and under 3000 cc were Jim and Peter, with Doc Steel fourth and Dave Price eighth.

Many of those who had completed the hill climb, including the Morgan team, waited at the top to watch the next competitors – until they realized that the time to the next control at Dunoon was now very short. Thus began a mad dash at high speed, helped by the police controlling other traffic, to reach the control and then on to rest for the night in the various hotels. The 'mad dash' become known as the Dunoon Grand Prix and the black tyre marks from the skidding competitors were visible for all to see the following morning.

On the Wednesday the route returned to England where a tricky section at Boot, consisting of a six-mile distance from Hardknott Pass to Wrynose Pass, had to be covered within a time of from fifteen to eighteen minutes, catching out several competitors. The route now made for Blackpool for an overnight stop, following a control at Blawith, but not before a final driving test on the promenade. This comprised a sharp dash to a figure of eight through pylons, a compulsory reverse and a sprint to a finishing line with a foul line twenty-five yards beyond. Peter Morgan set second fastest overall time here to Ian Appleyard's famous white Jaguar XK120, NUB 120, although of course the rally had several classes.

On Thursday the rally entrants made for Wales, through the Elan Valley to Llandrindod Wells and the Drover's Arms speed trial at Eppynt on War Office property. This consisted of a dash around a 1.9 mile road circuit, full of switchbacks and corners.

Thursday night was spent at Weston Super Mare, and on the Friday the survivors set off on a tight schedule to the finish at Bournemouth. Here the officials worked out which cars in the various classes would contest the deciding driving test the following day. The test took the form of accelerating to a chicane, through to a similar chicane, rounding a pylon at the other end and then returning to the finishing line after passing through the chicane again. A foul line was placed twenty-five yards back from the finish.

It was the leader of the rally and the leader of the class for open cars over 1500 cc, Ian Appleyard who set the target for the Morgans with a time of 73.58 sec. in the Jaguar. It seemed unlikely anyone would get close, but the Morgan team were in line for the team award if they were quick enough to beat the Jaguars. Jim Goodall was first of the Morgan team to go and he reached 74.42 sec., giving him an aggregate of 114.55 – second place to Appleyard's 109.61. Peter Morgan was next, and he achieved 75.4 sec., putting him in to second place with 112.99, and Jim into third. Now all depended on Doc Steel, and he made sure of the team award with a faultless drive, pushing the Jaguars into second place. Overall, he finished sixteenth, just one place ahead of Dave Price.

This was a tremendous achievement for the Morgan factory, following on from the company's successes in the RAC rallies of pre-war days. The power and manoeuvrability of the Plus 4 had been

Doc Steel performs correctly at the final test of the RAC Rally, to clinch the team prize for Morgan. (*Photograph: Doc Steel collection*)

The successful Morgan team. (*Photograph: Morgan Motor Co. collection*)

ably demonstrated, and the motoring sportsmen were impressed. If only they could get hold of them now that most of the factory output was going to exports to please the government.

Thinking about the RAC afterwards, Peter Morgan has always wondered whether he would have beaten Ian Appleyard had he used a two-seater rather than the Coupe, as the former weighed 1 cwt less than the Coupe, at 15 cwt. Doc Steel also had some cause to regret having the four-seater – because its fuel tank was of two gallons less capacity than the other models at nine gallons. As a result he had to stop more frequently for fuel and then race along trying to catch up with his team mates! A new set of front tyres was found to be necessary after the event.

The popularity of rallying was ably demonstrated by the huge number of entries for the Lancashire AC Morecambe Rally, held from 25 to 27 June, there being only thirty-five fewer than the RAC Rally itself. In Britain there were no speed limits for cars outside built up areas (the restrictions were lifted after the war), and traffic was light, allowing the competitive-minded motorist and navigator to enjoy hard driving to strict time schedules. Commercial vehicles were subject to speed limits, light commercials being restricted to 30 mph and some heavy lorries 20 mph, but many rallies were run in country areas where such traffic was seldom met. The rallies often included night runs, with hardly any traffic at all. There were many natural hazards on the roads of those days, including poor surfaces, level crossings where road and rail met, and hump-backed bridges where roads crossed canals. These bridges were relics from the era of the horse. They were usually narrow and often blind as to where the road went or what was on it, once over the canal.

Night rallies called for good lighting. Prior to 1951 all Morgans had two single filament headlights, and dipping of the beam to avoid dazzle was achieved by switching these two lights off and using a dipped central pass lamp. Early home market Plus 4s used this same system (certainly JNP 239 did), but in 1951 a double filament main beam/dip beam headlamp was introduced, with the central light now becoming a spot lamp.

The Morecambe Rally itself was won by the Leeds Jaguar dealer Ian Appleyard in his XK120, but in sixth place was Merton Biberfield from Prestwich, near Manchester, with his 1949 blue 4/4. He also won the starting control award for the Whalley start (other starts were from Birmingham, Leeds, London and Manchester). In a separate class for specials the Jaguar XK120 of another future Morgan driver, Jimmy Ray, came in fifth. Jimmy, whose family owned a confectionery business at Prescot in Lancashire, was a very keen rally driver and was to become one of the top drivers of the 1950s.

For some time a group of Morgan enthusiasts in the Derby area had been debating whether there should be a Morgan club. To gauge support an advertisement had been placed in *The Autocar* of 18 May. This produced several replies of interest and so it was agreed to have an inaugural meeting on 30 June at Kegworth. 'Bill' Parkes was keen to join, but was racing at Silverstone on that day so he telephoned his apologies, only to be told that there were three other enthusiasts who had agreed to go on to the meeting following the Silerstone races. Bill agreed to do likewise.

The Silverstone meeting was that of the Midland Motoring Enthusiasts Club. The five-lap scratch race for 1100 cc cars saw Jeff Sparrowe making an uncharacteristic spin in JUO 177, but he eventually finished third, beaten by Len Gibbs' usual pre-war Riley, and the very fast 747 cc two-seater of J. M. Allen

The Allen brothers, Nigel and Michael had fabricated this car under the guidance and assistance of a certain Colin Chapman, and it was called Lotus. The engine on this Lotus III was a desiamesed port Austin 7 and it made the little car virtually unbeatable in 750 formula racing.

Bill Parkes took to the track for the 1500 cc, five-lap scratch race but lost a plug lead on FNP 684 and had to retire.

In the sports car handicap race over six laps, Jeff Sparrowe found himself on scratch but was again unable to catch Gibbs' Riley, finishing second. Bill Parkes finished fourth behind Pratt's Bugatti.

Following the event it was a follow my leader drive from Silverstone to Kegworth for the Morgans of Jeff Sparrowe, Bill Parkes and Bill Allarton with his colleague Gordon Stratton. Bill Parkes was 'tail end Charlie' and recalls it was quite an exciting drive. At one stage the three Morgans went round one traffic island twice before locating the correct exit and Bill was somewhat relieved that a watching policeman did not record his number.

The meeting was successful, with Jeff Sparrowe elected as President of the new Morgan 4/4 Club. It was agreed the club would cater for all four-wheeler Morgans, including the new Plus 4.

A good turn-out for the inaugural meeting of the Morgan 4/4 Club. (*Photograph: Bill Parkes collection*)

The same weekend the BARC ran its fifth annual Eastbourne Rally as a two-day event, complete with midnight Concours d'Elegance under floodlights! Winner of a Second Class Award, and the award for best novice was J. A. McHarg with his Morgan.

It was one of the great motoring adventures of the time to travel abroad for a Continental rally and these events caught the public's imagination. There were no such things then as drive-on cross-Channel car ferries, and the average British holidaymaker considered himself lucky to reach the coast of England, Continental holidays being definitely for the future. Once over the Channel the formidable Alps were challenging to cross by car, using the steep, rough roads often with unguarded drops to the sides as they wound their ways through the passes or 'cols de montagne'.

These rallies, however, also demanded strict time schedules of the drivers as they raced up the 'cols'. Added to that was the unpredictability of the weather, such that the Continental rallies had a formidable reputation. HFS Morgan believed these events to be intrinsically dangerous, having seen these passes himself on various Continental trips, and had no wish for his son to take part – a wish Peter respected, perhaps reluctantly.

The French Automobile Club du Mont Blanc ran its fifth International Evian – Mont Blanc Rally on 27–29 July, starting at Annecy and finishing 950 miles later in Evian. Among the eighty-strong entries were ten British competitors, no doubt assisted with their entries by Roy Clarkson, from Halstead in Essex, who was the British contact for the event. David Price and his daughter Pamela decided to enter in their Plus 4.

It was the feeling of the competitors that the timing was even stiffer than the better known Alpine rally, with short distances between the controls over the 'cols' of the French Alps making it difficult to achieve the required speeds. The second stage of the rally included twelve 'cols' with six time controls, and it was on the Thones–Taninges section that the Prices lost two minutes – their only penalties of the whole event. From Martigny in Switzerland to Megeve in

France, the route was in the thick of tourist traffic and Pamela Price admitted that she put her hand hard on the horn button – and left it there!

The following morning there were five 'cols' to climb, one of which was crowded by cyclists (the roads were not closed), and the Prices' Plus 4 had a plug lead come adrift on the Col Galibier, just making the time control within the two minutes' extra allowance.

In the Annemasse hillclimb David Price made second fastest climb in the 2–3 litre class to Heyworth's Healey, and when all the results were compiled the Price Plus 4 had managed to finish first overall in this class, ahead of two Citroëns.

During his return drive to England, David Price's Morgan broke a steering damper, and he had to stop at a French garage for a replacement to be manufactured out of saw blade spring steel.

On 28 July the Aston Martin Owners Club held their St John Horsfall Race Meeting at Silverstone, starting with three heats of five-lap handicaps before a later twenty-lap final. In the first heat Jeff Sparrowe, with JUO 177, was on scratch along with David Blakely's 1496 cc HRG Le Mans. In the event the larger car finished just ahead of Jeff and both qualified for the final. Bill Parkes unluckily finished sixth in his heat and missed the cut-off for the final with FNP 684.

Come the final, over twenty laps, it was again Blakely and Sparrowe who dominated the event, finishing first and second and ahead of Basset's Allard.

Jeff Sparrowe leads Colin Chapman's Lotus Mk III and eventual winner David Blakely's HRG at Silverstone. (*Photograph: Jeff Sparrowe collection*)

There was another race between these two adversaries in Race 5, a five-lap handicap for post-war cars. Again the order at the flag was Blakely then Sparrowe, with third and fourth places going to two other HRGs.

Poor David Blakely was to achieve further fame – he was the unfortunate murder victim of Ruth Ellis, the last woman to be hanged for murder in Britain.

The very next day Jeff Sparrowe was hillclimbing at Brunton, near Ludgersall in Wiltshire at the BARC South-Western Centre's event. We believe this to be the Brunton event at which Jeff used the ex-Morgan factory Le Mans car to come first in the up to 1200 cc class, with a time of 36.75 sec. For 'economy', at this event, Jeff ran the Morgan on the registration plates from JUO 177.

HFS Morgan was approaching his 70th birthday (11 August). He decided that this was an appropriate occasion to announce that he would be appointing his son Peter to the position of Deputy Governing Director and Chairman of the Morgan Motor Company. He, himself, remained as Governing Director and George Goodall was Managing Director.

HFS Morgan was a very modest man, little given to niceties of conversation, and quite shy. Sonny McCann recently recalled that HFS would often stand nearby for a while before approaching him with a question – as if plucking up courage to interrupt his work. None the less, he was a very popular figure at the Morgan works, and, on his regular visits to the factory, he would always visit Mrs Brown's little sandwich shop at the works, for his lunchtime cheese sandwich and a cup of oxo.

His managing director was the exact opposite – an extrovert who could be very difficult to deal with as several Morgan agents found to their cost. Often giving the impression that it was he who owned the factory, George Goodall also had a reputation of being a strict disciplinarian, who insisted on everything being spick and span.

Peter Morgan had been intensely irritated by George Goodall's attitude, finding him difficult to work with, and even approached his father with his difficulties. HFS then explained to Peter just how good George had been during the difficult

Jeff Sparrowe at the BARC Brunton, in what we believe to be the ex-Le Mans 4/4. (*Photograph: Jeff Sparrowe collection*)

days of the Second World War in making sure the factory had secure work (HFS was a pacifist and disliked seeking contracts at this time).

Over the years the Morgan Motor Company itself had been enlarged by HFS Morgan and his advisors, into what was by now virtually an investment company, with car production very much a secondary consideration, reducing the necessity for the Malvern factory always to make an annual profit. That being said, HFS enjoyed his involvement with the factory that he had founded, particularly when involved in new designs or modifications.

Besides obviously having a works Morgan car, HFS had purchased a 3½ litre Bentley from a dealer in Bournemouth in 1936. It was then one year old, having initially belonged to the Earl of Southampton, and had an aluminium Park Ward saloon body. He was to keep this favourite Bentley, registered AAA 533, throughout the 1950s.

Over in Northern Ireland, Stanley Porter was back in action over the August bank holiday weekend, on Saturday 4 August, at Newtownards airfield circuit. The handicap event was run as three heats and a final, all of fifteen laps. Porter and his Plus 4 OZ 2343 contested the third heat with a handicap credit of two laps and finished second to Lindsay's ERA.

In the final Lindsay retired with mechanical trouble after one lap, leaving the race to Stanley Porter and Arthur Clapham (with a Ford special) who raced a wheel-to-wheel duel. It was Porter who took the chequered flag after 20 min. 55 sec. at an average speed of 54.24 mph. Second was Lovell-Butt's supercharged MG which just pushed Clapham into third place.

The West Hants and Dorset MC had an excellent entry of 147 cars for their Ibsley race meeting the same day, including two Morgans, both entered by Jeff Sparrowe. We have been unable to ascertain which of his two Morgans (JUO 177 and the Le Mans car) he actually raced and he did not feature in the results.

The first competitive event organized by the new Morgan 4/4 Club was a road rally, held on Sunday 5 August over a course of around 75 miles from Burton-on-Trent to Banbury, followed by some driving tests. The required average speed was high and Bill Parkes remembers covering eleven miles of a good main road section in nine minutes. Of course, there were hump-backed bridges taken perhaps a little too fast, and Bill's navigator was not amused by flying into the air, muttering various unquotable utterances. The best performance on the road section was by Bill Allarton – later to become the competitions manager of Joseph Lucas Limited. Bill Allarton had purchased a 1939 cycle-winged 1098 cc Climax-engined 4/4, reg. EAX 377, after returning from service in the Navy in 1948. He then competed with it in various sprints at Queensbury, Prescott and Shelsley, but without success. During the winter of 1950 he stripped the Morgan down to its last nuts and bolts and rebuilt it. Bill has always described his car a Le Mans Replica, but, as we have shown, it is one of the cycle-wing cars with conventional twin spare wheeled rear end.

The event was won by Graham Stallard, with his 1949 two-seater 4/4, MKX 239, with Bill Parkes second and Bill Allarton third. This was Graham Stallard's second 4/4, replacing his black pre-war 4/4, CUY 229, which he had managed to invert in a ditch.

Bill Allarton smiles as he sets off on the 4/4 Club rally. To the rear are the entries of D. E. Street and Stanley Dyke. (*Photograph: Bill Parkes collection*)

On Saturday, 11 August the West Essex CC put up with unrelenting rain for its second race meeting at Boreham airfield. The third event, over seven laps for 1100 cc unsupercharged and 750 cc supercharged sports cars, saw a goodly tussle between Harewood's MGPB, Colin Chapman's Lotus, Dickie Le Strange Metcalfe's Fiat Balilla, and Jeff Sparrowe's Morgan, with victory going to the MG, followed by the Fiat and the Morgan.

The same day, over the Irish Sea, at the Craigantlet hillclimb, the rain held off, and Stanley Porter finished third with his Plus 4, OZ 2343, in the over 2000 cc class, only ⅕ sec. behind the 2468 cc Graham of J. L. Kearney, but some 6 sec. behind the winner, C. E. Robb's 3917 cc Mercury Special.

Pamela Price borrowed her father's Plus 4, WHX 280, for the NW London MC driving tests at Redhill on 12 August, and drove well to take the ladies' award.

While *The Autocar* had managed a road test of Peter Morgan's Coupe, JNP 239, for the 27 April edition, the two-seater had so far not been tested by a motoring magazine. This was put right by *The Motor* when Joe Lowrey went to collect HUY 982 from the factory on Friday afternoon of 24 August. Not content with an ordinary road test, Joe had entered the car in that weekend's Cheltenham MC Rally, which included, within the five-hundred-mile rally route into Wales, a miles-per-gallon economy test as well as driving tests. Joe was accompanied by John Rowe of *The Light Car* magazine which was also produced by Temple Press. For the economy test the carburettor jets and choke tube were replaced by smaller ones (120 for 135 main jet, 180 air correction jet for 190, and 23 for 25 choke tube). This change had minimal effect on acceleration, but did reduce maximum speed. Averaging just over 30 mph in the Welsh mountains Joe recorded 38.6 mpg, but there was much coasting to save fuel. Joe went on to cover 1,900 miles in eleven days with the Morgan, and enjoyed it so much that he decided he wanted one, putting in an order on his return to the factory.

When the road test was published, in the 19 September edition of *The Motor*, an acceleration of 0–50 mph in just under 10 seconds, with a maximum speed of 84.7 mph was quoted following the performance test undertaken in Belgium.

Joe Lowrey had worked during the war for the Royal Aircraft Establishment, and had been using a HRG 1100. He had used this car after the war while reporting events for *The Motor*, and, when sent to a distant event, such as to report the Alpine Rally, he would himself enter other events on the way there and back, often with success. These were the happy days of being able to enter quite well-known events with everyday cars and actually get prizes.

Holland Birkett of the 750 MC was instrumental in organizing a six-hour relay race for teams of sports cars from invited clubs at Silverstone on 25 August. Any number of cars up to six could be entered. A coloured sash had to be carried by each team and transferred from driver to driver when they changed over at the pits. Little time was given for the new Morgan 4/4 Club to come up with a team, but they did manage to get one together. This comprised Jeff Sparrowe, with his ex-factory 1938 Le Mans car running as the 'A' car, Bill Parkes with FNP 684 as the 'B' car, Bill Allarton with EAX 377 as the 'C', and finally, club secretary, John Sutton Atkins' 1937 1122 cc Morgan, FPE 567, as the 'D' car. The team manager was the club competition secretary Douglas Whetton. A handicap of thirty-four credit laps was allocated, the Jaguars being the scratch team.

On the way to the circuit John Sutton Atkins' Morgan broke down with a recalcitrant fuel pump, but luckily another club member, Dick Pritchard, who was to run the pits, came to his assistance and got him to the circuit just before practice ended. He was quickly scrutineered and made his three practice laps. Meanwhile the rest of the team was already scrutineered, had practised and was preparing for the race.

The start at 12.30 p.m. was to be Le Mans style, and Bill Parkes was chosen to carry the sash for the Morgans.

From the start Bill maintained lap speeds of 63–64 mph, which lasted for the next sixty-five minutes. At 1.40 p.m. he began to slow and came in to the pits. He was replaced by Jeff Sparrowe. Bill's problem had been brakes and his car was taken to the reserve pits for his attention, assisted by Bill Allarton.

Bill Parkes before the start, with other team members around his car. (*Photograph: Bill Parkes collection*)

Jeff built up his speed until lapping at 65 mph but at 2.20 p.m. he signalled he was coming in and John Atkins took over the sash. Clearly the standard 1122 cc car would be slower than the two racers, and John lapped at just under 60 mph. Just five minutes later came the excellent news that the Morgan team was now in second place, behind the Aston Martins.

John Sutton Atkins' car now began to blow out a lot of oil smoke, suggesting piston ring trouble, so it was flagged in at 2.40 p.m., to be replaced by Jeff Sparrowe once more.

At 3.15 p.m. Bill Allarton took over the sash from Jeff and began lapping at 62 mph until 4 p.m. when his clutch gave out and he came in to hand over to Bill Parkes.

The VSCC Bentleys were now in the lead but Bill gradually whittled away at their lead until the Morgans were finally in front at 4.30 p.m. Bill came into the pits after another fifteen minutes to hand over once more to Jeff Sparrowe. Jeff kept up the pressure for the next hour but the VSCC Bentleys were able to retake the lead.

Once again it was Bill Parkes who took up the sash for the chase of the Bentleys, but at 6.05 p.m. his engine began making expensive big-end-going noises and he came in to the pits. Jeff Sparrowe went out again but, with just five

The successful 4/4 Club team. *Left to right*: John Sutton-Atkins, Bill Allarton, Bill Parkes and Jeff Sparrowe. (*Photograph: Bill Parkes collection*)

minutes to go to the chequered flag at 6.30 p.m., he was forced to come in with ignition problems.

With not a fit car left in the Morgan team, it was Bill Parkes who was sent out again for a slow final lap to bring the sash over the finishing line for a excellent second place. Bill Parkes had not anticipated two and a half hours of racing when he had agreed to be a member of the team for the six-hour race!

Everyone regarded the race as a great success, and the 750 MC decided it should be an annual event.

Bill Parkes was able to drive slowly home where he luckily found the crank to be undamaged and just requiring new bearings. He was back in action the following weekend at Silverstone for the SUNBAC meeting.

The Standard engine in Bill's 4/4 was prone to overheat its engine oil when racing but Bill was to cure this by fashioning a scoop out of plywood and fastening it to the numberplate to direct air on to the sump.

Bill was out of luck in his first race at the SUNBAC meeting on 1 September, finishing ninth in the scratch race for up to 1500 cc. There were, however, also four heats and a final of a forty-one-lap handicap race, the latter counting towards the *Motor Sport* Trophy. Bill was third in his heat and finished fourth in the final behind D. Chapman's Bentley, Dennis O'Malley Taylor's Jaguar XK120 and K. Downing's Connaught.

The three points from the final made Bill eligible for the next round of the *Motor Sport* competition at the MCC Silverstone meeting on 8 September, but Bill decided not to enter as he wanted to save his car for his forthcoming holiday which included a visit to the Nurburgring. He was to finish sixth in the *Motor Sport* competition, the winner of the *Motor Sport* Trophy being D. J. R. Chapman with his Bentley.

The MCC meeting did see a Morgan competing – that of Paul Hughes, out once more with CAB 652, which he entered in a one-hour high-speed trial, winning a First Class Award at 54.24 mph.

Although Joe Lowrey was now patiently waiting for his ordered Plus 4 to be manufactured, he was not to be the first motoring journalist to own one. That honour was to go to lifetime Morgan enthusiast Bill Boddy, the editor of *Motor Sport*. Bill had been enthusiastic about the new Plus 4 at its debut at the 1950 Motor Show and, as he already had an order in at the Morgan factory, he was eagerly anticipating the delivery of his car. When he went to the factory to collect his Morgan on 15 December, he was disappointed to find he had one of the very last 4/4s, rather than his anticipated Plus 4. Although he described his new car, registration PPB 184, as virtually obsolete, it served him well until he lost some teeth on the gearbox constant mesh pinion – to find no new ones were available either at Morgans or at the Moss Gear Company. He found this somewhat surprising for a car only a few months old.

Meanwhile, the Morgan directors had realized how disappointed Bill was not to get a Plus 4, so they pushed his name forward on the order book for one of these cars. A delighted Bill Boddy finally collected his blue Plus 4, chassis number P2162, registration KAB 303, on a very hot 2 July.

By 2 September he had covered an eventful 4,000 miles, and he documented his experiences for the October edition of *Motor Sport*. Bill found his Plus 4 to be very good fun to drive, being remarkably handy in traffic, able to hold a speedometer to 65 mph indefinitely and possessing very good acceleration, cornering stability and brakes. However, it was not trouble free and Peter Morgan was later to remark to Joe Lowrey that Bill Boddy would make an excellent factory tester as everything that ever went wrong on a Plus 4 happened on Bill's car. Bill, of course, documented it all in *Motor Sport*.

After just 1,350 miles the clutch refused to free, necessitating an engine-out repair at Malvern and replacement of the bent clutch operating eye bolt. Early attempts to solve this problem were by using a stronger bolt of 3% nickel steel but finally, on new Morgans from chassis number P2306 despatched in January 1952, this bolt was to be enlarged from 3/8in. to 1/2in. BSF, and the problem was no more.

After 1,750 miles the offside steering damper sheared and 220 miles later it was followed by that on the nearside, giving the dreaded wheel shimmy at just under 40 mph. This violent shaking in turn caused the radiator to leak. Bill, rather surprisingly, put up with the wheel shimmy for some further 2,000 miles (on one occasion being stopped five times by police), before having the dampers replaced.

While the steering dampers generally worked well, the increased suspension travel of the Plus 4 over the 4/4 was reducing their life expectancy and it was then a front suspension strip down to replace them. Bill Boddy awaited a redesign with some impatience.

He was not alone in his condemnation of these dampers. Stanley Porter had had several break before he cured the problem by drilling four holes in the broken portion and joining it to the chassis between two pieces of 'Balata' flat belting.

The original design consisted of a flat strip of spring steel, which was drilled for the centre pin, with a phosphor bronze washer riveted to the underside. Thus, if they broke the whole suspension had to be stripped. It was not until production of chassis P2410 (in mid-1952) that the phosphor bronze washer alone went over the centre pin, with the fragile spring steel bolted to it. It was now a simple method of undoing bolts to replace a damper. Any rally driver worth his salt would now carry a few spares within his tool box.

Bill had other problems with his Morgan, albeit less important. The accelerator did not fully open, the choke stuck, a bonnet bracket had broken, and the windscreen wiper became too hot to touch, leaking grease when working. The silencer joints had also blown a little, but, all in all, he enjoyed the Morgan. It was, after all, the fastest sports car on the British market at the price and he had no plans to change it.

On 6 September, Worcestershire farmer John Moore collected his black Coupe, registration KNP 5, from the factory. This car, chassis number P2216, was to become a noteworthy competition Morgan on road, trials hill and track.

Nearing completion at the factory at this time was an experimental blue Coupe, chassis P2227, which had an extra two child seats in the rear. HFS Morgan was always looking for new models and the increased length of the Plus 4 chassis compared with the earlier 4/4 made the four-seater Coupe a feasible proposition. This prototype was registered KNP 152.

In Ireland the Irish Motor Racing Club organized the Wakefield Trophy Meeting on the long Curragh circuit in County Kildare on 8 September. There was just one race which was to be run as a handicap but there were also separate scratch classes within it and the event attracted Stanley Porter with his Plus 4, OZ 2343. The race was of thirty laps, giving a distance of 147½ miles for the scratch cars, these being two single-seater HWMs, a Maserati and an Alta. Stanley received four laps credit and 3½ min. start, but this was not sufficient to hold Stirling Moss, with an HWM, who dominated the race. Stanley finally finished eighth, in 1 hr. 58 min. 22.2 sec., an average speed of 65.10 mph.

On 9 September Jeff Sparrowe took JUO 177 to the BOC Prescott hill climb for the International Meeting. The Arnott supercharger had been refitted and a lightweight louvred bonnet was being used, with a scoop to direct air to the SU carburettor mounted on top of the blower.

After one practice run, as Jeff returned to the paddock and switched off, there was a sudden fire under the bonnet. Fortunately extinguishers were to hand and there was little damage. The cause was a leaking petrol pipe. Sadly the high tension leads were burnt and a persistent misfire put paid to Jeff's chances in the competitive runs, recording 58.28 sec.

Two weeks later, at Shelsley Walsh, on 22 September, it was the turn of the Plus 4s to contest the hills, with Doc Steel and Peter Morgan entered in the production car class from 1501 to 3000 cc. Doc Steel had regularly visited Shelsley as medical officer for the Midland Automobile Club, so it was surprising that he would only record 55.19 and 53.51 seconds on his two runs, whereas Peter Morgan was streets faster, with 49.14 and 48.98 seconds. Doc Steel's engine was always run unmodified, although regularly serviced at the Morgan factory, but he believes that both Jim Goodall and Peter had had their engines worked on and balanced. Peter refutes this, and maintains he was just lucky to have a good ex-factory engine. But a margin of five seconds!

JUO 177 on fire in the Prescott paddock.
(Photograph: Jeff Sparrowe collection)

The following day Jim Goodall was in action with his Plus 4 at the Hagley and District LCC speed trials at Westwood Park near Droitwich. Jim finished second in the class for 1500–3000 cc sports cars to Ken Rawlings famous Vanguard-engined special 'Buttercup', which was being driven by S. K. Ridley.

The next weekend saw the East Anglian CC's Clacton Rally attracting the rallying enthusiasts to a long-distance overnight event, although one section in the Peak District had to be cancelled because police feared local residents would have their sleep disturbed. A remarkable coincidence saw two Morgan 4/4s, driven by two brothers, Alan and Ken Hobbs tie for points for the novice's award, with Ken finally getting the verdict. Alan won the class for open cars up to 1300 cc and David Price with his Plus 4, WHX 280, came second to ADC Gordon's HRG in the 1301–2500 cc class.

Alan and Ken Hobbs came from Stroud in Gloucestershire. In 1948 Alan had purchased a black 1939 Climax-engined 4/4, GAE 705. His brother Ken had obtained a new blue Standard Special-engined Coupe, JAD 722, the following year but then replaced this with one of the few 1939 4/4s fitted with the same engine, this red two-seater carrying registration GBH 458. Both brothers were die-hard Morgan enthusiasts and, like many other enthusiasts living in this area, they became keen trials drivers.

On 6 October the largest crowd yet recorded at Castle Combe came to watch the Bristol MC and LCC's national race meeting. The only Morgan was that of Jeff Sparrowe but he entertained

Doc Steel readies himself for the start at Shelsley Walsh. (*Photograph: Doc Steel collection*)

the crowd in a manner in which he had not intended when an axle half shaft broke during practice at Paddock bend, a fast right-hander. Luckily no-one was behind him, and he was able to stop safely.

As a result Jeff decided to have his half shafts and front stub axles crack tested before the following season.

Jeff was now happily using a single downdraught SU type D3 carburettor, fed by twin SU electric fuel pumps. This entailed a modification to the induction manifold and the use of a Bowden cable as the throttle control.

One day later the Morgan 4/4 Club held their driving tests at Queensford Aerodrome, Dorchester on Thames. The event was won by Graham Stallard with his 1949 4/4, MKX 239, with John Sutton-Atkins second in his 1937 Climax 4/4, FPE 567, and Stan Dyke of Newcastle under Lyme came third with his four-seater, KKC 888, which used fashionable white-wall tyres.

The 1951 Motor Show was held during October and saw, at last, the full range of Plus 4 models being exhibited, the four-seater Plus 4 making its show debut this year (chassis number P2232). All of the show cars were fitted with Coventry radiators and had the new pattern drilled Dunlop wheels (type LP658), to be fitted to all production cars from P2275 onwards. These wheels also featured slots for snow grips.

Much attracted to the new four-seater Plus 4 was Peter Silcock who was in the hotel business in Bexley, Surrey. He went to see Peter Morgan, and when he confirmed that he definitely would use it in motor sport, Peter Morgan agreed to sell him a new four-seater, namely P2219, which he collected at the end of the show and drove home. It was ivory, with red leather upholstery and registered KNP 377.

Once again the *Daily Express* newspaper was to sponsor the MCC's three-day National rally, beginning on 7 November with starting points at

Plymouth, Manchester, Leamington Spa, Norwich, Cardiff, Glasgow, London and Harrogate. This year the Morgan factory team did enter, Peter Morgan being passengered by Sonny McCann, Jim Goodall by Terry Hall, and Doc Steel by Dr Gavin Scott all in their usual Plus 4s, JNP 239, HUY 982 and JWP537. There was a large entry of over seven hundred and all 450 places were soon taken. The Morgan team elected to start from Leamington Spa. There was one other Morgan entry starting from there, that of Bill Parkes, navigated by Peter Homes. No doubt Gavin Scott was pleased to see his old car once more. Because of the special twin-carburettor manifold on FNP 684, Bill was classified into the 'specials' class. Two other Morgans were competing the Standard Special-engined 4/4 of Derek Howard, navigated by Brian Jepson, starting from Harrogate, and the Plus 4 of J. S. Eynon, navigated by E. T. Fletcher, and entered from Cardiff.

Both Stuart Eynon and Edward Fletcher were keen aviators. The owner of the car, Stuart Eynon, had served as a pilot in the RAF during the war before joining his family's Swansea-based confectionery and restaurant business. He had wanted a Lea Francis but that company was in financial difficulties, so it was a black two-seater Plus 4 Coupe that he had purchased. This was chassis number P2142, registered HCY 155, and purchased from local car dealer Arthur Bennett Limited in May 1951.

The rally had road sections of over 1,200 miles, followed by driving tests at the finish in Hastings. Of the road section the final 582 miles followed a common route from Penrith but, before that stage, each starting point had its own route. The Leamington Spa route initially made for Southend, and Bill Parkes remembers being passed by two of the earlier starting factory Morgans, one of which had been delayed by clutch problems.

Unrelenting rain made the road section particularly difficult for those in open cars and the

Doc Steel setting off in the *Daily Express* Rally. (*Photograph: Doc Steel collection*)

Welsh sections were the worst, with much flooding, particularly on the road to Knighton. Bill Parkes watched a Ford Pilot get through the first road flood and decided to follow. Peter Homes, driving, took it very slowly in bottom gear, slipping the clutch and keeping good revs, but the fan drew the water up and threw it about, drowning the electrics. Poor Bill had to get out and push. Before the Morgan was out, the water was through the floor boards, but luckily two or three cylinders fired using the starter and away they went, passing many cars attending to various problems also caused by water. Bill believes the heat from the special exhaust manifold expansion chamber had been sufficient to dry the plug leads.

Once away Bill took his shoes off to try and thaw out but no sooner had he done so than they came to an even deeper flood, estimated by some as being some fifteen inches deep. Yet again Bill was made to get out and push, but this time the water rose to above seat level, giving poor Peter Homes an unpleasant time.

Doc Steel in the Plus 4 always rallied with an extension attached to the exhaust pipe, to prevent suffocation of the engine when in deep water and was not unduly troubled. It is likely, however, that this was the rally in which the five hundred cigarettes he was carrying on the rear seat of his four-seater fell into the footwell just before the deep bit, being well and truly ruined.

The cigarette disaster was to stimulate him into replacing the rear seat with a fabricated tray, which bolted to the seat pan and was supported by stays bearing on the floor. A 9in. front edge would in future keep items securely in place.

Cigarettes were of course medically and socially acceptable at this time and chain smoking was one recognized way of keeping awake while driving through the long night sections.

The floods caused other makes worse problems, the low built Jaguar XK 120s, for example, having the interior carpets floating around inside the car. Some thirty cars retired during this section.

Once through the floods the cars began unavoidably to weave from side to side on braking as the sodden brake linings took time to dry but all of the Morgans safely reached Hastings without penalty.

Navigation for the road sections in rallies was fairly amateurish in those days. Bill Parkes took the issued MCC route book, an AA Members road book, a small paper pad and a 6*d.* notebook in which he and Peter Homes had planned out their own detailed route and mileages. They had an extra watch for timings. The Morgan team would meet up before the rally at Peter Morgan's house at Braeside, Wych Road, Malvern, to plan their route and itinerary. Terry Hall, navigating for Jim Goodall, always carried two stop watches but even in later years never had the famous Halda system for calculating average speed in regularity sections. Jim and Terry formed an excellent partnership. Terry could always tell when Jim was over-tired – he would go fast, then slow then fast again. Terry then knew it was his turn to drive and often Jim would be asleep before the clutch was in. Terry would fold the windscreen flat and drive fast to keep awake.

When really tired in major rallies they would stop and lie down in the road for five to ten minutes and then set off more refreshed.

After the road sections there were just four driving tests left to sort out the winners (a regularity test during the road sections was scrapped because of criticism of the timings recorded). Sadly, many were caught out, including Doc Steel who failed to complete the pylon test correctly. Also Peter Morgan, who made an uncharacteristic error in the acceleration and braking test. Overall, however, the event proved successful for the Morgans. Jim Goodall had driven faultlessly throughout and won the class for open cars up to 3000 cc, with Doc Steel third. Bill Parkes finished second to Ken Rawlings 'Buttercup' in the specials class, and Derek Howard took the starting control award for Harrogate. Not a bad result for five Morgans in a rally of 450 competitors.

Derek Howard and Bill Parkes had demonstrated that the Standard Special-engined 4/4s were still a force to be reckoned with in rallies. News filtering through from Portugal revealed a further 4/4 success for Carlos Baeta in winning the 1,350 mile long Third Tour of Portugal, beating a Lancia and a Porsche into second and third places, the latter being a post-war newcomer to the ranks of the sports car.

The enthusiastic Morgan 4/4 Club ran a night

rally during 1 and 2 December. There were starting points based in Manchester, Gloucester and Hereford and the twenty-four starters then joined up for a common route into Lincolnshire and Derbyshire, before finishing at Leicester after three hundred miles.

A Daimler rather surprisingly took first place, but Stan Dyke claimed second in KKC 888 with Alan Hobbs third in CAE 705. The Morgan concours d'elegance trophy was taken by B. M. Lee's 1938 4/4.

Derek Howard continued his success by finishing second in his class in the Intervarsity Rally and then, on 9 December, in atrocious weather (rain, hail, snow and floods) he finished third in the Manchester University Yorkshire Cup Rally, behind two MGs. Over half the competitors failed to finish.

The competition year ended for Morgans with the traditional post-Christmas MCC Exeter Trial, beginning on Friday evening 28 December, and finishing in Bournemouth the following day. The usual Morgan works team was entered, Peter Morgan with the Coupe JNP 239, Jim Goodall with the two-seater, HUY 982, and Sonny McCann with Jim's old 4/4, BWP 47. Also competing were the 4/4s of Joe Huxham (FOH 812) and Paul Hughes (CAB 652) and also two Plus 4s, those of Peter Silcock and London Morgan agent Basil Roy, who traded from Great Portland Street.

Peter had found his four-seater, KNP 377, a bit of a handful on the poor-quality tyres of the time. As a result he had fitted oversize rear tyres to make it grip better. Jim Goodall spotted them on one occasion but luckily the scrutineers never did.

The night of 28 December was cursed with a ferocious storm, with flooding on some roads, and the observed sections were very greasy. The works team were fast and sure. All three took First Class Awards, and the MCC team

Joe Huxham coaxes FOH 812 up Cocknowle Hill in the Exeter. (*Photograph: Quadrant Picture Library*)

Sonny McCann with navigator Terry Hall on Fingle Bridge, BWP 47 having three-wheeler front wings. (*Photograph: LAT Photographic*)

championship. Paul Hughes took a Second, and the others Thirds.

Overseas

United States of America

In early 1951 Morgan Plus 4s began to appear in America, via two distributors, one on the west coast and the other on the east. The western distributor, Angell Motors of Pasadena, California, we have mentioned in the chapter on 1950.

The new distributor for the eastern half of the USA was Joe Ferguson, of New York City, who traded as Fergus Motors Inc., and he took his first cars, beginning with P2114, in February 1951. He was to remain a loyal agent for Morgans for the rest of his life (he died in 1967).

Joseph Bell Ferguson (known as J. B.) was the elder brother of Harry Ferguson, the tractor magnate, to whom we have previously referred. They were born (Joe in 1882) in Northern Ireland, south east of Belfast. Both trained as engineers, and Joe went into the motor trade in the early years of the twentieth century, his brother Harry coming to work for him.

In 1909 J. B. visited the USA for the first time seeking an American automobile to import to Northern Ireland to rival the Ford. He chose the Flanders, which was not a great success. While he was away his brother used his premises, from which he developed, constructed and eventually flew his own aeroplane.

Harry was to leave his brother's business and pursue his own desire to create the world's best tractor, also running a motor garage, which continued as the Belfast Austin agency into the 1950s.

J. B., on the other hand, wished to design the world's best automobile, a passion he retained all his life. In 1915 he built three running chassis of his own design, the 'Fergus', and one was shipped to New York for exhibition at the Grand Central Palace Motor Show in 1916 where it was very favourably received, being very advanced, including an overhead camshaft engine with hemispherical combustion chambers among other novel features.

The First World War put paid to any thoughts of production but after the Armistice Joe decided to continue his business and creative designing in the USA, emigrating and setting up business, initially in a Newark, New Jersey factory. He later moved to New York City.

J. B. started with dealerships in Plymouth and Desoto cars, later taking on the small American cars, the Bantam and Crosley. Prior to the Second World War, J. B. was dealing in British cars, namely Austin, Morris and Standards.

Following the Second World War, Fergus Motors handled Austin, Standard, Studebaker, Singer, Renault and Saab, as local dealer for New York City. In 1951 J. B. took on the twelve-state distributorship for Borgward, the German cars of Dr Carl Borgward, and he also began to handle Morgan sports cars, this time as the eastern distributor. The showroom was in Broadway, in the centre of New York City.

In the business with his father was Joe Ferguson Jnr. Recently he described his father as a hard-headed businessman who put his business, and his burning desire to build his special automobile, very much first, followed by his strong Christian religion – with his family an afterthought.

Unlike the Californian distributor, Angell Motors, Joe Ferguson was pleased to promote and advertize the newly imported Morgan. In various sports car race programmes, such as the programme for the Watkins Glen races on 15 September, there appeared adverts from Fergus Motors to attract budding motor sports enthusiasts for the Morgan.

The newly imported Morgan Plus 4 was also very competitively priced for the USA market, at the following prices, f.o.b. New York as of November 1951 indicated: Morgan Plus 4 $2,100, MGTD $2,125, Jowett Jupiter $2,850, Allard chassis $3,245, Porsche convertible $3,895, Jaguar XK 120 $3,945, Nash-Healey $4,000 approx., and Aston Martin DB2 convertible $5,800. Many enthusiasts began to try the 'best value for money' Morgan and considered using it competitively in the expanding number of races run for sports cars by the SCCA.

California, in particular, had ideal weather conditions for open air motoring, and sports cars became very popular there. Indeed, in 1947 Roger Barlow of International Motors, John Von Neumann of Competition Motors (VW and Porsche dealers) and Taylor Lucas had founded the California Sports Car Club (CSCC) to cater for sports car drivers. Their events were very popular.

One of the first Californians to compete with a Morgan Plus 4 was Leo Caton of Hollywood, who had previously been racing motorcycles for

Fergus Motors premises in New York. (*Photograph: Morgan Motor Co. collection*)

several years. One of his first competitive events with his two-seater was at the Sandberg hill climb organized by the Southern California Region of SCCA on 16 December. This event replaced one scheduled for October, but called off on the day by officers of the Highway Patrol. The half-mile hill climb was held on part of the Old Ridge Route, climbing through the Angeles National Forest fifty miles north of Los Angeles, and was a very 'clubby' affair complete with lodge at the top serving refreshments. Plenty of practice was allowed for the thirty-two entrants, at least three runs being undertaken by each competitor before the timed runs, and Leo Caton finished second with a time of 39.88 sec., behind a supercharged MGTC, in class 2 (1500–2000 cc). There was another Morgan competing – a British-registered three-wheeler F-Super, driven by Walker Edminson (reg. HVC 567).

Imports to the USA of Morgans for 1951 totalled forty-seven as interest in the marque began to develop. This should be put into context, however, by the 3,790 MGs imported in the same period.

Australia

The weekend of 24 and 25 February was a busy period for Western Australian motor sport enthusiasts, with the WA hill climb championship being held at Mundaring Weir on the Saturday, and a race meeting at Mooliabeenie on the Sunday. Many drivers from other States were also attracted – arriving early for the forthcoming Australian Grand Prix. There was no success for Colin Uphill at the first venue, but at the second he did taste success once more, for in the five-lap handicap he finished in first place.

Also competing at Mooliabeenie was another Standard-engined 4/4, that of Johnny Motteram, who finished fifth in the sports car trophy handicap. His lap times of 2.33 to 2.37 were some 15 seconds slower than Colin had recorded – pointing to the excellent work Colin had achieved in preparing his Morgan, its engine being kept in standard form apart from twin carburettors and extractor exhaust system. Johnny Motteram had been a keen motorcyclist, but his mother was not so keen and so she had bought him the Morgan to keep him off two wheels.

Johnny Motteram at Mooliabeenie. (*Photograph*: Daily News)

Colin Uphill at Mooliabeenie in his stripped and lightened 4/4. (*Photograph: Colin Uphill collection*)

The final event at Mooliabeenie was the ten-lap State road racing championship handicap. It was won by Syd Negus with his Plymouth Special, but, in second place, was the irrepressible Colin Uphill and his Morgan.

This year the State of Western Australia had the honour of holding the Australian Grand Prix, which was to be held as part of the Commonwealth Jubilee celebrations at Narrogin on 5 March. The well-established 2.2-mile round the houses circuit was doubled in length by adding a rectangular loop of existing roads to take the track out into the country. Forty-four entries were received, one being the Morgan of Colin Uphill, and another a Morgan Plus 4 for Bill Richards.

For the 24-lap (105.6 mile) race Colin was given 25½ minutes start over the scratch man, a visiting Scot named Colin Murray, driving a Maserati 6C. The Bill Richards' entry failed to start. Bill had actually entered on behalf of a young engineer named David Van Dal, but David had been called to an engineering meeting at Melbourne and had to withdraw.

Colin set off very well, and was still leading the field after five laps, but he then had to make an unscheduled five-minute pit stop, rejoining in fifth place. The problem had been a broken fuel line at a solderless nipple, which did not take long to fix once he had stopped. He continued once again, and now had an uneventful drive to the finish, finally finishing in ninth position overall, and sixth on handicap. The winner was Warwick Pratley's Ford V8-engined G Reed Special.

This was to be the last race for Colin Uphill's Morgan. He converted it back to completely standard trim, and sold it. Johnny Motteram was to purchase the 'go faster' twin Solex carburettors and special inlet and exhaust manifolds and lightened bodywork parts.

On 21 October the action returned to Mooliabeenie. In the ten-lap handicap for the Sunbeam-Talbot Trophy Colin Uphill was driving Bill Richards' demonstrator Plus 4, and Johnny Motteram his own 4/4. Only four cars completed the distance, one being Colin's Plus 4, which finished third. Johnny completed just two laps. The winner was Syd Negus' reliable Plymouth Special.

In the five-lap handicap race Colin finished sixth of the seven finishers. Johnny retiring after just three laps, but in the three-lap scratch race Johnny got his car to complete the distance and took the second place in the 1500 cc and below class, lapping just a second slower than the Plus 4, which finished sixth in the above 1500 cc class.

Six weeks later, on 9 December, a Picnic Meeting was held at Mooliabeenie combining several fun events with some racing. There were two Plus 4 Morgans entered, the demonstrator of Bill Richards, and the new red two-seater of David Van Dal, reg. 2–936, which he had purchased new from Bill's showroom. David was proud of his Morgan and kept it spotless. Initially he had no plans to race it, but talk in the bar with friends convinced him to enter a sports car race, so he had joined the WASCC and obtained a licence. He had to withdraw his entry from the Australian Grand Prix earlier, but had no excuse this time. He had made some padded covers to prevent any damage to the headlamps.

The first events were standing quarter mile sprints, David beating Bill's time of 20.15 seconds by nearly a second.

After some gymkhana type events came the proper races. The three-lap handicap had a massed start, fastest cars in front, and when handicaps were taken into account David discovered he had won this event from Sid Taylor's TS Special (Dodge-engined single-seater) although he did not cross the line first.

The five-lap handicap also used a massed start, and David nearly lost his Plus 4 in a 'whizzie' at the entrance to the straight. Again, when the handicaps were checked he had finished first, once more just in front of Sid Taylor.

There was also a scratch race of three laps, and David did not do badly in this either, finishing second although Sid Taylor took his revenge for earlier defeats by taking the spoils.

David had enjoyed his most successful racing debut. He was sad to find that the Morgan's radiator grill had been damaged by a flying stone, so he designed a mesh grill in a tubular frame to protect the radiator better for future races.

CHAPTER THIRTEEN

1952

1951 had been a good year for Morgans in motor sport, and many enthusiasts were keen to get hold of the rally-winning Plus 4. Times were still difficult, however, with the bulk of production bound for export at the Government's behest, and with the existence still of the BMTA's Covenant which restricted resale of new cars for two years. One way around the big delay in obtaining a new Morgan was to purchase a chassis and have it bodied locally. Several chassis were to be purchased for this purpose in 1952 by enthusiasts.

Fuel was still pooled, of just 72 octane, now some seven years after the end of the war, and this of course restricted engine development and the ability to tune.

As from late 1951 a new form of radiator grille was introduced, with the badge plate fixed outside the bars. One of the first to be despatched in this form was P2267, bound for Carr's Motors in Liverpool where it was to be prepared by Jimmy Ray for rallying for the 1952 season. Non rallying enthusiasts had thought Jimmy quite mad to exchange his prestigious Jaguar XK120 for the more basic Morgan, but rallying was Jimmy's passion and the Jaguar proved too much of a handful on foggy Welsh roads. Registered in mid-December 1951 as MLV 58, this green Morgan with distinctive red chassis was to become an impressive rally machine in Jimmy's hands.

Jimmy soon had the engine balanced at Laystall Engineering's Liverpool branch works, and while the engine was out, stronger clutch springs were also fitted. The traditional 'blow up' Moseley 'float on air' cushions on a wooden frame of the two-seater Plus 4 did not appeal to Jimmy, so he had some bucket seats upholstered locally at Len Dickinson's in Liverpool. Although these seats were somewhat heavier than the originals, Jimmy was keen to keep his Morgan light, so the floor boards were replaced with thinner plywood. A crude heater, manufactured from half-inch convoluted copper tubing taking water from the engine's cooling system was fastened along the bulkhead, and proved a boon for half-frozen navigators, who could rest their feet thereon, at least keeping these reasonably warm on winter nights.

Jimmy liked to focus the central spot lamp pointing downwards. It was then immensely useful when taking hump-backed bridges in the dark, giving advance warning of the direction taken by the road on the other side while the headlamps were still pointing uselessly at the sky. It was to become a 'trademark' for Jimmy's rally cars.

Several other Morgans were also acquired by keen rally drivers at the beginning of the year, the Plus 4 being the car to have.

We have previously mentioned the Reece cousins Peter and Jack. They were both very keen motoring sportsmen, and also directors of the Liverpool Ford agency, Blakes. Their rallying successes in Fords were noteworthy, so perhaps it was not surprising that with the RAC Rally approaching in March Jack Reece should receive a phone call from the Morgan Motor Company offering him and his cousin Peter their own Plus 4 Morgan, to be part of a second Morgan team entry for the RAC Rally. Jack was to be responsible for selecting other team members for a similar deal from the factory. With a plethora of rallying talent in the North West this was not too difficult. Bob Dickson, a Standard-Triumph dealer in Carlisle, and Dennis Done, another Standard Triumph dealer (Chester), agreed to complete the team. Perhaps there was some support by Standard-Triumph for these entries. Three chassis were ear-marked for their cars. P2315, P2318 and P2321. Two were to be despatched in chassis form to be completed locally, P2315 going to Davies Brothers in Chester on 6 February, for Dennis Done, and P2318 going to Carr's Motors in Liverpool on 14 February for the Reece cousins. The third chassis was to be completed at the Morgan factory (finally leaving for J. W. Hodgson & Company in Carlisle on 20

March) and was to become Bob Dickson's car. All three were registered by the Morgan factory on 12 March as KUY 474, 475 and 476 (chassis P2315, P2318 and P2321 respectively).

These three cars all received some aluminium panelling as part of the sheet metal work and were therefore known as lightweights. All three were to be painted ivory and, with red upholstery and wheels, they were to make a magnificent sight as a team.

Yet another North West motor trader to purchase a Morgan for rallying was Ken Bancroft, who ran the Premier Garage at Droylsden, Manchester. His Morgan, P2329, was despatched on 22 February, to the Manchester Morgan agents 'The Colmore Depot' and registered NTJ 943 on 1 March. Coloured green, this two-seater was fitted with Vanguard engine V216ME.

Built alongside Ken Bancroft's car within the Morgan factory had been chassis P2328, and this was to be Joe Lowrey's Morgan. During the long wait for the Morgan since placing the order in 1951, Joe had been debating the final colour scheme with the sales department. The factory standard colours of Nile Blue, British Racing Green, Black or Carnation Red, all with sensible black-coloured leather upholstery did not appeal, so finally the factory sent Joe the ICI paint colour card and asked him to choose his own. He chose grey, with red seats, and he collected his new Morgan on 26 February. It was registered KUY 284.

Also being completed in early 1952 was a new car for Peter Morgan. Peter was convinced he would do better in races and rallies with a two-seater rather than continuing to use the Coupe, but wanted something a little special. Investigations at Standard Triumph revealed they would let him have an experimental Vanguard engine equipped with developmental inlet manifolds suitable for twin SU Carburettors. This engine, number X540E (prefix X for experimental) had been built in 1950. We suspect it was one of the engines evaluated for the Triumph TRX, as shown at the Motor Show of that year (certainly X536E was), and as such would have produced circa 71 bhp at 4,200 rpm. Presumably it had been standing around at Standard Triumph's Banner Lane plant since those days.

The engine was fitted to chassis P2316, a green two-seater, which was registered KUY 387 on 29 February. Peter Knight of the SU Carburettor Company adjusted the jetting of twin SU carburettors for the factory.

The tuning of this special engine by the SU Company led to regular Le Mans racer Robert Lawrie being tipped off that it might be possible to enter a Morgan for this year's 24-hour race in June. Rob Lawrie ran a business in London supplying explorers and mountaineers with their specialized boots and clothing. Indeed he was to supply the following year's successful Everest expedition. Rob's personality and his life in the world of explorers gave him a wide circle of friends, and he could choose his teams to accompany him to the Le Mans from these. In 1949 he finished tenth in an Aston Martin, co-driven with Dr Dick Parker. In 1950 he was seventeenth in a Riley with Geoff Beetson, and in 1951 eleventh in a Jaguar XK120 with Ivan Waller as co-driver.

Rob made an approach to Morgan for a car for Le Mans and the factory agreed in principle to lend him one. As a result he was able to put in his entry just before the closure date of 29 February.

Back to the competitions of early 1952. Jimmy Ray took his rallying seriously, and rather than just use a friend as a navigator he preferred to pick an expert from among the talent within the very active Liverpool Motor Club, which was based around the Reece cousins. For a Yorkshire Rally in February, Jeff Dixon accompanied Jimmy, but was soon to regret it as the replacement plywood floor was not up to the job. Jeff went through it and had a very uncomfortable ride fending off melting snow coming in from below.

On 23 and 24 February the Cambridge University Automobile Club ran its Lent Term Rally, starting in bright clear weather in Leeds. The rally proved very tough, with no clean sheets from the fifty-four starters, but Derek Howard struggled through to win with his black 4/4 Coupe.

The same weekend saw Stanley Porter in action in his Plus 4, OZ2343, in the Newry MC's Spring Trial, which besides trials sections also included driving tests. He collected a First Class Award.

Stanley was back in action on 15 March, this time on the race track at Ards airfield for the opening meeting of the Irish season, organized by the 500 cc Motor Racing Club of Ireland. The open handicap event was split into four heats, two semi-finals of five laps and a final of ten laps and Stanley was entered in heat 2 in OZ 2343. In this heat he finished second to Robin Scott's Ford Special, and this was also the order after the semi-final. The final was also won by Scott, but this time Stanley finished third, behind Jimmy McKay's Ford Special.

The Bolton-le-Moors Car Club held its popular Bolton Rally and Driving Tests on 16 March, including thirteen timed tests and also a timed test on a skid pan! Jimmy Ray and Derek Howard excelled, Jimmy producing second f.t.d. on test 8 and Derek likewise on test 11, Derek finishing fourth overall to take a class award with his 4/4. Jimmy finished eighteenth in this star-studded event (139 competitors) and took a First Class Award also, being fourth in class. Biberfield's 4/4 finished down the field but fifteenth in class.

The following week Jimmy decided to replace the clutch operating eye bolt (fitted with 3/8in. 3% nickel steel originally) with the improved 1/2in. version now used by the factory, and this was despatched to him on 21 March. Jimmy was now preparing for the forthcoming RAC Rally, and this was just a precaution to prevent failure of this component.

The following day, 22 March, the English motor racing season opened at Goodwood with a BARC members meeting. A new chicane had been built beyond Woodcote corner somewhat narrowing the course. It was to become a favourite spot for photographers! Jeff Sparrowe entered with JUO 177 for the scratch race up to 1100 cc, and his Morgan was noted to have a stiffening strip beneath the track rod. The race was won by Mike Hawthorn's Riley, with Jeff third behind the other Riley of Len Gibbs.

Jimmy Ray in the Bolton Rally and driving tests. (*Photograph: Jimmy Ray collection*)

The 1,800 mile RAC International Rally this year was held between 31 March and 5 April, with competitors starting at Hastings and Scarborough. The finish was to be at Scarborough, and there were 242 starters, of which nine entered Morgans, all Plus 4s.

As usual the works Morgan team consisted of Peter Morgan, passengered this time by his wife Jane, Jim Goodall with Terry Hall and Doc Steel with his son Robin Steel. Peter was in his twin-carburettor Vanguard special-engined two-seater, KUY 387, Jim in HUY 982 and Doc Steel in his four-seater, JWP 537. The team carried reversing lights to deal with night-time driving tests (strictly speaking illegal lighting at this time).

The other semi-official works team of the three lightweight ivory and red two-seaters, KUY 474, 5–6, were driven by their owners Dennis Done, Peter Reece (navigated by cousin Jack) and Bob Dickson. Also entered was Jimmy Ray with MLV 58, Ken Bancroft with NTJ 943, and Dave Price with WHX 280.

The conditions were somewhat wintry for the Hastings starters as they battled through snow drifts with the help of snowploughs, to meet up with the Scarborough starters at Silverstone. Sadly, on arrival, they discovered the Silverstone speed test had been cancelled because of the weather, leaving somewhat disgruntled competitors to make for Castle Combe for the night-time driving test. Fastest here was Ken Bancroft, with Peter Morgan also good.

In freezing conditions and strong winds the competitors moved on into Wales for a speed test at Llandulas over the 2.2-mile military road on Mount Eppynt, with passengers carried. Peter Reece and Doc Steel were good performers here.

The route now passed through Llandrindod Wells to Bwlch-y-groes and on to Blackpool for a 'scissors' test. This time it was Jim Goodall who

Jeff Sparrowe goes wide at Goodwood chasing eventual winner Mike Hawthorn, and Len Gibbs, both in Rileys. (*Photograph: Jeff Sparrowe collection*)

starred, Ken Bancroft also doing well. After a night's sleep it was on in to the Lake District for three non-stop sections, and it was Ken Bancroft who was leading the rally overall on arrival in Edinburgh after an excellent drive.

The following morning the entrants left Edinburgh for the famous Rest-and-be-Thankful speed hill climb.

Peter Morgan was fastest here in his class, but Ken Bancroft still led the rally overall despite the radiator boiling, this being put down to a suspect head gasket.

The route now took the competitors to the finish at Scarborough, where the first thirty-six were to undertake further speed regulating tests on Oliver's Mount over the following day to decide the overall winners.

Having successfully disputed their given time for the Rest-and-be-Thankful hill climb the Reece cousins luckily managed to join the other selected competitors for the Oliver's Mount deciding tests.

When it was all over, it was Goff Imhof's Cadillac-engined Allard J2, followed by three Jaguar XK120s that took the open class. Peter Reece finished fifth, just ahead of Peter Morgan. Ken Bancroft managed to finish tenth, just ahead of Jim Goodall. Jimmy Ray was 13th, Dennis Done 18th and Doc Steel 19th. Bob Dickson finished 37th and Dave Price was 39th. The all-important team prize did go to the works Morgan team, however, for the second year in a row – a tremendous achievement for the Malvern factory.

The Malvern Urban District Council was very impressed, and duly arranged to hold a dinner in honour of the team at the Malvern Winter Gardens on 8 May.

The ivory and red Morgan team of Reece, Done, and Dickson had also impressed everyone who saw them during the rally, driving throughout as a team in close formation. Even their performance was not perfect, however, as on one occasion they arrived at a road junction one behind the other only for each to disappear up a different exit road! We think these three Morgans were all fitted with separate red bucket seats, a non-standard fitment.

Ken Bancroft leads the rally competitors through Thirsk towards Scarborough. (*Photograph: Quadrant Picture Library*)

Jimmy Ray on Oliver's Mount. The special front seats are visible. (*Photograph: Jimmy Ray collection*)

On 6 April, the day after the RAC Rally finished Jeff Sparrowe continued to uphold the merits of the 4/4 by taking the under 1100 cc open class at the BARC's Brunton hill climb in Wiltshire with a time of 34.9 seconds, some 10 seconds faster than the second-placed Singer.

There were seven Morgans entered for the Easter MCC Lands End Trial, starting on Good Friday 11 April. Excellent weather led to fifty-eight of the 144 cars starting claiming Premier Awards after Bluehills Mine had been excluded from the results, including all the Morgans except L. Sandercocks Climax-engined 4/4 which sadly retired. The victorious Morgans were those of Joe Huxham, with FOH 812, Basil Roy and Peter Silcock with Plus 4s, and the factory team of Peter Morgan, Jim Goodall and Sonny McCann. No doubt the last two named were in their usual cars, HUY 982 and BWP 47 respectively, but Peter now had a choice of KUY 387 or JNP 239 and we are unsure which he used. The Morgan team also proved victorious in the team competition, collecting the one-make team prize.

Jeff Sparrowe was racing at Castle Combe on

Joe Huxham climbs Beggars Roost on his way to a Premier Award in the Lands End Trial. (*Photograph: Quadrant Picture Library*)

Easter Saturday at the Bristol MC and LCC's meeting. In the six-lap sports car event he had little opposition in JUO 177, and beat Parker's Riley by over a minute. All racing drivers for this season had to wear approved crash helmets in the interest of safety.

Also starting on Easter Sunday was the Ulster AC's Circuit of Ireland rally, which covered a strenuous one thousand miles over four days, including driving and regularity tests. Joe Lowrey had entered in KUY 284. He started off well and in the regularity test held on the second day Joe put up the best performance in the open car class, but then began to slip down the order as tiredness took a hold. After the finish it was a ferry boat to the mainland and then a fast overnight drive to London – to clock in for work, this being the third night without sleep for Joe and his navigator.

The London Motor Club ran two popular rallies for the enthusiast, these being the London Rally, and the 'Little Rally', the latter being a days rallying in Surrey and Hampshire. One hundred and fifty entries were received for this event held on 19 April, including many of the top British drivers. When the results were announced the

Jeff Sparrowe cuts the corner closely at Castle Combe. (*Photograph: Jeff Sparrowe collection*)

Plus 4 Coupe of P. G. Mallam, navigated by M. A. Taylor, had won the Club Challenge Trophy.

Stanley Porter entered his Plus 4, OZ 2343, for possibly its last appearance in his hands for the Cairncastle hill climb in Co. Antrim organized by the 500 Motor Racing Club of Ireland on Saturday 3 May. He also had entered his 4½ litre Invicta in the same class, for cars other than racing cars of over 1750 cc and proved invincible in this, with the Morgan third behind a Jaguar.

During his ownership of the Plus 4 Stanley had achieved many excellent motor sport results. He had not been a fan, however, of the flexible rubber engine mountings for the Vanguard engines, and had replaced them following an Irish race in which excessive engine movement broke through a radiator hose, losing him a certain place.

He replaced the front mountings with those from a Jeep, and the rears from a Morris Commercial. This claimed the additional benefit of being able to use a steel front exhaust pipe rather than the standard flexible type, which was prone to leaks. He believed flexible engine mountings to be 'just another Americanism' that had unfortunately become accepted in England.

Once again the *Daily Express* newspaper sponsored the BRDC International Trophy Meeting at Silverstone, which was held on 10 May. There were several changes to the event this year, including the previously one-hour sports car races now being limited to seventeen laps of the outer-circuit for the larger capacity classes, and sixteen laps for the smallest class, cars of 1101–1500 cc. Unlike previous years there was no under 1100 cc class. The Le Mans start was still being used.

Just one Morgan had entered – Jeff Sparrowe

Derek Howard lifts the dust during the Morecambe Rally. (*Photograph: National Motor Museum*)

Ken Bancroft and his Morgan receive some admiring looks by winning the Morecambe Rally. (*Photograph: Quadrant Picture Library*)

with JUO 177, his opposition in the up to 1500 cc class being an Austin A40, two Cooper-MGs, two Lester-MGs and three Jowett Jupiters.

It was two of the MGs that took the lead in the class at the start, but Jeff kept ahead of the others, including the Jupiters. Then Jim Mayer's Lester-MG blew its engine comprehensively at Stowe corner, sending competitors spinning in all directions on its oil. At the finish the class was won by Cliff Davis in his Cooper MG, in 37 min. 2 sec., followed home by Gerry Ruddock's Lester-MG, George Phillips' Jupiter and then Jeff's Morgan. Overall Jeff was in twenty-first place out of the twenty-six finishers from the thirty-two starters, the winner being Stirling Moss in a C-Type Jaguar.

Glorious weather accompanied nearly three hundred competitors in the Lancashire Automobile Club's Morecambe National Jubilee Rally, held from 16 to 18 May. Starts were held at Birmingham, Bristol, Leeds, London, Manchester, Whalley and Glasgow, and the event attracted entries from the drivers of three Plus 4s, and seven 4/4s running in separate classes. Some confusion was caused by Derek Howard taking part in his new all black Plus 4, two-seater (registered as CJX 318 on 9 May), when he had actually entered his previous black 1949 4/4 Coupe. This brought the Plus 4 contingent up to four.

Ken Bancroft was driving NTJ 943, Peter Reece KUY 475, and Jimmy Ray MLV 58, and they had also entered as a Morgan team. Within the 4/4s, the 1937 Climax car of G Barker and the very late 1951 Standard-engined car of J. Smith were in the Knowldale Noggins team, along with Clarke's Alvis. The other 4/4s were the 1936 Standard-engined car of J. M. Williams (presumably a re-engined car), Merton Biberfield's 1949

1267 cc 4/4, F. C. Cole's 1098 cc Climax-engined 1936 car (also presumably re-engined) and F. G. Hill's 1949 1267 cc car.

After the first day the four Plus 4s were all leading the class for sports cars of 1301–3000 cc, Ken Bancroft being ahead of Peter Reece, Derek Howard and Jimmy Ray. The glorious hot weather was causing major problems for many of the other competitors who suffered boiling radiators and fuel vaporization problems on the long ascents of the Lake District passes. The Saturday was especially hot, and when the cars returned to Morecambe for the final test, the Morgans had confirmed their complete domination of the event. Ken Bancroft had made up for his disappointment in the RAC Rally by finishing first overall, collecting the Morecambe and Heysham Challenge Trophy.

He also took home the Morecambe and Lancaster Challenge Trophy for the best performance by an open sports car. Over twenty XK120 Jaguars had also taken part, so this was a considerable achievement.

Peter Reece took the class award with KUY 475 but the Morgan team just failed to take the team award (having been leading after the first day), this going to the three MG TDs of the BARC. The MGs also took the 1300 cc sports car class ahead of the 4/4s.

The same weekend also saw the speedmen in action. On the Saturday (17 May) Jeff Sparrowe contested the five-lap scratch race for sports cars of up to 1100 cc at the BARC Ninth Members Meeting at Goodwood. A depleted field saw Jeff finish third, behind Len Gibbs' Riley and R. Watling-Greenwood's RWG. In the programme the Morgan is said to have been green – it was probably JU0 177 which ran in that colour for a while, or less likely the Le Mans Morgan.

On the Sunday the speedmen moved to Prescott for the BOC National hill climb. Just one Morgan was entered, Bill Parkes' 4/4 FNP 684. He recorded 57.69 sec., finishing fifteenth in the class for up to 1500 cc unsupercharged or 1100 cc supercharged, the winner being Gerry Ruddock with his Lester-MG in 51.20 seconds.

While Joe Lowrey had been very pleased with his Plus 4 he felt the back axle was unnecessarily of too low a ratio for the characteristics of the Vanguard engine, which was not designed for operating at high engine speeds. When he learned that a 3.73 to 1 crown wheel and pinion had been developed by Salisbury to fit the forthcoming Le Mans entry and was to be made available as an alternative for new Plus 4s, he arranged for one to be fitted to his own car KUY 284. It returned to the factory for this to be done on 20 May, and while the car was there Joe had the steering dampers replaced with the latest easily replaceable style.

Trials with the Le Mans entry at MIRA had highlighted the inadequacy of the normal back axle ratio for sustained high-speed running, as required for the long Mulsanne straight at Le Mans. Indeed Rob Lawrie would have preferred an even higher ratio than the 3.73 to 1 but Salisbury had nothing suitable. This ratio came from a 41-tooth crown wheel and an 11 tooth pinion (3.727 to 1).

Bill Parkes entered the Maidstone and Mid-Kent MC's Silverstone meeting, held in glorious weather on 24 May, but was forced to retire from the seven-lap scratch race for sports cars up to 1500 cc with flooding petrol and overheating oil, the event being won by Peter Gammon's special-bodied MG.

The same weekend the BARC's Yorkshire Centre ran its Scarborough Rally. Jimmy Ray, with MLV 58, beat Ken Bancroft with NTJ 943 to win his class. These two, together with Bob Berry's XK120 Jaguar, took the team award with their Red Rose team entry.

The Morgan 4/4 Club ran a Spring Road Rally on 25 May, attracting several club members for an enjoyable event. It was won by Les Newey in his 4/4.

The event was notable, however, for the appearance of a rather special Plus 4 – that of Barrie Phipps, whose family ran a fruit canning business near Pershore in Worcestershire. Obtaining a new Morgan was not easy, so Barrie's father purchased just a chassis. He was friendly with the owner of Black & White Garages at Harvington near Evesham, and he arranged with them for Radpanels, who produced the bodies for Dellow Motors, the manufacturers of Dellow trials cars, to body the car. As such it had a tubular steel body frame, with aluminium panels and normal

Morgan steel wings. This four-seater was registered KU7 714 on 9 April 1952 and given to Barrie as a twenty-first birthday present. It was painted pale green, with dark green wings.

Another new Morgan, this time produced completely at the factory, was a leaf green two-seater, chassis P2395, registered KWP 127. It was purchased by Basil de Mattos of Laystall Engineering in London, and he took it down to these works in May for the engine to be given the Laystall treatment (balanced and blueprinted). Somewhat to his annoyance he found that even after all this treatment the engine (V259ME) would only just produce the 68 bhp claimed by the Standard Motor Co. for normal units.

Also finishing on 25 May was the Lisbon Rally over in Portugal, which had attracted several British entries among the ninety-eight starters, there having been a London start point (on 20 May). The route near Porto became particularly difficult among the mountains, with many time controls to catch out those having problems. Upon arrival at Estoril there was a special test in which the two leading Porsche 356s of Noguiera and Martorell recorded the best times. Third in the test, though, was the impressive Plus 4 of D. Magalhaes. The final test consisted of a regularity test over the 1½ mile Estoril circuit and the results confirmed the success of the Porsches. Fifth overall was D. Magalhaes, and he also beat the Aston Martin DB2 of Hansen to clinch the class for cars up to 3,000 cc.

Six Morgans were entered for the MCC's second Edinburgh Rally, held over the Whitsun holiday period on Friday 30 and Saturday 31 May. The Morgan factory team consisted of Peter Morgan, Jim Goodall and Sonny McCann, all in Plus 4s. Jim Goodall was in HUY 982, and Sonny McCann had borrowed Doc Steel's four-seater, JWP 537. Peter Morgan could have been in either JNP 239 or KUY 387 (we have yet to identify which car he used). Completing the Morgan entries were Basil Roy and Peter Silcock in their Plus 4s and Merton Biberfield with his 4/4.

Eighty-seven cars converged on Harrogate after the overnight runs from the three starting points at London, Bristol and Buxton, then making for the Pennines for the first driving tests, the works team being particularly impressive here. Further tests followed as the route wound on to the finish at Edinburgh for the final test in which Peter Morgan and Jim Goodall were fastest overall. When the results were announced Peter Morgan and Jim Goodall had won First Class Awards, with Peter also taking the class award. Second Class Awards were taken by Merton Biberfield and Basil Roy, with Sonny McCann collecting a Third. The team award naturally went to the Morgan team.

On Whit Monday, 2 June, the BARC held an international meeting at Goodwood, but the rather sparse programme attracted just one Morgan entry – that of Jeff Sparrowe with JUO 177 for a seven-lap sports car handicap race. Sadly, JUO 177 was off form and the race was taken by Lamb's Healey Silvertone from Jim Mayer's Lester-MG.

Jeff's Morgan now had rather weird looking bonnet scoops fitted to the front of the lightweight bonnet, the idea being to direct cool air on to the supercharger when fitted. The bonnet was also propped open about ½in. at the front for the same reason. Jeff had been running unsupercharged in this event, however.

The Royal Scottish Automobile Club's Tenth Scottish Rally also began on Whit Monday, continuing over 1,058 miles until the finish at the club's headquarters in Glasgow on the Thursday. There were just two Morgans within the ninety-eight entries for the event. Jimmy Ray was in his Plus 4, MLV 58, as usual, and Edinburgh motor sport enthusiast, William Kerr Stewart, was competing in a Plus 4 as well. He was also a member of the Scottish Motor Racing Club's team, with Hughes' Allard and Herrald's MG Y type.

The first day took the competitors from Glasgow to Inverness, by way of a timed ascent of Rest and Be Thankful, and a restart with acceleration test on Cairn O' Mount. There were twelve competitors in the open class for 1301–2200 cc and when William Stewart came into Inverness he had scored the maximum possible forty marks for these two tests, thereby leading the class at the end of the first day.

On the Tuesday the route started and finished in Inverness but was noted for a test at

Aultnamain in which the competitors were required to average 32 mph for thirteen miles. Once again Stewart finished the day with a maximum score.

The cavalcade set off to the south west on the Wednesday with an acceleration, braking and reversing test in the grounds of Taymouth Castle, before the day's journey finally finished at Oban. Jimmy Ray did well in this, and began to creep up the class positions, while William Stewart had an indifferent day, although he still led the class, tying now with Murray's Frazer Nash Le Mans Replica.

The final day's journey back to Glasgow included Campbeltown circuit, Inveraray and Rest and Be Thankful, but the latter was now tackled downhill, with a braking test initiated by a traffic light being changed to red. Again Jimmy Ray was on form, but when the results were announced the following day it was William Stewart who had hung on to the class award, with Jimmy Ray third, behind the Frazer Nash. Stewart's team, the Scottish Motor Racing Club, was also victorious in the team competition.

On 7 June The Eight Clubs (Hants & Berks MC, Harrow CC, Cemian CC, Chiltern CC, 750 MC, Lagonda Club, Lancia MC & AC Owners Club) ran a race meeting at Silverstone using the reorganized Club circuit of 1.608 miles. It used the outer circuit from Woodcote through Copse and Maggotts to a sharp bend at Becketts from whence a runway was taken back to Woodcote once more. Two Morgan Plus 4s were entered, those of londoner A. J. Range of the Cemian CC and A. R. Morton of the 750 MC.

In the one-hour high-speed trial for 1501–3000 cc cars Range's Plus 4 (reg. XMY 238) was one of only four cars to complete the required thirty-two laps (51.46 miles), the others being a supercharged Alfa Romeo, a 2½ litre Riley and a similarly-engined Healey.

A. R. Morton's first event was a five-lap handicap where he was given 45 seconds start over the two scratch Jaguars but the race was won by the two 1½ litre HRGs of John Gott and Nancy Mitchell, with Morton third in his Plus 4, LWK 517.

This Plus 4 two-seater had been delivered to

The start of the one-hour high-speed trial, with Range's Plus 4 looking rather odd with painted wings and no headlights. (*Photograph: Guy Griffiths*)

the Coventry Motor Mart on 28 December 1951, being purchased new from there by A. Morton, who was a local enthusiast. The car carried chassis number P2287.

Two races later came a five-lap scratch race and both Morgans were entered, but again it was the HRGs that proved victorious. This time the Le Mans lightweights of David Blakely and Mrs Bluebelle Gibbs beat Morton into third place again.

The final race to feature a Morgan in this well-organized event was another five-lap handicap, but this time an Allard took the spoils from Peter Gammon's well-sorted MG which had started on scratch. Finishing fourth was the Plus 4 of A. J. Range.

Range's Morgan had left the Morgan factory on 19 September 1951 as one of two rolling chassis collected by North London dealers Motourists Ltd. Range's car, P2224, was then bodied as a four-seater, while the other, P2222, was to become Bernard Clarke's Plus 4, PKK 769, although for some reason it was nearly a year before the latter was completed.

While these Plus 4s were circulating Silverstone a group of 4/4 Club members had travelled to Queensferry for the Chester MC's half-mile sprint on Summers Steelworks Drive. Bill Parkes did best, recording 33.8 sec. with FNP 684, to finish fourth equal in the up to 1500 cc class. Bill Allarton managed 37.0 sec. with EAX 377, and Stan Dyke's 1949 4/4, KKC 888, clocked 38.2 sec. Also competing was Peter Reece's petite wife Doreen in their Plus 4, KUY 475, clocking 31.6 sec.

The Le Mans 24-hour race was to be held on Saturday and Sunday 14 and 15 June. Rob Lawrie had chosen his friend John Isherwood as his co-driver (he had been with his team's Le Mans entries in 1949 and 1950 but had not driven there before). Testing at MIRA had caused Rob Lawrie some concern about the back axle ratio, as we have previously mentioned, and also allowed John Isherwood to undertake some speed tests on the straight. However, he mistook the cone markers and started to decelerate in the wrong place, rather upsetting the rest of those present!

All entrants had to use the same fuel – 80 octane petrol (containing 15% alcohol and 10% benzole), restricting any possible tuning. This fuel was to be supplied by the organizers at the circuit.

The regulations for the race allowed pit stops for refuelling, for oil and for water, no more frequently than every twenty-eight laps (243 miles). Presumably an enlarged fuel tank was therefore fitted to the Le Mans entry by the Morgan factory. The Morgan was also fitted with two large regulation fuel fillers on the tail that would allow the regulation lead seals to be fitted. It was to be prepared for the race by Rob's engineering brain Ivan Waller. He was concerned that the radiator might lose water through the overflow pipe, so he arranged for a pipe to conduct the overflow to a bottle on the passenger seat, an early concept of a sealed system. A wire mesh stone guard replaced the normal slatted sort, to protect the radiator further. It appears that the engine oil filler was extended to protrude through the bonnet, allowing easy replenishment, the bonnet itself being held shut by two bonnet straps. Quite which factory car Rob took to Le Mans we have not been able to prove conclusively. However, we do know that it was green, that it had twin carburettors and had taken part in other rallies and trials, so we suspect it was Peter Morgan's own car, KUY 387.

John and Rob drove down to Le Mans in the Morgan together. Rob had many friends to meet on the way, virtually making it a holiday, taking his time to reach the circuit and enjoying much French food on the two-day journey! Within his team of helpers was Ivan Waller as above, helped by Kevin Walton, an engineering officer from the Royal Navy. In charge of time keeping was mathematician Ian Hogg, who was completely unflappable and had a dry sense of humour.

After scrutineering, the nominated drivers were required to undertake night practice on the circuit, which was closed for the purpose on three nights between 10 p.m. and 2 a.m. (during the day anyone could drive on the roads, which added to the fun). Ivan accompanied John so that he could tell him of braking, gear change points etc., the aim being consistent lap times. John's practice was enlivened by the throttles sticking open just after the Dunlop bridge on the downhill approach to the Esses, but as the same thing had already happened to Rob he knew to drive on the ignition switch.

For the race itself it was decided each driver would do four-hour shifts, with Rob Lawrie undertaking the start as he was the more experienced of the two. The Automobile Club d'Ouest had set a minimum distance for the Morgan to cover before being eligible for index of performance awards of 209 laps (2,819 km).

At 4 p.m. on 14 June Rob Lawrie sprinted across the track by the pits to the waiting Morgan for the Le Mans start. He got away without problem and settled down to his four hours of driving consistent lap times.

Sadly, however, the Vanguard engine was not up to the strain of endurance racing, and Rob was forced to stop on the corner just beyond the pits after around twenty laps with the Morgan clouded in oil smoke, making expensive sounding noises. It turned out that a valve head had broken off, in turn breaking a piston, so the Morgan was out of the race.

Poor John Isherwood was denied, therefore, his moment of glory driving in a Le Mans 24-hour race as the disaster happened before the first pit stop and driver change. Indeed this was to be a rather sad finale to Rob Lawrie's series of Le Mans drives, for he raced there no more.

On Saturday 21 June heavy rain storms and long periods of drizzle did not help the competitors racing on the short triangular circuit at The Curragh in Ireland. Competing in the first heat of the car handicap was Bill O'Brien who impressed all, his 4/4 being amazingly steady in the atrocious conditions. In the final it was Frank Bigger with his XK 120 that stormed through the field to win.

A popular form of enjoyable low key competition driving was to enter a driving test, and the Lancia MC's team driving tests were particularly enjoyable, with each entered one make team

Rob Lawrie gets away at the start of the Le Mans 24 hour race. A 2½ litre Ferrari is alongside, in front of a Lancia and several Renault 4 CVs are visible behind. (*Photograph: Louis Klemantaski*)

setting one of the tests. The Morgan 4/4 Club entered three teams each of three cars for this event held on 22 June at Bovington Aerodrome. The 'A' team included Graham Stallard driving his newly purchased ex-factory car, CAB 652, Paul Hughes, its previous driver, having left employment at the Morgan factory during May to seek his fortune elsewhere. The other two team members were Bill Parkes, with FNP 684, and Stan Dyke with KKC 888. This latter Morgan had been purchased for Stan and his sister to share, by their father in Liverpool in 1950, but Stanley was able to buy out his sister during 1952 when she got married. This 1949 Standard-engined four-seater always looked impressive – in club events the previous year it had even sported whitewall tyres.

The 'B' team contained the cycle-winged 4/4 of Bill Allarton (EAX 377), the 4/4 Coupe (FOE 547) of Warwick garage owner John McDonagh and John Sutton-Atkins with FPE 567.

The 'C' team entry of the 4/4 Club consisted of Miss Aileen Jervis with her Le Mans replica JTT 703, which she had run unsupercharged since November 1950, Ernest Cox with his two-seater EXJ 867, sporting aero screens, and Pat Otterway with his 4/4, FBT 246.

Morgans were particularly suitable vehicles for driving tests as the results demonstrated, with the 'A' team winning the event, the B team finishing runners-up and the 'C' team not far behind in sixth place. In the individual classification Graham Stallard and Bill Parkes were third equal, just pipping Stanley Dyke, who was fifth.

It had not seemed so rosy just before lunch, when Bill, having just finished a reversing test, discovered his gear lever stuck in reverse. Lunch was abandoned and with the help of several club members, in particular John McDonagh, the lid was removed from the gearbox; three people levered on an impressively long screwdriver provided by John until eventually, with a loud bang, the gear disengaged and all was well once more.

When *Autosport* appeared at the newsagents on 27 June it contained an advert from Jeff Sparrowe offering his famous 4/4 JUO 177 for the price of £750, reflecting its success and the amount of preparation he had put into it. Jeff failed to sell

Rob Lawrie at speed. The radiator overflow pipe can be seen protruding from the rear of the bonnet, and passing into the passenger compartment, where it entered a reservoir bottle on the seat. (*Photograph: Louis Klemantaski*)

The victorious 'A' team at Bovington. (*Photograph: Stanley Dyke collection*)

it, and its racing career in his hands was to continue for a while longer.

On Saturday 28 June the Midland Motoring Enthusiasts Club ran their Silverstone meeting, and both Bill Parkes (FNP 684) and Bill Allarton (EAX 377) decided to have a go.

Bill Allarton found himself up against just two other starters in the five-lap scratch race for sports cars up to 1100 cc. Underwoods ex-Gerard TT Riley led until Bill took the lead on the inside at Woodcote. A neck-and-neck battle between these two then enthralled the spectators, with Bill proving the winner. Len Gibbs' Riley, which had started slowly, finished third.

In the five-lap scratch race for up to 1500 cc

Bill Parkes suffered plug trouble and had to retire, the race going to Peter Gammon's amazing MG.

Two six-lap sports car handicaps closed the days racing, and Bill Parkes made up for his previous disappointment by finishing third, Peter Gammon's MG once again the victor.

Bill Allarton wins at the MMEC Silverstone meeting. (*Photograph: Stanley Dyke collection*)

On Friday and Saturday 11 and 12 July the South Wales AC ran their seventh Welsh Rally, attracting one hundred and five competitors who started from either Tenby, Shrewsbury, Cardiff or Cheltenham. Jimmy Ray was navigated by Ian Hall for this event. He finished as a member of the winning team in the team prize competition, along with Peter Reece in a Ford Zephyr and John Cunningham in a Jaguar XK 120. In the under 1500 cc open car class Ken Hobbs came second in GBH 458 to Ridley's MG.

Winning the Cheltenham start award was a new name among the Morgan Plus 4 drivers, that of Geoff White whose family were Birmingham funeral directors. Geoff himself at this time was an apprentice in the motor trade, and he had purchased a red Plus 4, registered MOH 453,

Jimmy Ray, with Ian Hall navigating, tackle the final tests of the Welsh Rally at Cardiff. (*Photograph: National Motor Museum*)

Geoff White doing the Aberystwyth tests of the Welsh Rally. (*Photograph: Charles Dunn*)

from the Colmore Depot (Birmingham Morgan agents). This was chassis number P2202, which left the factory on 23 August 1951.

For this event he was passengered by his sister Pat, but over-exuberance in the final tests in Cardiff caused him to bend the front lower crosshead tube back under frantic braking. Despite the wheel being slightly out of alignment he finished the event and drove home, where the crosshead was put right and sleeved to make it stronger. The bent tubular bracing strut leading from the chassis to the bottom of the kingpin was also replaced by a length of duralumin 'angle iron' which Geoff believed was a better alternative to the component fitted at Malvern.

Being a keen motor enthusiast, Geoff was also to fit a hand throttle to the dashboard of his car, additional to the usual foot pedal. This was to help with driving tests. He also fitted a rather ingenious rear reversing light. This was made from a fog lamp let into the rear spare wheel's hub cap, and having 72 watt power, achieved by coupling both filaments of a 36/36 watt headlamp bulb together. The bulb was also shot blasted to give a good spread of light behind the car.

Also starting on 11 July was the 1952 version of one of the most famous Continental rallies – the Alpine, organized by the AC de Marseille et Provence. Attracting only the very best and bravest drivers, it took the form of a fast road race over Alpine mountain passes. Many had narrow, unmade roads with loose stony surfaces, still open to ordinary traffic, and often with unguarded sheer drops to rocks on one side for the unwary.

The daily stages were of 300–400 miles, allowing little time for food or rest. Temperatures varied from scorching heat in the Côte d'Azur to the chill of 7,000 ft. passes. The start was from Marseilles and the event raced through southern France and into Italy, Austria and Switzerland before finishing on Wednesday 16 July at Cannes, some two thousand miles later. Engine and chassis parts were marked to prevent any substitutions and only those wheels and tyres carried on the car at the start could be used.

Four Morgans had entered. One was the black Plus 4 of Derek Howard. Derek had been fascinated by the Provence area of France since reading an enjoyable book on this region. When, at a local Yorkshire BARC meeting, racing driver Tommy Wise mentioned that he was going to drive a Jowett Jupiter in this year's event Derek decided he too would have a go. He began preparation of the Plus 4 – the number plate he felt would impede the flow of cooling air to the sump and brakes, so it was removed and the registration number, CJX 318, painted on the nearside front wing. A protective metal sump guard was fitted to the chassis to deflect stones and rocks, and to direct air flow around the sump. This guard would also allow the car to 'bottom' on severe bumps without damage. Stone guards were attached to both front headlamps, and a 'winking' indicator system fitted using a French system purchased while previously in France (strictly speaking illegal in Britain at this time). Being a dentist, Derek had also arranged for a dental mechanic, more used to making false teeth, to make a replacement gear knob from denture material in the form of a handle that accurately fitted his hand. Derek's navigator was to be his future wife, Kath, entered under his pet name for her of 'Miss Jumbo'.

Not long before the event Derek was surprised to receive a phone call from the Standard Triumph Motor Co., asking whether he would like to join their entry of a team of Morgans!

When he agreed the company sent him a rev counter to fit to his Morgan, driven from the distributor drive. The black 5in. Smiths unit was redlined at 40, 45 and 55 hundred rpm. Derek also fitted a Smiths cream and brown kilometre speedometer to assist his Continental adventure.

The other three Morgans forming the Standard Triumph team were the special ivory and red lightweights KUY 474, 5 and 6, recently used in the RAC Rally. As we have previously mentioned two of these Morgans were owned by Standard Triumph dealers. Lyndon Mills, who was in charge of sales at Standard Triumph, had decided to help finance these entries, as well as participate himself.

Perhaps he had convinced the Standard Triumph board that this testing event might be useful to the company to reveal any weaknesses in the Vanguard engine design, and would also allow testing of the developments such as the distributor take-off for the rev counter (all three were so fitted). Whether there were other engine modifications we have been unable to ascertain, although we know that KUY 474 was running with twin carburettors some months later.

KUY 474, the Morgan belonging to Dennis Done, the manager of the Chester Standard Triumph dealership James Edwards, was to be navigated by Dennis, with Lyndon Mills himself driving. KUY 476 was to be driven by its owner Bobby Dickson, the Carlisle Standard Triumph dealer. KUY 475 belonged to the Reece cousins who were really Ford dealers. While they had previously undertaken some Continental rallies in Fords, they considered the Alpine to be too dangerous. Consequently, this car was offered to experienced racing driver and Leeds motor trader Peter Bolton, who also happened to have the local Morgan dealership. He was to be accompanied by Arthur Slater.

Lyndon Mills of the Standard Triumph Motor Company in the heat of Marseilles before the start of the Alpine Rally, alongside KUY 474. (*Photograph: Photo-Junior*)

Some eighty-five competitors left the start at Marseilles between 9 p.m. and midnight on the Friday for the 614-mile first stage run to Cortina, high up in the Dolomites. This stage included the climb of the Col d'Izoard, the competitors then travelling over Montgenevre into Italy for a timed standing kilometre on the Monza race track and an eighty-five-mile high-speed run on the Autostrada. The mountain passes were notably dusty and clean sheets were only achieved by thirty-three competitors, including the Morgans of Mills and Dickson. Twenty-six cars failed to survive even this first day.

The following day, a timed one hundred and ninety mile run over the Dolomite Cup circuit took place in intermittent rain – and this made the loose road surface particularly slippery and dangerous. Before the start there was a problem with one of the ivory Morgans which had blown an exhaust gasket thereby cooking the starter, so the other drivers made a screen around the car while it was push started.

The atrocious conditions proved too much for the Morgans. Mills' car lost a wheel, Dickson's broke its front suspension and Peter Bolton's Morgan dropped a stud out of the differential into the casing which produced a 'rat tat tat' noise. Peter and Arthur stopped and stripped the differential. They were able to carry on for a while but making 'a hell of a noise' as the case hardening had been damaged. They eventually retired when centres pulled out of two wheels.

Thus, all three of the 'Ivory Morgan team' had stopped, each having lost a wheel and all within fifteen miles of each other. As a result, the team was easily able to meet up together, and after a few drinks they telegrammed the Morgan factory 'All three Morgans have reverted to type' (referring to having become three-wheelers).

Derek Howard and Kath, meanwhile, had the misfortune for the driving-side front stub axle to fail. The car slid on its sump guard to the edge of the road, over the apex of the hairpin bend and down . . . until eventually the Morgan stopped before the final big drop. Local villagers helped retrieve the car, and a blacksmith was able to make up a new stub axle, to allow them eventually to return home safely to Bridlington. Following his return to England Derek sent the offending stub axle back to Peter Morgan for analysis, somewhat irritated by its failure.

Peter Bolton had a communication from the Morgan factory upon his return. George Goodall was clearly not amused by the team's telegram, and it was all Peter Bolton could do to hang on to his Morgan dealership.

Only twenty-three of the Alpine starters reached the finish at Cannes, of which just ten were unpenalized, thereby winning the coveted 'Coupe des Alpes'. Five of these cars were British including the Sunbeam-Talbots of Stirling Moss, Mike Hawthorn and George Murray-Frame, as well as Ian Appleyard's incredible Jaguar XK 120. Ian also collected the first 'Coupe des Alpes en Or' ever awarded, for three unpenalized runs over three consecutive years, a brilliant performance for the Leeds Jaguar dealer and his famous white car.

Continuing the Continental theme, David Price once more decided to take part in the Rallye Evian Mont-Blanc, which for 1952 was held from 24 to 27 July.

The event proved to be very tough, with just ten of the sixty starters finishing unpenalized.

David Price during the Evian Mont-Blanc Rally. (*Photograph: Photo-Junior*)

David Price had the misfortune for the advance-retard mechanism to seize within the distributor, slowing him somewhat, but he still managed to finish third in the class for 2–3 litre cars behind Hebrard's Salmson and Mrs Needham's Lea Francis.

On Friday 25 July the Cheltenham MC began their National Road Fuel Economy Contest which was sponsored by the *News Chronicle* newspaper. This event took in 828 miles of England, Wales and Scotland, including many hilly roads. It also required an average speed of 29 mph to be maintained, to the finish the following day. Joe Lowrey, who had taken part the previous year in the works car HUY 982, decided this year to enter his own car, co-driven by Charles Bulmer, also of *The Motor* magazine. He prepared the Morgan by fitting 'economy' jets in the carburettor as before, by using thin oils (SAE 5 for the engine), and also by removing the lowest of the four piston rings, which he believed to be a completely unnecessary extra oil ring. Running with his 3.73 back axle he made best times of the day in the standing start acceleration tests, and won the class for 2–3 seaters, recording a consumption of 57.8 mpg.

Joe had joined in with Alan Hobbs and M. Gunn to form a Morgan team, which won the team competition, with Hobbs 4/4 recording 50.64 mpg, and also taking the class for the best pre-war car of two or three seats.

At the beginning of 1952 the Government had further tightened the screw on the allocation of cars to the British home market by UK manufacturers, restricting sales to a quota of 60,000 (the lowest since 1923!). 'Export or die' was the message, and when the Morgan Motor Company reviewed their own results, it was clear that production of the three-wheeler F type would have to be discontinued. During 1951 a mere twenty-

Joe Lowrey on his way to recording 57.8 mpg during the Economy Run. (*Photograph: National Motor Museum*)

Jeff Sparrowe at Boreham, JUO 177 running in production sports car trim. (*Photograph: National Motor Museum*)

Hawes 1947 4/4, the winner, ahead of Freddy Dyke's ex-Dorothy Bean pre-war car. (*Photograph: Bill Parkes collection*)

six had been built, of which exports accounted for just nine, markets being found in Europe, Mexico and New Zealand. The problem was that there was no tax advantage in owning a three-wheeler overseas, so they were not easy to export.

The very last F type, chassis number F1301, an F Super, was despatched to the Southampton agent Bennetts on 29 July.

No doubt HFS Morgan was sad to see this Morgan go. The three-wheelers that he had designed, and with which he had made his fortune, had given him much pleasure over the years. Then, the Government began to remove the pressures on manufacturers to export such high percentages of their production. In July the British Motor Trade Association was able to announce that certain 'selected' models need no longer comply with their two-year covenant scheme preventing resale within two years of purchase – ironically the Morgan models were included.

For the August Bank Holiday race meeting, held on Saturday 2 August at Boreham, sponsorship was obtained from the *Daily Mail* newspaper, and the BBC *Light Programme* was to broadcast the main race for Formula 1 cars. Jeff Sparrowe had entered the one hundred mile race for sports cars up to 2,000 cc, the only Morgan at the meeting. After starting well to lead the up to 1100 cc class JUO 177 began to trail oil smoke, and Jeff had to stop at the pits for replenishment, not featuring in the awards at the finish.

The Morgan 4/4 Club ran its annual road rally on Sunday 10 August attracting eight starters for the ninety mile course from Burton-on-Trent to Banbury, with driving tests at the finish. The results gave the event to T. F. Hawes from Boughton in his 1947 4/4, DBD 921, with Stan Dyke second in KKC 888, and Aileen Jervis, navigated by Mary Freeman from the hospital radiography department, third with JTT 703.

The same day various car club members collected at Prescott for a novel Inter Club hill climb. Each invited team ran its fastest cars up the hill, their first run times being added together and given a handicap. There was also an individual class competition.

Six Morgans had entered for the fun. Merton Biberfield was in the Liverpool team with his blue Standard-engined 4/4. Peter Morgan, with KUY 387, and Basil de Mattos, with KWP 127 were in the MCC team. John Moore, with KNP 5, and Doc Steel using Jim Goodall's car, HUY 982, were in the MAC team. The other Morgan was a late entry for the Hagley and District Light Car Club's team, and was none other than OZ 2343, the early Plus 4 previously campaigned so successfully in Northern Ireland by Stanley Porter. Unfortunately, the surviving results sheets of this event held by the BOC do not clearly identify its new driver. A damp course reduced the speed of the first runs, with the Nottingham Sports Car Club proving to be the victors in the team competition, the MCC team finishing fifth, best of those containing Morgans.

In the class competition for cars between 2001 and 3000 cc Peter Morgan finished third with a

The Prescott paddock, with 0Z 2343 visible in front of Basil de Mattos' car. (*Photograph: Murray Hardy*)

time of 52.56 seconds behind two supercharged type 35B Bugattis.

Fifty-six cars assembled in Newmarket on Friday 22 August for the Eastern Counties CC's second Annual Invitation Rally, held over a route of 370 miles and finishing the following day at Felixstowe. There were two 1952 Plus 4s entered, those of A. D. C. Gordon (MYP 666) and D. Hastings (KWP 741), and both featured in the awards, with Hastings finishing equal third overall, and Gordon taking the class for open cars of over 1500 cc.

Sergeant Hastings was based at Lakenheath Air Base, near Brandon in Suffolk, and was one of the many American airmen stationed in England at this time. Clearly he was enthusiastic about British motor sport, for he had purchased a green Plus 4 two-seater, chassis P2427, registered KWP 741, and fitted with the optional 3.73 to 1 axle ratio. It was despatched from the factory on 31 July.

We have previously mentioned how the difficulty in obtaining new Morgans in Britain could be partly overcome by purchasing a chassis and having it completed elsewhere. Some quite interesting and successful Plus 4s were produced in this way. One such was that of Peter Gammon. We have previously referred to his amazing racing MG, which had started life as an ordinary MG TC and had been rebodied with a bomber aeroplane's nose before being tuned by John Lucas, who worked for Weslakes. Peter, a Surrey draper, had now managed to purchase the tuned Standard Vanguard engine recently employed by Peter Clark in his unsuccessful Formula 2 HRG single-seater, and he had decided to put it into a lightened Plus 4. A chassis was obtained, the original scuttle retained but reduced in height and the whole car panelled in aluminium. The paneller, who worked on the car in his shed at home, had a connection with Connaught Engineering, the well-known racing car manufacturers. We think it possible that the chassis was P2207, which was despatched to Connaughts at Send in Surrey on 5 September 1951. In the quest to save weight on the new car (registered SPA 7 in June), many engineering studs even had their centres drilled out, so it ended up weighing a mere 13 cwt.

The engine as originally prepared by Peter Clark had been reduced in capacity to 1991 cc by using 83 mm liners. The head, originally on twin Solex carburettors, had latterly been modified to take four Amals but Peter found this of no use, so another head was modified by John Lucas, who had access at Weslakes to a flowmeter, and also a smoke apparatus for swirl testing within the combustion chambers. Twin 1½in. horizontal SUs on a branch manifold were fitted, which, with a compression ratio of 7.8 to 1, gave an extra 20 bhp over an untuned Vanguard. A 4.1 to 1 axle was used, with 600 × 16in. rear tyres. Sadly, this Vanguard engine, now of 1998 cc, proved resistant to John Lucas' preparations, and overall was a great disappointment to Peter. John's much more successful work with MG engines led him later to form Barwell Engineering with Ron Golding, and they went on to prepare MG engines for the Lotus cars of Colin Chapman.

Another chassis (P2372) had been sold to Les Yarranton whose family ran a motor coach and garage business in Eardiston in Worcestershire. Les had previously used an MG TC for some rallies but fancied more power, hence the decision to buy the Morgan. Having a family motor coach business on hand meant body manufacture was not too difficult on the premises. His two-seater was registered KWP 926 on 18 August. The chassis had been despatched to his nearest agent, Bowman and Acock on 25 April, so construction was fairly rapid.

A third Plus 4 chassis (P2291) is of particular interest. It had been delivered to the north London agency, Motourists Ltd on 1 January 1952. They had advertized the chassis and the advertisement was spotted by Norman Clarke, a motoring enthusiast living in Cheshire. He had recently come into some money following the death of his father and had really wanted to purchase a factory built Morgan, having been impressed by the road test reports, but none was available, or likely to be available. He telephoned Motourists to see whether they could recommend a coach builder to complete the car. They suggested Cooper Motor Bodies of Putney. After a test drive on a chassis – a bit rough and unrefined – the deal was made.

Les Yarranton's Morgan nears completion at the family's coach garage. (*Photograph: Les Yarranton collection*)

Norman and his wife sketched out a saloon body, similar in style to the MGY type, that could be built around the standard Morgan wings and bonnet, and Coopers went to work. Progress was slow and required several visits and instalments of money, until finally the saloon was finished, painted grey and registered PMB 173, on 1 November. It had been an expensive exercise, but the car handled well, despite rather vague steering. The Morgan became popular with Norman's wife, although it was somewhat cramped inside.

This year the 750 MC's six-hour Relay Race was to be held over the Club circuit at Silverstone on Saturday 30 August and it included several Morgans within the various teams. The Morgan 4/4 club had entered a team of six cars this year, three Climax- and three Standard-engined 4/4s. The 'A' car was Jeff Sparrowe's JUO 177, the 'B' was Freddy Dyke's, ex-Dorothy Bean 4/4, EJJ63 and the 'C' car, the last of the Climax-engined Morgans, was John Sutton-Atkins' well-used 4/4, FPE 567. The Standard-engined cars comprised the 'D' car, FNP 684, of Bill Parkes, the ex-factory car, CAB 652, driven by Graham Stallard as the 'E' car, and the four-seater of Stanley Dyke, KKC 888, as the 'F' entry.

Norman Clarke's saloon Morgan. (*Photograph: Quadrant Picture Library*)

Peter Gammon's much modified Plus 4, SPA 7, was in the Hants & Berks MC team. Peter Reece was driving KUY 475, this time less rev counter and passenger seat, in the Liverpool MC team, and D. Llewellyn Rees had entered a supercharged Climax-engined 4/4 in the Harrow Car Club's team.

In charge of the 4/4 Club pits was John McDonagh, who ran the Bridge Garage at Warwick, and he decided that Bill Parkes would do the Le Mans start as in the previous year. The club had been given forty credit laps start over the scratch team of the SUNBAC XK 120 Jaguars.

Practice revealed problems with Freddy Dyke's car and it was sidelined for the rest of the day.

Bill Parkes made an uneventful start and set out for his thirty-six lap stint, coming in after averaging an excellent 59.5 mph to hand over to Graham Stallard with CAB 652. After lapping at around 56 mph, Graham began to slow after just eight laps, and was brought in on his ninth. He was replaced by Jeff Sparrowe who proved to be still the fastest of the 4/4 drivers, averaging 60 mph for his sixteen laps until disaster struck and a rear wheel detached itself at Beckett's Corner. A 'helper' had failed to tighten the wheel nuts adequately. Luckily Jeff managed to stop without incident. It was left to John Sutton-Atkins to leave the pits in FPE 567 and collect the sash from Jeff, so that Jeff could retrieve his wheel and make his way back to the paddock for repairs.

Atkins' car, which had had the spare wheels removed for racing and the aperture in the tail body work covered over, only managed four fairly slow laps (52 mph), so he came in and was replaced by Stanley Dyke with his immaculate 4/4, KKC 888. Having now fitted cycle wings to the front, he painted the exposed wooden engine bay sides silver, contrasting with the gleaming British Racing Green paintwork of the rest of the car.

Stan had added a few measures of benzole to his fuel to help his car go. Sadly, he had not realized that this dissolved rubber and the inevitable happened on his second lap when parts of the rubber fuel pipe blocked the fuel supply to the carburettor and he ground to a halt. After a while he restarted his car and made it back to the pits for further sorting, handing over to Graham Stallard once more for a further seven laps before he in turn handed over to Jeff Sparrowe in the refettled JUO 177.

John Sutton-Atkins' 4/4 in the paddock. (*Photograph: Bill Parkes collection*)

Twelve laps later Jeff handed over to Bill Parkes for his twelve laps, who then gave the sash to John Sutton-Atkins, whose 4/4 was going much better now, staying out for 17 laps at 55 mph.

Then it was Stan Dyke's chance to redeem himself, which he duly did, lapping at 56 mph average for the next sixteen laps.

Back to Graham Stallard and CAB 652 for twenty-three consistent laps at 57 mph, and then after a short spell of Bill Parkes (six laps).

Graham was out again for six laps, the last very slow. Bill was therefore sent out again for sixteen

Peter Reece about to receive the sash from his team mate in the 750 MC Relay Race. (*Photograph: Guy Griffiths*)

laps, each of 1 min. 39 sec. approximate duration (57 mph). Then Stanley Dyke was sent out for the final period of the six hours, again averaging 57 mph.

The Morgan team had covered 210 laps, but what of the other Morgans taking part? Of these Peter Gammon's SPA 7 was particularly noteworthy for being enthusiastically driven almost at the limit of control. For the last hour of the event, he was engaged in a duel with Chris Sears' rapid Lea Francis-engined Frazer Nash, although the latter kept just ahead at the finish.

The Harrow CC team, including Llewellyn-Rees and the supercharged 4/4, proved to be the most successful of the teams containing Morgans, running in sixth position with just half an hour to go. Unfortunately the Chiltern HRG team put on a late spurt, and they finished seventh.

The Morgan 4/4 team finished thirteenth, a bit of a disappointment after the previous year, but at least more team members were still running at the finish.

On the same day the MAC ran an International hill climb at Shelsley Walsh in glorious sunshine. The event attracted two Morgan participants. Local farmer, John Moore, had been persuaded to enter his black Plus 4 Coupe, KNP 5, by the regulars in his nearby local public house. Charlie Robertson, who hailed from Edinburgh, had purchased a red two-seater, chassis P2278, which had been despatched from the factory on 21 December 1951, and registered JSG 320. The Morgan had needed some attention to the rear springs, and to a gearbox oil leak, so Charlie had arranged for the factory to attend to these on 28 August, taking in the Shelsley meeting while he was in the area. Charlie recorded a best time of 51.86 seconds to John's 53.53, but the clear class winner was Ken Wharton with a Bristol-engined Frazer Nash in 42.26 seconds.

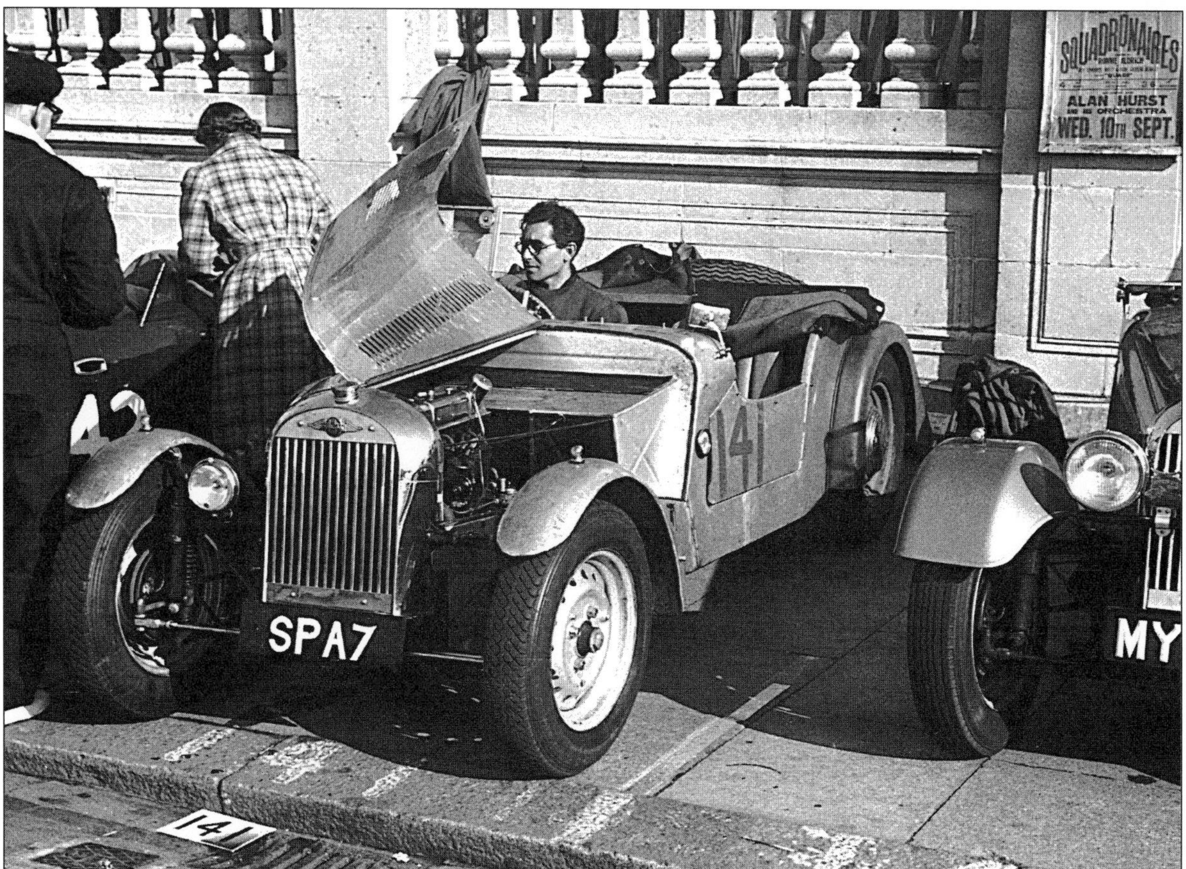

Peter Gammon at Brighton. (*Photograph: Guy Griffiths*)

The start of the second high-speed trial, with Peter Morgan in KUY 387 leading the Morgans of Jim Goodall (HUY 982) and Alec Gordon (0Z 2343). (*Photograph: James Brymer*)

John Moore had thoroughly enjoyed his day's motor sport and resolved to enter his Coupe for more motor sport events in the future.

Looking at the Shelsley times from the previous year, Peter Morgan's time of 48.98 seconds still looked most impressive.

Once again the Hagley and District LCC used Westwood Park near Droitwich for speed trials on 31 August, using seven hundred yards of the drive to Westwood Hall. Three Plus 4s were entered. Geoff White was in MOH 453, Sgt Hastings was in KWP 741, and G. A. Lewis completed the trio with his Plus 4.

Hastings managed 26.59 seconds to take third place behind Mr & Mrs Sutcliffe in a shared Mille Miglia Frazer Nash, in the class for sports cars of 1501–3000 cc.

On 6 September the Brighton and Hove MC ran its annual sprint meeting on Madeira Drive in Brighton. Peter Gammon was present with his MG special and his Morgan, recording 37.42 seconds on his first run, with the latter, some seven seconds behind class winner, Greene's Frazer Nash.

There was another Plus 4 competing – that of R. W. Cookson, but driven by Miss A. W. Cookson. This standard looking two-seater, MYP802, clocked 38.4 seconds.

East Anglian Morgan driver Peter Wren had also entered with his hybrid Riley-engined 4/4, but did not run.

The MCC ran this year's Silverstone race meeting on 13 September. Once more Peter Gammon had entered both his cars, the MG and the Morgan. Peter Morgan and Jim Goodall were present from the factory, with KUY 387 and HUY 982 respectively, the former Plus 4 sporting a 'metal spare wheel cover' according to *Motor Sport*.

Sonny McCann completed the Morgan factory team, driving another Plus 4, as yet unidentified.

Also entered was Basil de Mattos with his green Plus 4, KWP 127, and A. D. C. Gordon.

Londoner Alec Gordon was now the owner of the ex-Stanley Porter modified Morgan, OZ 2343, which he hoped would be somewhat faster than his previous Plus 4.

The MCC programme began with two one-hour high-speed trials. Peter Gammon took part in the first with his Morgan, collecting a Second Class Award. In the second event four Morgans did better, each collecting First Class Awards. These were the entries of Peter Morgan, who covered 61.39 miles, Sonny McCann with 54.77 miles, Jim Goodall with 58.78 miles and A. D. C. Gordon with 54.89 miles.

In the first five-lap handicap Peter Morgan and Peter Gammon found their Morgans to be evenly matched in the battle for third place, Peter Morgan finally taking the honours.

The second five-lap handicap saw Jim Goodall battling against Chris Sears' Frazer Nash for the entire distance, but neither finished in the places.

The MCC had also devised a rather unusual twenty-four-lap Relay Race, attracting seven teams each of three cars. Rather than handing over a sash to the various drivers, the next car waited in the pits with a spark plug removed. It could not start until the incoming team member had removed one of his own car's plugs and put it on the pit counter. Needless to say there were some rather burnt fingers and much bad language!

On scratch was the Morgan team of Peter Morgan, Jim Goodall and Sonny McCann but they were unable to catch the limit teams, and a Bentley team eventually proved the winner. Basil de Mattos was in his Morgan in a mixed team that also included an SS Jaguar and an HRG, but again no success.

The day's racing was concluded by the *Motor Sport* Handicap, in which Peter Morgan managed sixth place.

That Peter Morgan's KUY 387 should have challenged and beaten Peter Gammon's much modified SPA 7 should not come as too much of a surprise. Both cars had twin SU carburettor engines, and Peter Morgan had been undertaking considerable development of his experimental version. At one stage he had experimented with four Amal carburettors but, rather like Peter Gammon, he found these difficult to set up. Indeed he was advised that he would set the whole thing on fire if he persisted! HFS Morgan had also asked Harry Hatch to look over the Vanguard engine to see whether it was amenable to greater performance. Peter Morgan remembers that Harry thought the valve train was not suitable for high engine speeds and would benefit from much lightening.

Standard Triumph themselves had advised the Morgan factory that they were intending to introduce a 2-litre version of the Vanguard engine, which they currently had under development, and promised HFS that the Morgan company would have access to these engines. It was being developed for their own sports car.

Prescott was the venue for an International hill climb the day following the MCC meeting. Just one Morgan was entered, the Plus 4 of Peter Reece, who recorded a best run of 52.23 seconds – the fastest Morgan time recorded at Prescott to date, and giving him fourth place in the sports car class for 1501–3000 cc unsupercharged, behind an MG PB and two Healeys.

The London Motor Club's London Rally had been elevated to National status this year, attracting over three hundred entries for Friday the 19th until Saturday the 20th event, during which seven hundred miles were to be covered. As might be expected a good number of Morgans were attracted to the event, in fact no fewer than eighteen.

There were thirteen Plus 4s driven by D. W. Price Jnr (Dave Price's son), P. G. Mallam, Bernard Clarke, L. West, Robin Steel, Geoff White, D. J. Isaacs, G. A. Lewis, Sgt D. O. Hastings, Jim Goodall, Jimmy Ray, Alec Gordon and Jack Reece. The 4/4s were the 1125 cc car of G. R. Barker, J. Smith's Standard-engined car, Bill Parkes well-known FNP 684, M. C. Cartwright's 1100 cc car and E. C. Cameron's Standard-engined car. Jim Goodall, Jack Reece and Jimmy Ray were the members of the Morgan team.

While Jim Goodall and Jack Reece were probably in their usual cars (HUY 982 and KUY 475 respectively), Jimmy Ray now had a new car. Following the Alpine Rally, Dennis Done had decided to sell his lightweight KUY 474, and Jimmy had realized that this twin-carburettor ex-Standard Triumph sponsored car could be more potent than his own for rallying, so he had purchased it. His navigator was Jeff Dixon.

Bernard Clarke was also in a new Morgan, this being PKK 769, the newly bodied chassis P2222, which was originally despatched along with the chassis for A. Range's car to Motourists Ltd in North London on 19 September 1951.

There were two starts, from Croydon Aerodrome and Appleyard's garage in Leeds, with the routes meeting at Kidderminster. The rally proved to be a tough one, just four cars arriving back at Croydon Aerodrome unpenalized after the road section. There had been several crashes, one sadly fatal, and seventy-five cars retired.

One of the four unpenalized crews was Jimmy Ray and Jeff Dixon. When the driving test results were taken into account, it was found they had achieved victory overall, a tremendous achievement. This was not the only Morgan award, however, for Jim Goodall and his navigator Terry Hall took the Member's Trophy for the best performance by an LMC member. L. West and his navigator, D. B. Smith, took their class novices' award, and the team of Ray, Goodall and Reece were second in the team award. All these awards showed the motoring world how excellent the Morgan was for rallying, clearly the sportsman's choice for these events.

All had not gone to plan for Jack Reece and his navigator Barrie Davies, however. Lost, they had driven into a farmyard and thence into a barn to turn around. The barn doors were immediately closed behind them and an irate farmer informed them that they were the thirty-sixth so-and-sos to visit that night and what were they going to do about it? Eventually they negotiated their release!

Another driver facing problems was Robin Steel, the son of Doc Steel, driving the latter's Plus 4 at his father's suggestion. He entered a field to turn around, but found it sloped away from the entrance. A tractor was required to retrieve the Morgan and Robin retired, never to drive in a rally again.

On the same day that the London Rally was finishing the West Hants & Dorset CC ran a sprint meeting at Ibsley. Jeff Sparrowe impressed with his classic 'drifts' around Paddock Bend, but the bigger-engined cars took the spoils.

Exactly one week later the Eastern Counties MC ran a club speed trial on Snetterton Circuit (between Thetford and Attleborough in Norfolk), Sgt D. O. Hastings competing with his Plus 4, KWP 741.

Another two-day rally, starting on Friday 10 October and finishing on the 11th, was the MG CC's Weston Rally. The road section once again separated the men from the boys, the mist and keen frost on the Welsh hills playing havoc with time schedules. Sadly the Morgans were out of the prizes in this event, even Jimmy Ray making a hash of one driving test.

At Silverstone the last car race meeting of the year was held jointly by the North Staffs and Nottingham SCC, on 11 October. The weather was excellent and a good day's racing was held. The only Morgan to feature in the awards was Peter Gammon's SPA 7, which finished second in the unlimited sports car handicap to Dalton's MG TD. Also competing was Basil de Mattos.

On Sunday 12 October the 4/4 Club held its second annual driving tests, which were won by Bill Allarton in EAX 377, with Barrie Phipps second in his Plus 4, KUY 714. Plus 4s were accepted for membership of the 4/4 Club, despite the club's title.

The last week in October was the traditional date of the Motor Show, and there were some very interesting vehicles at Earls Court to interest the sports car enthusiast. Donald Healey had designed an attractive, modern looking sports car to take the Austin A90's 90 bhp 2660 cc engine. It was originally priced at £850 but on the eve of the show Leonard Lord, head of the recently formed British Motor Corporation, purchased the

Geoff White acknowledges the start officials as he leaves the Croydon Aerodrome start of the London Rally. (*Photograph: Charles Dunn*)

Alec Gordon in the Weston Rally. (*Photograph: National Motor Museum*)

Basil de Mattos at Silverstone. (*Photograph: Basil de Mattos collection*)

rights to the design and renamed it the Austin-Healey 100, dropping the price to £750 and thereby making this sports car the least expensive 100 mph sports car in the world.

Standard Triumph were also showing a sports car. Code-named 20 TS, this car had been built in a fairly short period by John Turnbull and chief chassis engineer Harry Webster. It used a chassis made from a left-over Standard Flying Nine frame with Triumph Mayflower front suspension grafted on to it. Naturally, this white car with red leather upholstery attracted HFS and Peter Morgan to the stand, and Peter was surprised to discover that it had a similar worm and nut type steering system to that he was trying to persuade his father to replace on the Morgan. The wheelbase was shorter than the Morgan (7 ft. 4 in.), and the back axle ratio 3.89 to 1 giving the little car a maximum speed of 90 mph. It was proposed to sell it at £555 plus purchase tax (the Morgan two-seater cost £565).

What made this car particularly interesting was the engine. This was Vanguard based but with an 83 mm bore, giving 1991 cc, and hence putting the new car into the all important under 2 litre class for racing. The compression ratio was 7.5 to 1 (still pooled petrol remember), giving 75 bhp at 4,500 rpm.

Ted Grinham, Standard Triumph's technical director, and deputy managing director was fully aware of the achilles heel of the Vanguard engine – the unusual valve spring system in which only the inner valve spring(s) acted to close the valves, the outer ones acting on a free floating valve cap to return the rockers. This system could not take high engine speeds, as confirmed by Morgan at Le Mans and then Sebring. It is such an odd system that it deserves some explanation.

During engine development for the original Standard Vanguard, a conventional valve/valve spring retaining system was used but it was found to produce too much tappet noise for installation into a luxurious saloon. As a result it was Harry Webster who suggested to Ted Grinham that the outer valve spring should just act on a cap to return the rockers, thereby reducing the load and hence noise of the 'tappets'. This system proved fine for the Vanguard, but meant that the valves were only returned by the 28lb of the inner spring for the inlet valve and 38lb for the exhaust, which had had an additional inner spring fitted from 1951. For the sports car owner tappet noise was of little consequence, so a conventional system could be used, with all the springs (approximately 70lb) returning the valves thereby reducing bounce and permitting higher engine speeds with safety.

A few years later, when Standard Triumph introduced their even more upmarket Vanguard Sportsman, the Vanguard valve retaining system continued to be used, but now with a double skinned rocker cover to reduce noise further.

Twin 1½in. SU carburettors (H4) were also fitted to the engine of the little Triumph sports car, which was attracting much attention on the show stand, although the mixture of a modern front end and short tail with exposed spare wheel was not to everyone's taste. One of those impressed was Bill Parkes, who immediately placed an order at the Worcester Standard Triumph dealer. It was to be over a year before he received his new car and it then incorporated many changes from the Motor Show prototype.

Ted Grinham was aware that Standard Triumph, being new to sports cars, needed someone to assess their new car properly before it went into production, so he had invited Ken Richardson, recently at BRM, to drive the car immediately after the show. Just a short drive around the Coventry factory and surrounding district was enough to convince Ken that the chassis was far too flexible for production, so Standard Triumph decided that he should be employed to oversee the new sports car, as developmental engineer.

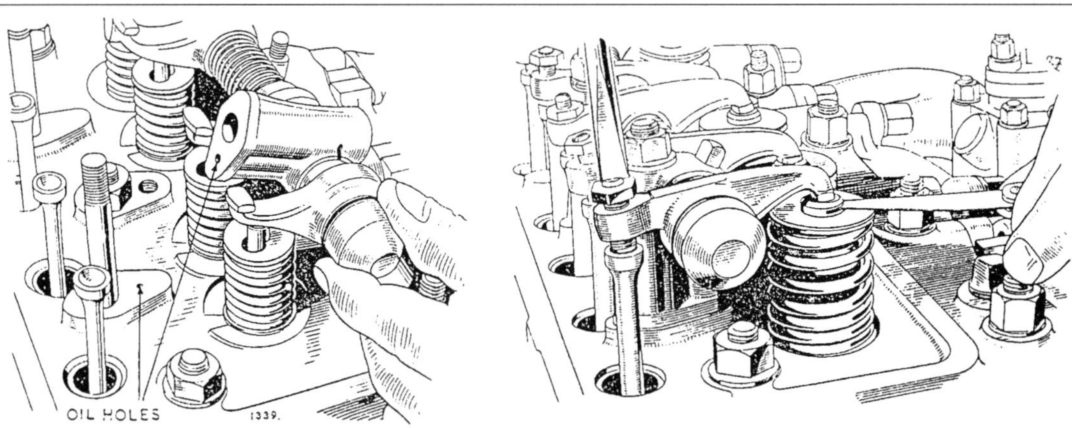

Adjusting rocker clearances.

Drawings from the Standard Vanguard workshop manual showing, to the left, the inner springs only being located onto the valve stems (the outer valve springs are removed) and, to the right, the outer valve spring being retained by a floating cap, which bears directly on the rocker arm, tappet clearance being between the cap and the top of the valve stem.

The Morgan Motor Company had exhibited their Plus 4 in the usual three styles of bodywork and also offered the 3.73 to 1 back axle as an option. Bill Boddy, writing in *Motor Sport*, believed this axle ratio completely transformed the car, and suggested Standard Triumph would be advised to use a similar ratio in their new sports car.

Also optional for the Plus 4 was a slightly higher compression ratio Vanguard engine (7.1 to 1), presumably achieved by shaving the cylinder head.

Once more the MCC held its National Rally sponsored by the *Daily Express* in November, from the 12th to the 15th. Underlining the popularity of rallies with motoring sportsmen, some 461 entries were taken, of which twenty-nine non-started. Naturally there were a few Plus 4s. The Morgan factory had entered their usual team of Peter and Jane Morgan with JNP 239, Jim Goodall and Terry Hall with HUY 982, and Doc Steel, navigated by Gavin Scott, with JWP537. They chose to start from the Kenilworth start point, as did Derek Howard, navigated by Ted Booth of the East Yorks Car Club, with Derek's ex-Alpine Plus 4, CJX 318, and Bill Parkes with Peter Homes in FNP 684.

Starting from Manchester were five Plus 4s. Jimmy Ray and Peter Reece were in their two of the Alpine cars – KUY 474 and KUY 475 respectively, Peter Reece being navigated by his wife Doreen on this occasion. Ken Bancroft was navigated by T. Platt in his Plus 4, NTJ 943. Also starting from Manchester were the entries of H. M. Mettrick and Harry Harrop, the latter being the licensee of a public house near Stockport.

The Norwich start had one Plus 4 – that of Peter Silcock. From the London start, the 4/4 of F. C. Cole and Alec Gordon's OZ 2343 were the only Morgan starters.

This year the weather was cold but sunny, making the 1,250-mile run to the finish at Brighton, including a common route for all the cars from Penrith, particularly easy, if not tedious. The Reeces, however, finished their rally near Tewkesbury, when KUY 475 lost a front wheel and ended in a ditch.

At Brighton several driving tests were held to sort out the winners, Derek Howard being particularly impressive in the 'garage' test. Mettrick's Morgan had no clutch after the first of the three tests and had to take maximum penalties on the last two.

When the results were announced it was Jim Goodall and Terry Hall who proved to be the top Morgan crew, finishing in overall third place, and taking the up to 3000 cc open car class. Peter and Jane Morgan were fourth, and took the up to 3000 cc closed car class. A magnificent seventh overall were Bill Parkes and Peter Homes, although their class (specials) went to the overall winner Dr Charles Hardman with his Dellow. Ken Bancroft finished fifteenth.

Derek Howard giving a characteristically impressive performance in the second test at Brighton. (*Photograph: L. A. T. photographic*)

Peter Morgan in the Brighton test, on his way to a class victory. (*Photograph: James Brymer*)

The Morgan team were pipped by two tenths of a point in the team competition to finish second to an MG team, and, to complete an excellent event for Morgans, Peter Silcock also took the post event concours d'elegance for open cars of up to £550.

The Morgan 4/4 Club held an ambitious second annual night rally over 29 and 30 November, with no fewer than four different start points. Twenty-two enthusiasts took part, eight with 4/4s seven with Plus 4s. A variety of other vehicles completed the field.

Graham Stallard won the open class with CAB 652, ahead of A. W. Taylor's Standard Special-engined 4/4 and Aileen Jervis in JTT 703. The closed car class went to Gordon Stratton in an Austin (!), followed by Sutcliffe's Porsche, the best Morgan being that of Peter Morgan (JNP 239), back in fourth place.

Morgans had had another good year in 1952, both at home and overseas. Real competition for the Plus 4 was now appearing on the horizon, however, with the Austin-Healey and Triumph sports cars newly announced at the Motor Show.

With the forthcoming completion of extra petrol refinery capacity in Britain it was announced that, at long last, branded petrol would replace pool petrol from February 1953. A raising of octane rating would give freedom for the development of proper competition engines, both by manufacturers and tuning establishments. Things were looking good for the motor sport enthusiasts for 1953.

Overseas

United States of America

For the Christmas/New Year holiday a west coast sports car enthusiast named Stephen Wilder had travelled back home to be with his family in the North East. He had recently disposed of his MG TC which he had rallied and raced, but had soon realized to be a very tired machine.

Impressed by the Morgan, he went to see Joe Ferguson at Fergus Motors and put in his order. He then went to the Ninth Annual Meeting of the Sports Car Club of America, Inc., held at the Henry Hudson Hotel in New York City on 19 January. Here all the news was of two forthcoming twelve-hour races, one at Vero Beach, Florida, on 8 March, under SCCA rules, and one, at Sebring on 15 March under 'Triple A' (American Automobile Association) sanctions. Stephen was not too interested in the heated politics of the occasion. He put in his application for both events and awaited the arrival of his two-seater Plus 4.

The Sebring twelve-hour race was the brainchild of Alec Ulmann. Alec had been to Le Mans in the 1930s, and when he went back there in 1950 as team manager for the Briggs Cunningham team he made up his mind to try and organize a similar annual long-distance endurance sports car race in the USA.

Coincidentally, Alec was also involved in a business converting ex-military aircraft into civil use, and he had been looking for storage space for this enterprise. This had led to the inspection of the Hendrick Field, located near Sebring in Florida, an ex-Second World War B17 bomber base. The long (1 mile) runways impressed him, and brought back memories of the Mulsanne Straight at Le Mans. It seemed ideal, so Alec began the organization, initially of a six-hour race for December 1950. He wanted the race to be open to international entries, and needed the approval of the Federation International d'Automobile (FIA) for this. Unfortunately, they would not recognize the SCCA (Alec Ulmann was their Activities Chairman) but wanted the events run under AAA sanctions, despite the fact that this organization was not really sport orientated.

There was thus an almighty bust-up between Ulmann and the SCCA, who threw him out. When he then dared to organize another event, this being the first twelve-hour Sebring race in 1952, again under AAA rules, they retaliated by organizing their own, the Vero Beach event, one week earlier.

Unfortunately for Steve Wilder, his red two-seater was not delivered in time for the Vero Beach event but he was able to collect it, accompanied by his mother's sister, in time for Sebring, Joe Ferguson allowing Steve to take the car, even though he had not paid all the required purchase price at the time.

Steve took the car up to Boston to show his family, and to try and persuade Art Eldredge,

Gus Ehrman driving Steve Wilder's Plus 4 leads J. Norcross' T type MG, in the early hours of the Sebring race. (*Photograph: Gus Ehrman collection*)

who had raced an MG TC at Watkins Glen, to be his co-driver. He also acquired a sturdy ex-aeroplane seat belt to fasten through the floor boards.

Failing to persuade Art, Steve headed south to Sebring, arriving for scrutineering at the last minute. He had hardly stopped before Gus Ehrman approached him and offered to be his passenger. Steve asked him just three questions: 'Have you raced before? Have you a helmet? Will it fit me?' As all replies were affirmative, Gus was to be co-driver.

Gus had been in the USA since 1948, racing MGs and was involved in the MG distribution business. He had been promised a drive at Sebring by Joe Ferguson, but had been let down. No doubt Joe had tipped him off that Steve was still looking for a co-driver.

Race preparation consisted of removing one of the spare wheels (only one required), installing the seat belt and putting on the race numbers. Steve had asked for, and been given, number 7, as it was easy to make out of Scotchlite reflective tape.

After practice they decided that Gus, being the more experienced, would take the Le Mans type start, and that four three-hour shifts would be used. Gus had also found a couple of people to help in the pits for refuelling etc.

Come the start (delayed from noon to 13.03 because of morning rain), Gus ran across the road, got in, and then nothing! He could not find the starter button, all his practice having been with the engine running! Eventually the 'S' button was located and the Morgan was on its way. There was no tachometer, so gear changes were done on 'sound', and down shifting was preferred for slowing down as brake fade was known to be a problem in long-distance races.

Thirty-two competitors had set off, but in class D (2000–3000 cc), there were just three starters. Besides the Morgan there was a supercharged 2½ litre MG and an Aston Martin DB2 but when the latter retired on lap 29 with back axle trouble, and the MG on lap 43 with engine problems, Steve and Gus knew they had the class trophy in the bag if they could keep going.

At the six-hour mark they were up to tenth position overall and by nine hours they were running eighth. It was just a matter of keeping going, and Steve remembers that he was easing off on the two one-mile long straights on the 5.2 mile circuit, also thinking now of the long drive home ahead of him (approximately 1,500 miles).

Eventually, at 1.03 a.m. on 16 March the flag was held out to signify the end of the twelve hours of racing, and the Morgan had duly won its class, having covered 128 laps and finishing ninth overall. The winner was the Kulok/Gray Frazer Nash Le Mans, with 145 laps.

Returning to the pits, Steve discovered his spare wheel had been stolen but the cost of this was reclaimable on insurance. The following day, having collected the trophy, Steve headed north. In Georgia the starter motor packed up and gradients were sought out henceforth for bump starts.

Back in Massachusetts, Hansen-McPhee installed a new starter, and tuned the engine. Two miles later a valve broke, embedding its head into a piston. Steve had been lucky that this, the Achilles heel of the Vanguard engine, had not shown itself until after the Sebring race meeting, and Morgan and their importer had meanwhile received excellent publicity from the victory. Incidentally, Joe Ferguson's son, Joe Jnr, had also competed at Sebring – in an Italian Siata, but he had retired with engine trouble.

Steve's car was eventually to be put right with parts located in Toronto, Canada, where several Standard Vanguards had been imported. Steve now headed west once more, to California, and here he lent the Morgan to *Road and Track* magazine for a road test, where a 0–60 mph time of 17.1 seconds was recorded. Not long after, Steve sold the car, having had his fill of enjoyment from this memorable red two-seater.

Apart from the Sebring 12-hour race, the venues for the racing of sports cars in the USA were somewhat limited. Traditional American racing favoured small oval tracks, but these were not popular with sports car enthusiasts who wanted European-style road courses, so that they could use the impressive acceleration and handling of their imported, nimble cars. Some country village elders were persuaded to introduce 'round the houses races', through the streets of their villages, and Watkins Glen in New York, Bridgehampton on Long Island, and Pebble Beach in California were examples of these.

The other popular alternative was to use airfield courses, as there were no purpose-built road race courses available in the USA at this time.

One such airfield course was in the Californian desert at Palm Springs, and, on 23 March, the CSCC ran a race meeting there over a 2.3-mile course. Entered for the ten-lap race for 'stock' sports cars from 1501–4500 cc, was Bill Pollack, who found himself up against a field of six XK 120 Jaguars. As might be anticipated Bill stood no chance, and he finished seventh. This was Bill's only drive in a Morgan. At this stage in his career he had been racing supercharged MG TCs, and was shortly to transfer to an Allard. It was not even his Morgan, but belonged to a dentist named Sam Cooms, who had asked Bill to drive it for him, to see how it would go. The drive itself was uneventful for Bill, except for constantly banging his knuckles on the windscreen wiper motor, which he felt was far too close to the steering wheel.

The major event of the meeting was the fifty-lap Palm Springs Cup, and Leo Caton Jnr had also entered his Morgan for this one. He managed to finish a creditable ninth, the winner being Chuck Manning's Manning Special. Leo was also third in class, behind an Aston Martin DB2 and a Ford V8-engined MG. Also entered had been future star Phil Hill in a Cunningham, but he retired.

On 6 April Leo Caton returned to Sandberg Hill for the CSCC's hill climb, and here he managed third in class behind a supercharged MG TC.

Two weeks later Leo was in action at Pebble Beach, on the Monterey peninsula, for the meeting organized by the San Francisco region of the SCCA. The Pebble Beach course was spectacular and beautiful, being held on private roads within the private community of Pebble Beach. The circuit was of 2.1 miles and included hills and hairpins, a fine downhill straight and roads lined by pine trees, to catch the unwary.

The third event was a one hundred mile race (43 laps) for cars of over 1500 cc, for the Del Monte Trophy (Del Monte Properties owned the site), and Leo Caton was entered. The race was won by Bill Pollack in an Allard, and Leo stood no chance against such power. In the class for cars from 1950–3000 cc he finished an excellent third, however, behind class winner Arnold Stubbs' Ferrari 212, and Barry Wagner's Healey Silverstone.

During this meeting, Leo Caton had the misfortune for a wheel to pull right through the retaining wheel nuts, something that the magazine *Road and Track* commented adversely upon when they printed the road test of Steve Wilder's Plus 4 in their September issue.

American sports car owners were less conservative in their car colour schemes than the more restrained British equivalent. As a result, the USA importers Fergus Motors and Angell Motors made an arrangement with the Morgan factory that, as from 20 May, they would change the colour of the interiors as follows: black cars to have red upholstery, with black hood and side curtains; green cars to have black upholstery, hoods and side curtains and red, blue or cream cars to have red upholstery hoods and side curtains.

Morgan owners continued to increase in number. In Ohio, enthusiast Clem Bauman took his new two-seater Plus 4 to spectate at the one-mile Bembridge sprint on 29 June, the car being too new to use in competition, he reasoned.

The next appearance of a Plus 4 in competition we believe to be that of J. I. Staley, on an airport circuit at Caddo Mills, Texas, where he finished third in class. This event was also the first event for another future star, Carroll Shelby.

While 'round the houses' races were popular with sports car racers in America, the speed of the cars, and the vulnerability of spectators meant it was only a matter of time before a disaster occurred. It happened during the Watkins Glen Grand Prix on 20 September, when the Allard J2 of Fred Wacker bounced off a curb, killing a seven-year-old boy who had been sitting there, and injuring twelve spectators. As a result the street circuit at Watkins Glen was to be used no more, and the whole concept of such events was severely criticized on safety reasons.

The difficulty facing the sports car racers was where they could now find venues to race in safety. To the rescue came General Curtis Le May, head of the USAF Strategic Air Command, who made an arrangement with the SCCA for SAC air force bases to be used. All proceeds from the race meetings were to be donated to various charities, including the SAC Airmen's Living Improvement Fund. The very first of these races was held at Turner base in Albany, Georgia, on 25 October 1952.

Back in California the SCCA, the Fresno Sports Car Club and the Madera 20–30 Club had arranged to borrow Madera airfield on 9 November for their race meeting. A 2.6-mile circuit was marked out using airfield runways and aprons. Some one hundred and twenty entries were attracted, including Leo Caton with his Morgan, running with an aero screen but in road trim with front bumper and hub caps.

The finale of the meeting was a thirty-lap race for over 1500 cc sports cars. Caton's claim to fame is that, on the last corner of the very last lap, he spun in front of the leaders who were lapping him! Bill Pollack's Allard J2 just managed to hold off Phil Hill's C type Jaguar in the melée.

Australia

There had recently been little Australian racing outside the State of Western Australia, where enthusiasts congregated around the Morgan dealership of Bill Richards in Perth, and where the 'round the houses' races provided venues for sports car racing.

In the State of Victoria Brylaw Motors of Melbourne were still importing Morgans, but there were few suitable venues for racing, with the result that hill climbing was becoming more popular with motor sport enthusiasts. Having purchased a second-hand Morgan Plus 4, registered UU 727, from an English army officer named Major Barker, twenty-year-old Richard Reynolds was keen to take part in motor sport. It is of interest that his mother's Alvis 12/50 had been driven in the very first Australian Grand Prix in 1928 by her brother and more recently Richard's brother had raced a Sunbeam Talbot, so motor racing was in the family's blood.

On 10 March Richard took his red Morgan to the Rob Roy hill climb, where he competed in the 1501–3000 cc sports car class against two 3 litre Alvis, a Riley, a Citroën and an Austin A90. His driving was consistent, giving times of 35.55 and 35.51 seconds to take the class.

There was also a keen group of motor racing enthusiasts in South Australia, in the Adelaide area, and one of them, Peter Hay, had purchased one of the very first Morgan Plus 4s to arrive in Australia, it having been despatched to Brylaw Motors from the Morgan factory on 6 February 1951. When Peter purchased this green two-seater (chassis P2106, engine number V3ME), it was second-hand, having previously belonged to the Managing Director of an Adelaide car distributorship. It had around 2,000 miles under its belt.

Peter was a member of the Sporting Car Club of South Australia, and the club was now able to run hill climbs at Collingrove, on property belonging to the Angas family near Angastown. The

Richard Reynolds on the slopes of Rob Roy. (*Photograph: Richard Reynolds collection*)

Peter Hay at Collingrove hill climb. (*Photograph: Peter Hay collection*)

750-yard course was formally opened on 15 March by the Attorney General. Some 6,000 spectators watched the competitors at this meeting but Peter did not feature among the winners.

Back in Western Australia the Great Southern Flying Fifty was once more held at Narrogin on 24 March, using the original 2.2-mile course, rather than the enlarged course used for the previous year's Australian Grand Prix. Some 12,000 people converged on the town for the racing, showing it had lost none of its popularity. Several competitors travelled long distances from South Australia to get there, one becoming stranded in the Nullarbor Plain in blazing heat with a burst radiator, finally arriving after temporary repairs and after requiring a rescue.

The racing started at 1.30 p.m. with a pre-1929 'old crocks' race, won by Barry Ranford Junior in a Chrysler. Then came the three-lap scratch races, and the under 1500 cc version was easily won by Eldred Norman (from South Australia) with his Maserati 6C (the one driven by Colin Murray the previous year). Second place was taken by Noel Aldous' MG TC and third went to Johnny Motteram's Morgan, now going better than ever.

Thirteen cars took to the line for the five-lap handicap. Limit man was Johnny Motteram, and he drove so well that no-one could get near him, Noel Aldous finishing second with the MG.

The final event was the Great Southern Flying Fifty itself, over twenty-three laps of the circuit, with handicaps.

Limit man was once again Johnny Motteram, given 12 min. 50 sec. start over scratch man Eldred Norman with his Maserati. Also competing was David Van Dal with his red Plus 4, which he had now prepared for racing. He had fitted larger valves, complete with double BSA valve springs and colletts. He had also shaved the cylinder head to raise the compression, and cut and welded a Vanguard inlet manifold to accept two Vanguard Solex carburettors which supplied 50/50 benzole/petrol mixture. He was given a handicap of 6 min. 10 sec.

Once again Motteram set a tremendous pace while behind him all was not so well. Claude La Motte's 'Fidget' had a carburettor fire, and Barker's Ballot retired with cooling problems. By the sixth lap the leader, Motteram, was being followed by Noel Aldous' MG with David Van Dal's Plus 4 in third position.

As the race progressed the faster, later starters began to come through the field. By the fourteenth lap, although Motteram and Aldous still led, David Van Dal was now being pushed further down the order.

The big excitement of the race was the tremendous progress of the Maserati as it tore through the field. Would it catch the reliable as clockwork Motteram was the big question, and in the event it failed by just half a lap, finishing second, but setting a record time for the circuit. David Van Dal finished ninth, having broken a valve spring.

Johnny Motteram had had an excellent day's sport and his motor had never missed a beat, a tribute to his preparation for the day's events, and no doubt he celebrated in style at the prize-giving ball that evening.

Easter Monday, 14 April, marked the inauguration of yet another 'round the houses' race in Western Australia 'The Northam Flying Fifty'. Northam was a 'wheat and sheep' town, some sixty miles east of Perth, and the 2¼ mile circuit had one straight of almost a mile in length.

Practice on Easter Sunday demonstrated that the circuit was extremely bumpy, several cars being thrown into the air. One, the supercharged MG driven by visiting South Australian driver Don Reimann, was travelling much faster than most, and Don lost it over the bumps, the car skidding on landing, straight into a tree, badly injuring poor Don. As a result the course was altered to detour around the Town Hall,

The over 1500cc three-lap scratch race at Northam. David Van Dal (no. 16) and a grid full of specials: 5: Dave Morphett in Sid Barker's Ford V8-engined Ballot 1: Syd Anderson's V16 Ford Special (2 V8 Ford engines coupled in tandem 7,800cc) 3: Sid Taylor's TS Special (3½ litre Dodge engine) 10: Syd Negus' Plymouth Special (3.3 litre Plymouth engine) 14: Frank Lawrence's Chrysler Speedcar (ex Barry Ranford) 9: Maurie Maurice's Chrysler Special. Behind and to the right of the gird can be seen the pits, with smaller-capacity cars awaiting their race. (*Photograph: Terry McGrath collection*)

thereby slowing the cars down and avoiding major bumps.

Two Morgans were entered for the day's races – David Van Dal's Plus 4 and Johnny Motteram's 4/4. The three-lap scratch races began the proceedings, one for cars of over 1500 cc and one for those of below. David took part in the former, and found himself on the grid surrounded by typical Australian specials of this era. He could make little impression upon them, the victor being Syd Anderson driving the incredible, but effective, ex-Eldred Norman double Ford V8-engined special.

After two more races came a five-lap handicap in which sixteen cars came to the line. Sid Taylor proved the victor with his TS Special, followed by Greg McEwin's fast HRG with David Van Dal and his Plus 4 in third place.

Then came the Northam Flying Fifty, a handicap race over twenty-three laps of the course. Sixteen cars took to the line, the scratch man being Syd Anderson with his double V8-engined special. Two Morgans were taking part – David Van Dal with a handicap of 4 min. 25 sec., and Johnny Motteram on the limit mark (6 min. 30 sec.).

Johnny set a cracking pace from the start, and indeed many thought he would hold his lead to the finish as he had at Narrogin. At half distance he was still well in the lead.

Meanwhile David Van Dal had been climbing

Johnny Motteram at Northam, about to be passed by Maurie Maurice's Chrysler Special. *(Photograph: Johnny Motteram collection)*

up the field from ninth place at the start until he was second to Motteram by the tenth lap. He was lapping consistently in around 2 min. 50 sec., but David must have thought he stood little chance of catching Johnny Motteram, who was lapping just three seconds slower, and was still some distance ahead.

Then on the eighteenth lap the progress of Johnny was interrupted by a broken battery terminal. He had dropped down to tenth before he got going again although the repair was completed within four minutes. This left David Van Dal in the lead, and the only question now was whether any of the back markers could get to him before the finish, in particular Maurie Maurice's Chrysler Special. David held on by ten seconds to take the race, Maurice finishing second and Noel Aldous was third with his MG.

David was delighted to receive the laurel wreath as victor, and also the Licensed Victuallers' Trophy after an excellent drive.

The Australian Grand Prix was also held on Easter Monday, but this year it took place in New South Wales on the Bathurst circuit. No Morgans took part, but in the six-lap Ferodo handicap held after the main event, for production cars (open and closed) the Plus 4 of D. McDonald made an appearance. He was clocked at 92.79 mph through the speed trap, but his last lap was very slow and he did not feature in the first eight finishers.

Richard Reynolds managed to find some circuit racing in the state of Victoria when he took part in the Nash Park Corio races held on 27 April. Nash Park was a one-mile virtually oval grass track situated on land owned by the Nash family some 4 miles from Geelong on the road to Melbourne. Sadly the racing was marred by the death of John Cooper, which occurred when he turned over his Jaguar XK 120, and the meeting was abandoned.

In South Australia Peter Hay was the only

Victory for David Van Dal, wearing the laurel wreath. Also congratulating themselves are his father, Sidney, and his pit crew, Bill Norgard. (*Photograph: Terry McGrath collection*)

competitor in the over 1500 cc sports car class, at Collingrove hill climb on 11 May. He recorded 47.5 seconds, and was actually eighth fastest overall, the fastest being Eldred Norman with his Maserati in 42 seconds.

On 17 May Reynolds was back at Rob Roy for the hill climb. In the morning he recorded 38.00 seconds to finish first in the class for sports cars from 1501 to 3000 (again his was the only entry).

Richard had fitted cycle front wings to his Morgan now, so after lunch he was able to remove these and enter the same capacity racing car class. He recorded 35.67 seconds to finish second behind E. Perkins' rear-engined Lancia special.

The injuries to Don Reimann at Northam led the Western Australia Sports Car Club and the Northam Car Club jointly to hold a benefit meeting for him at Mooliabeenie on 25 May.

Standing and flying quarter mile trials began the day with A. Herbert's 'stock' Plus 4 clocking 12.2 seconds (73.5 mph) for the flying quarter mile. David Van Dal clocked 11.4 sec. (79 mph) and Johnny Motteram 12.1 sec. (74.5 mph), showing just how competitive his car now was.

After some gymkhana events came the circuit races. In the three-lap sealed handicap event David Van Dal managed third place, behind winner Sid Taylor's TS Special, and Fred Coxon's Ford A Special. In the final event, a five-lap sealed handicap, David finished second equal with Syd Anderson (driving the twin Ford V8-engined special), behind Sid Taylor once more, with Johnny Motteram seventh. £110 was collected for the recovering Don Reimann during the day, an excellent achievement.

The Western Australia drivers congregated on Goomalling on Monday 2 June (Foundation Day) for the Fourth Goomalling Speed Classic on the usual L-shaped 2.2-mile course. In the under 1500 cc three-lap scratch race Johnny Motteram finished a disappointing sixth, his engine lacking its usual zip. In the over 1500 cc race Syd Anderson was unstoppable with the double Ford V8 special but David Van Dal did manage fourth place behind Sid Taylor's TS and Syd Negus' Plymouth special.

Johnny Motteram's luck failed to return for the five-lap handicap – he broke a brake cable, putting paid to his day's racing. David Van Dal finished seventh, the winner being the on-form Syd Anderson, with Colin Uphill second in the Topolino – a pretty little Ford 10 special he was now campaigning.

The main event of the day, the Goomalling Flying Fifty was to be a handicap race over fifteen laps of the circuit. Twelve cars came to the line, David Van Dal being the only Morgan driver, with 1 min. 45 sec. start over scratch man Syd Anderson. David's luck was also out, for he needed to pit with steering problems, rejoining when nothing wrong could be found, but then retiring on the next lap. It was later discovered that a faulty oil seal in the front offside hub had led to the brake linings swelling, locking the wheel.

David Van Dal was now to put his Morgan back into original trim and begin preparation of another specifically for racing. Not long after the running of the Northam Flying Fifty an impressed Bill Richards had called him into his 'office' (the Rosemount Hotel bar) and offered to supply David with a new Morgan for racing. This new red Morgan Plus 4 took the registration latterly used on his original car, 21–936.

There was a Morgan entered for the state of Queensland's Road Racing Championship held on 9 June on the old aerodrome at Lowood, some forty miles inland from Brisbane. The entrant was Jack Hicks, and he was continuing the Australian motor enthusiast's delight for building specials, for the four-wheeler he was racing was actually one of the last batch of Morgan three-wheeler vee twins to be imported into Australia in 1946. Chassis D1891 had been converted to a four-wheeler, and, with highly tuned Matchless engine, was reputedly capable of 106 mph on the fastest part of the 2.7-mile circuit.

In the six-lap under 1500 cc scratch race Jack finished second in 14 min. 27.2 sec., at an average speed of 67.50 mph, the winner being Stan Mossetter with a Riley special. In the Queensland Road Racing Championship over fifty-five miles it was again Stan Mossetter who was the victor, with the Morgan 5th and last of the finishers, some six minutes behind.

Richard Reynolds was also in action on 9 June but this time in a hill climb. This was at Templestowe for the Queen's birthday holiday meeting, only the second time that hill climbing had actually been held at this venue, and the first meeting since the surface had received a bitumen cover. As a result many record times were to be established. The hill was very twisty, with many steep gradients, including a one-in-three section (The Wall). The course was 1,060 yards long. There were just two entrants in the sports car class for 1501–3000 cc, and Richard proved to be the victor, recording 74.2 seconds to set a new class record, and beating Stapleton's Alvis saloon, which was driven by Clerk of the Course, Maurie Monk.

Aside from racing Richard was finding the Morgan to be fairly unsuited to ordinary Australian roads, which were often of very poor quality. The Morgan was regularly on ramps to replace damaged items, and he also discovered that the Morgan had previously been damaged during Major Barker's ownership.

Over in South Australia Peter Hay had been meticulously preparing his Plus 4 for further racing during the cold winter nights. The cylinder head, manifolds and ports were polished to a mirror finish, the carburettor jets increased in size and the throttle butterfly made thinner. The push rods were also lightened and polished, and new valves carefully fitted.

On 11 October Peter took his Plus 4 on to Sellick's Beach, near Adelaide, for the SA Sporting Car Club's speed meeting in front of 5,000 spectators. Racing was delayed for 2½ hours by a high tide and strong westerly wind, but eventually the sea left the course. A two-mile circuit

The tuned and much developed Vanguard engine fitted to David Van Dal's Plus 4. The two ex-Ford V8 twin-choke Stromberg carburettors and tuned stub exhausts are clearly visible. Upon the bulkhead lies the discarded ex-Citroën air filter, used with the original single Solex carburettor. These air filters were necessary in Western Australia because of the sand and dust. (*Photograph: David Van Dal collection*)

was produced for racing up and down the 80 yd. wide patch of hard sand, by placing 44 gallon oil drums at either end for hairpin turns. Peter was pleased that his car proved fast enough to beat a stripped, tuned MG TC. His best result was a fourth place in the top race in the programme, the unlimited handicap, which had attracted over forty starters.

Mooliabeenie was once again used by the WA Sporting Car Club on 19 October, David Van Dal and A. Herbert both being entries, but we have no results.

David Van Dal had been gradually developing his Morgan for racing. Most noticeable was the conversion from a Single Solex carburettor to twin twin-choke Strombergs, ex-Ford V8, which ran on a 50/50 alcohol/avgas mixture, and the use of tuned exhaust manifold stub exhausts to extract the gases.

Richard Reynolds was back at Rob Roy hill climb in Victoria for the twenty-ninth meeting, held on 4 November. This was 'Cup Day', the day of the famous Melbourne Cup horse race, and racing would therefore stop while the horse race was being run, to allow spectators to hear the horse racing commentary. This meeting was also the Australian Hillclimb championship meeting, so it attracted an impressive field. This time Reynolds recorded 36.34 seconds, but Stan Jones' Aston Martin DB2 was an easy class winner with 34.54 seconds, and Richard had to settle for fifth position.

Richard also had the pleasure of driving another Morgan at this event – the 1946 Matchless-engined three-wheeler belonging to Ian Stewart, who was physically handicapped and therefore preferred the hand throttle fitted to three-wheeler Morgan vee twins. The time was 42.33 seconds, and *Australian Motor Sport* described the climb as 'funereal'!

Racing in the state of New South Wales was difficult for the motor sport enthusiast, there being a lack of suitable venues. In 1952 the town of Paramatta, near Sydney, had held some races on circuits laid out in Paramatta Park. We know that S. Godfrey entered a Plus 4 for the 15 November meeting, but again have no results.

1952 had been a good year for Morgans in Australia, with good performances in several states. Development of several racing Morgans was continuing for events during 1953.

New Zealand

1951 had been a barren year for Morgan racing in New Zealand, but things were to improve in 1952 now that the new Plus 4 was available. The main agent in North Island was Independent Motor Sales Ltd in Wellington, run by Jack Shelly. Keith Roper, the manager of Nelson Car Sales, in Nelson on the South Island, made an arrangement with Mr Shelly to sell some cars. On 18 March 1952 a sales representative called Allen Freeman purchased a red four-seater, chassis P2290, which had left the Morgan factory on 31 December 1951. Allen kept his Morgan standard for he used it as his business car during the week, but at weekends he began to compete with the car. On 29 March he took the Plus 4 to the Saddle Road hill climb at Palmerston North on the North Island collecting ninth fastest time.

Over the weekend of 26 and 27 April he competed first on the Saturday in the Sundstrum Memorial Rally based at Dunedin in the south of the South Island, finishing nineteenth, and then on the Sunday he was grass-track racing at nearby Hampden, Otago, finishing in the places in several races.

He also competed in trials, and on 11 May he was second in the 150-mile trial based at Watrarapa, while the following weekend he was at the Wanganui Trial.

Meanwhile, having been impressed by the performance and handling of his old 4/4, Ted Reid of Dunedin had decided to purchase a new Plus 4. This was P2412, a green two-seater, and it was despatched from the Morgan factory on 26 June to T. R. Taylor Ltd of Invercargill, South Island.

Allen Freeman continued his motor sport with fastest time of the day at the Game Farm Road hill climb at Paraparaumu on 11 September, and also at the Flagstaff hill climb at Trentham on 18 October.

Next it was the New Zealand Championship Rally, held on 24 and 25 October, based at Manawatu in the North Island. There was no luck for Allen in this, however, for his navigator was ill for the last half of the rally and they finished sixty-first! The following day, however, Allen was back on the hill at Saddle Road, Palmerston North and recorded the fastest time of the day.

On Labour Day, 27 October, the Nelson Car Club ran a race meeting on the front (main) beach of Tahuna, using a course of four-fifths of a mile. Club member and local Morgan dealer Keith Roper entered his own Morgan, a red two-seater Plus 4, and thousands of Nelson townsfolk crowded the sandhills to watch him finish second in a rolling start ten-lap scratch race, behind Halsey Logan's HRG. On 8 November Allen Freeman took part in a forty-mile night trial, based at Lower Hutt on North Island, finishing third, and one week later he was back hill climbing, this time on Houghton Bay Road, Wellington, where he finished with fifth fastest time of the day, but winner of his class.

Meanwhile, Ted Reid was finding his new Plus 4 a joy to throw around on the gravel roads that abounded in New Zealand at this time, so predictable was its handling, allowing slides to be taken at speed with confidence. On 22 November he entered the South Canterbury Car Club's hill climb, taking home the first place award in his class.

CHAPTER FOURTEEN

1953

January 1953 heralded a rise in the cost of the road fund licence for cars of £2 10*s.* 0*d.* (£2.50), the new rate being £12 10*s.* 0*d.* Thankfully there was no thought of returning to a tax based on horsepower.

Within the month the BMTA Covenant system was to be totally abolished, allowing the resale of motor vehicles to take place without consideration of the time they had been owned by the original purchaser. Morgan and other sports cars had been made exempt from this scheme during 1952 as we have previously mentioned, but now there was total freedom for the second-hand market.

This winter's MCC Exeter Trial slipped, datewise, from the end of December to start on Friday night 2 January, finishing the following day and having three starting points: Stratford on Avon, Virginia Water and Launceston. 166 cars started this traditional event, including no fewer than twelve Morgans.

The Morgan factory had entered Peter Morgan in his Coupe, JNP 239, Jim Goodall in HUY 982, and Sonny McCann in the short chassis 4/4, BWP47. Joe Huxham was in his usual 1098cc Climax-engined 4/4, FOH 812, Derek Howard was giving trials a try in his black ex-Alpine

John Moore on Simms in the Exeter Trial. An extra large spare wheel is being carried, presumably as a spare for the similar rear wheels. (*Photograph: Morgan Motor Co collection*)

Basil Roy going well during the Exeter Trial. (*Photograph: Quadrant Picture Library*)

Plus 4, CJX 318 and John Moore was using his Coupe, KNP 5. The Hobbs brothers were in their two 4/4s, the Climax car, GAE 705, being driven by Alan and the Standard car, GBH 458, by Ken. Les Newey was also in a Standard-engined 4/4. Three more Plus 4 drivers completed the entry – Basil De Mattos in KWP 127, Basil Roy in MLP 816 and D. L. Markham.

Good weather, but with a frost, ensured good driving conditions on the hills, although Simms defeated Jim and Sonny in the Morgan team. When the results were announced, Peter and Joe Huxham were the only Morgan drivers with Firsts, Jim, Sonny, John Moore, Alan Hobbs, Basil de Mattos and Basil Roy all taking Seconds, and the other three took Third Class Awards.

As we have indicated, this Exeter Trial was really part of the MCC's 1952 trials year and, as Peter Morgan had previously won First Class Awards in the 1952 Lands End Trial and the 1952 Edinburgh Rally, this latest success in the Exeter gave him three Firsts for the year. He was thus delighted to be awarded his second much coveted MCC Triple Award for such a magnificent achievement.

Not only that but the Morgan factory team was awarded the MCC's 1952 Team Championship for its success in those same three events, demonstrating once again that Morgan was a name to be reckoned with in this type of motor sport.

Continuing the trials successes was Sgt Hastings with his Plus 4, in the Eastern Counties Motor Club's Sporting Trial, held on 18 January. He finished third, behind Alex Cleghorn's Dellow and Jacobs' Land Rover, which presumably was only allowed two-wheel drive.

This was probably the last competition event for Hastings' Plus 4, KWP 741, for it was shortly to return to the Morgan factory for an overhaul and preparation for shipment to the USA.

Presumably Sgt Hastings' English tour of duty was coming to an end.

Bill Parkes took the navigator's job for Graham Stallard in CAB 652 on 18 January, for the Worcestershire MC's Rally. The combination proved very successful, for they were second overall, and first in their class.

Perhaps the greatest adventure for the Continental rally enthusiast was the Rallye Automobile Monte Carlo, where crews would battle through the snow and ice of winter roads, over the Alpine passes to the exciting Mediterranean town of Monte Carlo completing some two thousand miles of testing motoring in four days.

This annual event had caught the imagination of the British public and was well reported by newspapers and wireless.

Taking part this year was a Plus 4, entered by Roy Clarkson, to start from Munich on 20 January. This Morgan, however, looked nothing like the normal product from the Malvern factory, for it had a closed coupe body, similar to the Touring design of the 2.3 litre Ferrari that Roy had rallied in 1951.

Roy, a dental surgeon based in Halstead, Essex, had been a keen trials and rally competitor since pre-war days. He moved his practice down from his native Scotland after the war and also formed the East Anglian Motor Club. In 1950 he helped fellow Scot, Gregor Grant, launch *Autosport* magazine and it was Grant who persuaded Roy to buy the Ferrari. He considered that the car handled well but was not particularly fast.

Roy Clarkson's Ferrari, with Carozzeria Touring superleggra body work. (*Photograph: Roy Clarkson collection*)

The overall performance of the new Plus 4, however, had impressed Roy on various events and he had also got to know Peter Morgan quite well.

When regulations for rallying indicated a class for four-seater grand touring cars, Roy thought that a body like the Ferrari but fitted to a Morgan chassis, would fit the bill. The regulations for the Monte had banned open sports cars after 1951, but individually built closed versions of open cars in series production would be allowed for 1952 and 1953. Sydney Allard won the 1952 Monte outright in his saloon bodied Allard, so Roy aimed to have his car completed for the 1953 event.

As a result, he purchased a Plus 4 rolling chassis, P2483, which was delivered to the Halstead Motor Company on 13 October 1952. From there it was taken to the premises of Adams and Robinson, Sunbury on Thames, which were shared with Maurice Gomm.

Charlie Robinson, who had an enviable reputation for his skills in multi-directional panel work, started work on two bodies using photos of Clarkson's Ferrari. He copied the Carozzeria Touring superleggra, or ultra-light, technique of aluminium panelling hung on a light tubular superstructure, welded to the car's chassis. The second body was fitted to a Jowett Jupiter chassis for fellow rally enthusiast Philip Fotheringham-Parker, who must have had plans for the same event.

Unfortunately, Robinson's firm got into financial difficulties. Work on the Jupiter stagnated and the Morgan was only finished by Maurice Gomm stepping in. In the hurry to get the car completed, insufficient care was taken when working on the special fuel tank trying to correct a leak, and it exploded, necessitating another to be made from scratch.

Nevertheless, the completed Morgan, registered VNO 600, was an excellent job, weighing just 14½ cwt. A number of features helped keep weight to a minimum, including perspex rear and side windows.

The interior was fitted out to barely accommodate four people, with access to a space for soft luggage above the fuel tank. A small panel in the tail allowed access to a compartment just big enough to take a spare wheel, with the tyre deflated!

A special radiator, with a slim header tank, allowed a low bonnet line. Its mounting in the car, however, would prove problematical at first until the front of the chassis was boxed to improve rigidity.

Under the bonnet was the standard 2088 cc Vanguard unit. Roy's dental mechanic, Alan Blyth, did most of the work on the car during its subsequent career, including engine tuning under Roy's direction. (Roy wished to avoid putting oily fingers into patients' mouths!)

After three days and nights of solid work to ready Roy's new car for the Monte, there was little or no time for testing. It was too late to catch the ferry with the Morgan but Silver City Airways flew them across the Channel in a Bristol Freighter.

The Munich start was reached just in time but thick fog soon hampered progress on the route. On a wide autobahn, Roy and his co-driver found it impossible to navigate in the poor visibility and they became hopelessly lost. A motorcycle policeman rescued them and tried in vain to find them hotel accommodation, so they ended up spending a night in the cells!

So much time had been lost that they were to retire from the rally. However, it was decided to motor on down to Monte Carlo to gain more experience with the car and join in the end of rally parties. Success with the Morgan would come later.

Philip Fotherington-Parker's Jowett Jupiter body was not finished in time for the event, and he obtained a drive in a Sunbeam-Talbot. It was to be four years before it was finally completed.

February could be a tricky month to run rallies as the Cambridge University AC and Yorkshire Sports Car Club found with their two rallies.

The Cambridge UAC's third Lent Term Rally, held in February, became known as the 'Miniature Monte'. This was very apt as every competitor had penalties at the end of the road sections, with snow, ice and a temperature of 10° below freezing doing the damage. After leaving the two starting points at St Neots and Leeds, the initial route was by main roads but the Pennine sections and bleak Yorkshire Moors caught out many, although Derek Howard was keeping up among the leaders of the seventy-eight strong field.

Thirty-six finished, and the winner was Leeds garage owner Ken Lee in an MG TD. Derek Howard was fifth overall, and Barrie Phipps eighth in KUY 714. Member of the winning Leeds University II team was J. M. Hulme with a Standard-engined 4/4. He was eleventh overall.

The YSCC's Annual Rally this year was not using the usual special tests but was relying upon the road sections to sort out the winners. Sixty-eight starters set off from Harrogate on 13 February, beginning at 9 p.m. on a cold clear night to face a route much modified by snow and ice which had closed many roads. Despite the easier new route, Jimmy Ray got stuck on a snow-covered hill near Steamer although Peter Reece managed to crawl to the summit.

By the early hours only twenty-four competitors were still running, drifting snow causing havoc, and much of the route had to be hastily deleted. Twenty-two clocked in at the finish, all with mammoth penalty scores. The winner was Peter Bolton in a Sunbeam-Talbot but two Morgan drivers had struggled through to win First Class Awards. These were Derek Howard in CJX 318, and William Whiteley of Poole in Wharfedale, who was driving his blue 1952 Plus 4, reg. PKK 256. This car, chassis P2402, had originally been delivered to Tonbridge in Kent on 20 June, although Yorkshire-based Whiteley is listed as the first owner.

There were so many rallies now that an enthusiast could find an event every weekend. As with all motor sport in Great Britain, these events were run under the jurisdiction of the RAC. There were various categories of events available. The most minor were those put on by car clubs, just for the participation of their own members, such as those we have previously reported run by the Morgan 4/4 Club. These were termed 'Closed' events by the RAC, entries being closed to club members only.

The next, more ambitious, type of event for a club to put on was termed 'Closed Invitation', meaning that club members, plus members of other invited clubs, could participate. Such rallies included the Cambridge University and Yorkshire rallies that we have just reported. In order to make sure of invites to these events the keen rally competitors, such as Jimmy Ray, Derek Howard and now Barrie Phipps, were members of several car clubs.

'National' classified rallies were more important rallies, designed for the experienced rally driver to enter. Finally, there were 'International' classified rallies, of which the RAC was the only British event, the Alpine, Tulip and Monte Carlo being well-known Continental examples.

To try and produce some form of championship for keen rally drivers, the British Trial Drivers Association (BTDA) had introduced an annual Silver Star competition for the best six performances in eight major or national rallies, and a Gold Star competition for the best performances in international rallies. They also had separate categories for ladies.

In 1952 the Silver Star had been won by Dennis O'Malley Taylor with his Jaguar XK 120, Jimmy Ray being the runner-up. For 1953 Jimmy had his sights on the Star itself.

The Lancia Motor Club ran a spring rally with driving tests on a fine spring day on Sunday 8 March. Several Morgans were among the awards, Bernard Clarke and Barrie Phipps being sixth and eighth respectively and collecting First Class Awards and L. Brisacher taking a Second Class Award home. The same weekend the Cumberland SCC ran its third Keswick rally over the Saturday and Sunday. Bob Dickson finished runner up with KUY 476, just ahead of Peter Reece in KUY 475.

For the Oxford University MDC's Rallye Rapide, held over the following weekend, there were two Morgan entries, both from the invited club of the Cambridge University AC. Barrie Phipps finished tenth overall, and fourth in class with KUY 714, while Graeme Anton and his Plus 4 finished 27th out of the fifty-five starters.

Graeme Anton, from Ombersley in Worcester-

The 'Dellow' bodied Plus 4 of Graeme Anton, with rear-hinged doors. (*Photograph: Graeme Anton collection*)

shire, had limped his way into the Morgan factory during 1952, while recovering from injuries sustained serving in the army. He wanted a Plus 4, but was told by Peter Morgan and George Goodall that few were destined for the home market because of the Government's export policy. He was, however, offered a chassis, which he decided to accept, and P2440 was collected from the factory on 18 July 1952.

As Graeme worked in Kidderminster he was familiar with the nearby Dellow company, so he approached Lionel Evans at Radpanels, the company that made Dellow car bodies, and he agreed that they would body his Morgan chassis for him. It was panelled in aluminium over a tubular frame, as had been Barrie Phipps' car, but Graeme's two-seater had unusual rear hinged doors. Graeme painted it turquoise green, it was registered LAB 274, and when he went up to Cambridge University in October 1952 he become a keen competitor with it in their events.

A large crowd gathered at Blackpool on Sunday 15 March, for the Bolton-le-Moors CC's driving tests which this year attracted 287 entries, although only 150 were permitted to start. When the results were announced, Peter Reece in KUY 475 had held off Derek Howard in CJX 318 to take the trophy for best performance of a standard car, Howard taking the class and participating in the team award, which went to the BARC second team.

Meanwhile, back at the Morgan factory, HFS Morgan had built another four-seater Coupe. With chassis number P2612, and registered MAB 696, it was tested by Charlie Curtis during the week of 16 March. Behind the four-seater body was a locker containing the spare wheel. The lid could be lowered to carry luggage – or a crate of pullets perhaps!

The interior of HFS Morgan's four-seater Coupe, as photographed in 1954. (*Photograph: Quadrant Picture Library*)

The Morgans of Graham Stallard (CAB 652) and Les Yarranton (KWP 926) at the Herefordshire MC's Welsh Rally. (*Photograph: Les Yarranton collection*)

HFS was to use this Coupe as his works car throughout the 1950s and was now contemplating adding this model to the Morgan factory range.

The MG CC's Scottish Centre ran a Spring Rally on 22 March, with seven road sections and seven driving tests to sort out the competitors. Charlie Robertson took home a Second Class Award with JSG 320.

The Herefordshire MC's third Welsh Rally was held over the two days of 21 and 22 March and attracted five Morgan entries. The three Plus 4s comprised Les Yarranton with his cream Plus 4, KWP 926. Alan Hobbs also entered a Plus 4, and Barrie Phipps was in KUY 714. Bill Parkes was in FNP 684 and Graham Stallard in CAB 652, making up the two 4/4 entries.

Alan Hobbs's interesting Plus 4 had been acquired from a Bristol garage that had taken it in part exchange and wanted a quick sale. It was a rather odd car, chassis number P2213 which had originally been supplied to Coventry and Jeffs Limited of Bristol on 19 September 1951 as a rolling chassis.

A rather unusual two-seater body had been built to the order of a Bristol doctor, there being just one spare wheel behind a luggage locker. The Morgan was white, and registered OHW 273.

The forty-nine competitors were flagged off by the Mayor and Mayoress of Hereford on the Saturday evening, facing a five hundred mile drive through Wales on second- and third-class roads, at a required average of 30 mph, before finishing at Leominster the following afternoon for the usual driving test.

The class for open cars of over 1500 cc was taken by Alan Hobbs, with Les Yarranton second. Bill Parkes took the Specials class.

The following day marked the beginning of the 1953 RAC International Rally. Of the 204 accepted entries, there were eleven Morgans, all Plus 4s. As usual, the Morgan factory's team consisted of Peter Morgan, Jim Goodall and Doc

Steel in their three cars, KUY 387, HUY 982 and JWP 537. This year they were navigated by Jane Morgan, Terry Hall and Sonny McCann respectively. There was also another Morgan team entered, comprising the three Morgans of Ken Bancroft, Jimmy Ray and Geoff White. Ken was navigated by T. Platt in NTJ 943, Jimmy was in KUY 474, navigated by K. Dunn, and Geoff White was in MOH 453, with Hamilton Evans as his navigator.

Completing the Morgan entries were Alec Gordon and P. Steiner in OZ 2343, H. Mettrick and E. Curtis in MYP 666, John Moore and Terry Langford in the former's Coupe KNP 5, J. Rodley and J. Castle in MYP 338 and finally the Neil sisters in KYS 41.

Miss Andie Neil and her sister Christine hailed from Scotland and had been rallying a Standard Vanguard with some success. Their cream two-seater Morgan, chassis P2508, had been delivered to Carr's Motors in Liverpool on 25 November 1952. Rather unusually, home for the Neil sisters was actually a farm at Tollcross, quite near the centre of Glasgow.

There were two starting points, Hastings and Blackpool, and from each start the first leg led to Silverstone. Here a half-mile sprint down the main straight of the club circuit towards Woodcote concluded with a brake test, there being a line sixty yards beyond the finish that was not to be crossed. This caught out several, including Doc Steel, who slid over the line and was consequently rebuked by his team leader for this lapse of concentration.

Doc Steel fails to stop and slides over the line at Silverstone during the braking test. (*Photograph: Doc Steel collection*)

From Silverstone the entourage headed for Castle Combe for a night driving test. Peter Morgan was outstanding as was Geoff White, but poor Doc Steel continued his nightmare by going into the bays in the wrong order. Luckily he realized his error, and finally did the correct test, but in a somewhat slow time. His passenger, Sonny McCann, was subsequently chastised by Peter Morgan for not looking after his driver properly.

The next venue was Prescott Hill Climb, for a night climb of part of the hill, and then, following a control at Haverfordwest, they made for the Welsh section, including a test at Llandrindod Wells. Geoff White was fastest overall here.

The Tuesday dawned bright and sunny for the drive north to Blackpool, where they were greeted by sea mist on the promenade. This made the pylons for the driving test virtually invisible but this did not stop Jim Goodall and Peter Morgan from making very fast times. Jimmy Ray was even faster, but penalized for a finish line infringement.

After a welcome night in bed the crews set off for the Lake District and the 'consistency test' in which three road sections had to be covered as quickly as possible, with the slowest time to count. Peter Morgan was again outstanding in these hill starts, with Jim Goodall not far behind.

Since leaving Blackpool the planned route was new to the crews – they had received a supplementary Road Book as they left the start that morning, and had had to navigate the course as they went along.

The route took the crews through Stranraer and on to Turnberry for a night driving test, Peter Morgan again being very quick. Following Turnberry the field made for Barnard Castle for a Night Navigation exercise, the controls to be visited being difficult to locate from the route book given to the crews at Blackpool.

After breakfast there was a tricky route to follow to Buxton, by way of another consistency test in the Pennine hills. Many had difficulties with this section which was not helped by the pouring rain.

After a quick lunch at Buxton the crews were allowed to pick their own way to Hastings for a night's rest.

The following morning, Friday, the cars made for Goodwood and further driving tests. Of the

The two Morganing sisters from Glasgow, Andie and Chrissie Neil, at Goodwood. (*Photograph: L.A.T. Photographic*)

148 cars still in the rally, Peter Morgan was best of the Morgan drivers and after the Goodwood driving tests he was in sixth overall position. These tests caught out several other Morgan drivers, however, for Geoff White selected the wrong gear, John Moore had trouble finding his, and Alec Gordon stalled his engine.

The best one hundred drivers took part in the final two deciding tests at Hastings on the Saturday, this being a very cold day complete with mist and rain. On the final test Peter Morgan misunderstood the starter and went off to a false start, with inevitable penalties.

When it was all over it was Ian Appleyard who had won the rally, driving his famous XK 120 Jaguar. There was also a Jaguar success in the team competition, in which Ian was supported by Messrs Grant-Norton and Grounds. This was not a good event for Morgans, with none finishing in the first twenty.

When he returned home to Worcester, Doc Steel was on the receiving end of much ribbing from his friends, who claimed he had messed up the driving tests purely to get his name in the motoring magazines!

The Government announced a revision of purchase tax on new cars as from April, this time in the motorist's favour, with a reduction from 66⅔% to 50%. Coupled with the availability of branded petrol since February, this meant that the world of the motoring enthusiast was definitely improving. This was amply demonstrated by the increase in numbers of available events for the sportsman.

Easter was packed out with events for enthusiasts. Good Friday, 3 April, marked the traditional start date of the MCC's Lands End Trial, which this year had a record entry of 426 vehicles, of which 166 were cars. There were just five Morgans, however: two 4/4s and three Plus 4s. The 4/4s were FOH 812, driven by Joe Huxham, and BWP 47, driven by Sonny McCann. The Plus 4s were those of Basil Roy (probably MLP 816) Jim Goodall (HUY 982) and John Moore (KNP 5). Despite snow on the Friday night and showers of sleet and rain on the Saturday, Sonny McCann managed a First Class Award, the others taking Seconds.

Several events took place on Easter Saturday. The Pembrokeshire MC's hill climb at Lydstep near Tenby was unfortunately plagued by snow and sleet blasting over the half-mile course. Best Morgan performance was that of Mrs Doreen Reece who also made best time of the day by a lady driver.

In Scotland the Scottish Sporting Car Club's Highland Three Days rally commenced in Glasgow, attracting an entry of fifty-two. Again blinding snow made life difficult on the first day's drive to Gleneagles, with many penalties for the crews on the road sections. There were several driving tests on route.

On the Sunday the route began and finished in Gleneagles, but wind and rain again made life unpleasant. The final day was a little easier on the competitors, with Ian Jeffrey and his HRG proving the overall winners, ahead of Standard dealer Bob Dickson's Standard Vanguard. The ladies' award was taken by Andie Neil, passengered by her sister Chrissie in their Plus 4, KYS 41, and Charlie Robertson was in the winning team with JSG 320.

Over in Northern Ireland Easter Saturday also marked the start in Belfast of the one thousand mile Circuit of Ireland Trial, organized by the Ulster AC. Several Morgans took part in this strenuous four-day event. The first day was fairly uneventful for the Morgans but then things began to go wrong.

The second day began with a regularity test,

Charlie Robertson awaits the start of the special test on 'Rest and be Thankful', where he was second fastest. (*Photograph: Morgan Motor Co. collection*)

with a set 24 mph average for the forty miles of most primitive Irish roads in the Sheehy Mountains of Co. Cork. During this test John Howe ran into the back of Desmond Titterington's Sunbeam Talbot when the latter stopped suddenly after missing a turning, and the steering damage to John's Plus 4 proved terminal.

The next special test was a novel timed descent of a mountain pass near Ballyduff, which had a loose road surface causing much sliding. An excellent time in this was recorded by Albert Acheson's green Plus 4, registration KUY 625.

Albert's car was chassis P2350, which was registered KUY 625 on 27 March 1952, but was not despatched to the Belfast agent Victor Ltd until 25 April 1952. Quite why there was this delay we do not know.

On the third day, Easter Monday, the crews faced a twenty-seven hour drive right round the west coast of Ireland to the final control at Bangor, Co. Down. Albert Acheson was caught out early on by a secret control after a hump-backed bridge, and received 100 penalty points. At the timed hill climb of Corkscrew Hill, Lisdoonvarna, Albert was second in class behind Frank Bigger's Jaguar. Fourth fastest was Jim Eaton's Morgan Plus 4.

Jim, a Londonderry baker, was driving P2510, a two-seater Plus 4 despatched to Victor Ltd on 15 November 1952 and registered locally as UI 4920.

Jim Eaton with his Morgan before the start of the 1,000 miles Circuit of Ireland Trial. Adjoining the Morgan on the Belfast cobbles is a Jowett Jupiter and a Citroën. (*Photograph: Jim Eaton Collection*)

For this event Jim had fitted extra lights, and removed the hubcaps. He had previously owned and rallied an MG TC.

The long run around the coast proved difficult for the tired crews, and many cars began to show signs of contact with the scenery. Jim Eaton suffered the dreaded steering wobble after both steering dampers sheared, and he limped into Sligo at 15 mph, having collected many time penalties. The dampers were repaired at a wayside garage during the night by bolting lengths of rubber cut from an old tyre above and below the broken strips.

Following the deciding driving tests on the Tuesday at Bangor it was Lisburn driver Wilbert Todd and his Dellow who won the event, none of the Morgans featuring in the awards.

After his experience with steering dampers in this event Jim Eaton was to reinforce these items thereafter on his Morgan with pieces of flat industrial belting, then in general factory usage.

Roy Clarkson was continuing with the development of his special Morgan, and took it to the West Essex Car Club's sprint meeting held at Snetterton on 12 April. Originally the WECC had wanted to use the popular circuit at Boreham, but racing had had to be abandoned at that venue, so the replacement ex-airfield circuit at Snetterton, between Thetford and Attleborough, was booked. Sadly heavy rain made sprinting difficult along the 880-yard stretch of the circuit.

On 18 April Roy was back at Snetterton, this time for the Aston Martin OC's race meeting, held on the full 2.7-mile circuit, and this time in glorious sunshine.

Although Roy did not feature in the results of this closed to club event, the car motored quickly, despite rear wheel patter and brake fade. This was a useful test for Roy before the forthcoming Tulip Rally, due to start on 27 April.

Down in Hampshire, the West Hants and Dorset CC ran their first meeting of the year, also on 18 April. It was held on the 2.2-mile airfield circuit at Ibsley, near Ringwood. Two 4/4s were entered for the five-lap race for up to 750 cc supercharged, and up to 1500 cc unsupercharged. The drivers were Jeff Sparrowe, in JUO 177, and Joe Huxham, in FOH 812. Neither could keep

Joe Huxham struggles to keep ahead of Donald Beauman's Riley at Ibsley. (*Photograph: Guy Griffiths*)

up with the very fast ex-Mike Hawthorn Riley of Donald Beauman which won the event after Peter Gammon's yellow MG special spun.

Another event taking place on 18 April was the London MC's Little Rally. Once again the event attracted a big field, 240 entries being accepted despite being a closed invitation event. There were seven Morgans, five Plus 4s and two 4/4s. In the former group was L. G. Brisacher with MXH 946 (although he actually non-started), M. C. Cartwright with NBJ 971, Alec Gordon with OZ 2343, Geoff White with MOH 453 and Bernard Clarke with PKK 769. The latter group consisted of Bill Parkes with FNP 684 and another Standard-engined 4/4, PPU 286, the entry of R. H. Minall.

Bill Parkes was truly outstanding, finishing class winner of the 'specials' class, with a points score equivalent to second overall, and taking home the 'Breakheart Trophy' as reward for his efforts. Alec Gordon was also excellent, finishing third in his class. His team, comprising himself, Geoff White and Bert Westwood's Dellow came second behind a team of Jaguars in the team competition.

The following weekend the Rhyl and DMC ran its two-day North Wales Rally, attracting some sixty competitors to the Chester or Rhyl starts. There was an interesting regularity test on the Horseshoe Pass, where there was a timed descent of the new pass and an ascent of the old pass on the Saturday, with the drivers having to repeat their times to the nearest half minute the following day, but going in the reverse direction. Jimmy Ray excelled here, with just five seconds difference in times for a test taking over 14½ minutes.

Breakfast was taken in Rhyl prior to the final driving test, and Jimmy Ray, in KUY 474, took the Rhyl Motor Trader's Trophy, with his passenger Jeff Dixon taking the Chilwell Davies Shield for best navigator. Best club member award went to Barrie Davies in a Morgan.

The 1953 'Tulpen Rallye' attracted 237 starters. There was just one Morgan, the special of Roy Clarkson, and he was passengered by Gregor Grant, the editor of *Autosport*. There were seven starting points, The Hague, London, Brussels, Basle, Paris, Hamburg and Stuttgart, with Clarkson choosing Brussels. All the routes converged at Spa and from there led to the first test at Clervaux – a downhill speed test, with engine off! Later, during the 42 kilometre special stage between Willer and Schweighouse, dense fog made driving very difficult, and Gregor Grant as co-driver found himself on a grassy patch overhanging a precipice, before luckily realizing his mistake.

In Switzerland, the fabulous Col de la Faucille, an ascent of 10,600 metres, formed the third special test. Here, Clarkson and Grant were second in class to the Bill Banks and Mike Porter's Bristol.

The fourth special test was a climb of the Ballon d'Alsace, and here Clarkson was truly outstanding, being first in class, some 4½ seconds ahead of the Banks' Bristol.

With the bulk of the event over, and now on the return leg, there was to be cruel disappointment for Roy and Gregor, for the radiator header tank burst. Despite getting the blacksmith in the Alsatian village of Friedland to look at the car, it was beyond immediate repair, and the Morgan had to be retired.

At the finish of the rally, the technical committee went to town on many of the cars, eliminating several for having non-standard non-production fitments. As a result a Dutch driver's Jowett Javelin became the winner, with the Banks' Bristol runner up. Quite how the very non-standard Morgan would have fared, if it had finished, is an interesting speculation.

Ever since the 1952 Motor Show, Standard Triumph had been working on improving their

Roy Clarkson's Saloon Morgan after the Tulip Rally. (*Photograph: Roy Clarkson collection*)

new sports car, including the engine, under the direction of Ken Richardson. We shall discuss this in detail later, but one spin-off was an improvement also in the Vanguard engine, and engines from number V574ME were supplied to a revised specification. The first Morgan to be built with the improved Vanguard engine was P2641, which was despatched on 6 June, fitted with engine V584ME.

The revised specification included a better crankcase breathing system, so future Plus 4 owners no longer had little pools of oil on the garage floor after a hard drive.

The North Devon MC ran its third Ilfracombe Rally over the weekend of 9 and 10 May. Included in the eighty-three entries was a new name to Morgans, that of Taunton GP, Dr John Spare. John had begun in motor sport in 1948 with a Vauxhall 12, then concentrating on trials in 1949 and 1950 in a Ford-based trials car. After some class wins in rallies in 1952 with a Standard Vanguard, he had hankered after something more competitive, and so had travelled to Carlisle to purchase KUY 476 from Bob Dickson. It was now fitted with standard Morgan seating, with 'float on air' Moseley cushions over a wooden frame.

There were starting points at Ilfracombe, Plymouth, Bristol, Bournemouth and London, the routes then converging at Ottery for a night run across Exmoor and Dartmoor. There were several tests *en route*, and the event finished with further tests on the pier at Ilfracombe.

Overall winner was Plymouth Vauxhall dealer George Turnbull, with a modified 4/4 fitted with twin reversing lights for the night tests. John Spare won the over 1300 cc open car class, and also had the best aggregate time for the pier tests. Barrie Phipps had to make two attempts to get into one of the test garages on the pier with KUY 714.

A bumper entry of 280 cars was received for the Morecambe Coronation Year National Rally, organized by the Lancs AC on 15–17 May. There were eight starting points: Birmingham, Glasgow, Leeds, Bristol, Manchester, London, Morecambe or Whalley, from whence the crews departed on the Friday, the routes converging at Higher Hodder. At the timed hill climb at Birdie Brow, Harry Harrop was in the top few with his Plus 4.

In to Morecambe for the tests on the

promenade to finish the first day and John Spare was second fastest behind Ian Appleyard's Jaguar.

The Saturday began with further driving tests in the rain on the promenade, before setting off for the Lake District. There was a delay at Wrynose – the Jowett company were testing their Bradford vans there at the time, but eventually all returned to Morecambe for the final driving tests. In the first test, John Spare and Derek Howard tied for second behind Ian Appleyard.

In the second test, Jimmy Ray was fifth fastest, with Derek Howard just behind.

When the results were announced it was Ian Appleyard who had won the event, with Jimmy Ray taking the class award for open cars of 1301–2,600 cc, after finishing tenth overall. Derek Howard was twelfth and won the W. W. Turner Challenge Trophy for his performance in the Saturday afternoon tests. Completing the Morgan prizes was Annie Neil, who took home the ladies' prize. First Class Awards were won by Harry Harrop, Geoff White, Doc Spare and Gerry Hoyle the Southport Morgan agent. Whiteley, Alec Gordon, J. D. Waddell and V. Thomas had only rally badges for their efforts. All were in Plus 4s.

Geoff White's Morgan was now a smart white. It had been returned to the Morgan factory for repainting, but the previous red paint had not been completely removed beforehand, so various areas such as the bonnet louvres were an interesting pink colour.

Three Morgans took to the hill at Prescott for the BOC's National Meeting on 17 May, over the usual 880-yard course. The sole Morgan representative in the class for sports cars up to 1500 cc was 'Bill' Parkes with FNP 684, recording a time of 59.17 seconds to finish in fifteenth place. In the class for 1501–3000 cc sports cars J. H. Cunningham's 1952 Plus 4 recorded 55.56 seconds, finishing fifth, while John Moore and

Whiteley in action during the Morecambe Rally. (*Photograph: National Motor Museum*)

his Coupe KNP 5 were not much slower, with a time of 55.92 seconds, finishing eighth.

John Cunningham, of the Warrington brewing family, was usually to be seen in Jaguar XK120s. We think it was his brother Ted's Morgan that he was driving on this occasion.

The 1953 MCC Edinburgh Rally began on Friday 22 May, the sixty-five car crews leaving Kenilworth from 11.57 p.m. onwards at minute intervals for the 457-mile journey north to Edinburgh. Breakfast was taken at Harrogate, and then the MCC introduced various driving tests on the Pennine roads before lunch was finally taken at Carlisle. Mist and rain made time-keeping particularly difficult on this section. The bedraggled crews then made for the final destination of Edinburgh. There were further tests *en route*, and a final test on Observatory Road, in which Jim Goodall excelled in HUY 982.

The Morgan team entry this year comprised Jim Goodall with HUY 982, Sonny McCann with BWP 47 and John Moore with his Coupe, KNP 5. Peter Morgan was also participating with KUY 387 but he was not in the team. Entries were not prolific this year and, besides Morgan, there was only one other car team, a mixed Dellow/Jowett Javelin affair.

When the results were declared Jim's excellent drive had won him the class award and the Morgan team had also taken the team prize. Besides Jim Goodall, First Class Awards were also taken by Basil Roy and Joe Lowrey, the latter driving KUY 284 through the Edinburgh Rally to get to Glasgow for the forthcoming Scottish Rally, which he had entered and intended also to report for *The Motor*.

The Whitsun holiday's sport for the Morgan enthusiast continued on Easter Monday with a race at Thruxton, a hill climb in Jersey, and the start of the Scottish Rally.

Peter Morgan gets away without difficulty on the restart test at Talla Linn reservoir in the Edinburgh Rally. *(Photograph: James Brymer)*

At Thruxton the Bristol MC & LCC co-promoted a race meeting with the Sporting Owner Drivers Club on a glorious sunny day. The first race was for sports cars up to 1200 cc and saw Jeff Sparrowe in JUO 177 among a large field for this six-lap event. At the start, Archie Scott-Brown in the Tojeiro JAP, took an easy lead, which he held to the finish. Behind him there was a terrific fight for second place between Jeff, Watling Greenwood in his RWG, and Metcalfe's Fiat, places changing with every lap. At the flag Jeff was just beaten by Watling Greenwood, finishing finally in third position.

Jeff Sparrowe was also competing later in the meeting with his Cooper Bristol but had the throttle stick wide open, controlling the projectile on the ignition switch until finally retiring.

The weather was even hotter in Jersey for the Bouley Bay hill climb. L. R. Olver's Plus 4, J518, had minimal opposition in the class for production cars from 1500–3000 cc, although causing some alarm for spectators when the front tyres appeared as if they must roll off the rims, such were the low tyre pressures he was using.

The Royal Scottish Automobile Club's Scottish Rally was this year renamed the Coronation Scottish Rally, for obvious reasons, and this four-day rally also began on Whit Monday, at the RSAC's headquarters in Glasgow. 143 entries were received, there being several Morgans. Included were two lady entrants – Andie Neil, presumably with her sister Chris navigating, in KYS 41, and top rally driver Mrs Nancy Mitchell, who was due to drive Peter Reece's car, but she non-started. The male entrants were Jimmy Ray with KUY 474, Joe Lowrey with KUY 284, William Whiteley with PKK 256 and Gerry Hoyle. Gerry Hoyle was the Morgan agent in Southport, having purchased Life's Motors from the original agent Billy Life, who had set up the agency in 1926. Gerry was driving a 1953 Plus 4. This year the Morgans were placed in the class for open cars of 1501–2500 cc, there being sixteen starters in this class.

Three teams contained Morgans. Whiteley was with Clapham's Jowett Javelin and Hobson's Austin A40 in the Ilkley MC squad, Jimmy Ray was with Doc Hardman's Dellow and Frank Ground's Jowett Javelin in the quaintly named 'Scorched Earth' team. Andie Neil was in the Scottish Sporting Car Club's all ladies team, along with Charlotte Sadler's Rover and Agnes Balfour's MG.

This year the rally was to be based at the famous golf course of Gleneagles, so, being keen golfers, Jimmy Ray and his passenger Brian Horrocks took along their golf clubs, hoping for a game one evening.

The start, however, was at the Glasgow headquarters of the RSAC, from whence the competition headed for Rest and Be Thankful for a hill restart test and a timed hill climb. A cloud burst greeted the competitors and they had difficulties in seeing the course, let alone climbing it. Jimmy Ray did manage to secure second fastest time in class, a good start for him.

The storms caused much damage, washing away roads and depositing mud and rocks onto them but eventually the tired crews arrived at Gleneagles for an overnight stay.

Luckily the following day was much brighter and it began with a regularity test of maintaining 26 mph to an unspecified point within fifteen miles. Having completed this, the competitors made for Taymouth Castle for a braking and reversing test. Again, Jimmy Ray was on form, setting second fastest time of the day behind a Jaguar. Joe Lowrey lost his gear knob but finished third in class behind Ray and Gerry Hoyle.

Following this test it was back to Gleneagles. Jimmy Ray and Brian Horrocks were one of the first crews back – so that they could take to the golf course. Sadly three hundred miles of driving meant the game was of no distinction!

The Wednesday began with a car parking test at Gleneagles, with Jimmy Ray and Gerry Hoyle best in their class. From here the entrants made for Cairn O'Mount where a restarting test was held in appallingly wet conditions. Jimmy Ray was best of all at this. Back at Gleneagles after 308 miles, the competitors faced an acceleration and braking test in which Jimmy again led his class, only being beaten by an Allard for best time overall. Lowrey and Whiteley came second and third to Ray in their class.

The final day had just 138 miles of motoring for the rally competitors, before the finish at Glasgow, after a total of 976 miles for the four days. At Taymouth Castle, on the way to Glasgow, the RSAC ran its traffic light braking test, as in 1952.

When the results were announced it was Jimmy Ray who had comfortably won his class, ahead of Davis's Healey. Third, fourth, fifth and sixth equal were the Morgans of Gerry Hoyle, William Whiteley, Andie Neil and Joe Lowrey. An impressive showing of the Morgan's suitability for top class British rallying. There was no overall winner selected but if there had been, then Jimmy Ray would have finished fourth, behind a Jaguar, a Healey and a Cooper MG.

Excellent weather and a resurfaced road helped Ken Wharton to a new Shelsley hill climb record on 6 June, when he recorded 36.60 seconds in his supercharged 1100 cc JAP-engined Cooper. Just one Morgan was participating in this MAC event, that of Geoff White, who recorded 49.60 seconds in MOH 453, but this was not as quick as three supercharged Bugattis which, therefore, took the awards in the 1501–3000 cc sports car class.

The following weekend Geoff White took to the hills again, this time at Prescott, but his was not the sole Morgan entry, as he was accompanied by John Moore with KNP 5. Of the two, Geoff proved to be the fastest, recording 53.95 seconds to finish fourth in the class for sports cars of 1301–2500 cc unsupercharged or 751–1300 cc supercharged.

John Moore recorded 56.06 seconds to finish eighth in class, the class leader being a supercharged 1172 cc Ford-engined Dellow.

There was a good turnout of Morgans for the MCC's fourth Silverstone meeting on 20 June. The first two car events were the traditional one-hour high-speed trials. In the first John Moore took his black Coupe KNP 5 to a First Class Award. Bernard Clarke had the bad luck to run a big end in his Plus 4 and had to retire.

In the second high-speed trial, which was run in heavy rain, both Peter Morgan in KUY 387 and Jim Goodall in HUY 982 collected First Class Awards, covering 58.87 and 58.23 miles

The start line of the first handicap event of the MCC Silverstone. *Left to right*: Jim Goodall (51), Rogers' Riley (11), Powell's supercharged Mercedes (90), Basil de Mattos (96), John Moore (10). (*Photograph: Quadrant Picture Library*)

respectively. After these high-speed trials came a scratch race and then some handicap events. John Moore was limit man in the first of the handicap event, and did not give up the lead to Everard's Aston Martin DB2 without a struggle, finishing a worthy second.

After the other handicap events came the team handicap Relay Race, contested by four teams of three cars, each driver having to unscrew a sparking plug at the end of his stint and give it to the next team member. The Morgan team consisted of Peter Morgan, Jim Goodall and John Moore, and they finished third behind the teams of MGs and Bentleys. John Moore in particular was impressive for his 'on the limit' cornering style in the Coupe.

On the south coast, the Plymouth Motor Club ran its eighth Presidential Trophy Rally over Friday night, 26 June, and through the following day, finishing on Plymouth Hoe. Outright winner, despite the fog, was Doc Spare in KUY 476. He also took home the Morgan cup, and the Bridgwater start award. George Turnbull was also successful, collecting the Plymouth MC's own Morgan award, presumably in his 4/4.

Following the 1952 achievements of the Morgan 4/4 Club's entries in the Lancia Motor Club's Inter One Make Driving Tests, the 4/4 Club once again decided to enter the maximum of three teams for this year's event at Thruxton aerodrome, on 28 June. The 'A' team was to comprise Stan Dyke with KKC 888, Bill Parkes with FNP 684 and Graham Stallard with CAB 652. The 'B' team was to be Peter Morgan with KUY 387, John McDonagh with his 4/4 Coupe, FOE 547, and Aileen Jervis with JTT 703. The final team was to be Les Newey and Alan Taylor in 4/4s and Les Yarranton with his Plus 4, KWP926.

Barry Phipps, the 4/4 Club's selector, had asked a new Morgan driver to be reserve. This was Ray Meredith, who had now acquired the Bill Allarton 1100 cc Climax car, EAX 377, recently repainted red, by Bill. Ray had previously been using the ex-Bill Parkes 1933 MG and had now fancied something a little more competitive for motor sport, hence journeying by train to Chester to purchase Bill Allarton's car and driving it back home.

Not long before the event, Barrie Phipps received the bad news that Stan Dyke had damaged

The victorious Morgan 'A' team. (*Photograph: Bill Parkes collection*)

Derek Howard and 'Miss Jumbo' at Marseilles before the start of the Alpine Rally. (*Photograph: Photo-Junior*)

the front end of his 4/4 and would be out. A reshuffle was made, with his place being taken by Peter Morgan. Les Yarranton moved into Peter's place and Ray now had a drive in team C.

Just before the competitors were due to report to the circuit there was a storm over the area and poor Alan Taylor, still on his way to the venue, slid into a Rolls Royce. Thus Barrie was one short again. Among the spectators he espied Bill Boddy of *Motor Sport* but he did not have a competition licence. Luckily Ross Lomax was present, complete with his 1938 4/4, JK 7381, and the required licence, so he made up team C.

As usual, each invited club had submitted a test, giving all a chance, and the early rain made wheelspin and slides a feature of the first tests that were attempted.

When all the tests had been completed, the Morgan 'A' team had won the event, the 'B' team was third and the 'C' team eighth. In the individual classification, Les Yarranton was first overall, Graham Stallard second, Bill Parkes fourth and Peter Morgan fifth. Once again the Morgan had shown itself to be a superb driving test competitor.

Francophile, Derek Howard, passengered by 'Miss Jumbo', once again decided to have a crack at the Rallye International des Alpes, the 1953 event beginning at Marseilles on 10 July and finishing after some two thousand miles of narrow Alpine roads at Cannes on 16 July. The black Plus 4, CJX 318, was in the same trim as in 1952, except it was now running on Dunlop racing tyres, these being loaned to Derek by Dunlop, just for the Alpine rally.

The first stage was of 584 miles, to Cortina

Derek Howard sets off on the first stage (*Photograph: Photo-Junior*)

d'Ampezzo, the cars starting at one-minute intervals from 9.30 p.m. onwards, under floodlights on the Vieux Port.

The Morgan had been motoring well but towards the end of the stage disaster struck, when Derek came around a blind bend in the middle of the road to face an ancient Lancia taxi travelling in the opposite direction. Somewhat half asleep, Derek instinctively swerved to the left, forgetting that on the Continent one drove on the right of the road!

There was the inevitable collision and Derek cut his nose quite badly on the Morgan windscreen. A well-meaning passer-by decided he would benefit from a tourniquet around his neck to stem the bleeding, until Kath convinced him otherwise.

The car was clearly out of the rally, with the radiator pushed right back, but it proved possible to manhandle the radiator away from the engine, and Derek and Kath managed to coast downhill into Cortina, where a doctor was located among the skiing community to attend to Derek's injuries.

Following the success in 1952 of the Inter Club Hill Climb at Prescott, the BOC had decided to make this an annual meeting, attracting over one hundred cars for the 1953 event on 12 July. Ten Morgans, all Plus 4s, were entered as members of various teams, these being as follows. From the North West came Harry Harrop in the Lancashire and Cheshire Car Club team, Jimmy Ray in the Liverpool MC team, and Hector Sinclair representing the Chester MC. From the Midlands came Doc Steel, Peter Morgan, Jim Goodall and John Moore, all from the Worcestershire Motor

The bonnet flaps as Roy Clarkson pushes VNO 600 up Prescott hill. (*Photograph: Richmond Pike*)

Club. Basil de Mattos represented the MCC and Roy Clarkson was in the London MC team.

Torrential rain early in the day made the course very slippery, particularly the first half of the 'Esses', but all the Morgans climbed well, although one shifted a little sand on the outside of 'Orchard'. Roy Clarkson had trouble with a loose bonnet on the special-bodied Coupe, VNO 600, recording the slowest of the Morgan times with 60.74 seconds, while Peter Morgan was the fastest with 55.54 seconds, attracting audible gasps from the marshalls at Pardon Hairpin as he blasted his Coupe, JNP 239, up the hill. This time proved fast enough to give him third overall in the individual performances for the class for 2001–3000 cc behind two Bugattis. Jim Goodall and Doc Steel were fourth and fifth.

Hector 'Jock' Sinclair, who had competed for the Chester MC, was the proprietor of the Zetland Garage in Southport. He was a keen motor sport enthusiast and had recently been competing in a Connaught sports car. Jock, however, had now purchased Peter Reece's ivory Morgan, KUY 475. Peter Reece, meanwhile, was dealing in second-hand sports cars at Blakes in Liverpool, so he could usually locate a Morgan for his own events.

At the Standard Triumph factory in Coventry the first of the production Triumph sports cars was completed on Wednesday 22 July, a left-hand drive car bound for Canada. The new sports car, soon to be known as the Triumph TR2, differed considerably from the original Triumph 20 TS, development of which had been taken over by Ken Richardson after the 1952 Motor Show. As it was to compete with the Morgan, as well as donate its engine to the Plus 4, this development deserves some amplification.

The original concept of Sir John Black was for a 90 mph sports car costing approximately £550, and therefore using as many components from existing Standard Triumph models as possible, to keep the costs down.

Ken Richardson had immediately ordered a redesign of the composite Standard Flying Nine/Triumph Mayflower chassis, which was far too flexible to give acceptable road-holding. Walter Belgrove had also undertaken a redesign of the rather odd rear end of the car with exposed spare wheel, changing this to give a modern car boot, with spare wheel beneath. The rather vague steering was replaced by a more accurate cam and lever system, and the Lockheed hydraulic brakes were increased in size to 10in. front and 9in. rear. Bill Boddy would have been pleased that the final drive ratio was also changed to 3.7 to 1.

Morgans of course were more interested in the engine, which now produced 90 bhp, compared with 73 bhp of the previous year's 20 TS prototype. Important to this development was the availability, from February 1953, of branded petrol of higher octane ratio than the previous Pool petrol. This allowed the Triumph experimental engineers to raise the compression ratio from 7.5 to 8.6 to 1 without needing to alter the combustion chamber shape. In turn, this raised the power output to approximately 80 bhp, and development was now concentrated on the camshaft and valves. First the valve lift was increased from 0.36in. to 0.375in., and then the timing modified from that of the Vanguard (10–50, 50–10) to 15–55, 55–15 giving more overlap. This took the power output up to 84 bhp. Increasing the size of the inlet valve from $1\frac{1}{2}$in. to $1\frac{9}{16}$ diameter gave an extra 3 bhp, and fine refinement of the distributor curve and carburettor settings gave the full 90 bhp. Inevitably various inadequate design features had been exposed during this considerable raise in power of the Vanguard engine. The first weak link was found to be the cylinder block, which tended to crack below the intermediate head stud bosses. This was remedied by extending the casting so that longer studs could be fitted threading into the stiff crankshaft chamber beneath. These were also increased in diameter from 7/16in. to 1/2in. Still cylinder head gaskets were failing, so the wire-based figure of eight seals beneath the cylinder liners were upgraded to resin coated steel. Improved and stressed conrods were installed, using 7/16in. big end bolts, and Vandervell idium-coated lead bronze bearings proved better than the previous Vanguard white metal type.

High-speed testing showed a tendency for No. 1 exhaust valve to break. This was found to be due to bending of the camshaft, increasing the load on the valve, and was remedied by increasing the size of the front of the camshaft.

High engine speeds also showed the inadequacy of the Vanguard's proprietory AC system of crankcase ventilation via the induction system. It was replaced by a breather pipe on the side of the engine, shaped to prevent oil loss due to suction or surge.

Most of these modifications were undertaken by engine design engineer, Lewis Dawtrey, who worked closely with Ken Richardson at this time, and in May 1953 Ken had driven such an engine in a prototype TR2 to a speed of 124mph over the measured mile on the Jabbeke high-speed road in Belgium, a major delight to Sir John Black and the Board.

Morgan were pleased that they were to receive these engines but various modifications needed to be made to the TR2 version to satisfy the Morgan factory's requirements. These included the removal of the TR2's crankshaft pulley extension fan, and replacement with the Vanguard crankshaft pulley, the fitting of Phase I Vanguard engine mounting plates and thermostat housing, and the continued use of a graphite block type clutch withdrawal bearing assembly, rather than using the TR2's hydraulically operated ball bearing type clutch withdrawal system.

Engine numbers of engines fitted to TR sports cars were given the prefix TS, for Triumph Sports, and the usual suffix E (for engine). The first engine supplied to Morgan specification was given the number TS1ME, the ME suffix indicating Morgan engine.

We suspect that it was during July or August that the Morgan factory actually received this first engine. Its arrival coincided with design thoughts by HFS Morgan on a new Plus 4 front end, brought about as a result of several pressures. First there had been comments from Morgan customers that the exposed front suspension easily became dirty, spoiling the finish of the car, and making it difficult to keep presentable.

Second, Joseph Lucas Ltd., the suppliers of headlamps, had advised that they intended to concentrate future production on flush fitting 7in. units, the remaining customers for free standing headlights therefore facing a considerable price rise. Thirdly, the newly introduced sports cars competing within the same market, such as the new Triumph and Austin Healey, were bang up-to-date in their streamlined styling, making the Morgan look very old fashioned.

Also to be considered was the fact that the twin SU carburettors fitted to the TR2 engine, even with the removal of the AC air filters as used in the Triumph, made the offside of the engine some 3in. wider than with the single Solex carburettor on the Vanguard engine. Consequently, there was not a lot of room to spare under the offside bonnet in the current Plus 4s for this new engine.

HFS Morgan decided, therefore, to build this new engine, TS1ME, into a developmental Plus 4. He had calculated that fitting a cowl over the radiator could allow the extra under-bonnet room he required. At the time time he set about designing new front wings that were more enveloping in style. These contained 7in. headlamp pods, similar to those of the post-war Rileys, and the shape of the wing continued forward to cover the front suspension area.

Meanwhile, at Shelsley, the MAC ran a rather novel gymkhana and hill climb on 25 July, combining various driving tests (including blindfold) with the hill climb. John Moore proved outstanding, finishing second overall in KNP 5 to a Dellow. Also competing were Bill Parkes with FNP 684, Doc Steel with JWP 537, Barrie Phipps with KUY 714, Les Yarranton with KWP 926 and Graeme Anton with LAB 274. In the team competition Bill Parkes, Barrie Phipps and Les Yarranton came second, representing the Worcestershire MC.

On Sunday 9 August twenty-one members of the Herefordshire MC took part in a run of thirty-four miles with seven driving tests. The open car class was taken by Les Yarranton, with KWP 926, who was gaining a formidable reputation for his ability in driving tests.

The same day, the Morgan 4/4 Club ran its Burton to Banbury Rally. Of the seven entries, Bill Parkes had to non-start because of business commitments, leaving Barrie Phipps to take first place in KUY 714. Second was John Pither with his British Racing Green Plus 4, XME 110, and third was Ray Meredith, driving his ex-Bill Allarton 1098 cc Climax 4/4, EAX 377.

The Aston Martin Owners Club ran an interesting fourth St John Horsfall Race Meeting at Silverstone on 15 August. The club was using the 750 Motor Club's circuit of two and a half miles, in which the course took to the cross runway from Maggots to Club corner for a tight hairpin, returning back along the runway to join the usual club straight into Woodcote. Several Morgans were entered for the meeting.

Each car was given a set speed for the half-hour regularity trial which opened the meeting, and Barrie Phipps with KUY 714 and John Moore with KNP 5 finished in runner-up positions, both being set 60 mph targets. Also entered was the Ford-engined 4/4 of D. I. C. Brunt which was set a rather high 55 mph.

In a five-lap handicap for sports cars John Moore found himself on the limit allowance of 1 min. 45 sec. start over scratchman J. Swift's C-type Jaguar. He successfully held the lead for three laps, but was then caught by the field, finishing out of the places.

The last event of the day was a fifteen-lap handicap relay race, attracting ten teams competing for the David Brown Challenge Cup. The Morgan 4/4 Club had entered a team, comprising John Moore, Geoff White with MOH 453 and B. M. Lee, but the latter non-started and Barrie Phipps took his place. The scratch team compromised three Allards and the 4/4 Club team had three and a half minutes start on them.

Each car had to complete five laps carrying the team sash before handing over to the next, and excellent racing resulted. Geoff White became engaged in an almighty scrap for sixth place, with Fowler's Le Mans Aston Martin and Constable's MG TD, before handing over to Barrie Phipps. In that position he continued the battle but the 4/4 Club team finally finished seventh when the MG CC's final MG TD overtook Barrie, and sped up to fourth for the MG team.

The 750 MC's annual six-hour handicap Relay Race was once more held at Silverstone on 29 August, this time using the 750 MC's new circuit as recently used by the AMOC. The race attracted some forty-one teams, of which three contained Morgans. This year the Morgan 4/4 Club had entered two teams, one of 4/4s, and one of Plus 4s. The 4/4 team, which had thirty-one credit laps, consisted of Stan Dyke in KKC 888 as 'A' car, Ross Lomax's Climax two-seater JK 7381 as 'B' car, with Ray Meredith's ex-Bill Allarton 1098 cc Climax car, EAX 377, as the 'C' car. The 'D' car was Les Newey's Standard-engined two-seater, Bill Parkes with FNP 684 was the 'E', and the 'F' was Jeff Sparrowe with JUO 177. Pit manager was Dick Pritchard.

The Plus 4 team was given twenty-one credit laps, and consisted of John Moore in KNP 5 as A car, John Pither with XME 110 as 'B', Geoff White in MOH 453 as 'C', Les Yarranton in KWP 926 as 'D' and finally Barrie Phipps in KUY 714 as 'E' car. Pit manager was Gordon Stratton.

The only other Morgan participating was the re-engined 4/4 of D. I. C. Brunt, carrying an 1172 cc Ford engine, running as 'E' car in the Herefordshire MC's team.

The day of the event proved to be very wet. Torrential rain just before the start caught out many of the entries, the start proving to be very ragged. Dick Pritchard sent out his team in letter

Stan Dyke laps with caution in the Silverstone rain. *(Photograph: James Brymer)*

order, Stan Dyke taking the first stint and recording a very commendable lap time of 2 min. 40 sec. considering the conditions.

Many a marker barrel was set flying by the field as they slid and spun their way around the circuit. Brunt had a 'touch and go' moment at Woodcote corner. Later in the event, Bill Parkes recorded 2 min. 39 sec. and finally Jeff Sparrowe got down to 2 min. 31 sec.

After three and a half hours the Morgan 4/4s were in ninth position, so Dick Pritchard decided to use his faster cars to try and improve this position, and they finally came in a respectable eighth, just four laps behind the winning team of King MGs. The Plus 4 team finished in twelfth position, with the Herefordshire MC's mixed team finishing nineteenth.

This very wet race had been the first taste of racing for Ross Lomax. He had purchased his 1938 Climax-engined two-seater in 1950 from an ex-Daimler apprentice, who had rebuilt it fully. Ross then replaced the Solex carburettor with a Zenith type having an accelerator pump. The flywheel had been lightened, then the complete crankshaft, flywheel clutch unit had been dynamically balanced. The con-rods were polished, a Fram oil filter fitted, and a stainless steel exhaust added. A cooling fan, which was belt driven, steering dampers and Girling hydraulic shock absorbers continued the modifications. A new set of Easiclean pattern road wheels had replaced the originals.

Ray Meredith had also thoroughly enjoyed his two stints of racing and the practice the day before. He looked forward to more racing in the future.

The last Sunday in August was once again the date for the Hagley and DLCC's speed trials, along the drive at Westwood Park, near Droitwich. Just two Morgans were entered, the Climax-engined 4/4 of J. Fiander in the class for sports cars between 751 and 1200 cc, and KWP 926, the Plus 4 of Les Yarranton, in the 1501–3000 cc class. Neither finished in the

Ross Lomax paddles his way past the Silverstone pits in the 750 MC Relay Race. (*Photograph: James Brymer*)

Les Yarranton prepares to start at Westwood Park. (*Photograph: J. H. Miller*)

awards, and the suitability of the short seven hundred yard course for the faster racing cars was called into question by a Maserati, which finished in the hall's courtyard!

A mammoth entry of 339 cars contested the London MC's London Rally, held on 11 and 12 September. The road section of 710 miles was not completed by anyone without penalty, but Jimmy Ray navigated by Jeff Dixon in KUY 474 had collected only one penalty point for arriving three minutes late at a checkpoint. As in the previous year, they won the event, with a brilliant performance.

There had been three starting points, Leeds, Birmingham and London, from whence the entrants made for Kidderminster and the rally proper. The entire entry then headed into Wales where three routes had been plotted, shaped like a clover leaf, each 'loop' being tackled by a portion of the entry, which then moved on to the next loop, until all were completed. The finish was at Croydon.

Jimmy Ray and Jeff Dixon give an impeccable performance to win the London Rally. (*Photograph: Jimmy Ray collection*)

Also successful was Doc Spare in KUY 476, who captured the Committee's Trophy for runner-up in the winner's class.

At Snetterton, on 12 September, the Aston Martin OC ran a programme of ten races in ideal

Doc Steel and John Dodds in reverse mode during one of the tests in the *Birmingham Post* Rally. (*Photograph: Doc Steel collection*)

weather. Most of the events were for the top racing cars of the day, but the five-lap race for sports cars up to 1100 cc did feature a Morgan – the 4/4 of Peter Wren, fitted with a Riley engine. Peter finished third of the four starters, being unable to stay with the two modified MG P types of Moore and Rash.

On 18 and 19 September the Midland AC ran an invitation rally, sponsored by the *Birmingham Post* newspaper. Nine Morgans were entered among the 66-strong field. Six formed two teams for the Worcestershire MC. In the 'A' team were Peter Morgan, Jim Goodall and Doc Steel, navigated by Sonny McCann, Terry Hall and John Dodds, respectively. The 'B' team consisted of Les Yarranton and Desmond Thompson in KWP 926, Barrie Phipps and Henk Piest in KUY 714, and Aileen Jervis with Mary Freeman in JTT 703. Also competing was John Moore with KNP 5 in the MAC 'A' team, Geoff White and Hamilton Evans in MOH 453 and Les Newey with W. Taylor in Les's 4/4.

The 480-mile route proved difficult, with only twenty-eight crews completing the night section in Wales without penalty. The daylight section included several transmission trying driving tests alongside the lake at Llandrindod Wells and at Shelsley Walsh.

When the results were announced the Morgan marque had confirmed its superiority in rallying. Peter Morgan had won the event overall, taking the MAC challenge cup, but we are not sure which of his cars he was using. In the class for open cars over 1300 cc Jim Goodall in HUY 982 took the class award, with Les Yarranton third. The ladies' award ('Regent' Challenge Trophy) was collected by Aileen Jervis and the team prize went to the Worcester MC 'A' team.

The Cambridge 50 CC had found a rather unusual hill climb venue at Great Chishall, near Royston, in that the road surface was loose, making it more like an autocross event or trials hill if it rained. Luckily it was sunny on Sunday 20 September. Taking the class for closed cars was

Roy Clarkson in VNO 600, beating Playford's Healey by half a second.

One week later on 26 September another hill, this time the Ulster AC's annual event at Knockagh in Northern Ireland, was the venue for a hill climb in which a Morgan again took an award. The Morgan in question was KUY 625, the Plus 4 of Albert Acheson, but it was being driven by Joe Taggart. He clocked 73 seconds, enough to bring him second place in the class for open cars between 1301 and 2300 cc, the winner being the HRG of Alan Brown. Stanley Porter was also present, competing with his 4½ litre Invicta.

Sadly for the East Anglia Motor Club, thick fog upset the night navigation section of their Clacton rally, held on the 26th and 27th, as well as delaying the start of the driving tests at Wormingford, and causing the abandonment of the high-speed test at Snetterton. This did not stop Bernard Clarke's Plus 4 (PKK 769) putting up fastest time in one of the tests, and winning the large capacity open-car class. Second in class was a new name to Morgan rally drivers – Hugh Denton, with his Plus 4 two-seater, JNV 654. Hugh was from Rushden in Northamptonshire and involved in the leather shoe industry. His new Morgan, chassis number P2712, engine number V588ME, had been supplied to Grove (Kettering) Ltd and was registered on 28 August.

The Lancashire and Cheshire CC also ran its popular Lakeland Rally, which actually took place in North Wales, on 26 and 27 September. One hundred and thirty competitors took part, leaving the starts at Manchester, Birmingham and Llandudno on the Saturday morning, the routes converging at Ruabon in North Wales for a common rally route, the finish being at Llandudno with the usual arrival test on the West Promenade. On the Sunday a further fifty miles rallying was undertaken, with final eliminating tests back in Llandudno once more.

There were several Morgans taking part, with Derek Howard, Alec Newsham and Harry Jacoby recording excellent times in the driving tests. Only Harry Jacoby featured in the awards, however, taking the Tom Leigh Trophy for Class C2. Harry was a motor trader in St Helens and he had taken over Jimmy Ray's old Morgan, MLV 58. Alec Newsham was the proud owner of a red two-seater, OKC 208, which he had purchased new from Gerry Hoyle, the proprietor of Life's Motors of Southport. It carried chassis number P2554. Alec lived at Blackburn and was involved in the fish and chips business. He was becoming a top flight rally driver, competing most weekends.

Meanwhile, HFS Morgan had been busy at the Morgan factory with the design of the front of the new TR-engined Morgan, which had been allocated chassis number 3000. Peter Morgan, however, was none too impressed with the end result – he thought the light units resembled bean cans let into the wings, and he felt that the new grille could be improved upon. As a result, he asked Felix Day of Mudguard Supplies, who supplied production wings for the Morgan factory, whether he could manufacture a slightly different design using a curved light unit let into the front wings. He also visited Charlie Cummings in the sheet metal shop to see whether he could fabricate a more rounded grille.

Visiting the factory in September, on the return from a holiday in the West Country, was the pre-war Sheffield Morgan agent Freddie James (he had lost his business when it received a direct hit from a German bomb during the blitz on Sheffield on 12 December 1940). HFS was delighted to see him and showed him around the factory, including the new ivory Plus 4 in the tour.

'What do you think?' HFS asked.

'I think it's bloody awful,' Freddie replied, with typical Yorkshire bluntness, and he went on to comment how much better it would be if the lovely curves of the old Aero three-wheeler could somehow be introduced to the radiator cowl.

It was too late to alter the new model significantly, and production was begun with a view to showing the new model at the forthcoming Motor Show. All were two-seaters. With this new design the previously windscreen-mounted wiper motor was moved under the bonnet and many Morgan drivers were relieved that their previously vulnerable knuckles were to have an easier time in the new cars.

An even more novel Morgan, registered for the road as XEV 795 on 25 September, was a Plus 4 van! It was built on chassis P2479, which had been despatched to Basil Roy on 7 October 1952.

The owner, Sandy Lumsdaine of Little Waltham in Essex, was keen to avoid the crippling 66⅔% purchase tax on new cars, and realized that goods vehicles carried a lower 33⅓%. By the time the van had been constructed the rates had dropped even lower to 50% and 25% respectively, these having replaced the higher rates in April.

There was a penalty to pay for Sandy's initiative in avoiding the new car purchase tax – the van had to conform to the speed limit for goods vehicles weighing under 1 ton – just 30 mph.

In later years this unusual Morgan was to be raced, the aluminium van body, built by Buckland, not being particularly heavy. The spare wheel lay loose on the van floor.

No doubt the noise of the Moss gearbox in a van was considerable. It certainly could be intrusive in Plus 4 Coupes, with the result that the Morgan factory had made an arrangement with the Moss Gear Co. Ltd, back in August for the quietest gearboxes after test to be marked with three stars, so that they could be reserved for Coupe installation.

On 4 October the Worcestershire Motor Club ran an autumn rally, which contained fourteen tests within its route. Several Morgans took part, and the event turned into a Morgan benefit. In the small class for open cars Graham Stallard came first of the twelve entries, with CAB 652. Three other 4/4s had taken part, those of Aileen Jervis (JTT 703), George Perks (FGW 415) and F. R. Turner (GTN 148).

George Perks came from Pershore, and had purchased his four-seater Climax-engined car second hand in the late 1940s. It was a 1938 car, chassis number 660.

In the larger open class just four entries were received, three Morgans and an Allard. Les Yarranton came first, and set the best performance of the rally with KWP 926, while Barrie Phipps was not far behind with KUY 714. Jim Goodall was third in HUY 982.

The following week Barrie Phipps continued his rallying successes at the MGCC's Western Rally, accompanied by Hugh Denton and Doctor John Spare. Hugh Denton came away with the Nuffield trophy for his performance in JNV 654, while Barrie in KUY 714 tied for the Birmingham start award. Doc Spare, in KUY 476, took the Bristol start award. Three entries and three awards was an excellent performance for Morgans.

The following day, 11 October, the Morgan 4/4 Club ran its annual driving tests at Honeybourne Aerodrome in Worcestershire. Barrie Phipps was here again, completing his full weekend of competition in KUY 714, coming away with second place.

First place was taken by Geoff White in MOH 453, with John McDonagh third in his 4/4 Coupe, FOE 547, fourth was Peter Morgan and fifth Les Yarranton. Eighteen club members took part, each tackling seven tests.

The Morgan 4/4 Club had been invited to enter the MGCC (Midland Centre) Autumn Round Trial, held on 18 October in the Bridgemouth area. Nine club members decided to have a go, these being John Pither, Les Newey, Aileen Jervis, Dick Pritchard, Graham Stallard, Les Yarranton, Barrie Phipps, Hugh Denton and Stan Dyke. Newey, Yarranton and Phipps retired, but John Pither did manage a First Class Award.

The Motor Show was held at Earls Court from 21 October until 31 October. Five Morgans were displayed, of which three were two-seaters with the new front-end treatment. Two were left-hand drive, being chassis numbers P3001 (blue) and P3002 (red) respectively, and one was right-hand drive (P3003, which was ivory with green upholstery). The other two cars shown were a conventional four-seater (P2743) and a Coupe (P2746). All were fitted with Vanguard engines as no further supplies of the TR engine had yet arrived. Thompson track rod ends had replaced the original Harrisflex type, these having been introduced on production Morgans as from P2725 in September.

Because the new front end only appeared on the two-seater, the impression was given to some motoring journalists that the four-seater and Coupe were to remain with the old style. This was incorrect, as four-seaters and Coupes were under construction to the new configuration. The last of the old vertical radiator style Morgans was to be a Coupe, P2756, which was tested by Charlie Curtis during the week of 9 November.

Advertizing photographs issued to the motoring magazines showed one of the new fronted right-

The new Morgan two-seaters on the Morgan stand before the opening of the Motor Show. (*Photograph: Quadrant Picture Library*)

hand drive cars in front of the Malvern Hills. Some prints were supplied 'reversed' to show a left-hand drive version, with the number plate on the print repainted with the letters Morgan. The give away is the position of the tax disc!

The price of the Morgan two-seater was £565 basic. Also at the Motor Show was the new Triumph TR2, listed at £555, making it now the lowest price high performance 100 mph sports car in the world. Naturally, it caught the attention of the enthusiasts. Also making its debut was the MG TF, priced at £550. Among the component stands, Michelin were showing car versions of the revolutionary radial Michelin 'X' tyre. Dunlop had their recently introduced tubeless tyre on show, together with the disc brakes that had helped Jaguar at Le Mans.

After each Motor Show, the Society of Motor Manufacturers and Traders arranged a Test Day

The Morgan factory's publicity photo of the new two-seater, in correct right-hand drive print. (*Photograph: Morgan Motor Co. collection*)

at Goodwood for journalists to test their latest products. Wilson McComb, an assistant editor at *Autosport*, had ended his 1952 Test Day with a

Plus 4, and he was keen to try out the new car. Morgan had on-hand the prototype TR2-engined two-seater (P3000), which Wilson found had considerably improved performance over the old model, but as always he particularly enjoyed the way in which the Plus 4 could be thrown into corners with complete safety.

The London Gliding Club's headquarters at Dunstable was the unlikely scene of motor sport on Sunday 25 October, when the Sporting Owner Drivers' Club ran an Autocross over a P-shaped grass course. Competitors started in pairs and had five timed runs each. Two Morgans proved successful in the open class over 2000 cc. P. Isaac's Plus 4 Coupe, MXK 946, was first, with P. Norgard second.

Norgard, from Barnstead in Surrey, was running his two-seater, NYF 452, which had been despatched on 19 March to Conway Motors. It was chassis number P2548.

This year's *Daily Express* MCC Rally, the fourth, was held from 11 to 14 November. There were 542 entries, of which 401 actually started. Eighteen Morgans had been entered. Starting from Plymouth were the Plus 4s of L. Griffiths, Doc Spare (KUY 476), H. S. Bailey and Derek Howard (CJX 318), the latter being entered into the 'modified' open class. Starting from Manchester were the Plus 4s of Alec Newsham (OKC 208), A. J. Ridy, Harry Jacoby (MLV 58) and Jimmy Ray (KUY 474), the latter also being entered in the 'modified' open class. From Kenilworth came Hertfordshire farmer Alex Blair (NXY 859), Les Yarranton (KWP 926), Barrie Phipps (KUY 714), John Moore (KNP 5), Roy Clarkson (VNO 600), and Bill Parkes (FNP 684). All were in the non-modified open car class 1551–2600 cc except John Moore who was in the non-modified closed class, Roy Clarkson, who was in the modified closed class and Bill Parkes, who

Peter Morgan prepares to leave from the Leicester control at Castle's Garage on the Wednesday evening. (*Photograph: Quadrant Picture Library*)

Roy Clarkson leaves Lampeter Control on the Thursday evening. (*Photograph: Quadrant Picture Library*)

was in the open specials class. Entered from Cardiff were Doc Steel (JWP 537), Jim Goodall (HUY 982) and Peter Morgan (JNP 239), Peter's Coupe being in the unmodified closed class. From Glasgow the Neil sisters were entered in KYS 41, and, surprisingly, there were no Morgan entries from the Norwich and London starts.

Two Morgan teams had entered – the factory team of Peter, Jim and Doc Steel, and a team of John Moore, Barrie Phipps and Les Yarranton.

Derek Howard was the only Morgan non-starter but Roy Clarkson had a little trouble convincing the scrutineers at Kenilworth that the side lights on his special-bodied Morgan (which was now painted blue) were actually working.

The first part of the route was individual to each starting point, the common route beginning from Wednesday evening at Harrogate. The Morgan factory team's route included a control at Leicester.

From Harrogate the route took the entrants via Ripon to Scotch Corner, Barnard Castle and then the first test, a brake test, at Stanhope. From Stanhope the route progressed via Bellingham to a control at Hawick, and then on to an acceleration test at Newcastleton. By now the weather conditions had deteriorated, with poor visibility, horizontal rain and a biting wind. Doc Spare retired here, having left the road on an acute bend. The route now went through Penrith and Appleby to Kirkby Stephen for a regularity test, in which Les Yarranton put up best performance in KWP 926.

Thoroughly soaked, the crews took their cars now towards the Skipton control, through flood water near Hubberholme that came through the floor boards, and then onwards to the Chester control during Thursday afternoon.

From Chester the route led into Wales for the Bwlch-y-groes special test, the climb to the restart

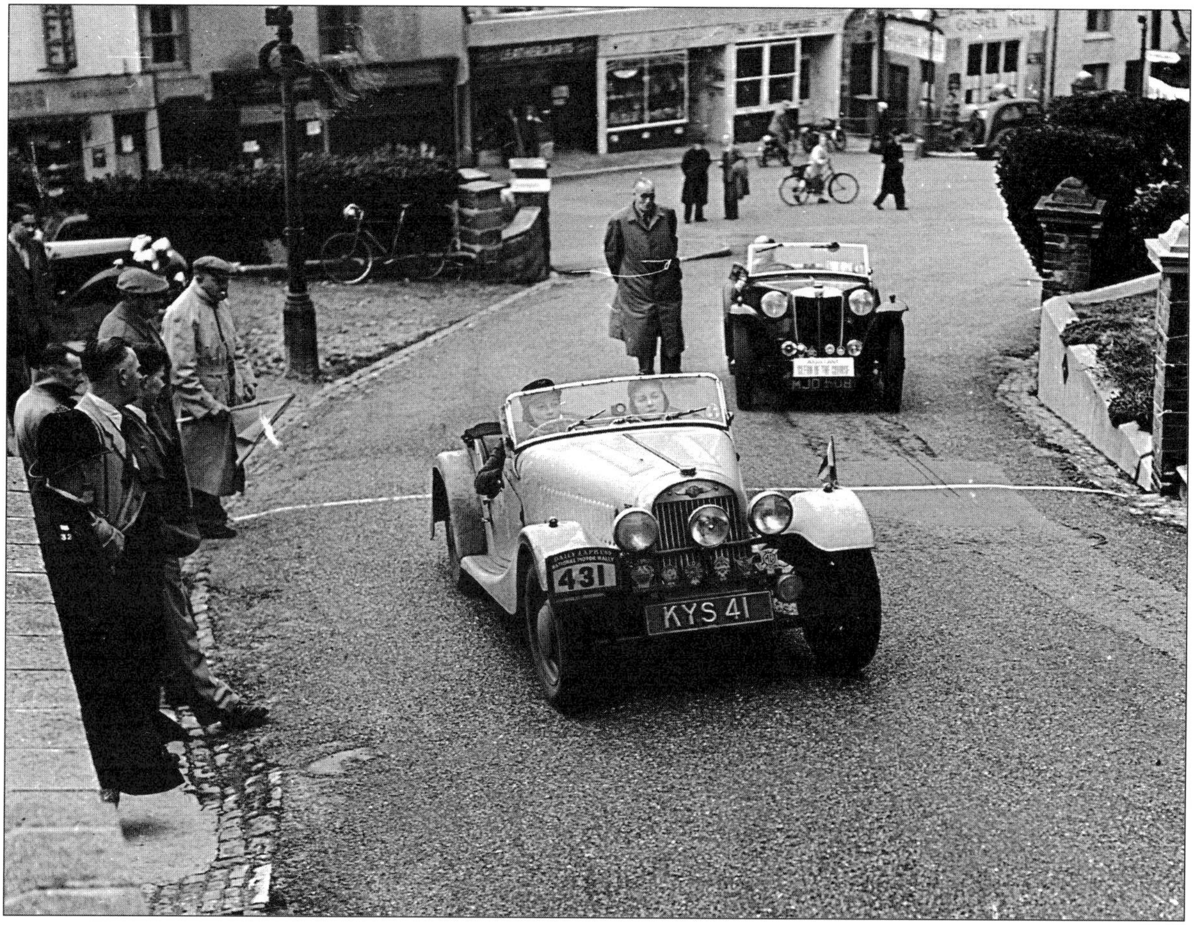

The Neil sisters start the Hastings hill test. (*Photograph: Quadrant Picture Library*)

test proving more difficult for the later numbers who encountered it in darkness and driving rain.

Through a wild night the route continued past the Elan Valley and around south west Wales to Lampeter.

A miserable rally ended for a very wet Bill Parkes during the next stage, when the big ends failed on the way to Ystalyfera. The route now left Wales for Tewkesbury, then headed south for Stockbridge in Hampshire before the final control near Hastings. The tired crews were now faced with a hill test, on which was a pylon that they had to pass and then reverse past on the other side, before completing the hill climb. Many had problems here, but Jim Goodall set best time.

There were three more deciding tests, the Morgans doing particularly well in these, and then it was time for the Friday night Lord Mayor's reception. The following day saw the concours d'elegance, and the rally results were finally announced.

The overall winner was to be the driver who had the best performance over and above the standard marks of his class. As the saloon classes had the biggest spread of marks, the winner and the two runners-up were all from this group. The winner was Frank Downs (Sunbeam-Talbot), but second was Roy Clarkson in his saloon Morgan. Third was ex-Morgan driver Horace Roberts – in a Ford Zephyr.

The open car class for 1550–2600 cc went to Barrie Phipps in KUY 714, followed by Harry Jacoby in MLV 58. Jimmy Ray was the sole finisher in the modified class for 1550–2600 cc, so obviously he won that class.

In the team competition the Yarranton/Phipps/

Moore team took the open class, and to cap an excellent result for the Morgan company the Neil sisters took the ladies' award.

Following the publication of these excellent results, the BTDA were able to announce the results of their rally Silver Star competition, of which the MCC rally had been the final qualifying event. Winner was Jimmy Ray, way ahead of John Cunningham and Ian Appleyard with their Jaguars. The winner of the Silver Garter for the ladies was Andie Neil.

Once again the Morgans had demonstrated their rally abilities to the motoring world.

Over in Ireland the Ulster AC ran its last trial of the year in Co. Antrim on 21 November. Albert Acheson had reclaimed KUY 625 for this event, but did not feature in the results.

The Morgan 4/4 Club's third Annual Night Rally was held over the weekend of 28 and 29 November. Twenty-seven entries were received, thirteen Morgans and fourteen assorted vehicles from the other invited clubs, this being the 4/4 Club's first closed invitation event.

There were four starting points, Manchester, Hertford, Gloucester and Sutton Coldfield, and thick fog played havoc with the early part of the event. Only seven competitors finished the course and noted top rally drivers such as Les Yarranton, Geoff White and Barrie Phipps were among the retirements. Absolutely outstanding was 4/4 Club member A. L. Dyke but he was driving his MG! He was delighted to take home the 4/4 Club's Patron's Trophy, donated by HFS Morgan. The Committee's Trophy went to George Perks with his 4/4, FGW 415, and class awards for the small capacity open cars went to Mayall's MG, followed by the two 1100 cc 4/4s of Graham Stallard and Aileen Jervis. No Plus 4s finished. The team award was taken by the 4/4 Club's 'B' team, George Perks, Aileen Jervis and Graham Stallard, which were actually the only Morgans to finish.

Dr John Spare had his Morgan running efficiently once more on the occasion of the Torbay Motor Club's second Torbay Rally, held on 5 December. Forty-three started, but Doc Spare excelled in the driving tests and ended up winning the rally in KUY 476.

Another Winter Rally was held by the Worcestershire Motor Club on 6 December. Six Morgans took part, F. R. Turner with his 4/4 GTN 148, Graham Stallard with the ex-factory car CAB 652, Barrie Phipps with Plus 4, KUY 714, Jim Goodall with HUY 982, Les Yarranton with KWP 926, and finally Aileen Jervis with JTT 703.

Les Yarranton took the class, with Jim Goodall second, just ahead of Aileen Jervis.

The Bugatti Owner's Club ran a two-day Welsh Rally at Tenby on 12 and 13 December, the start being at Worcester. John Moore finished in third place after an excellent performance in KNP 5.

No doubt the rally drivers were delighted that the white reversing lights so essential for nocturnal driving tests were made legal by the introduction of the Road Vehicles (Reversing Lights) Regulations 1953, towards the end of the year. The 1st of January 1954 was also to mark the legality of flashing direction indicators, which some, such as Derek Howard, had imported from the Continent and had been using for some time. They remained an optional fitment, however.

On Boxing Day the MGCC ran its Kimber Trophy Trial near Bristol, using a thirty-mile route including several trials hills and tests. Intermittent rain made the hills slippery and difficult, but ex-trials driver Doctor John Spare showed the MGs how it should be done, finishing an excellent Morgan year for himself by collecting the Cecil Kimber Trophy for the best performance by a standard car.

Doc Spare on his way to winning the MG Car Club's Kimber Trophy Trial. (*Photograph: Doc Spare collection*)

The 1953 competition year thus came to a close. It had been quite a good one for the Morgan sportsmen, especially in rallies, crowned by the achievement of Jimmy Ray in winning the BTDA Silver Star.

Trials enthusiasts were now preparing for the MCC Exeter Trial, to be held on 1 and 2 January, the low-down torque of the Vanguard engine, as always, being particularly useful on trials hills.

Back at the Morgan factory, Peter Morgan was making arrangements for the TR2 engine in P3000 to be exchanged for the twin-carburettor experimental Vanguard engine currently fitted to KUY 387, in early January. The front end also was to be converted to the new cowled type, using the more rounded grille, as developed by Peter and Charlie Cummings, and the new front wings with raised headlamp pods supplied by Felix Day to Peter Morgan's request. Incidentally, these wings were to bring the headlights of the Morgan into compliance with the legal requirements introduced in 1950, for headlight centres to be not lower than 2ft. 2 in. from the ground in vehicles built after January 1952, in an attempt to reduce dazzle. The previous HFS-designed 'bean can' light pods were unfortunately some 2in. too low, although this does not seem to have hampered sales.

Some good news came for the Morgan company, with the announcement by Standard Triumph that there was to be a price rise of £40 for the Triumph TR2 sports car as from 1 January, thereby making the Morgan the cheaper two-seater sports car. The future Morgan buyer had seen, however, that the Plus 4 was to change, with a new modern front end and a TR2 engine. This meant that the last few old style radiator Plus 4s became 'last year's model', and proved difficult to sell, with some requiring updating by the factory in later months to take the new front end and, in one case, the TR2 motor.

Jim Goodall's car, HUY 982, was also being booked in to receive a new front end in January, along with a 3.73 to 1 back axle. However, no further TR2 engines had been received, so he was going to have to wait a little longer for the new engine.

A mere 305 Triumph TR2s had been built during 1953, with most being exported, leaving around fifty for distribution to dealers on the home market for demonstration. As a result none had yet competed in motor sport, but 1954 was to be different as production began to increase and the sportsmen got hold of them. 1954 promised to be an interesting year for the Morgan factory, with such strong opposition.

It is difficult if not impossible to be certain just how many Morgan Plus 4s were to be built with the interim HFS-designed front wings and cowl before the later Peter Morgan version took over for the future. This is made particularly difficult because several of these Morgans did not apparently sell with the Vanguard engines fitted. They were returned to the factory for the engines to be replaced by TR2 engines and for an update of front-end bodywork to the new style during 1954. Charlie Curtis' testing records show that all late 1953 production (some forty cars) was apparently fitted with the HFS-designed front wings, with production still continuing into the early months of 1954.

Overseas

New Zealand

The Nelson Car Club returned to Tahuna for a two-day beach race meeting, this time held on a tidal back beach, on 1 and 3 January. A regular circuit, oval but narrower at one end, was used for these annual New Year meetings, which attracted a large part of Nelson's population to watch the racing from the adjacent sand hills. A dyke was bulldozed to keep the tide at bay.

Keith Roper was once again entered in his Plus 4, which was considerably lightened by removing all lamps and mudguards, and doing without a windscreen. He finished third in the Nelson Electroplaters Cup handicap for cars of over 2,000 cc, behind Shuter's V8 Special and a Jaguar XK 120.

The feature race of the first day was for the Auto Parts Cup, and this time Keith's rapid Morgan finished second, again behind Frank Shuter's exciting V8 Special. Sand could be tricky to race upon, forming ruts in the corners, and Keith spun through 180 degrees during one race.

Allen Freeman continued his Morgan motor sport on 24 January at Nairarapa for timed standing and flying quarter-mile sprints. He recorded 19.55 seconds for the former and achieved 83.5 mph for the latter.

On Saturday 31 January, the Canterbury Car Club managed to organize a major 150-mile road race over a two and a half mile circuit of public roads at Mairehau in Waimairi County. Naturally Allen entered his red Plus 4, and was to receive twenty-three minutes' handicap start over scratchman Ron Roycroft's Alfa Romeo P3 monoposto.

Before the main race, there was to be a twenty-mile (8 lap) open handicap, the entrants of which could not enter the main one hundred and fifty mile race. Among the sixteen entrants was another Morgan – the red Plus 4 two-seater of Keith Roper. Unlike Allen, Keith had been tuning his car by raising the compression ratio, regrinding the camshaft and possibly by fitting twin SU carburettors. His handicap was 1¼ minutes start over two scratch XK 120 Jaguars.

Keith stormed through the field, and won the event in 25 min. 27⅖ sec., over 20 seconds ahead of second-placed Rudd's MG TD. He also made fastest time.

Next was the one hundred and fifty mile race, with Allen up against nineteen other assorted vehicles. For this long-distance race he had replaced the usual engine oil with Castrol 'R' vegetable oil, and fitted an oil cooler. He had also fitted a one size larger main jet to the single Solex carburettor and discarded as much weight as possible. At the finish, it was Roycroft's Alfa Romeo that had made fastest time (average 66.6 mph), coming through the field to take first place.

Initially, Allen was credited with an excellent second place but, following protests concerning lap scoring, he was 'relegated' to third, with a time of 2 hr. 46 min. 33 sec., at an average race speed of 55.8 mph.

On 14 February Allen was back hill climbing,

Allen Freeman passing the pits at Mairehau, during the 150-mile race. (*Photograph: Allen Freeman collection*)

Dr George Cowie's Coupe, with a Sunbeam-Talbot. (*Photograph: George Cowie collection*)

Allen Freeman at his pits after winning the Ohakea Trophy Race. George Cowie is one of the admirers. (*Photograph: Allen Freeman collection*)

this time at Plimmerton, near Wellington. He won his class and made fourth fastest time of the day.

On 14 March the Manawatu Car Club organized an ambitious race meeting on the airfield at Ohakea. The first car race was a twenty-mile (10 lap) handicap race for fully equipped sports cars. Two Morgan Plus 4s were entered – Keith Roper with his tuned, red two-seater, and Dr George Cowie with his black Coupe.

George Cowie had purchased his new Coupe from Independent Motors, having decided from *The Autocar* buyer's guide that it was the ideal vehicle with which to replace his Jowett Javelin. Jack Shelly had seemed surprised that anyone would want a Morgan, particularly as he himself had recently visited England and had found the small size of the Morgan company and the traditional methods of construction unimpressive.

It took Keith Roper seven laps to lead the race, overtaking three cars on lap five, and four cars on lap six, and he held this position to the end, also setting fastest time. Finishing in fifth place was George Cowie, behind a V8 Special, a Jaguar XK 120 and a Railton.

The big race of the day was the Ohakea Trophy Race, over fifty miles, and twenty-nine cars lined up for the start. Keith Roper was entered, as also was Allen Freeman, running his four-seater as set up for Mairehau.

By the eighth lap of this twenty-five lap handicap event Allen had taken the lead. He held on to the finish despite an impressive drive through the field by Ron Roycroft in his P3 Alfa Romeo, who finished second and obviously set the fastest time. Keith Roper finished eleventh but some believed the recorded lap times to be incorrect and have suggested he was actually second.

One week later Allen was near Auckland for the North Island hill climb championship held at Wairamarama. He finished with fourth fastest time of the day, and came second in class.

He was back at Saddle Road hill climb on 28 March, making second fastest time of the day.

In April Allen showed his versatility by finishing third in a half-day trial held at Lower Hutt, and then later came first and second in two races held on the half-mile mile trotting horse racing track at Kaiapoi.

Allen was now completing negotiations to purchase from England the ex-Peter Collins Cooper 500. Probably his last Morgan event was therefore the Flagstaff hill climb at Trentham on 9 May where he made third fastest time.

Meanwhile Ted Reid had entered his Morgan for the Dunedin 'round the houses' races held on 1 June. In the thirty-mile sports car handicap he came in fifth, and in the twenty-five mile stock car handicap he made third fastest time, finishing third.

On 26 September Ted finished second in the 2000–3000 cc open class of the Otago Sports Car Club Patmos hill climb and first in the stock class for the same capacity.

He was equally at home at the same club's grass hill climb on 7 November, making fastest time of the day and winning the class for cars of 1500 cc and above.

One week later, the Wellington Car Club ran its Plimmerton hill climb. Dr George Cowie had entered his Morgan, and also his 2.5 litre Riley, necessitating running back down the hill to collect the other car. He recorded 38.2 seconds with the Riley to take the class for touring cars of 1500–2500 cc, and recorded 34.75 seconds with the Morgan, to finish second in the class for sports cars over 1500 cc, behind McBeath's Special.

United States of America

Sixty-nine cars took part in the Long Beach California MG Club's time trials, held on a 1.7-mile road course at Costa Mesa on 15 February. T. E. Decker had a walk-over in the class for 1950–3000 cc cars, recording a rather slow 3 min. 1.6 sec. with his Plus 4.

A new West Coast distributor was appointed this year, Cavalier Motor Cars Ltd. of Crenshaw Boulevard in Los Angeles, which took over from Angell Motors. Their first Plus 4 (P2568) left the factory on 4 March.

A keen sports car enthusiast named Mike Rothschild, from New Jersey, had set his sights on entering the 1953 Sebring 12-hour race. Looking through the results of the 1952 event he decided a Morgan looked likely for further success, so he had placed an order with Fergus Motors Inc. for a two-seater and then entered the race. Mike was not new to motor sport, having been racing a Singer, fitted with a Jeep engine. He also had an

Ted Reid makes fastest time during the Otago club's grass hill climb. (*Photograph: Ted Reid collection*)

excellent mechanic to help him with his racing, namely Eddie Brown, who had previously worked on midget speedway cars. For the Sebring endurance race, the Morgan's standard exhaust system was replaced by a special made out of copper, but otherwise there was little done to the car, apart from careful preparation.

One week before the event, Mike and his English wife 'Honey' set off in the Morgan for Sebring, where they met up with the rest of the pit crew, and Jack Nile, the other driver.

Practice proved to be not uneventful for the Morgan, for the special copper exhaust disintegrated and was therefore discarded for the rest of the Sebring adventure. More seriously, the engine dropped a valve, which necessitated the head coming off, and then replacement using a Ford valve and a Pontiac valve spring. When this combination proved trouble-free during the rest of practice, Mike decided to pull the engine down once more. He replaced all the valves with the same components, thereby making the engine much more suitable for racing.

This year there were to be fifty-one starters, of which eight were in class D, for 2–3 litre sports cars, including a team of Aston Martin DB3s from England, much to the pleasure of Alec Ulmann. Reliability is the key to endurance racing, however, so Mike concentrated on planning for regular lap times, his wife Honey being in charge of their time-keeping.

George Eyston was this year's honoured starter and at 12 noon on 8 March he set off the field with the usual Le Mans start.

All was well with the Morgan until early in the fourth hour when Jack Nile lost control of the car and it vaulted a hay bale coming into the back straight, eventually coming to rest on top of a standpipe. He needed to jack up the car and replace a bent wheel before the car could be persuaded to leave its perch, losing around thirty minutes of valuable time. Thereafter the Morgan continued gamely on its way, although the exhaust problem contributed to an annoying tendency for the car to burst into flames each time it came into the pits!

Mike and Jack finally completed 119 laps within the twelve hours, finishing twenty-third overall and third in class, behind the one surviving Aston Martin and Peter Yung's Ferrari 225.

The problem now was for Mike and Honey to get the Morgan home, a mere 1,300 miles, for the Morgan engine was none too happy, having developed a tendency to blow out oil (subsequently it was found to have three cracked pistons). As a result the sidescreen had to be taken off to reduce the fumes inside the car but this in turn allowed Honey to get quite bad sunburn. They made it but their last few dollars went on some more oil for the engine, rather than a welcome, warming cup of soup for the occupants (snow fell as they travelled north and the temperature got colder).

A long parade of European cars wound from New York City's Central Park to the Grand Central Palace on 4 April to mark the opening of the second International Motor Sports Show. Inside was a truly beautiful array of European and American cars and among them was Joe Ferguson with the Morgan in its first major American show. European imports were now big news in the USA as this show demonstrated.

American enthusiasts were also keen to copy European rallies, such as the Monte Carlo, which they had read about in their motoring magazines. In Washington DC the SCCA ran a small one-day rally on 19 April, with R. T. Carruthers proving the victor in his Morgan. Also, on Friday 24 April the Connecticut Sports Car Club attracted over sixty cars to its two-day rally. There were starts in Alley Pond Park, Long Island; Grant's Tomb, New York; Norwalk, Connecticut; and in Massachusetts. One hundred and sixty-three miles were covered before a night's sleep at Pittsfield, Massachusetts. The following day saw the crews on a route of 165 miles of winding, hilly back roads through Massachusetts, New Hampshire and Vermont before finishing in Claremont, New Hampshire, with a banquet. Two MG TDs were first and second, but Mr & Mrs David Stewart of Westport, Connecticut, finished third in their Plus 4.

On the Sunday many of the contestants made for Thompson, Connecticut (approximately 150 miles north east of New York City) for motor racing. This circuit had originally been a half-mile speedway-type oval but during the last year Bill Proctor, Bill Lloyd and George Weaver had modified it to make it suitable for sports car racing. They added a road section which included a hill and a hairpin bend, thereby increasing the circuit length to 1½ miles. No Morgans featured in the results of Sunday's race.

Bridgehampton, on Long Island, New York,

was one of the 'round the houses' racing circuits, using public roads. On 23 May the SCCA ran a race meeting there but it was clear that the days of round-the-houses racing were virtually over. Bob Wilder was sadly killed practising an Allard LM, and then the racing had to be stopped when Harry Gray crashed his 'C' type Jaguar, narrowly missing some spectators.

However, in Sullivan County, New York, the nearby towns had found a circuit with an 8.5 miles lap distance that they hoped would be suitable for sports car racing. Several clubs inspected it but turned it down. The course was very narrow, two miles were unpaved, trees encroached to the very edge of the track and gravel formed the surface of two of the corners. Eventually the Jersey Sports Car Club decided to take it on and the local township of Callicoon enthusiastically helped to improve the circuit for the racing to be held on 28 June.

Mike Rothschild now had his Plus 4 fully operational once more. His was the only Morgan entered but he failed to feature in the results. There were also several accidents and doubt was expressed on the future of this circuit on safety grounds.

Over on the West Coast on 16 August the SCCA ran a race meeting at Moffett Field, a Blimp base south of San Francisco. Leo Caton from Hollywood was in action once more in his Plus 4 and finished an excellent fifth in the two and a half hour long race.

On the other side of the country, in New York, the AAA ran an FIA-sanctioned meeting at Floyd Bennett Field in Brooklyn, on 29 August. It was very hot (100°F), which softened the runways and made life difficult for both drivers and cooling systems. The second race on the programme was the Brighton Beach Trophy race over twenty laps of the 2.4-mile course and was for production sports cars of over 1500 cc, attracting twenty-three entries. One was Mike Rothschild with his Plus 4. Mike was unable to catch the bigger engined cars, and the Jaguar XK 120 of Russell Boss duly finished first, but Mike did win class D for 2000–3000 cc entries.

One week later, the North East racers were once more at Thompson, Connecticut, for the SCCA's National event on 6 September. Event 7 was a ten-lap race for classes B, D & E, and included in the Class D entries was the Plus 4 of Harry R. Beck Jnr of Delaware. Also, making its debut in the USA, was an Austin Healey, driven by Randy Pearsall. Both the Plus 4 and the Austin Healey impressed with their handling on the 1.5-mile track and finished in that order behind the class winning 2.7 litre Ferrari of William Spear.

A sprint meeting was held at Niagara Falls in New York, on the border with Canada on 26 September. The two Plus 4s of Jim Ottman and Ed Kowalski managed to beat several supercharged MGs to take the class for 1500–2500 cc in this drag race meeting.

Back at Thompson, P. Kinsolving managed a third in class at the race meeting held there on 1 November.

In California a new name was beginning to appear in races with a Morgan, this being that of Charles Thompson, a Beverly Hills doctor. On 8 November he took part in the SCCA's races held on the SAC base of March Field, near Riverside, finishing sixteenth overall out of nineteen finishers in the main race, although first in his class.

In November a new, purpose-built motor racing circuit was opened at Willow Springs, situated in the California desert north of Los Angeles. The CSCC used it for hill climbs on 13 December, and attracted a young commercial kitchen designer to enter his every-day Plus 4. He finished in the top three in his class. His name was Lew Spencer, and he was just at the beginning of a great future with Morgans and motor sport.

Towards the end of each year, the American sports car enthusiasts would eagerly scour the motoring magazines for reports of the British Motor Show, to learn whether any new sports cars had been developed or any modifications to current models had been introduced. This year the redesign of the Morgan front end did not go unnoticed and, as in England, the new styling was either liked or hated.

One of those who did not approve was the Technical Editor of *Road and Track*, John Bond, who wrote, 'I say the Morgan Co. have gone completely "off their rocker" with their unhappy attempt at restyling the radiator shell.' No doubt Fergus Motors and Cavalier Motor Cars were able to advise the factory further on the future saleability of their new design. As Triumph TR2 sports cars were now beginning to be imported into the USA, the fact that the Morgan was also to receive the same engine was good news for the American motor sport enthusiast.

Australia

The year 1953 began with the opening of a new Australian motor racing circuit – that at Port Wakefield in South Australia. A combined race meeting for cars and motorcycles was held on 1 January. Situated some forty miles north of Adelaide, just east of Port Wakefield itself, this small 1.3-mile circuit was purpose-built for racing, and was to be operated by Brooklyn Park Speedway SA Ltd.

Motor racing enthusiasts from far and wide entered for the day's races, among them several Morgan drivers. Local racer Peter Hay had further modified his Morgan for this event. The body was now much lightened, the bonnet being completely discarded and replaced by a small alloy engine cover which featured an air scoop directing air to the carburettor. The cylinder head had been shaved, raising the compression such that the petrol required a fair dose of benzole to prevent pinking. A Lucas magneto had replaced the distributor, and this allowed the batteries and dynamo to be removed, the normal fan belt being replaced by a smaller one. Cooling ducts were fitted to the brakes.

Also entered from South Australia was another Morgan driver, with the most appropriate name of Gavin Sandford-Morgan. Before buying his Morgan he had managed quite a bit of racing, using a variety of vehicles including MGs, vintage Bentleys, a Ford V8-powered Bugatti and a ditto powered Alfa Romeo. He had been impressed by the Morgan of Peter Hay, and consequently purchased a blue 1951 Plus 4 second-hand from a garage in Hamilton, Victoria which had sold a few to local sheep grazing families. He drove it back the three hundred and fifty miles to Adelaide.

The Port Wakefield meeting was to be his first event and preparation consisted of little more than fitting a straight through exhaust system.

Also entered for the event was David Van Dal from Western Australia, with his second red Morgan, which he had now considerably developed. The cylinder head was ported and polished, larger inlet valves were fitted and the head was copper

The paddock at Port Wakefield. No. 42 is the Morgan of Gavin Sandford-Morgan, behind No. 33, Vin Maloney's MG TC special. (*Photograph: Terry McGrath collection*)

Peter Hay holds off Bob Brown's MG TC at Port Wakefield to win the first race. (*Photograph: Peter Hay collection*)

plated. The Vanguard camshaft was reground with 20/70 timing. A small alloy engine cover replaced the bonnet, and featured a large scoop to direct air to the two carburettors. In view of its shape this scoop led to the Morgan being christened the 'letterbox Morgan'. The engine was fuelled by a 50/50 alcohol/avgas mixture delivered through two Ford V8 type Stromberg carburettors, as previously mentioned.

A new beefed-up clutch operated by a new fork withdrawal system was fitted. The sparks were delivered by a Lucas Vertex magneto with 27° advance, set at 11° static (38° at 2,500 rpm).

At the rear, tubular shock absorbers replaced the original lever arm system, and the rear body panel was closed in over the spare wheel gap.

David's Morgan was shipped along the coast to Adelaide, while he travelled the 1,800 miles with Syd Anderson in his Studebaker, Syd being another of the considerable contingent of racers from Western Australia making the long journey. On arrival David collected the Morgan from Rowland Motors in Adelaide and drove it to the circuit. The noise from the four unsilenced stub exhausts was somewhat embarrassing, but no-one complained and policemen even saluted him.

Also entered for the event, this time from the state of Victoria, was Ian Stewart with his Morgan three-wheeler, but we do not think he actually made the trip (along with many other Victoria entrants).

The first event, a ten-lap scratch race saw Peter Hay in with a field of mainly modified MG TCs. Peter took the lead, and held it to the end, beating both Bob Brown and Steve Tillett with their hot MG TCs to win this, the first race to be held on the new track, his fastest lap being at 62 mph.

The second event, another ten-lap scratch race brought David Van Dal to the line together with some larger machinery. All appeared well as he went into the first corner, but then, as he looked up from the rev counter, he noticed a wheel rolling down the road – it was his offside front!

Luckily the other drivers missed David, and at the end of the race the car and errant wheel were returned to the paddock, the stub axle having broken. With David were the support crew of Sid Taylor's TS Special, and they put an announcement over the public address system for a Morgan stub axle. Peter Hay came forward, and his offside front corner was removed by the TS men and refitted to David's car.

Luckily the middle part of the programme was for motorcycles, so David's car was able to be running again before the later car races.

Two twenty-lap handicaps restarted the motor racing after the motorcycle races. The second should have featured four Morgans, but obviously that of Pete Hay was unavailable and Ian Stewart had also non-started, so just those of Gavin Sandford-Morgan and David Van Dal represented the marque in the race. Gavin Sandford-Morgan, who had been pleased with the performance of his car in practice, particularly when compared with the tuned MGs, was soon troubled by loud and expensive-sounding noises from his engine. His day's racing was done and he returned to Adelaide on a tow rope.

David Van Dal did finish, but he was unable to beat his handicap, the race going to his friend Colin Uphill and the Topolino, ahead of an MG TC.

Celebrations continued for days in Adelaide long after the finish of these inaugural Port Wakefield races. Following this David Van Dal collected his Morgan, and towed it using a self steer 'V' bar to Melbourne some 800 miles further east for practice on the newly resurfaced Phillip Island circuit.

Gavin Sandford-Morgan soon dismantled the engine of his Plus 4, finding a broken exhaust valve, the head of which had destroyed a piston. Despite this setback he had enjoyed his racing, and began to prepare for future events.

Peter Hay, his car returned to one piece by the TS support crew, purchased two new large SU carburettors and fabricated a manifold for them. The car went much better and he looked forward to racing once more. Unfortunately, he was transferred to Sydney on business where he found no suitable venues for racing, so he returned his car to almost standard trim and sold it. The little alloy engine cover was purchased by Gavin Sandford-Morgan for his own car, along with the neat aluminium cycle mudguards.

David Van Dal in the Port Wakefield paddock in the 'Letterbox' Plus 4 (*Photograph: Terry McGrath collection*)

David Van Dal was back in Western Australia for the street races at Narrogin on Monday 2 March, having accompanied the Letterbox Plus 4 on its way back from Melbourne to Freemantle on the *SS Manoora*.

He had now removed the twin Stromberg carburettors and replaced them with the previously used type of cut and welded Vanguard manifold using two Vanguard Solexes. The problem with the set up of the Strombergs had been that the fuel float chambers were not in line with the carburettor bodies, so that the mixture was weak on right-hand turns, and rich when going the other way. New manifolds for the Strombergs, with the float chambers to the front were eventually to be constructed.

In addition to David Van Dal there were two other Morgan entrants at Narrogin, these being Johnny Motteram with his faithful 4/4, and Ted Barker with a Plus 4.

Ted Barker, known as 'Limpy' because his left leg was somewhat shorter than his right, was a qualified motor mechanic in Western Australia. Doubtless he had noticed the successes of David Van Dal in the Bill Richards sponsored Morgan, and decided he too would do well to race a Morgan.

Following the usual traditional, and colourful, parade of drivers the first race to feature a Morgan was the three-lap scratch race for cars of over

Bruce Mutton's MG TC and Johnny Motteram's Morgan cast deep shadows as they wait to start in the strong Narrogin sunshine. (*Photograph: Johnny Motteram collection*)

1500 cc. Syd Anderson proved impossible to pass in his double Ford V8 Special and took the flag, but David Van Dal came home in an excellent second place, ahead of Syd Negus's Plymouth Special.

The following three-lap scratch race for cars of under 1500 cc was notable for the MG TC of Bruce Mutton turning over and pinning him beneath, as he attempted to negotiate the S-bend on Fairway Street. Luckily he was found to be unhurt once the car was righted, and even competed again later in the day.

Yet another accident occurred at the same spot in the five-lap Memorial Pool Handicap when Colin Uphill crashed into a tree while driving his Topolino, injuring a spectator in the process. Colin suffered head injuries, and then burns, the latter being received when a well-meaning helper dragged him out of the car, and leaned him against the hot exhaust pipe.

The baking hot weather took its toll on the number of starters for the Great Southern Flying Fifty, with just eleven taking to the line, of which only seven finished. Noel Aldous took his third victory of the day in his gold monoposto MG TC Special, while Ted Barker finished sixth after a steady drive.

Richard Reynolds was back at Rob Roy hill climb on 8 March. He drove well once again to win the sports car class from 1501–3000 cc, beating two Holdens with a time of 34.65 seconds.

The following day Richards was at Templestowe for the Victorian Sporting Car Club's fifth hill climb at this venue. He recorded 72 seconds to take the class, and established a new record with this time.

Richard's Morgan was doing well in these hill climbs. The engine had received the usual extra performance treatment, with a shaved head to raise the compression, and polished inlet and exhaust ports with the former matched to the inlet manifold. The flywheel was also reduced in weight. At some stage twin Stromberg carburettors were fitted, these being of the type used on Holden cars. They worked well but had a horrendous appetite for Shell Racing Fuel.

The poor Australian roads continued to take their toll on Richard's car, and as spares were difficult to come by, it was through the help of his friends and acquaintances that the mechanical problems were largely overcome. The front crosshead bracing struts to the chassis were particularly vulnerable, with the result that these were replaced several times. The tubing used was increased in size each time, until they approached one inch in diameter before breakages ceased. Dust, mud and oil also played havoc with the front suspension, and Morris 8/40 rear axles were found suitable to machine into replacement centre pins.

Having purchased an early Plus 4, Richard was also faced with the problems caused by the small size of the eye bolt in the clutch sleeve. Eventually this worked loose, and was to be replaced by bigger and yet bigger versions.

Richard did write to Peter Morgan regarding spares, but the high cost of getting them to Australia made him reluctant to purchase. Australians were well used to making do with whatever was available locally to repair their cars.

In South Australia Gavin Sandford-Morgan was also developing the performance of his Plus 4 for racing. The cycle wings and one-piece bonnet purchased from Peter Hay were fitted, and painted blue to match Gavin's car. A second cylinder head was shaved ⅛in. to raise the compression ratio, and then polished, and a 'log' type inlet manifold was fabricated and fitted with a pair of 1½in. SU carburettors. A rev counter was driven from a belt to the crankshaft, and the car's instrumentation was generally improved.

The chassis also received attention. The front crosshead was sleeved with heavy gauge steel tubing to make it more rigid, and the steering damper blades were replaced with saw steel of greater thickness. Cracks were discovered in the chassis side members just in front of the bulkhead, so reinforcing plates made from redundant number plates were welded in for strengthening.

Gavin considered the Burman steering to be woefully inadequate, and began to think of any way this component could easily be replaced.

He took his Morgan to Collingrove hill climb for the Easter meeting. The car went well, but was beaten by another 'hot' Plus 4, this being the property of M. J. Thomson who lived in Snowtown in South Australia.

Thomson's Morgan was chassis number P2176, a green two-seater, engine number V42 ME, which had originally been despatched from the Morgan factory on 9 July 1951 to Kar-Fix Engineering of Adelaide. He had purchased it second-hand, with 14,000 miles on the clock and immediately wrote to the Morgan factory for an instruction manual, which was despatched in February 1953. His performance at Collingrove suggests he had studied it well for he had considerably improved the Plus 4's performance.

In Western Australia the Easter holidays were also the dates for the Northam street races. Three Morgans were entered, these being the 4/4 of Johnny Motteram, David Van Dal's 'Letterbox' Plus 4 and the similar model of Ted Barker. David Van Dal had of course won the previous year's Northam Flying Fifty, and was therefore a likely front runner for this, the second Northam meeting. He had contracted with the oil company Shell to use its recently introduced Shell X100 engine oil, but all was not well during practice, for the engine's bearings failed. David and his crew worked through the night repolishing the crank and mains, and fitting new shells. They also replaced the little end bushes and piston rings, and decided that the new oil was too suspect to continue to use. As a result they decanted trustworthy Mobil Delo 40 into X100 tins, and filled up the sump with this. It is believed the Shell oil company never knew of this deception.

Easter Monday, 6 April, was actual race day, and some 10,000 spectators congregated in the Northam streets for the racing, the track being over a different circuit to the previous year.

The first race was a four-lap scratch race for 'A' division cars of over 1500 cc. David Van Dal produced a magnificent performance, such that he won the race in 10 min. 25 sec. from Syd Anderson's double V8 Ford-engined special, and Sid Taylor's TS Special.

Following this race was the 'B' division four-lap scratch race for the smaller engined cars. Johnny Motteram was the only Morgan entry, and he finished fourth behind three MGs. The six-lap handicap again had David Van Dal among the awards, for he finished third, the winner being Syd Negus.

The Flying Fifty handicap race, over twenty-five laps was the final event on the programme. Johnny Motteram was famous for his deceptively fast drives in these long-distance street races, and soon went into the lead. Further back, driving off virtual scratch position, David Van Dal was desperately trying to pass Sid Taylor's Dodge-engined TS Special under braking as of course it had far more power than the Plus 4 on the straights. Brakes were not the Plus 4's finest point, especially on a street circuit with its many right-angled bends. Brake fade set in, and a startled David Van Dal found himself zipping past Sid on the inside! He then slid all four wheels across the corner to the straw bales on the outside, which the Plus 4 then mounted and started to shred. Poor Sid suddenly found his cockpit full of hay, could not find his gear lever, or indeed the road, and David was away. It did not last, however, and David's impressive drive later came to an end when he was forced to ease up, and then retire with shot bearings.

After twelve laps Johnny Motteram was still in the lead, but then he unfortunately clipped the curb as he turned into the home straight. The Morgan mounted the pavement and ploughed into a lamp standard dead centre; and Johnny's race was over.

Luckily bales of hay cushioned the impact and saved Johnny from serious injury, although he did receive an injury to his right elbow and shock. The car was extensively damaged, and later burst into flames while it was being towed away, although these were quickly extinguished.

The second race meeting to be held at the Port Wakefield circuit in South Australia was the ANZAC meeting held on 25 April. Three Plus 4s were entered, those of Gavin Sandford-Morgan, M. J. Thomson and a newcomer to Morgan, Derek Jolly, who was also entered with his more usual racing Austin 7.

Gavin was delighted with the performance of his Morgan during practice, and looked forward to the racing, hopeful of victory.

Over 8,000 spectators came to watch the day's racing. Two of the Morgans, those of Sandford-Morgan and Jolly, had entered for the twenty-lap open handicap event for racing and sports cars. The race proved to be a disaster for Gavin, for his engine dropped a valve yet again, this occurring on the very first lap, no less, putting an end to his day's activities. Derek Jolly also did not feature in the top seven.

Next followed an eight-lap handicap for sports cars and production cars. With the absence of Gavin's car, just Thomson's Plus 4 represented the Morgan marque. He had better luck and finished third behind Reg Spark's race-winning MG TC, and C. Smith's Terraplane.

Gavin was very disappointed and frustrated by the valve gear failure. It was all too much, and he vowed to get to the bottom of the problem. As a result he decided to write directly to the Standard Triumph Motor Company in England. To his surprise he was to receive a reply by return air mail from none other than Ted Grinham. He informed Gavin that the company had experienced exactly the same trouble during the development of the Vanguard engine for its new Triumph sports car. He enclosed drawings of the valve gear modifications required to eradicate this problem, in which conventional valve retaining split collets were used.

Meanwhile, the day after the Port Wakefield meeting Richard Reynolds was racing on the oval grass track at Nash Park Corio once again, this meeting having been organized by the Western District Car Club. In one of the over 1500 cc handicap heats Richard was second to Ted Gray's Alta-Ford V8, but then he went and improved on this position with a first place in a heat of the open handicap race. In the final of the latter Richard again finished first, beating K. Cantwell's Buick special into second place and the ex-Morgan three-wheeler driver Cec Warren who was in a JAP-engined Speedcar, into third.

The Victoria Sporting Car Club held its sixth hill climb at Templestowe on 17 May, and Richard Reynolds entered to try and defend his seventy-two second class record. It was a classic encounter and his record was broken no fewer

At Goomalling Ted Barker, John Cummins and David Van Dal inspect the engine of the 'Letterbox' Plus 4. Note the twin Solex carburettors, and stub exhausts. *(Photograph: Sid Bannister)*

than six times, thrice by Harry Firth's MG TC, and thrice by Reynolds himself. At the end of the day it was Firth who recorded 65.62 seconds on his third run to take the class and set a new record, while Richard's 69.56 seconds gave him second place.

In the afternoon, off came the cycle wings and other items of unnecessary weight from the Plus 4, and Richard took part in the racing car class. Again he finished second, with a time of 67.80 seconds, behind Geoff Brown's Willys-powered midget racer.

Some 3,000 spectators ignored the heavy rain to watch the street racing at Goomalling on 1 June. The large crowd proved difficult to control, and there was a false start to the proceedings while the course was cleared of spectators. Three Morgans were entered in the programme – David Van Dal with his 'Letterbox' Plus 4, Ted Barker with his own tuned Plus 4 and Arthur Littlejohns from Narrogin with his Plus 4.

David Van Dal's engineering training obviously enabled him to be up to the minute with the latest tuning ideas built into his Plus 4's engine. One of his friends and helpers was John Cummins, who had been an apprentice at the Rolloy Piston Co. Pty Ltd under the supervision of the famous Bob Chamberlain. Bob had, with his brother Bill, designed and built an extremely advanced 1100 cc four-cylinder 8-piston supercharged racing two stroke, 'The Beetle', in 1929, and was well versed in racing technology. Also counted among David and John's friends were Phil Irving (Vincent chief designer), and Charlie Dean (Repco experimental engineer), so many informative and exciting evenings and weekends were spent discussing racing engines and car set up. Sadly, David became a spectator at

The Riley rack and pinion steering fitted to Gavin Sandford-Morgan's Plus 4. (*Photograph: Gavin Sandford-Morgan collection*)

Goomalling, for his engine 'blew', despite using a hard chromed crank and new lead-bronze bearings. The main race of the day, the Flying Fifty, was won by Noel Aldous in his highly effective monoposto MG TC Special. The only Morgan entered was that of Ted Barker, who finished an uneventful seventh.

A spin at Garage Corner, within sight of the finish, deprived Arthur Littlejohns of a certain victory in the five-lap sports car handicap. He finally finished fourth.

The weather was much better at Rob Roy with a fine day on the occasion of the Coronation Day meeting, held on 2 June. Richard Reynolds was flying, and took his Plus 4 to a class win in the sports car class with a time of 33.40 seconds. In the afternoon's racing car competition he improved his time to 32.70 seconds, and finished a very respectable third in class behind Alf Beasley's Lea Francis, and Lex Davison's Alfa Romeo.

The same day Gavin Sandford-Morgan and M. J. Thomson were battling at Collingrove hill climb in South Australia. Gavin and his helpers had modified the valve spring retaining system on the Vanguard engine to include collets – something Gavin had decided to do even before receiving the letter from Ted Grinham. Thomson's Plus 4 was the one flying on this occasion, however, for he took the over 1500 cc sports car class with a time of 45.80 seconds, Gavin being second exactly two seconds slower.

Gavin Sandford-Morgan now turned his attention to the Morgan's steering. He decided to try and fit a rack and pinion system, and looked at those used on the Morris Minor, and the Riley RM series. He decided on the latter, for the steering arms were pivoted from the centre of the rack, rather than from either end with the Morris version. Gavin felt that the Riley system might create less bump steer effect when used in conjunction with the Morgan sliding pillar suspension. In the event it turned out to be an excellent modification, giving greatly improved steering and handling, and making the troublesome and crude steering dampers unnecessary. In later years Gavin was to wonder why it took the Morgan factory so long to try similar components on its production cars.

On 11 October Gavin took his modified Plus 4 to Collingrove. Again he was slower than Thomson, recording 45.9 seconds, against Thomson's 45.3, but progress was certainly being made.

The following day the two South Australian Plus 4 drivers were at Port Wakefield for the Labour Day Speed Meeting. In the eight-lap Maughan Thiem handicap for sports and touring cars the two Morgans were on scratch, and at last Gavin tasted success, storming through the field to a well-deserved victory, collecting £10 and the trophy presented by the Maughan Thiem Motor Co. Ltd (local Singer dealers).

Gavin was delighted, and decided he would now turn his attention to the carburation and the exhaust design on his Plus 4. He decided to consult the local guru, Ron Uffindell, for his advice and expertise on these matters.

On Saturday 11 October the WA Sporting Car Club managed to get permission to use the Caversham airstrip once again after a lapse of several years, to run a 'Speed Classic'. A crowd estimated at 10,000 were not disappointed by an exciting day's racing. Four Morgans were entered, these being the Plus 4s of David Van Dal, A. Herbert, Arthur Littlejohns and Ted Barker. Ted's blue Plus 4 had been 'breathed' on under the influence of David Van Dal, and had a 'letterbox' type air scoop supplying twin Solex carburettors, together with magneto ignition.

There were three heats to the three-lap production car handicap and Littlejohns finished in third place in the first to qualify for the final. He improved his position in this by finishing second behind Ron Shaw's Fiat 1100.

The five-lap open sports car handicap concluded with David Van Dal the victor, beating Noel Aldous into second place, with Peter Morgan's MG third.

The event had proved to be a great success, with various charities benefiting from the takings, and Syd Negus as President of the WA Sporting Car Club hoped to run further events in the future.

In New South Wales a new name appeared on the Morgan competition scene when Burt Colley took part in the quarter mile sprints organized by the Vintage Sports Car Club (NSW) at Castlereagh on 18 October. In the class for modern cars over 2000 cc his Plus 4 recorded a rather slow 19.23 seconds to give him fifth place.

Back in Western Australia, the WA Sporting Car Club managed to arrange another Caversham Speed Classic on Saturday 5 December. The first event was a three-lap production and sports car handicap, and David Van Dal managed second place behind Ron Shaw's Fiat 1100.

David was second again in the five-lap open sports car handicap, behind newcomer A. Walker and his MG.

In both of the above events it is likely that David was using the Bill Richards Motors Plus 4 demonstrator, rather than the 'Letterbox' Plus 4, which was of course heavily tuned, and could hardly be called a sports car any more.

The following event was a five-lap handicap for racing cars and this resulted in a fine win for Ted Barker who managed to stay ahead of Syd Anderson's double Ford V8 Special and Peter Morgan's MG.

A three-lap unrestricted capacity sealed handicap was the next event. Only three cars finished and Ron Scott's Fiat unfortunately turned over. Syd Anderson was the victor, followed by the Morgans of Arthur Littlejohns and David Van Dal.

The main race on the programme was the twelve-lap handicap Caversham Speed Classic itself. At half distance Ted Barker had drawn out a commanding lead following a superb drive, but then engine trouble intervened and he was forced to investigate in the pits. Although he got going again it was to no avail, and the race was won by Noel Aldous and his MG.

Among the spectators had been Johnny Motteram who had just returned from his honeymoon in Palm Beach with his new wife Shirley. The newlyweds were quizzed as to Johnny's future racing plans, but they confirmed that he had now retired.

The year of 1953 had been a good one for Morgans in Australian motor sport, with several extremely well prepared cars doing well. Major competition was on the horizon for 1954, however, as exports of Austin Healeys and Triumph TR2s began to arrive in enthusiasts' hands.

Canada

Canadian Morgan enthusiasts were now able to purchase new Morgans from two agencies – McGrail Motors of Montreal, and Windsor Motor Cycles in Ontario, the latter continuing to sell and service Morgans for very many years.

It was wet for the annual summer race meeting organized by the Sports Car Club of Toronto, at Edenvale airfield, seventy-five miles north of Toronto. Just three cars contented the five-lap Class D (2000–3000 cc) race, these being the Plus 4 of Alan Weed, a Hillman Minx and an MG TC, but the latter two had both been re-engined with side-valve Ford V8 60s. It was these two that took the lead, but on lap three of the one and three quarter mile course they both spun off, leaving Weed to make the fastest lap and win the race.

There was a Le Mans start for the one-hour Formula Race (handicap). Alan Weed held sixth position by lap ten, but finally finished eleventh on handicap.

APPENDIX

The Morgan Factory through to 1953

It is well documented how Morgan sports cars are produced today. These methods having been scrutinized and described by many authors, and, due to the generosity of the Morgan Motor Company, it is possible to tour the factory oneself and see just how the cars are manufactured.

The early days, however, have not had the same thorough investigation. Indeed, many authors have paid scant regard to these days and often the comments they do make are not borne out by the available facts.

Researching the early days is of course difficult, as time has now taken away the employees who could tell us about the manufacturing processes used. Some information is available within the Morgan factory archives; local newspapers, together with some motoring magazines, contain snippets of information in back issues. Some early plans also still exist at the Worcester County Record Office.

During the 1980s Dennis Rushton and one of the authors (J.A.) interviewed several ex-factory employees regarding the factory layout, and the former also surveyed the structural construction of the factory buildings. The information generously given to us by these ex-employees, particularly Reginald Thomas (from 1913), E. T. Vine (from 1915), Charlie Curtis (from 1917), Derek Evans (from 1930) and Percy Sambrook (from 1933) has allowed us to assemble this record of the factory layout and the changes made over the years. We are also indebted to the researches of Martyn Webb, whose interest in the early days of HFS Morgan's garage enterprise has helped us, and also to the Morgan Three-Wheeler Club for access to a series of well-known photographs taken in each shop of the Morgan factory in 1929–30.

In the following history, we have also included information about the Morgan family, itself, if we felt it relevant or of interest.

The story starts in 1905 with the purchase by twenty-three-year-old HFS Morgan of the house named Chestnut Villa on Worcester Road, Malvern Link, at the junction with Howsell Road. Adjacent to the house was a plot of land in which a few small buildings stood, but which was of a suitable size and location for the construction of a motor garage. HFS duly applied for planning permission for such an enterprise on 8 March 1905, having gone into partnership for this venture with his friend Leslie Bacon.

Approval was granted on 4 April for the single-storey building of 72ft. by 38¾ft., giving a total floor space of 2,790 sq ft, with toilets adjacent to the rear.

The building proceeded quickly, and on Saturday 20 May 1905 the new garage opened, with advertisements in the *Malvern Gazette* newspaper to publicize the new venture.

Photographs taken on this occasion, probably by HFS's father Prebendary H. George Morgan, who was a keen photographer and who had also doubtless financed the business, show HFS Morgan and Leslie Bacon with their various hire vehicles, which included the 22hp Daimler that was to initiate their local bus service.

The photograph of the interior shows a typical garage for the period, with a parking area for up to forty cars, and a small machine shop at the rear, on the right looking in, with a 3hp electric motor powering various items of garage machinery. There was also an inspection pit. A door at the rear led to a yard behind the works.

The Worcester Road façade contained three sets of double windows, having unusual semi-circular upper window framing, and also an entry door of similar styling, but this time containing a group of three windows. The name plate was in bright gold script on a scarlet background.

This façade was to greet many Morgan enthusiasts over the following years, and was to remain virtually unchanged for over seventy years, although the rear of the premises underwent many developments during the ensuing period.

Malvern Gazette advertisement.

Few changes to the garage were made over the next five years or so – until the decision was made after the showing of the Morgan three-wheeler at the 1910 Olympia Show to begin production.

The original prototype was designed and produced by HFS Morgan in 1909, and finally registered for road in June 1910. Much of the work was undoubtedly undertaken at Malvern College and Repton School under the direction of William Stephenson-Peach, the engineering master at the College. There is some evidence that the chassis was produced at the Derby firm of J. Smith and Company, where the bevel box and sliding axles were cast and machined, and the chassis assembled by Thomas Jones, machinist and engineer. The chassis tubes came from Repton School (where Stephenson-Peach had been engineering master prior to moving to Malvern) and were drilled and pegged into the bevel box etc. before being brazed in (brazing was rather crude and unreliable in those days). HFS Morgan had been a regular visitor to follow progress of his brainchild.

With the decision to manufacture the Runabout, the troublesome bus service was suspended. Clearly, however, the works were of inadequate size, so HFS hunted around for others to take on or help the manufacturing process.

The design of the three-wheeler allowed construction to be very simple. The chassis could be assembled completely separate from the body, and stored until required. The bodies were simple, mainly of wood, with minimal metal work, and could be easily manufactured by any coachbuilding enterprise.

They could be added to the completed chassis virtually as the last step in manufacture. Upholstery, at this time, was negligible.

To the east of the factory, along Worcester Road there was a coachbuilder, William Clare, whose premises were on the corner with Spring Lane (the site is currently a garage). It seems likely he was approached to make some bodies, while the Morgan works was adapted for chassis assembly, machining and finishing.

The demand following the 1910 Olympia show for the single-seater Runabout was disappointing, and barely adequate for the factory to begin production. A photograph taken in the machine shop

The interior of the Morgan garage. HFS is visible leaning on a partition. The car to the left is a Lanchester. (*Photograph: Morgan Motor Co. collection*)

A view of the garage from Worcester Road, HFS's house just visible to the right. From left to right are a Daimler bus, a Wolseley, a Lanchester (HFS driving), a Star (Leslie Bacon driving) and another Lanchester. (*Photograph: Morgan Motor Co. collection*)

shows few machine tools – mainly lathes, and hardly sufficient for vehicle manufacturing. Clearly further investment was urgently required.

It is likely that Leslie Bacon decided to leave the business at this stage. Clearly the Runabout venture was still very risky.

The 1911 Olympia Show saw the debut of the two-seater and the orders at last flocked in. Also successes in competition were now being a considerable help to selling the three-wheeler, and when Harry Martin won the first International Cyclecar Race at Brooklands in March 1912 at a canter, over one hundred orders were placed on that day alone. Expansion was now justified and, on 10 July 1912 HFS applied for planning permission to extend the factory. As HFS had married Ruth Day, daughter of the Vicar of Malvern Link on 12 June, the opportunity was also taken to expand Chestnut Villa by adding a scullery!

The extensions to the factory buildings were built to enclose the windows at the side of the machine shop, which were now removed to allow walk-in access. Two Crossley gas engines were to be fitted in here to power the expanded range of machine tools.

The plans also show some other free-standing sheds in existence behind the factory on HFS Morgan's land. The rectangular building on the Howsell Road side, adjacent to the toilet block behind the factory, is in exactly the same spot as the brazing hearths occupied in later buildings when under one roof. Perhaps they were in separate sheds at this time.

The Worcester Road end of the main building continued to be used for chassis manufacture.

Working with HFS Morgan since 1911 as works manager was Alfie Hales, who can be seen on both the above photographs. Alfie had moved from Birmingham to be with HFS and spoke with a strong 'Brummie' accent. He lived in a house on Redland Road, to the rear of the factory, as

The small machine shop. (*Photograph: Morgan Motor Co. collection*)

did many employees. Redland Road ran parallel to Worcester Road, skirting the gardens of the Worcester Road houses, including HFS's house and factory. It then turned north through 90° to run parallel to Howsell Road, with houses on both sides, and the back entrance to the Morgan factory was on the apex of this bend. Immediately opposite was a vacant site, surrounded by wooden boards, which was conveniently used as a backdrop for many publicity photographs of Morgan three-wheelers.

Alfie was 'one of the boys' who enjoyed his pint of beer, and was a mean crown green bowler. He curled his forelock with his wife's curling tongs, and was a popular works manager, tough and rugged but fair. If he did not have a Runabout ready for collection by an agent, he would disappear into his office near the gas engines to avoid them.

Also joining HFS, in 1912, was Harry Jones,

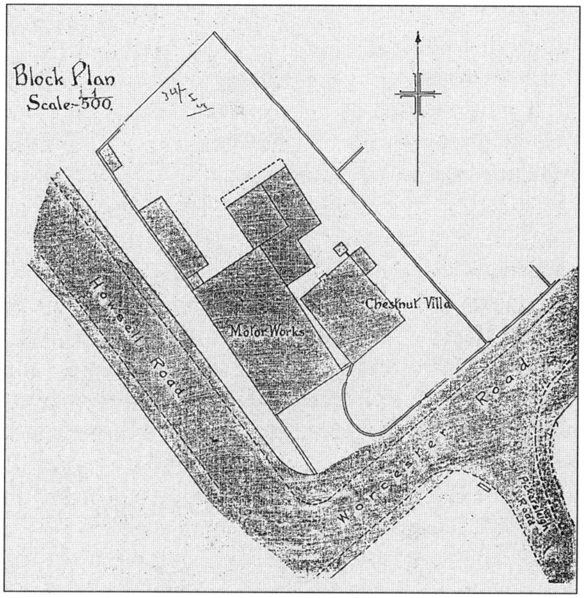

Planning application, dated 20 July, showing extensions to the original motor works.

Extended machine shop in 1912. Note the walk-through area replacing two of the side windows (compare with the 1911 photograph). Works manager Alfie Hales is the slightly blurred figure to the right. (*Photograph: Morgan Motor Co. collection*)

The erecting shop in 1912, with three-wheeler chassis under construction. HFS Morgan and Alfie Hales stand near each other, close to the brick support for overhead belt-driven shafts. (*Photograph: Morgan Motor Co. collection*)

later to become a company director in charge of servicing.

Much of the money for the extensions and extra machine tools no doubt came from HFS's father, Prebendary H. George Morgan, and he was to become chairman of the newly formed Morgan Motor Company which was incorporated on 1 April 1912, with HFS as managing director.

In 1913 a new business (Langley's) was set up in the house next to the rear entrance of the Morgan factory in Redland Road, taking over the complete first floor and half of the ground floor of this property. The other half of the ground floor was occupied by a printer (Stevens). Edmund Langley traded as a tin and coppersmith, and he was to take on the role of manufacturing all sheet metal products for HFS Morgan. Bare body frames in wood from William Clare's works in Worcester Road were taken by truck to the house for panelling with sheet metal. Langley also manufactured fuel tanks. Once Langleys had completed their work it was a simple task to carry the bodies out of the house and through the rear entrance of the Morgan factory for finishing and attachment to waiting chassis.

In 1913 HFS also began experimenting with water-cooled engines, which obviously required radiators. Although the first few radiators were bought in, these were also to be manufactured by Edmund Langley.

It was during October 1913 that Reginald Thomas joined Langleys at the age of fourteen for a five-year apprenticeship, and he was able vividly to remember the layout of this ultimate 'cottage industry', during the period he worked there.

The ground floor of Langleys was used for panel beating and was equipped with blocks and wheeling machines; the bodies from Clare's were panelled here. Upstairs fuel tanks and radiators were produced and repaired. There were little stoves on benches for heating the irons for soldering etc., and stove pipes through the roof to extract the smoke and fumes from the stoves. Radiators were built from tubes, to which gills

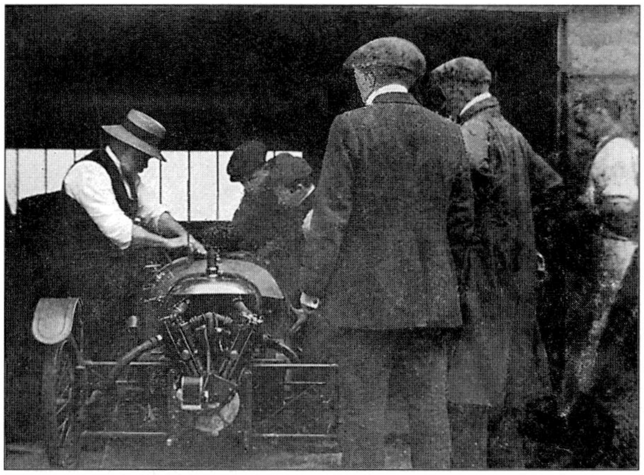

Dorothy Morgan took these unfortunately somewhat battered photographs. The first shows Edmund Langley (wearing straw hat) at work on the Morgan entry for the French Cyclecar Grand Prix. HFS is watching from the foreground.

The second shows HFS's Hupmobile (two speeds, just as in the Morgan three wheeler of this period) at the rear of the factory. To the right can be seen a house at the junction of Redland and Cromwell roads.

Three-wheelers galore outside the Worcester Road entrance, November 1913. (*Photograph: Morgan Motor Co. collection*)

were added by hand. They were then boxed up into the top and bottom spacing plates, with wires down each tube to prevent solder from clogging the tubes. The final tops and bottoms were then added, the former being produced by Langley by wheeling on a block.

Fuel tanks were again manufactured by soldering sheet metal.

A frequent visitor to her brother's factory in 1913 was Dorothy Morgan, and, in June 1913 she took a series of photographs at the factory, some showing recently built wooden sheds at the rear. No doubt these were used for completion of the Runabouts – painting, final assembly and despatch. One of these photographs shows Edmund Langley making final adjustments to the body of HFS Morgan's racer, destined for the Cyclecar Grand Prix in France on 13 July.

Success in the 1913 French Cyclecar Grand Prix by Gordon McMinnies resulted in many new orders. As a result the decision was made to purchase additional land on which to expand the factory. In November 1913 negotiations were completed to purchase just over two acres from Lord Beauchamp, with a frontage of 240 ft. The site was at the far end of Pickersleigh Road which was the road just opposite the Worcester Road factory.

For the Olympia show beginning that 24 November, the Morgan factory produced its full range of three-wheelers. Photographs taken before despatch clearly show the characteristics of the Worcester Road frontage, and also the layout of Redland Road opposite the rear entrance to the factory yard.

Order books were now bulging and HFS wasted no time in drawing up plans for the new site with local builder Martin Wilesmith. Over seventy employees were now working for the Morgan factory and HFS envisaged expansion soon to employ one hundred. Profits had risen from nil in 1911 to £1,314 in 1912, to £4,797 for 1913, excellent growth for the company.

Despite the onset of the First World War in 1914, it had little impact on production for some time, and indeed profits rose to £10,450. Some fifteen cars per week were being manufactured at the beginning of this year, but this dropped as workmen began to enlist in the Army.

The construction of the new shops at the Pickersleigh Road site went ahead, and by May 1914 George Morgan was reporting a potential capacity now of twenty to thirty vehicles per week, although 50% of the employees were now enlisted in the armed forces. As the government had yet to require the Morgan factory to manufacture for the war effort the expanded factory continued to make the Runabout.

Three-wheelers lined up in Redland Road, and photographed from by the rear entrance to the factory. (*Photograph: Morgan Motor Co. collection*)

The first two shops to be built at Pickersleigh Road took over the finishing and painting of the three-wheeler bodies. Completed chassis were now pushed along Pickersleigh Road to be united with the finished bodies, before returning to Worcester Road for despatch

There had been one 'hiccup' during the construction of the new factory – a proposal to develop a burial ground on Lord Beauchamps' land adjoining the factory.

HFS warned the local population, with a letter in the *Malvern Gazette* in June 1914 that access to this site would be through the Morgan factory, and that it would be quite unrealistic to expect the factory to stop work during funerals. The project was abandoned.

Mr E. T. Vine joined the stores in 1915, which were situated at Worcester Road, at the back of the main building. Entry was past the gas engine and up a couple of steps.

By August 1917 we believe that various sheds behind the main Worcester Road building may have been united into a single brick-built extension. Certainly this is how Charlie Curtis remembers the Worcester Road site on his arrival at that time as a mechanic in the repair shop. Wooden bodies were now being built by Morgan workmen at the rear of the Worcester Road Morgan factory as Clare's had ceased trading in 1916 but Langleys were still responsible for sheet metal work.

On 15 November 1916 the Ministry of

The first shop in the new Pickersleigh Road factory was used for finishing bodies. Here a steering column is being fitted. Today this shop is converted to offices and stores. (*Photograph: Morgan Motor Co. collection*)

Munitions had issued an order prohibiting manufacture of motor vehicles, without a special permit – usually given for export market only, and in early 1917 petrol became restricted to those 'engaged on work of national importance'. As a result the production of new Morgans fell to just two or three a week. Langley soon found himself unable to continue with the Morgan work and consequently sold his patterns to HFS Morgan, who set up his own sheet metal shop within the Worcester Road factory. The Morgan factory was now mainly producing munitions, and HFS was able to purchase extra machinery for the machine shop at favourable government terms.

Langley continued to trade in Redland Road into the 1920s and his premises still exist – now converted into two houses, with little sign of the former activities, except for the odd dark roof tile hiding the previous exit of a stove chimney.

HFS was by now a family man, and his daughters were brought up in Chestnut Villa, adjacent to the Worcester Road factory. His eldest daughter, Sylvia, was born on 2 May 1913, and she formed a particular friendship with the scrapman 'Scrappy Johnson' rushing to give him a fond embrace on his frequent visits. Mr Johnson, however, was not the cleanest of individuals and, on several occasions, Miss Morgan required a new white muslin smock after his departure.

At the age of five Sylvia was given the great honour of laying the foundation stone for an extension northwards of the existing blocks at Pickersleigh Road, destined for the future production of Morgan chassis. Beneath the foundation stone, laid on 5 March 1919, was placed a silver half crown.

This new block, which was to accommodate the brazing hearths, linked with the second shop,

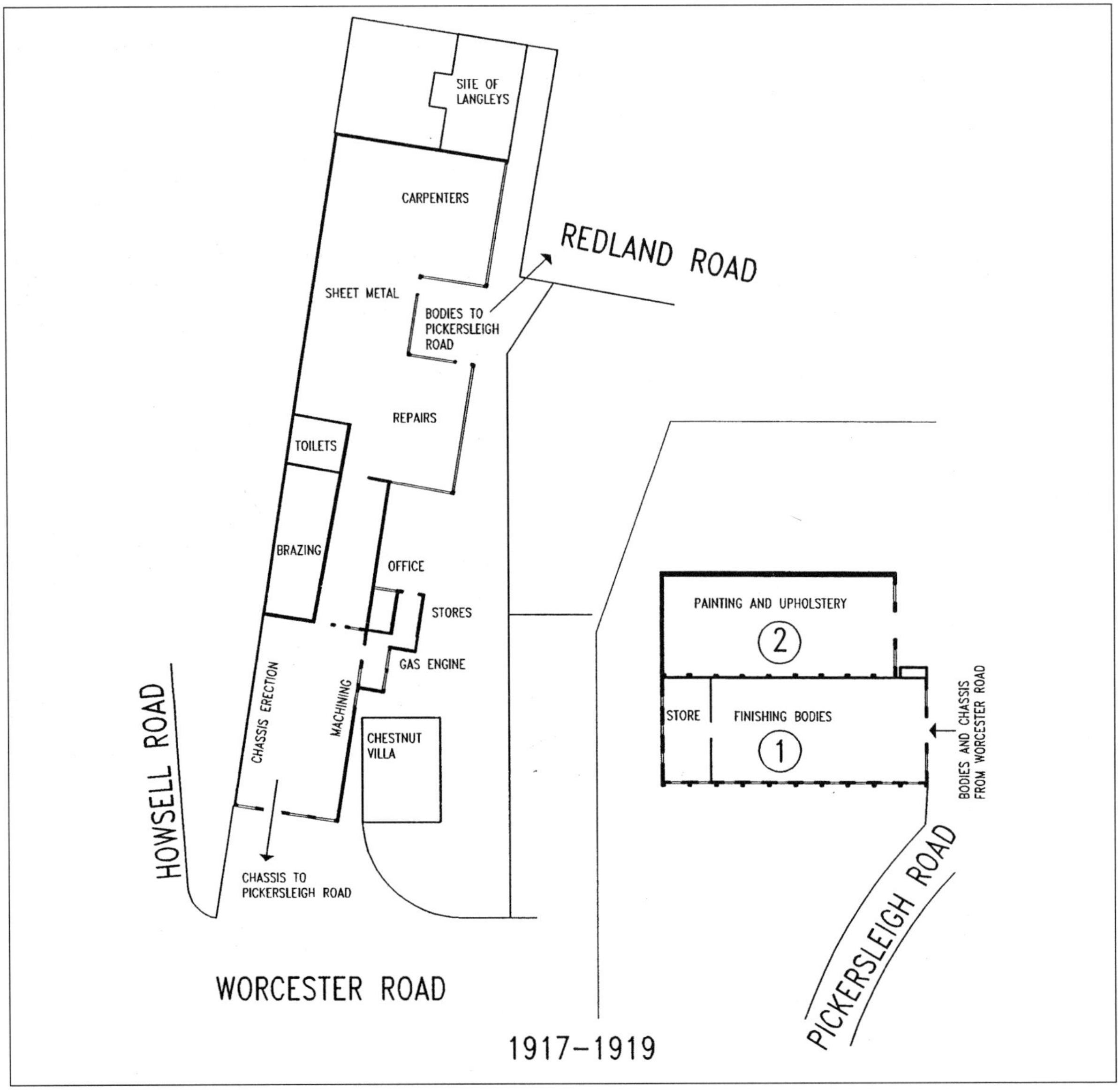

which was now to be reallocated for chassis erection, newly constructed chassis frames being carried round the corner from the brazing hearths. The area near the south entrance to this shop was to be used as the finishing shop for mounting completed bodies onto chassis and finishing the Runabouts.

The first shop at Pickersleigh Road was to be converted into offices and stores, and received a small porch for an entrance.

The plan was for chassis production now to be centred at Pickersleigh Road, while the woodwork and sheet metal shops manufactured complete bodies at Worcester Road. These were then to be transported by an ex-WWI Crossley Lorry to Pickersleigh Road for finishing and painting, prior to fitting to the running chassis as described above.

Besides the northern extensions, which increased the frontage onto the lane fronting the edge of Morgan's land (later to become Pickersleigh Avenue) two further full length rows of shops were to be built at the rear joining on to the eastern end of shop 2. These were initially to be for finishing and painting the bodies arriving from Worcester Road.

On a somewhat sadder note, during April HFS Morgan, while in the company of Freddie James (soon to become the Sheffield Morgan agent in place of his father Billie), had slipped on some grease while walking in the Worcester Road machine shop. In an attempt to save himself he had instinctively put out his hand, unfortunately catching two fingers of his right hand in a capstan lathe. As a result his third and fourth fingers had to be amputated.

On Thursday, 16 October 1919, HFS organized an opening dinner dance in the new paint shop at Pickersleigh Road. Over three hundred employees and friends were present for the festivities to hear HFS welcome them 'to the largest cyclecar factory in the country', with capacity for forty Runabouts per week.

There were replies from Alfie Hales, the works manager, and three Morgan agents, Billie James from Sheffield, Stan McCarthy from Homac's Agency in East London, and Albert Horrocks from Bolton, all wishing the new venture every success.

The new Pickersleigh Road works now had a floor space of 30,400 square feet, giving a total floor area of over 50,000 square feet for both sites.

HFS also announced that arrangements had been made for his Runabout to be built in France, under licence, at the Paris premises of Darmont and Badelogue, the French agents.

The Pickersleigh Road works were to be lit by electricity, but, according to Percy Sambrook, HFS had electricity lines laid from his old factory in Worcester Road to his new complex, as it was cheaper to purchase it there than to use the different local supply normally supplied to Pickersleigh Road.

It may seem surprising that a traditional Edwardian motor factory was being constructed, rather than a more modern state of the art American style production line as introduced into England by Ford at Trafford Park, Manchester, in 1914. We are sure that the Morgan directors were aware of such systems, but had rejected them on several grounds. First, the Morgan Runabout was very simple to manufacture, and cheap to produce

The chassis erection shop *c.* 1919–20, photographed through the southern entrance. The chassis brazing hearths are beyond the foreman's office, to the left. (*Photograph: Morgan Motor Co. collection*)

This is the same view as above, but with bodies now fitted to chassis, for finishing prior to despatch. Note the absence of any separating wall at this time between this shop and the adjacent body finishing shop. This photograph has been published many times before – but incorrectly in reversed form! (*Photograph: Morgan Motor Co. collection*)

conventionally. Second, a production line could be expensive to install, and the Morgan family were using their own money. Thirdly, as George Morgan pointed out in a letter to *The Light Car* during the war, the best way to compete with American know-how was by producing something uniquely British that the Americans were unable to produce – a sporting cyclecar being such an item. Such a philosophy is still consistent with Morgan production today.

On 3 November 1919 the Morgan world was delighted by the news that Ruth Morgan had given birth to a son, Peter. The Worcester Road factory duly celebrated with a party in the woodworking shop.

Demand for the Morgan three-wheeler remained high. Indeed, orders for the whole of the 1921 output were placed at the 1920 Olympia show. HFS was to consider whether to expand the Morgan factory further, and finally in 1922 decided to add a further two rows to enable construction of the bodies to be moved to

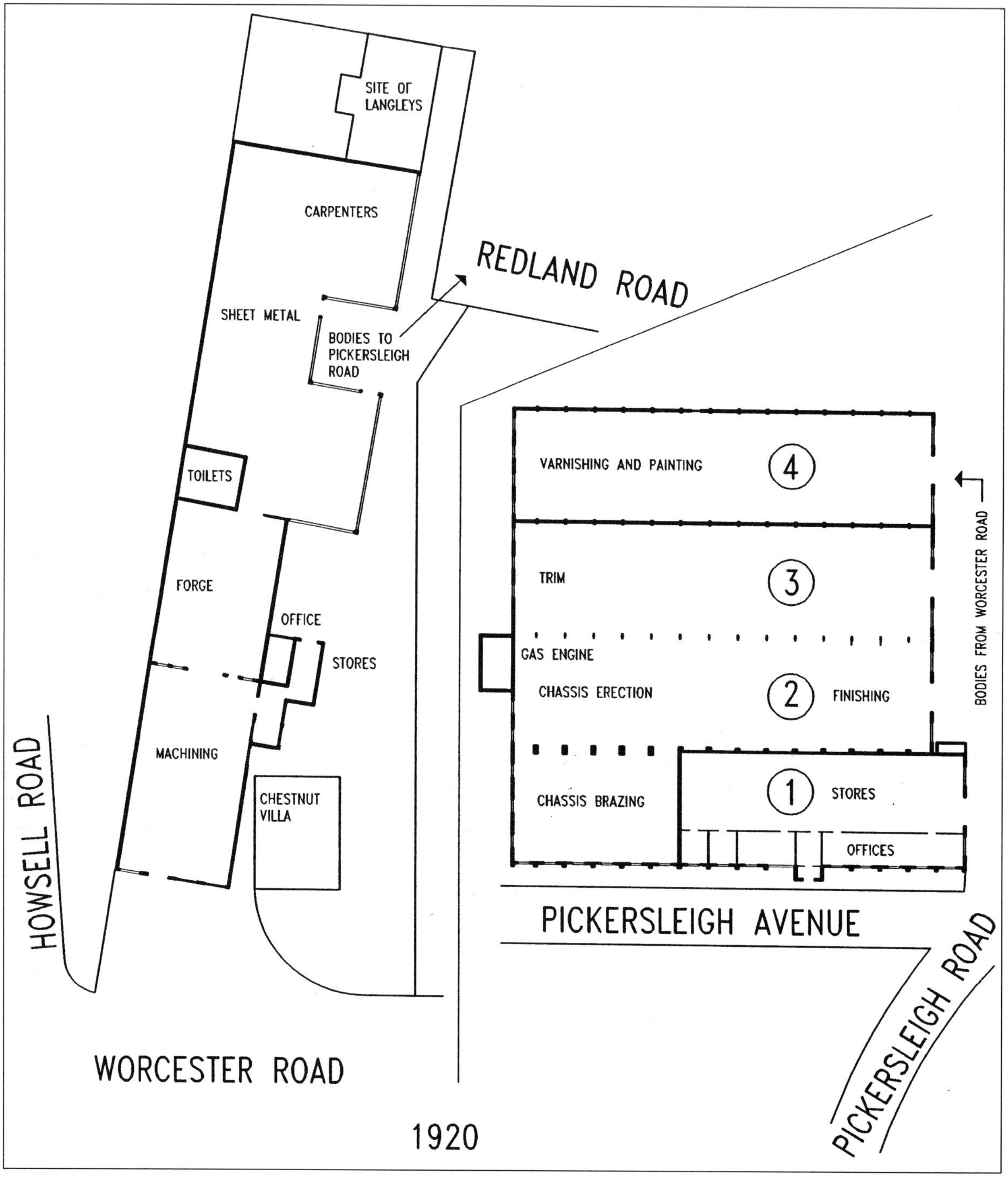

Pickersleigh Road. These two new buildings were further extensions to the east (rows 5 and 6), but slightly offset to the north compared with the previous rows.

The Pickersleigh Road factory in 1920, photographed from across what was to become Pickersleigh Avenue, and showing the north-west corner of the factory. Four rows of sheds are visible, and a gas engine is housed in the small shed attached to the north wall to pump air to the brazing hearths. Note the different type of roof glazing for the original factory (to the right). (*Photograph: Morgan Motor Co. collection*)

This was a courageous step, as competition from small cars such as the new Austin Seven, was causing many inferior cyclecar companies to fold. Prices of Morgan Runabouts were reduced to stay competitive, and order books remained full.

The southernmost third of row 5 was built with a higher roof compared with the rest of the row, with no roof glazing. It was destined to become the despatch shop, with the sheet metal shop going into the rest of row 5 behind the partitions.

The body shop was destined for row 6, along with the wood mill.

HFS was pleased with the way his workforce had supported him and made the move so trouble free. As a result he organized an evening dinner dance at the new factory one Friday evening in early 1923. Each employee was allowed to bring a friend and some five hundred thoroughly enjoyed dancing to Mr Noond's orchestra. Two buses brought employees from Worcester to the event.

During an interval in the dancing HFS addressed his employees, remarking how, three years previously, he had wondered whether the new

Sheet metal shop employees after transfer to Pickersleigh Road. (*Photograph: Mr Vine*)

Pickersleigh Road factory extension then opened would be too large, yet here he was, with an expanding business opening further extensions. HFS went on to pay tribute to his workforce for not striking, or even thinking of striking, but instead pulling together to make the business grow.

Alfie Hales, responding, said he was sure that they could not find a kinder or more generous master than Mr Morgan, and that they also thanked Mrs Morgan for her kindness to them. He was sure she would help anyone.

'For he's a jolly good fellow' was heartily sung, and three cheers were given to Mr & Mrs Morgan.

Remaining behind at Worcester Road was the machine shop and, for a while, the repair bay, but the latter had certainly transferred to Pickersleigh Road by the late 1920s.

Meanwhile HFS, Ruth and their family continued to live at Chestnut Villa. A passageway from the house into the adjacent factory had been built at some time since the war, giving HFS an escape route from the factory into his house if he wished not to meet any visitors! HFS was very kind and generous to young enthusiasts. Morgan racer Ronnie Horton remembered HFS's model railway at the top of the house with enthusiasm and also a musical cigarette box which gave the game away if the odd cigarette was being scrounged.

The children had enjoyed growing up close to the factory in Chestnut Villa, and Peter still remembers the fascinating sounds of the gas engines being started every morning. In 1925, however, the family moved a short distance up Worcester Road to a larger house with considerable grounds – Fern Lodge, where they were to live for the next ten years.

HFS was by now quite a wealthy man, and he was to invest wisely for the future, realizing that the motor business was quite precarious, and having seen many competitors go under. In 1922 he did indulge, however, in his first Rolls Royce, a Silver Ghost, chassis number 76SG, which had an open H. J. Mulliner's body.

Artist's drawing of the Morgan factory site at Pickersleigh Road, as used in sales material by 1926.

Harry Jones sits on the running board of a Family on the south side of the factory, the additional two rows of shops opened in 1923 being visible behind, slightly offset. Charlie Curtis walks away. (*Photograph: Harry Jones collection*)

The Wisteria-shrouded Fern Lodge garage. Left to right are HFS Morgan's Aero, and his Rolls Royce followed by the Morgan-bodied Alvis of Ruth Morgan, and Peter Morgan's 'racer'. Note the stork radiator mascots on the adult cars. Peter Morgan's pedal car was also built at the Morgan factory and featured in-line seating for two. The transmission was based on that of a tandem bicycle. To the right of Peter's car is the wing wherein Bobbie stabled her pony. (*Photograph: Morland Braithwaite Ltd*)

Sadly, poor Alfie Hales was taken terminally ill with cancer and had to leave the company probably during 1927. Alfie was well respected and had done an excellent job, and HFS was greatly saddened to lose his right hand man; he died on 8 December 1927. It was Ruth who suggested to HFS that George Goodall, who ran the service department at the Hereford motor trader 'Fryers', would make a suitable successor.

Alfie Hales had been employed on a bonus system, his pay depending on the performance of the factory in making Morgan Runabouts. As a result, he had done very well out of the Morgan Motor Company. George Goodall was not prepared to accept this system, and it has been said that factory production of three-wheelers subsequently suffered as a result.

By 1926 the Morgan company was using an artist's drawing of the six rows of shops at Pickersleigh Road as part of its advertizing literature. Artistic licence meant that the differing roof heights and roof glazings were overlooked.

In 1928 HFS decided to use his factory facilities to build the body on an Alvis TG12/50 chassis that he had purchased for Ruth. Delivered in April 1928, it was finally registered for the road in October (chassis number 6695).

During 1928–29 a series of photographs were taken at both factory sites, which are worth studying.

The three photographs taken at Worcester Road contain one showing the view through the main entrance, which shows the machine shop's lathes. This should be compared with the original interior of the factory in 1905. To the left, sliding axles are visible being machined.

The other two Worcester Road photos are taken looking through the partition into the second shed which is now revealed as being fully roofed.

Bevel boxes and clutches are being prepared in the upper photograph and in the lower hubs and propshafts.

At Pickersleigh Road, the original first shop to be built (in row 1) was now the stores and offices, as indeed it is today.

Inside the Worcester Road main building.

Views into the second shed of the machine shop.

Looking into the stores from the southern entrance. The doors to the left enter offices. Cecil Jay is standing to the centre (row 1).

The wall at the end of the stores separated this shop from the chassis brazing area, which also fronted Pickersleigh Avenue.

Row 2 was used for chassis erection, and was a full-length shop. Three-wheeler chassis were assembled on wooden stands, now cemented into position in the floor (previously mobile). The remains of these are still visible today (now in part of the repair shop).

Row 3 was sub-divided into three sub-sections. The section nearest the southern entrance we sadly have yet to identify. In the centre was the repair bay, which also contained wheel building benches.

Through a partition was the third sub-section the trim shop.

Row 4 was used for painting and varnishing.

Row 5, nearest the southern entrance, contained a higher roofed area, the despatch shop, and, through a partition, the sheet metal shop.

The sixth row contained the bodyshop, where the wooden body frames were manufactured, and, at the northern end of this row was the woodmill, where wooden components for the frame were produced.

Separate, to the north of the wood mill, was the wood store, where wood from the timber merchants was matured and stored.

The factory was to remain in this format for the next few years.

Body construction for the twin-cylinder three-wheeler proceeded separately from the chassis, as we have already mentioned. The body frame was built in the body shop in row 6, and carried by two employees through an intervening door into the sheet metal shop in row 5. From there it progressed into row 4 for painting and varnishing, then into row 3 for trimming and was finally united with an appropriate chassis in row 2, in the finishing shop close to the southern entrance to this row, where electrical work was also added. The finishing department would then test the car,

The chassis-brazing hearths, with the distant wall being the dividing wall from the stores (first shop) (row 1).

Looking through the southern entrance of the chassis assembly shop. Note the fixed wooden assembly stands, and the ease with which completed chassis could be stored whilst awaiting bodies (row 2).

The repair bay, from the southern aspect, with wheel-building bench on the left (row 3).

The trim shop, at the northern end of row 3.

The paint and varnish shop, looking towards the southern entrance (row 4).

The despatch bay, looking in from the southern door. Note the higher roof line, and lack of roof glazing for this shop (row 5).

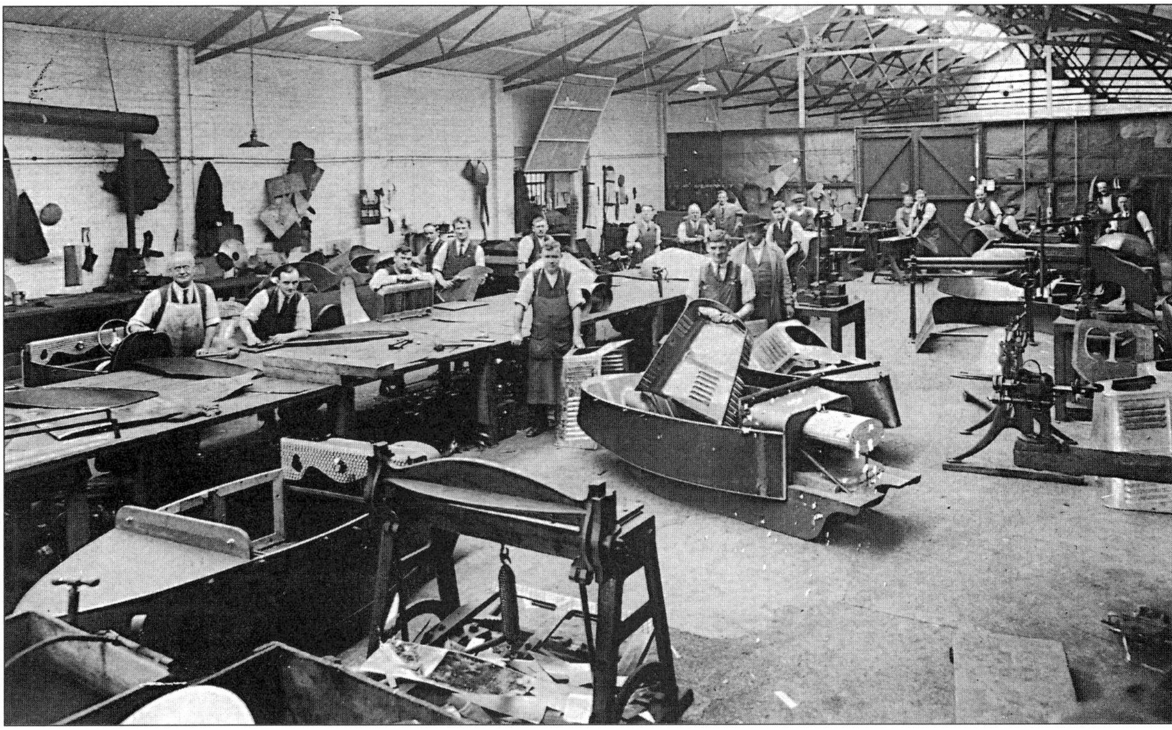

The sheet metal shop, looking back towards the despatch shop. The foreman, Mr Sambrook, is wearing the bowler hat (row 5).

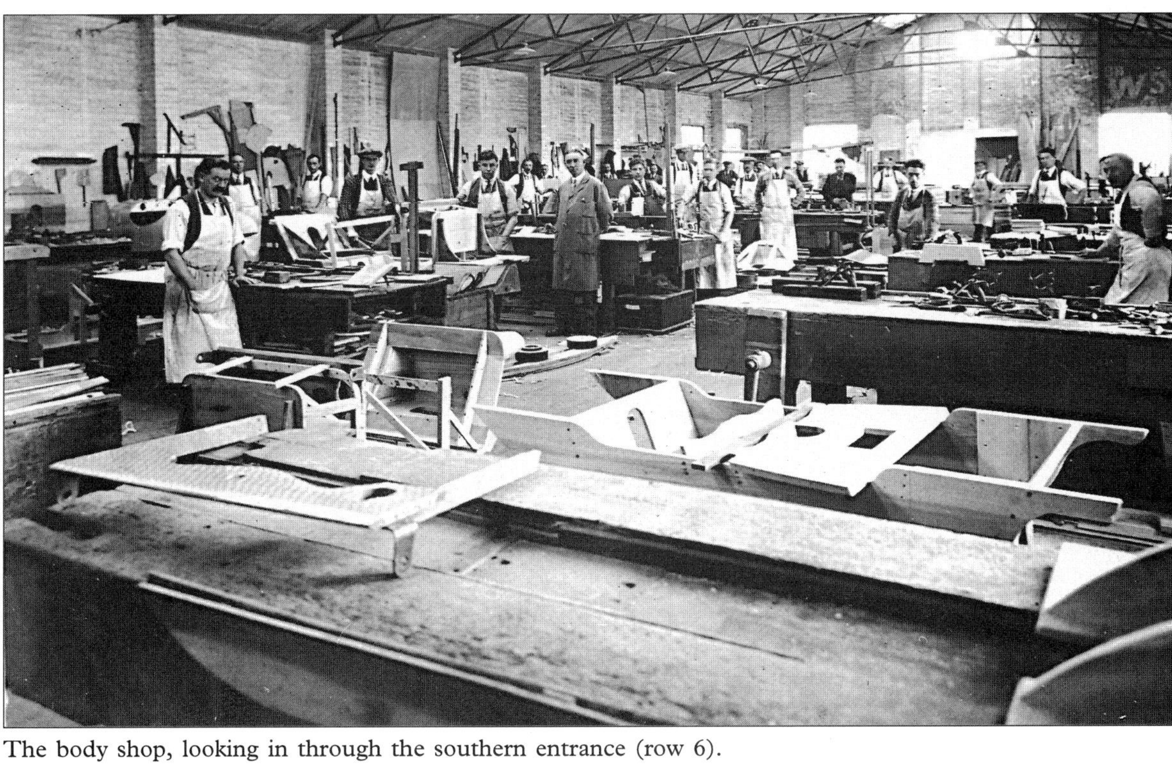

The body shop, looking in through the southern entrance (row 6).

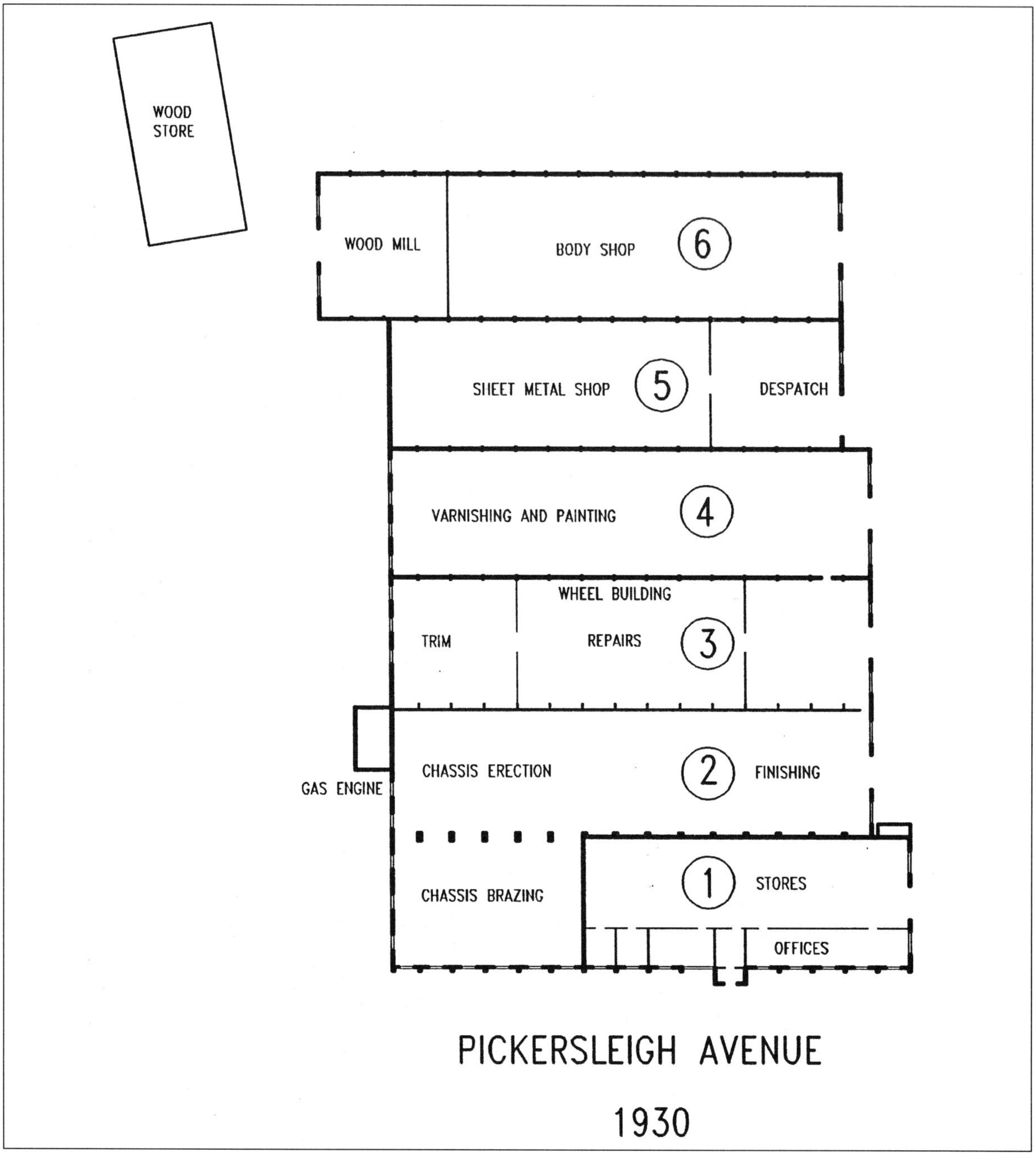

commonly a quick trip around the factory's encircling roads and yard, before taking it to the despatch shop. Each body was given a body number in the body shop, recorded by the foreman with the name of the man who had built it. Each department needed this number for its own work, and, as payment was on a piecework basis, this acted as a check on quality and quantity.

By the early 1930s the two-speed Morgan was no longer state of the art, and, despite the introduction of a three speed and reverse gearbox in 1931, sales began to slide. While work was going on in the experimental shop (thought to be adjacent to the repair shop) on a four-cylinder three-wheeler, HFS contemplated contracting from two sites to just Pickersleigh Road. Construction was begun of a seventh row, eventually to house the machine shop.

Meanwhile, other interesting projects were undertaken at the factory. Following the success of the Morgan body on the Alvis, HFS bought another chassis for the firm to body – this time a Rolls Royce Phantom II, despatched to HFS via agents George Heath Limited in Birmingham at the end of January 1930. The factory were able to complete an open five-seater body from plans produced by HFS. It was painted sky blue with the whole of the top of the body and bonnet chrome plated.

Another interesting project was the refurbishment of the Morgan family's boat, an open river boat of around 20ft, moored on the River Severn at Pixham Ferry. Used on many Sunday afternoons by the family, this boat, named 'Cu-ee', was submerged a couple of times when the river level rose above the moorings and needed cleaning and to be refurbished at the factory! Trips up the River Severn to Worcester would take the boat past the chimneys of Lee and Perrins Worcester Sauce factory. HFS would often remark to Peter how great it must be to make and sell a product not subject to the ups and downs of the motor trade.

The Morgan catalogue for 1931 showed an extra row, the seventh, on the redrawn artist's impression of the Morgan factory, but this was a premature extra row, as the seventh row was built in two halves, the southern end first.

Quite when the southern half was built we have been unable to ascertain, or why this row was built in two halves.

By 1933 the full seventh row had been built. Initially HFS just used it to store old machinery and cars, and at one time it housed a 1896 Pennington three-wheeler, an AJS three-wheeler, a Carden Cyclecar and HFS's first Rolls Royce, which Derek Evans, who now worked in the repair shop, regularly had to start up and check over.

Wheel building ceased in 1933 when Dunlop Magna wheels were introduced on the three-

Artist's drawing of the Pickersleigh Road site as used from 1931 onwards. Note the extra row, and the roof legend 'Morgan Motors'. Both are 'artistic licence'.

Aerial photograph of the Pickersleigh Road site, taken from the south west in the early 1930s. Note the various roof glazings used, the higher roof for the despatch bay, and the half constructed seventh row. (*Photograph: Aerofilms*)

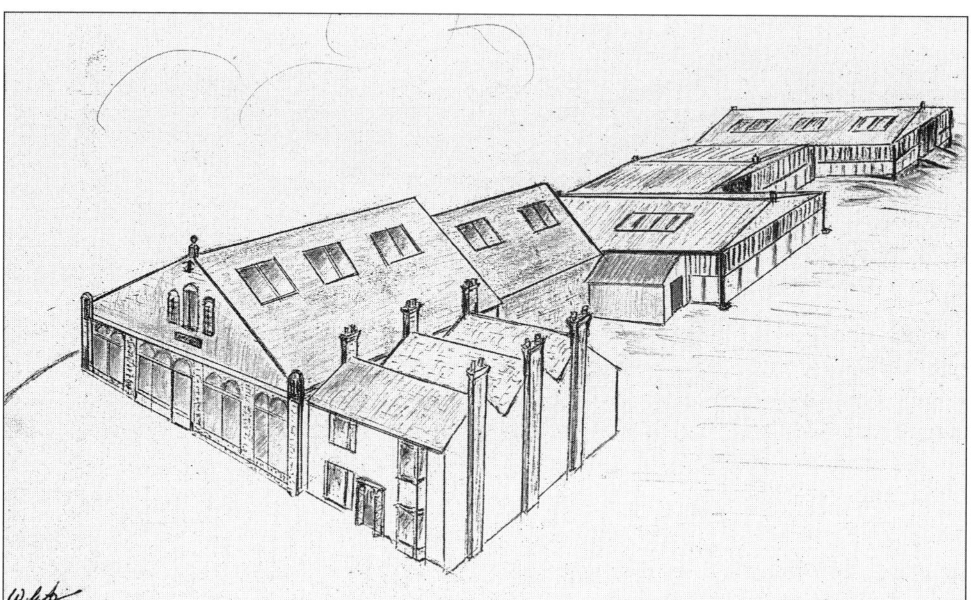

A drawing by Gordon Acock of the layout of the Worcester Road factory site, when acquired by Bowman and Acock in 1936. Of note is the original 1905 building, the later brick built extension, and the many wooden structures in the distance. Chestnut Villa is on the right

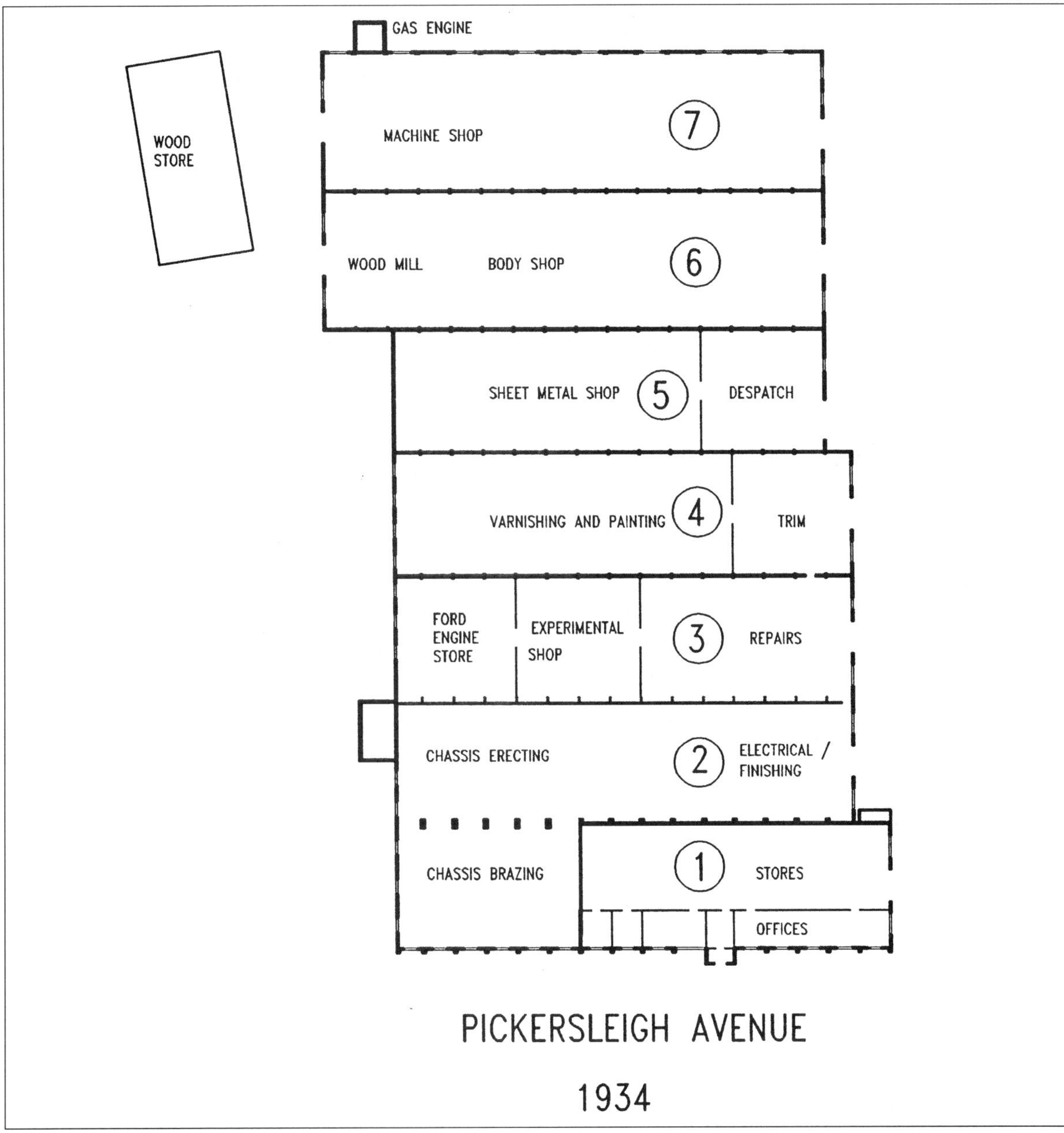

wheeler, and the next change in production methods occurred in 1934 with the introduction of the Ford-engined 'F' type three-wheeler.

Whereas with the twin three-wheeler the chassis and body were built separately and only united in the finishing shop, with the F type this was not possible. A rolling chassis was assembled in the chassis assembly shop, complete with engine, and this was then pushed into the body shop for the erection of the wooden body onto the chassis. From there it was pushed into the sheet metal shop for panelling, then painted, and upholstered and then finally completed in the finishing shop. The Ford engines needed a larger storage area than the twins, so the trim shop at the north end of the row 3 became the engine store, and the trim shop was relocated at the southern end of the paint shop in row 4.

Behind the developmental F type, photographed alongside the eastern wall of the machine shop, can be seen the gas engine house. (*Photograph: Morgan Motor Co. collection*)

A view inside row 2 from the southern entrance, probably in late 1936. The new layout is not yet in operation, for cars awaiting despatch are to the left (excluding AUY 33!), but to the right chassis are being constructed. Note the open-plan layout during this transitional time. (*Photograph: Morgan Motor Co. collection*)

It was probably in 1934 that the machine shop finally transferred from the Worcester Road factory into vacated row 7, the machinery being transported aboard the old, long suffering, Crossley lorry. At last all the factory was on one site, and HFS was soon to sell his original factory to Bowman and Acock, who kept the link with the factory by becoming Morgan distributors.

Attached to the north-eastern corner of the machine shop was a small shed housing a gas engine. This engine performed three functions: it ran an electric generator for the factory lighting; it drove a shaft to supply power to the woodmill by means of pullies; and it also drove an overhead drive shaft within the machine shop from which all the machines took their power via belt drive. When this engine broke down in winter, as it frequently did, then all the employees were sent home. Not surprisingly it was replaced by the normal electricity supply within a few years.

With three-wheeler demand falling rapidly, the introduction of the four-wheeler sports car came just in time to save the factory from further contraction. The fact that the four-wheeler was just a modification of the 'F' type three-wheeler design meant that production methods were virtually identical. However, the four-wheelers took up more room within the shops and a reorganization was soon required. The continuing fall in twin production meant that much fewer numbers of the three-wheeler chassis needed to be built, so it was decided that in future these should be brazed in a corner of the machine shop. The brazing hearths could now be removed from their site adjacent to the stores in row 1, and the repair shop was to be moved into this area, and the adjoining part of row 2. The chassis erecting shop was now moved into row 3, where the repair shop and experimental shop had been, and adjacent to the engine store. The despatch bay now moved to where the chassis assembly and finishing shops had been in row 2, freeing the whole of row 5 for sheet metal work. The new layout was to remain in this form until the onset of the Second World War.

In 1935 HFS and Ruth Morgan finally left Fern Lodge in Malvern and moved to Cannon Hill, Braywick, near Maidenhead in Berkshire. This was a large, early Victorian house with extensive grounds including a stream and a pond. Peter Morgan was to learn to drive around the grounds in the redundant Ford-engined prototype four-wheeler.

With his family now growing up rapidly HFS chose to rent large houses in Cornwall for the family's August holidays over the next few years. In 1935 and 1936 the Morgan family took over Morfa Lodge at New Polzeath, together with family friends. A photograph taken at the beach reveals HFS's Morgan-bodied Phantom II Rolls Royce (chassis number 138XJ, registration UY 8853). Also present is his daughter Sylvia's Hillman Aero Minx four-seater, WP 4756, which was the indirect inspiration for the rear suspension of the 4/4.

For 1936 Peter Morgan was allowed to take the ex-George Goodall F Type two-seater (registration BG08) with him on holiday and he was lucky not to turn it over on Polzeath Hill, driving a little too fast.

Chairman of the Morgan Motor Company since its inception in 1912, and the man who had backed his son with both capital and encouragement in the difficult early days, Prebendary George Morgan died on 11 November 1936 at the age of eighty-four. This sad event led to a reorganization of the Board, with HFS Morgan becoming Chairman and Governing Director. Managing Director was to become George Goodall, with Harry Jones continuing as Service Director.

George Morgan, the vicar of Stoke Lacy had, throughout his own motoring years, always used

The Morgan family and friends on holiday in Cornwall. Note Sylvia's Hillman Aero Minx (WP 4756) and HFS's Rolls Royce (UY 8853). *(Photograph: Morgan Motor Co. collection)*

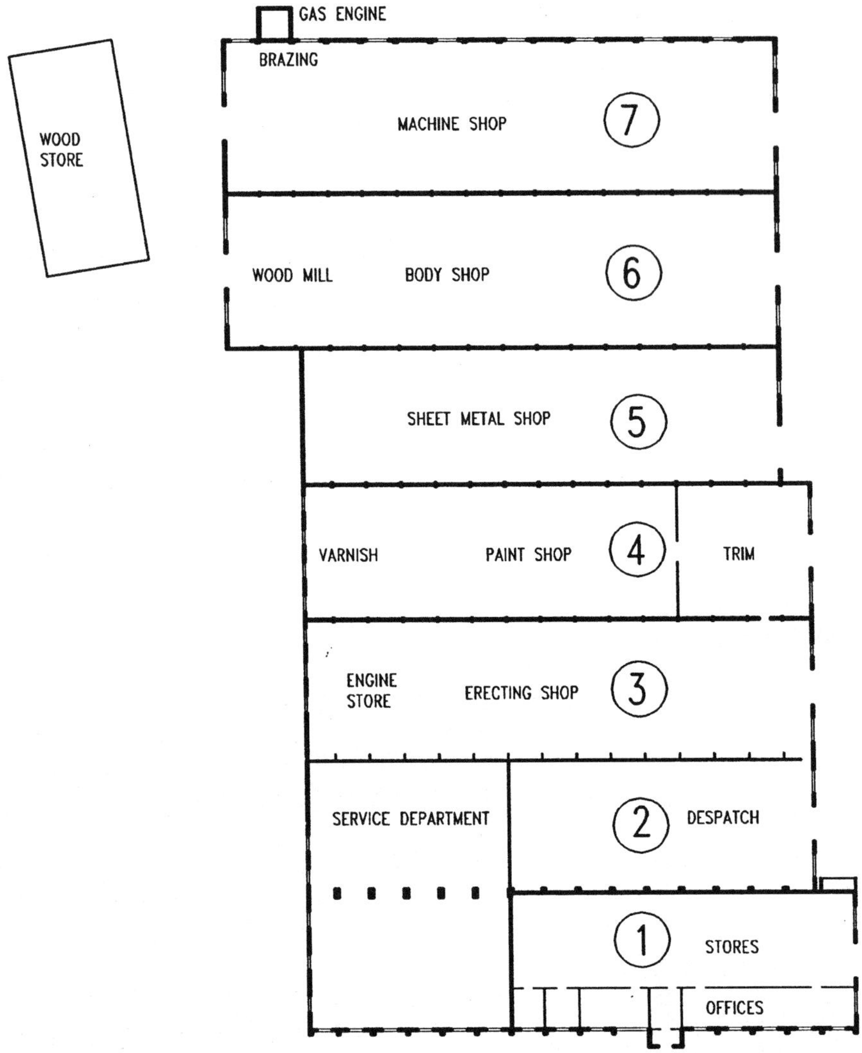

PICKERSLEIGH AVENUE

1937 – 1939

open cars. Perhaps this influenced his son in the models he chose to build.

In his will he left all his shares in the Morgan Motor Company to his son HFS, representing 600 preference and 100 ordinary shares.

For the family's August Cornish holiday in 1937 and 1938 HFS rented a house at Daymer Bay overlooking Padstow across the estuary. On these occasions Peter borrowed a 4/4 – the prototype WP 7490 in 1937, and his trials car BUY 754 the following year.

On one of these expeditions Peter took a 4/4 onto the beach to engage in figure of eights. Unfortunately a rear wheel came off – he had forgotten to tighten the nuts when fitting the competition wheels – and he had to ask some bathers to lift the car while the wheel was returned to its rightful place.

The Morgan family on holiday in 1937, with Peter and HFS Morgan in WP 7490. Ruth Morgan stands behind, with Peter's sister to their left. (*Photograph: Morgan Motor Co. collection*)

Back at the factory, an unfortunate fire in the woodmill led to some disruption of production during this period, but a good relationship with the Wilesmith wood mill near the Malvern Link railway station helped tide the company over until insurance repairs were put in hand.

A new up and down planer, a spindle machine and a circular saw were provided by insurance.

Apart from this episode, there was no change in the layout within the factory until the onset of the Second World War in September 1939, when production of cars ceased, and many of the workers were requisitioned to work on aircraft production elsewhere. The machine shop was kept busy on Government contracts, many new machines being acquired, and this shop made such items as breech block and other parts for

The Morgan family on the beach in 1938. Peter Morgan is wearing shorts and standing next to his trials car BUY 754. HFS Morgan's Bentley (AAA 533) is also visible. (*Photograph: Morgan Motor Co. collection*)

Oerlikon anti-aircraft guns, hydraulic undercarriage for aircraft, shell cases etc. Mr E. T. Vine found himself making tops for milk churns.

Only two other departments were eventually retained for Morgan car use – the repair shop and the stores.

Much of the rest was empty, and Mr Vine remembers several shops being used to store the furniture of those living in areas particularly vulnerable to enemy action.

HFS Morgan had left George Goodall to take charge of any sub-letting of the factory required by the country's war effort. HFS was a pacifist by nature and hated anything to do with war; indeed he had been optimistic it would not happen. Prior to war being declared he had, however, given an option to the Mond Nickel Company to move into his house should hostilities commence, and now duly found himself moving out of Cannon Hill and into a rented home in Braywick Road, San Stefano, where he resided for the duration of the conflict.

In June 1940 Sir Alan Cobham's company, Flight Refuelling Limited took over some of the factory, having been advised that their earlier base at Ford airfield in Sussex was to be requisitioned by the Royal Navy. Work was now to be undertaken at Malvern on the problems of wing icing, with the nearby satellite RAF base at Defford serving as the test aerodrome. Initially the Company was able to share offices with the Morgan Motor Company, and based its workshops within several shops, including some in rows 2, 3 and 6.

Peter Morgan visits his father at San Stefano whilst on leave from the army. He is accompanied by his wife Jane and dog Nan, and is driving BUY 754. (*Photograph: Morgan Motor Co. collection*)

Over at Coventry, however, the Standard Motor Company was heavily engaged in the manufacture of aircraft parts for the war effort, manufacturing Mosquito fighter bombers, Beaufighter fuselages, and Oxford trainer aircraft. Standard now needed extra space for aircraft carburettor manufacture, and duly requisitioned two rows (4 and 5) of the Morgan factory for this purpose.

This reduced the space available to Flight Refuelling Limited, who were now restricted to the carpenters' shop (row 6). With the help of the Ministry of Aircraft Productions (MAP) Capital Assistance Scheme they acquired the land farmed by Mr Wokey adjacent to the southern aspect of the factory and Wilesmiths built thereon several single storey buildings of which those nearest the road were to become drawing offices and for administration. This land had belonged to the Beauchamp estate.

Flight Refuelling had also lost their aerodrome at Defford, and had now taken over Staverton, some twenty miles away.

The Standard Motor Company was also finding the factory accommodation a bit cramped and inhospitable so they built a canteen for their employees adjacent to the factory to the north on land previously owned by the Morgan company, but requisitioned during the war. They also installed solid fuel central heating to row 4 and 5 of the main factory, replacing the old 'Tangy' coke stoves.

The Morgan factory was by now covered in camouflage paint and two underground air raid shelters had been built in the north eastern and south eastern corners of the grounds. There was also a ground-level circular water tank, to assist any fire fighting that might prove necessary.

The southern entrance to the carpenters' shop had been increased in size to allow in major aircraft components, and Flight Refuelling at one stage had a virtually complete Handley Page Hereford bomber within this shop. One poor employee of this company sadly lost his life when an insecure Rolls Royce Merlin engine slipped, crushing him.

After the war it was some time before production of cars could recommence, but the machine

The inaugural meeting of the Morgan Three Wheeler Club on 23 September 1945 at the Morgan factory. The building with the corregated roof behind the telegraph pole is the ex-Standard Motor Company canteen. (*Photograph: Morgan Three Wheeler Club*)

shop kept busy on contract work. Flight Refuelling Limited finally left for Littlehampton in 1947, selling their offices etc. to Chance Brothers (glass manufacturers) who also purchased the Standard Motor Company canteen.

Once production restarted the factory returned virtually to the pre-war layout, and methods of production. An extra store (rough store) had been built during the war years adjacent to the other outside storage, and there was now a small canteen at the north end of row 4, to be run by Mrs Brown.

Peter Morgan, who had married his first wife Jane on 1 December 1940, the honeymoon being abbreviated due to a wartime recall, joined the Morgan factory full-time in 1947. He was responsible for developing the successful Plus 4 model, which started in production in 1950. The introduction was not without its problems, however, as the Elektron castings for the clutch bell-housing proved trickly to machine, the magnesium alloy starting several small fires until the machining of this metal was better understood.

The 29th of July 1951 was the birth day of a son, Charles, to Peter and Jane, and no doubt the Morgan family was pleased that a third generation might wish to continue to operate the family business.

Following the end of the war HFS and Ruth Morgan had purchased Oakwood, a house situated on the old Cannon Hill estate. They were to remain in this house for the remainder of their lives. 11 August 1951 saw the seventieth birthday of HFS Morgan, and he took the opportunity to promote Peter to Deputy Governing Director and Company Chairman.

Having reached his allotted three score years and ten, HFS began to plan for the future of his company after his time on earth was over, and he instructed his Company Secretary, Major

Kendall, to arrange for the Company to pass into the ownership of his children.

There was little change in production methods or layout for the next two decades. Change comes slowly at Malvern and even the introduction of spray painting did not come easily. All cars up to 1952 were hand-painted, and the foreman of the paint shop, Harold Jauncey, a skilled hand

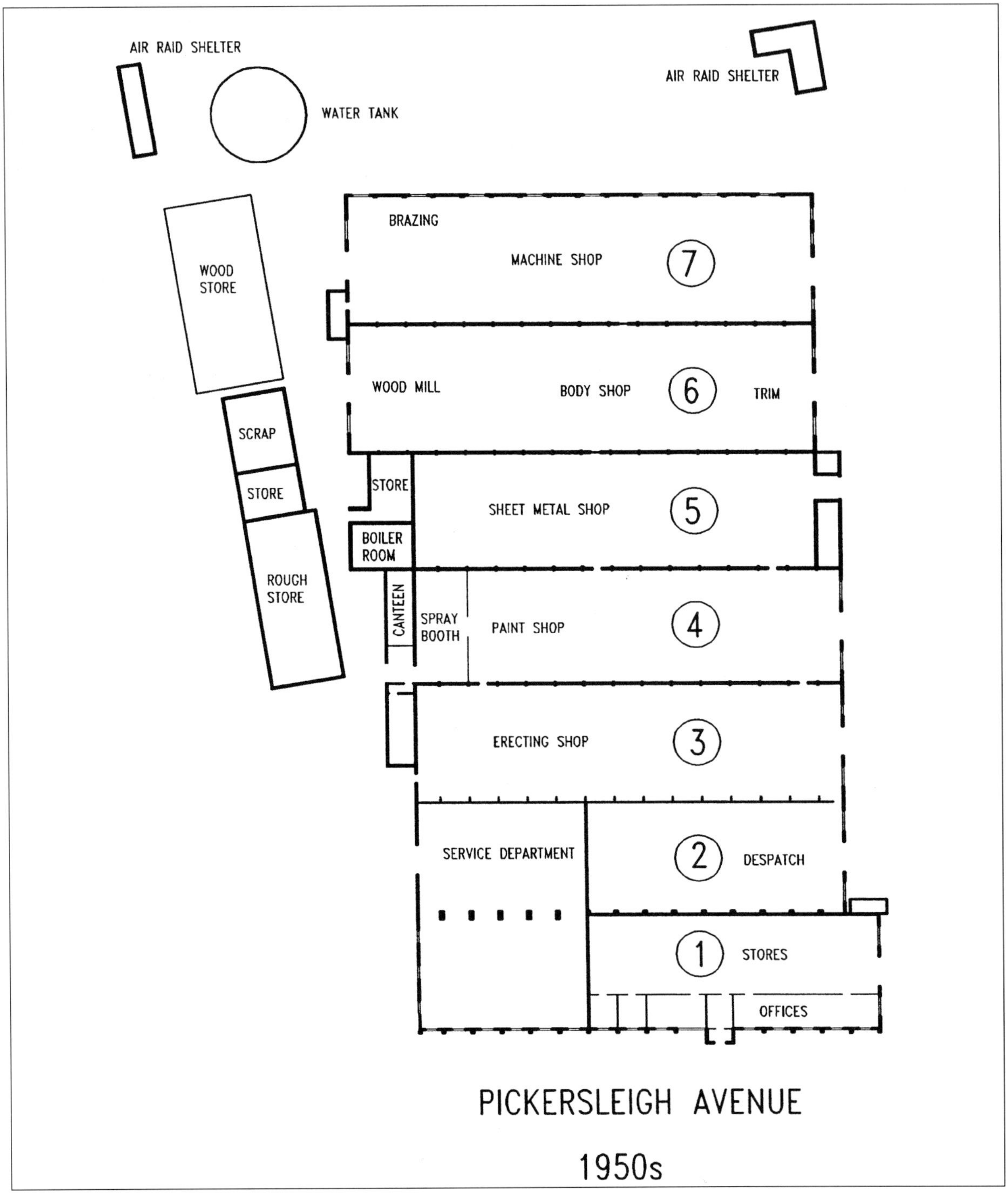

painter and liner, did not want to know about spray painting. Even after a spray booth was fitted to the north end of row 4 in 1953, he still preferred to finish cars by hand, and special cars, such as show models, continued to be prepared in this way for many years.

Since the successful days of three-wheeler production in the 1920s the Morgan factory had contracted considerably. From the remaining single site at Pickersleigh Road of approximately 18,000 square feet, production was roughly five or six cars per week. The factory was operating at a trading loss, supported only by the other profitable components of HFS Morgan's company (investments). In the years 1949, 1950 and 1951 these losses were £1,551, £618 and £2,683 respectively, but following an increase in sales for 1952 a profit of £3,543 was achieved. Despite the introduction of the more up-to-date cowled radiator models at the end of 1953 this failed to prevent a reduction in sales, and a loss of £372 was recorded for this year.

The Morgan factory was visited in the summer of 1953 by an American Thurber C. Phillips, who was collecting his Plus 4 two-seater for a European tour. He was fascinated by the factory and its 'ancient' production methods, so much so that he asked George Goodall how the company managed to stay in business when producing just six cars a week. Goodall replied, 'It's very simple really. We've been successful for many years by following this simple principle: We never make more cars than we can sell and we never sell more cars than we can make.' Several years later Thurber was still trying to work out the logic of this.

Acknowledgments

The publication of this book would not have been possible without the help and encouragement of many. We are particularly grateful to Peter Morgan and the Morgan Motor Co. Ltd., and also the National Motor Museum. To list all who assisted us with our research would be nigh impossible, but we would especially like to acknowledge help from the following:

Morgan Factory History: Reg Thomas, E. Vine, Charlie Curtis, Derek Evans, Percy Sambrook, Dorothy Morgan, Martyn Webb, J. Smith and Co., Martin Wilesmith & Co., Sylvia Morgan, Gordon Acock, Flight Refuelling Ltd., Graham Robson, Companies House, Derek Day. We are particularly grateful to Dennis Rushton for his help, and for the layout drawings.

Other Chapters: British Patent Office, GEC Diesels Ltd., Ford Motor Co. Ltd., Henry Laird albums, Harry Jones albums and Mrs L. Jones, 'Jim' Goodall, 'Joe' Huxham, Derek Evans, Charlie Curtis, Raymond Harris, Geoff & Mary Margetts, Rivers Fletcher, Lancelot Prideaux-Brune, Alan Archer, Gordon Acock, Tom Bryant, Bill & Margaret Billingham, Stanley Woods, Wilfie Fitzsimmons, Brendan Lynch, Sydney Booth, Bill Alexander, Peter Pidgeon, Roger White, Bill Boddy, Denis Jenkinson, Sonny McCann, Graham Robson, Ken Hill, John Gutteridge, Larry Ayres, Roger Comber, Mark Aston, Major Charles Trevelyan, Peter Garnier, Hermen Pol, Frans Vrijaldenhoven, John W. Artley, Martyn Stendall, John Macklin, David Render, Tim Bee, Horace and Hilda Roberts, David Whyley, Reg Hellier, Terry Hill, Ian Titterington, Harry Webster, Ken Richardson, Jeff Sparrowe, Bill Parkes, Mrs G. Scott, David Burgess-Wise, Ted Dennis, Marshall Watson, Dr William Steel, Peter Musitano, MIRA, Bill Piggott, John Smith, Derek Howard, Ian Dussek, P. Biberfield, Jimmy Ray, Bill Allarton, Ken Hobbs, Ian Hall, Stanley Dyke, Ross Lomax, Roy Clarkson, Edmund Nankivell, Joseph Lowrey, John Moore, Peter Silcock, Jack Reece, Doreen Bennett, Robin Steel, Barrie Phipps, Alan Smith, Basil de Mattos, John Isherwood, Ivan Waller, Aileen Jervis, Geoff White, Peter Bolton, Peter Gammon, Les Yarranton, Roger Moran, Barry Isles, Guy Griffiths and Michael Hammond of Axfords, Graeme Anton, Jim Eaton, Dr John Spare, Jock Sinclair, John Pither, Ray Meredith, Alec Newsham, Freddie James, Alex Blair, Pat Kennett, Bruce Cripps, Chris Rowe, Tim Cree, Chas Smith, LAT Photographic, Kathy Farrell and Quadrant Picture Library, Maurice Rowe and *The Motor* archives, Hereford & Worcester CC record office, Dublin Public Library, Glennis Lyons, Janet De Souza.

Australia

We are particularly grateful to Terry Wright, Terry McGrath and Terry Doyle. Also, Mrs J. Boughton, Russell Boughton, Colin Uphill, David Van Dal, Peter Hay, Gavin Sandford-Morgan, Johnny Motteram, Richard Reynolds, Leon Sims.

The State Libraries of Western Australia, South Australia.

USA

Impossible without the help of Jim Sitz. Also we wish to thank Gerry Willburn, Joe Ferguson Jnr, Gordon Mackenzie, Ken Breslauer, Gus Ehrman, Stephen Wilder, Bill Pollack, Mike and Honey Rothschild and Lew Spencer.

New Zealand

Ted Reid, Allen Freeman, Dr George Cowie, Tony Shelly, Graham Vercoe, Mike Stephens.

Sri Lanka

Malith Mendis

The following car clubs also contributed: Chester Motor Club, Motor Cycling Club, Bugatti Owners Club, Royal Automobile Club, Royal

Scottish Automobile Club, Sixty and Worcestershire Motor Club, Midlands Automobile Club, Hagley and District Light Car Club, The Alvis 12/50 Register, Ulster Automobile Club, Lancashire Automobile Club, Morgan Sports Car Club, British Automobile Racing Club, 750 Motor Club, Automobile Club d'Ouest, Royal Irish Automobile Club, Morgan Three-Wheeler Club, Western Australia Sporting Car Club, Sporting Car Club of South Australia, Rolls Royce Enthusiasts Club.

Index of Names